Practical Guide to Cooking, Entertaining and Household Management

By the same author

FEAST WITHOUT FUSS

Practical Guide

to

COOKING,
ENTERTAINING
and
HOUSEHOLD
MANAGEMENT

PAMELA HARLECH

M

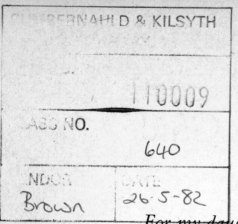
For my daughter, Pandora

ISBN *0 333 31002 0*

First published in the U.S.A. *1981* by
Atheneum, New York

Published in Great Britain *1981* by
MACMILLAN LONDON LTD
London and Basingstoke

Associated companies in Auckland, Dallas,
Delhi, Dublin, Hong Kong, Johannesburg,
Lagos, Manzini, Melbourne, Nairobi,
New York, Singapore, Tokyo, Washington and Zaria

Printed in Great Britain by
BUTLER & TANNER LTD
Frome and London

ACKNOWLEDGEMENTS

I have learned so much from so many people over the years, and so many have helped me with this book, that it is impossible to thank them all. I would, however, particularly like to thank the National Fisheries Institute in Washington, D.C., and the United States National Livestock and Meat Board, as well as the Good Housekeeping Institute for all their help with the information on American meat and fish, and the Flour Advisory Bureau Ltd. in London. Special thanks to Anne Dare of the Meat Promotion Executive in London for her particular help and guidance and the permission to use their meat charts; to Eddie Kohut of the Akron Meat Market in New York City, for his patience and knowledge in answering my many questions; to Harry Hutton, head meat buyer for Harrods, Ltd., London; to Mrs. Ruth Thompson of the Oak Tree Herb Farm in Nesscliff, Shropshire, who gave me valuable information and advice about herbs and spices, to Mr. Blagden and Des of John Blagden (Fish Market), to Mrs. Georgina Boosey of British *Vogue,* an extremely helpful editor of specific chapters, to Jane Fellowes for many hours of typing, and a very special thanks to my editors Judith Kern and Caroline Hobhouse, without whose patience, knowledge and sense of humor this book would never have been finished.

I would also like to thank the following people who have allowed me to reproduce their recipes: Aldo Bigozzi, Fiona Charlton Dewar, Tamasin Day-Lewis, Jane Grigson, Fernanda Neves, Sri Owen, Craig Claiborne and Virginia Lee.

ACKNOWLEDGEMENTS

The author and publishers wish to thank the following who have kindly granted permission for the use of copyright material:

Jonathan Cape Ltd. on behalf of the Executors of the Estate of Mrs. C. F. Leyel for the recipe "Candied Rhubarb Leaves" from *A Modern Herbal* by Mrs. M. Grieve, edited by Mrs. C. F. Leyel;

Bruno Cassirer (Publishers) Ltd. for extracts and the recipe "Hare à la Royale" from *Cooking with Pomiane* by Edouard de Pomiane;

William Collins, Sons & Co. Ltd. for the recipe "Spinach and Meat Soufflé" from *Kitchen Essays* by Lady Jekyll;

David Higham Associates Ltd. on behalf of Jane Grigson for recipes "Sea Bass Anisette with Pernod Mayonnaise" from *Fish Cookery*, published by the International Wine and Food Society, and "Artichauts à la Barigoule" and "Broad Beans in the Touraine Style" from *Vegetable Book* published by Michael Joseph Ltd.;

Sri Owen for her recipes "Semur Daging" and "Sayur Bayem" from *Indonesian Food and Cookery*, 1980, published by Prospect Books Ltd.;

Sphere Books Ltd. for the recipe "Stir Fry Cabbage and Shredded Pork" from *The Chinese Cook Book* by Craig Claiborne and Virginia Lee.

INTRODUCTION

This book is not meant to give the reader an encyclopedic knowledge of cooking, entertaining and housekeeping, nor is it meant to be a scholarly thesis on these subjects. Instead, I am trying to give practical answers to the questions I am asked daily by my friends and readers of my column as well as give some added information on the chemistry of cooking, the methods of cooking, and related subjects. The answers I give are from my own daily experience over the past twenty-five years and from many years of reading cookbooks I have collected over the years, including those as early as the seventeenth century, up to the modern day.

Another purpose for this book is to help those Americans who come to live in England, whether for three months, three years or for life, and vice versa. I know many American women whose husbands are sent by their firms to live in England for a short time—they are completely lost when trying to shop. The Americans and the British butcher their meat in totally different ways, and the cuts are called by different names. For this reason you will find both diagrams and charts giving the comparable cut. In addition, I have included an Anglo-American list of products that are available in both countries as well as equivalent terminology. In the recipes you will find the British equivalents listed second both in weights and in measures, and then the metric conversions. In the fish chapter, there are some fish that are available either only in America, or only in Britain. I have tried to indicate these as well.

As far as the recipes themselves are concerned, I have not attempted to be all-inclusive. Any good book such as the *Joy of Cooking,* the *Doubleday Cookbook,* Mrs. Beeton or Constance Spry will give "how to cook French-fried potatoes," etc. Instead, I decided to put in unusual recipes that I love, that my guests have loved and that are different. As mine are very personal choices, and since I love using herbs and spices, many of the recipes include interesting combinations of them, in particular from the Middle East. I have also included recipes from some of my favorite cooking writers, and I thank them for their permission to do so.

I am not trying to teach a cooking course, but I've included the basic whys and wherefores one must master. I hope that these recipes give the readers as much pleasure as they have given to my family and friends over the years, and that at least some of their questions will have been answered.

Cooking and entertaining should be fun as well as hard work—particularly entertaining. If it isn't—don't do it. Nothing is more depressing for one's guests than to know that their hostess thinks it is a trial to have them. Making a guest feel wanted and content does not require money. It needs only care, a tiny bit of thought and thoughtfulness, and a great deal of joy in wishing to make people happy.

CONTENTS

Practical Guide to
Cooking, Entertaining
and Household Management

WEIGHTS AND MEASURES

AMERICAN, IMPERIAL AND METRIC MEASURES

The single most important difference between American and British cooks is in the way they measure ingredients. From childhood, the American cook learns to think in terms of the cup, which is used for dry ingredients like flour and bread crumbs as well as for semi-dry ingredients such as molasses and butter, and for liquids like milk and water. The British cook, on the other hand, is trained to use tablespoons for small quantities of both dry and liquid ingredients, but sticks to pounds and ounces, weighed on a food scale, for dry ingredients and to pints and fractions thereof for liquids.

Now, however, the metric system, using grams and milliliters—although not yet in general popular use—is gaining ground. Metric measurements are now always included in British cookbooks, and are appearing more and more in American books as well.

Because of the difficulty of converting British dry weight measures to

American dry volume measures, as well as the confusing differences between the American and British pint and between our tablespoons, it is probably wisest to learn and use the metric system, which contains no such pitfalls. The following tables are an attempt to guide you through the maze.

CONVERSION TABLES

Dry Measures

1 ounce (oz) = 28 grams (g)
1 pound (lb) = 0.45 kilograms (kg)
1 gram (g) = 0.035 ounce (oz)
1000 grams (g) = 1 kilogram (kg)

To make cooking easier, one must round off the number of grams in an ounce; I prefer rounding off to 25 rather than 30 grams to the ounce. The very small differences in the quantities involved will not make any difference in the flavor of your food, so long as you round off consistently.

To convert ounces to grams, multiply by 25; to convert grams to ounces, multiply by 0.035.

Liquid Measures

1 fluid ounce (fl oz) = 30 milliliters (ml)
1 milliliter (ml) = 0.034 fluid ounce (fl oz)

100 milliliters (ml) = 1 deciliter (dl)
10 deciliters (dl) = 1 liter (l)

To convert ounces to milliliters, multiply the ounces by 30; to convert milliliters to ounces, multiply the milliliters by 0.034.

The Imperial (or British) pint is 20 fluid ounces; the American pint is 16 fluid ounces. Therefore:

2 American pints =	1¾ Imperial pints =	4 cups = 1 liter
1¼ American pints =	1 Imperial pint =	2½ cups = 600 milliliters
1 American pint =	¾ Imperial pint =	2 cups = ½ liter (500 ml)
½ American pint =	8 fluid ounces =	1 cup = ¼ liter (250 ml)

AMERICAN, BRITISH AND METRIC TABLESPOON MEASURES

Americans measure dry ingredients in level tablespoonfuls while the British measure them in heaping tablespoonfuls. Therefore:

2 American tablespoons = 1 British tablespoon

Liquid tablespoons must, obviously, be level for both Americans and British.

1 tablespoon liquid = 15 milliliters
1 teaspoon liquid = 5 milliliters
3 teaspoons = 1 tablespoon

ONE AMERICAN CUP MEASURES FOR STANDARD INGREDIENTS IN METRIC AND IMPERIAL EQUIVALENTS

American cup	Grams	Ounces
Allbran	50	2
Apples, cooking, pared and sliced	125	4
Applesauce	225	8
Apricots, dried	175	6
Barley, pearl	200	7
Bananas, sliced	175	6
———, mashed	225	8
Bread crumbs, dried	100	4
———, fresh	50	2
Bran, natural wheat	50	2
Butter	225	8
Cabbage, raw, shredded	100	4

American cup	Grams	Ounces
Cheese, cottage	225	8
———, Cheddar, coarsely grated and tightly packed	100	4
———, cream	225	8
Cherries, whole glacé	200	7
Chestnuts, fresh and shelled	200	7
———, dried	175	6
Cocoa powder	100	4
Coconut, shredded	85	3½
Cookies (sweet biscuits)	100	4
Cornflour	140	4½
Cornflakes	25	1
Currants, dried	150	5
Dates, whole, pitted and dried	175	6
Figs, dried	175	6
Flour, all-purpose (plain) and self-rising	125	4
———, whole wheat	140	4½
Honey	350	12
Jams	300	11
Lard or drippings	225	8
Lentils	200	7
Macaroni, uncooked	100	4
Marmalade	300	11
Mayonnaise	225	8
Milk, fresh	225	8
———, evaporated	250	9
———, condensed	300	11
———, powdered, low fat	85	3½
Mincemeat	300	11
Mixed peel, loosely packed	175	6
Molasses (treacle)	350	12
Muesli	150	5
Mushrooms, fresh, sliced	50	2
———, canned, drained	150	5
Noodles, uncooked	75	3
Nuts: almonds, whole, blanched	150	5
almonds, flaked	100	4
almonds, chopped fine	150	5
almonds, ground	100	4
cashews, whole, shelled	150	5
Brazils, whole, shelled	150	5

American cup	Grams	Ounces
hazelnuts, whole, shelled	150	5
peanuts, roasted	150	5
walnuts, halved	100	4
pine nuts (kernels)	200	7
Oats, rolled	75	3
Oils	215	7½
Olives, green stuffed	150	5
———, ripe black	175	6
Onions, chopped	150	5
Parsley, chopped	85	3½
Peaches, fresh, sliced	150	5
———, canned, drained slices	225	8
Peas, frozen	125	4
———, split, dried	200	7
Potatoes, raw, diced	175	6
———, cooked and mashed	225	8
Prunes, dried, with pits	200	7
———, cooked and pitted	225	8
Raisins, seedless	150	5
Rhubarb, raw, sliced	200	7
Rice, long grain, uncooked	200	7
———, short grain, uncooked	215	7½
Sago	175	6
Salmon, canned, drained and flaked	175	6
Semolina	200	7
Spaghetti, broken, uncooked	100	4
Strawberries, whole, fresh	150	5
Suet, shredded	125	4
Sugar, granulated	200	7
———, superfine granulated (castor)	200	7
———, confectioners' (icing)	125	4
———, moist brown, packed solid	200	7
———, demerara	200	7
Tapioca, seed pearl	175	6
Tomatoes, canned with juice	225	8
———, fresh, peeled and quartered	150	5
Tunafish, canned, drained and flaked	200	7

ACCURATE MEASURING

Always measure dry ingredients with the nested, dry measuring cups rather than the one-cup liquid measure.

To measure *cornstarch/cornflour, baking powder, salt* or *baking soda/ bicarbonate of soda,* dip the measuring spoon into the container and fill, heaping full. Then level it off across the top with a straight-edged knife.

To measure *solid fat* and *shortening,* pack it solidly with the back of a spoon into a measuring cup (to eliminate all air pockets) until it comes above the rim of the cup. Then level off with a spatula or straight-edged knife. To make measuring easier, have the solid fat or shortening at room temperature rather than cold and hard from the refrigerator.

To measure *granulated, superfine (castor)* or *confectioners' (icing) sugar,* lift the sugar from the container into the cup with a spoon or scoop and level off with a spatula. Do not tap or shake it down. *Brown sugar* should be packed firmly into the cup before leveling off.

Before measuring *flour,* always sift it once, then lift the sifted flour into the cup with a spoon or scoop until the cup is heaped full. Then level it off with a spatula. *Do not tap or shake the flour.* It undoes the work of sifting. To measure *oil* and *syrup* use an ordinary liquid measuring cup and make sure when you pour it out to use a brush and scraper to remove every last drop of the measured amount.

LENGTH

The American and British standard yard of 36 inches (in) is slightly shorter than the meter (m), which is equal to 100 centimeters (cm) or 39 inches.

1 inch = 2.54 centimeters
1 foot = 30 centimeters
1 yard = 0.9 meters

TEMPERATURE

Oven Temperatures

	Fahrenheit	Celsius (Centigrade)	Gas
Very Cool	250° F	130° C	Mark ½
	275° F	140° C	Mark 1
Cool	300° F	150° C	Mark 2
Warm	325° F	170° C	Mark 3
Moderate	350° F	180° C	Mark 4
Fairly Hot	375° F	190° C	Mark 5
	400° F	200° C	Mark 6
Hot	425° F	220° C	Mark 7
Very Hot	450° F	230° C	Mark 8
	475° F	240° C	Mark 9
	500° F	250° C	Mark 10

To convert Fahrenheit to Celsius: subtract 32, multiply by 5, divide by 9.
To convert Celsius to Fahrenheit: multiply by 9, divide by 5, and add 32.
Water freezes at 0° C; water boils at 100° C at sea level.

Temperature Conversion

Celsius	to	Fahrenheit	Celsius	to	Fahrenheit
−17.7° C		0° F	55° C		131° F
−15° C		5° F	60° C		140° F
−12.2° C		10° F	65° C		149° F
−6.6° C		20° F	70° C		158° F
−1.1° C		30° F	75° C		167° F
0° C	(water freezes)	32° F	80° C		176° F
5° C		41° F	85° C		185° F
10° C		50° F	90° C		194° F
15° C		59° F	95° C		203° F
20° C		68° F	100° C	(water boils)	212° F
25° C		77° F	110° C		230° F
30° C		86° F	120° C		248° F
35° C		95° F	130° C		266° F
40° C		104° F	140° C		284° F
45° C		113° F	150° C		302° F
50° C		122° F	200° C		392° F

THE HOUSEHOLD

THE CARE AND CLEANING OF
FURNITURE AND OBJECTS

General

Carpets marked by furniture: To restore the pile where carpets have been pressed flat by furniture legs, remove the furniture and lay a wet towel, folded twice, over the spot. Then steam it gently with a hot iron. This ought to lift the pile.

Formica: To remove stains, make a paste of baking soda (bicarbonate of soda) and water and apply it to the stain. Leave it for a minute or two, then rub to remove. The baking soda (bicarbonate of soda) won't scratch the surface of the formica.

Gilt: To restore color to gilt, use a little onion water applied with a sponge. (Onion water: Skin and chop 2 to 3 onions and boil them in 2 cups (475 ml) water for approximately ½ hour. Strain through a very fine strainer or muslin. Use *warm*.)

Glass on a picture: First dust it, then put 1 tablespoon denatured alcohol (methylated spirits) into a small bowl of water (2 cups; 475 ml), wring a sponge out in it and wash the glass, being careful not to wet the frame when cleaning edges and corners. Then dry with a clean linen towel and polish with a lint-free soft cloth or chamois.

Grass cloth wall coverings (Hessian): Vacuum first, then remove grease marks with a commercial spot cleaner. (Test it first on a spot which doesn't show. It might take out the color, making the fading worse than the grease spot.)

Hairbrushes: To wash hairbrushes, dissolve 1 teaspoon of baking soda (bicarbonate of soda) in a quart of water. Comb the hair from the brushes, then dip them, bristles down, into the water and out again. Keep the back of the brush and the handle out of the water, because the baking soda will leave a residue on the plastic. Repeat this until the bristles look clean. Then rinse the brush in a little cold water, shake it, wipe the back of the brush and handle with a towel. *Do not wipe the bristles.* For combs and brushes with non-natural bristles, denture powder is most effective.

Heat marks on polished wood furniture: *Either* rub, in the direction of the grain, with brass polish sprinkled on a cloth and then repolish; *or* place several thicknesses of blotting paper over the marks and press firmly with a hot iron, lifting the paper from time to time. Then apply a little paraffin wax and polish lightly with a clean, soft cloth. A third method is to rub the mark with a mixture of olive oil and denatured alcohol (methylated spirits).

Alcohol stains on wood furniture:
1. Make a paste of 1 part salt and 1 part linseed oil. Rub on the stain and leave for 1 hour, then remove.
2. Moisten cigarette ashes with furniture polish; apply to the spot and rub lightly with your fingers. Wipe off and rub the surface.

White spots and rings on furniture: Rub with liquid polish. Then dampen a cloth with turpentine, rub dry and buff.

To high-polish a dinner table: Rub the table with cold linseed oil in the following manner: Depending on the size of the surface, put 1 or more teaspoons of oil in the middle of the table and rub it well all over the table top with a piece of linen (never woolen) cloth. Then take another piece of linen and rub the table for 10 minutes; after that rub the table with a third cloth until the top is absolutely dry. If you do this every day for several months, you will find your wood surface has developed a permanent and beautiful luster, unattainable by any other means and equal to the finest French-polish finish. The table will then require only dry rubbing with a linen cloth for about 10 minutes twice a week to preserve its perfect polish. A hot dish will not mark it, even if you do not use an underpad or a trivet with your table-cloth.

Lucite (Perspex) table tops, shower doors, etc.: Wash with a warm detergent. For stubborn marks, add a teaspoonful (5 ml) of baking soda. Rinse very thoroughly. Polish with a Lucite polish.

Marble:
1. To clean marble, dip a quarter of a lemon in salt, rub, allow it to stand for a few minutes. Wash off with soap and water. OR
2. Make a solution of peroxide and a few drops of ammonia. Rub it on the marble and allow to set for several hours. Repeat if necessary. OR
3. To polish marble, moisten some ordinary chalk with water and gently rub the marble surface.

To protect paint: To protect surrounding paint when polishing brass knobs and knockers, cut out a piece of cardboard which will fit around the base of the brass object. Extend the cut with slits to allow it to pass over the knob or knocker.

Papier-mâché: Wash the object gently with a sponge wrung out in tepid water—*never use soap*. Then dry off with a cloth and polish with a little dry flour rubbed on with a chamois or other soft cloth.

Parquet floors:
1. To take out ordinary spots, wash with a soapy cloth, dry well, then polish.
2. If the stains are very deep, take an old razor blade and scrape carefully along the grain of the wood, then rub with denatured alcohol (methylated spirits); put on floor polish (preferably beeswax and turpentine), leave for a short time so that it soaks in, then polish.
3. If the floor is very dirty, but there is a little polish left, take a pail of Ivory Snow and water, or soap and water—but *never a detergent*—and wash thoroughly, brushing in the same direction as the grain of the wood. Dry well and leave for a while. Then boil some linseed oil, and with an ordinary pencil eraser on a flat piece of wood with a short wooden handle, apply it all over the floor, again rubbing with the grain of the wood. Leave it overnight to dry thoroughly, then polish. This should make the floor as good as new.

Pewter:
1. To restore luster to pewter, use linseed oil and a pumice stone.
2. Gently rub stubborn stains with fine steel wool, but first check one spot to be sure the steel wool doesn't mark the metal.
3. Rub with a mixture of mild scouring powder, such as Ajax, and olive oil.

Substitutes for copper and brass polish:
1. A slice of lemon with baking soda.
2. Ketchup.
3. Salt and vinegar.

Sheepskin rugs: Boil 2 pints (1 liter) of water with 6 ounces (175 g) pure soap flakes and 2 fluid ounces (50 ml) olive oil and stir well. Fill a sink with warm water, pour in the mixture and add 2 fluid ounces (50 ml) glycerine. Wash the rug in this. Then give the rug just *one* rinse, leaving some of the soapiness in the skin. Squeeze out all the excess water and towel dry. Hang out on the line. When almost dry, rub it with ½ pound (225 g) fine oatmeal and flour mixed in equal parts to help restore it to fluffiness. When dry, comb it carefully.

Teak: Natural oil-finished teak should not be cleaned with ordinary furniture polish but with teak oil—and then only about two or three times a year, or there will be a build-up of unattractive looking polish. For heat marks or stubborn stains, rub the spot with a solution of equal parts linseed oil and cleaning fluid. Wipe off.

Tortoise shell: To clean, rub in a little olive oil, then polish with a soft cloth.

Umbrellas badly stained with mud can be cleaned by sponging them with ordinary vinegar.

Varnished woodwork: Use plain cold tea—it is by far the most effective cleaner.

Glass vases and decanters: It is important to clean all vases thoroughly or the bacteria in the residue from the last flowers will harm the new, fresh flowers. Put some strips of newspaper in the bottom of the vase or decanter. Pour in 2 fl oz (50 ml) vinegar mixed with 1 tablespoon salt. Shake and leave to soak for a few hours. Then drain and wash with warm, soapy water and a wire brush. Drain and turn upside down to dry. If the decanters have glass stoppers, both the decanter and the stopper must be thoroughly dry before inserting the stopper, otherwise it will get stuck and break when removed. To preserve flowers, add a little sugar or an aspirin to the water and the flowers will remain upright instead of drooping over.

Willow, cane and bamboo furniture: Use 4 ounces (120 g) salt and 1 tablespoon (15 g) baking soda for every quart of water. Wash the furniture, rinse well, then dry and rub lightly with linseed oil. To best protect this kind of furniture, apply one coat of white shellac.

Wooden Venetian blinds: These should be dusted once a week, starting at the top and working down. At least once or twice a year, wash each slat with a sponge dipped in a solution of equal amounts of fine soap and boric acid dissolved in warm water. Then dip the sponge into clean warm water and rub the soap off the wood. Dry with a soft towel.

Kitchen Equipment and Utensils

Aluminum double boilers: Put ½ teaspoon (2.5 g) of cream of tartar or vinegar in the lower compartment with the water to prevent discoloration.

Brillo pads: To keep them from drying out between uses, wrap them in a piece of aluminum foil.

Burned or stained enameled or aluminum saucepans: Fill with cold water and 3 tablespoons (45 g) salt. Leave to soak overnight. In the morning bring this water slowly to the boil and boil for 10 minutes. Then wash in hot, soapy water. Repeat until all particles and stains have lifted.

Care of a teapot: It should be rinsed out with boiling water directly after use and then well dried both inside and out. After washing, the teapot lid should be left off, or else the pot will acquire a musty, disagreeable odor, which will probably flavor the next pot of tea. If this odor does occur, put in a teaspoon of baking soda, close the lid and let it stand until the next day. Empty it out, wash thoroughly in boiling water and scrub with a small brush, then rinse and dry carefully.

Drain cleaner: For a noncaustic drain cleaner, mix 1 cup (8 oz; 225 g) salt, 1 cup (4½ oz; 140 g) baking soda (bicarbonate of soda), and 2 tablespoons (1½ oz; 30 g) cream of tartar. Put 3 to 4 tablespoons (45–60 g) down the drain, pour a cup of water on top, let it stand for 20 minutes then flush drains thoroughly.

Earthenware pots and dishes: Helen Lyon Adamson in *Grandmother's Household Hints:* "To prevent new earthenware pottery from being broken, put it in a kettle and cover it with cold water. Then boil the water. When it has boiled for a few minutes, throw a handful or two of bran into the water and set it aside, tightly covered. When the water is cold, remove the pottery. In this way the glazing will resist damage by acids or salt."

Glassware: When glasses develop chips on the edges, rub them smooth with fine sandpaper. To remove film spots caused by dishwasher detergent on glasses, add a little white vinegar to the rinse cycle.

Greasy iron pans: Sprinkle salt in the bottom and wipe with paper towels.

Greasy pots and pans: Place a large tablespoonful of cornmeal (20 ml) (instant porridge oats) into the pot or pan and let it stand to soak up the grease. Then rinse and wipe.

Kettles: Helen Lyon Adamson in *Grandmother's Household Hints:* "To keep them free from crusts, place a flat oyster shell in the bottom of the kettle and keep it there. The shell will attract the stony particles in the water to itself and prevent the formation of crust in the kettle. This is also useful as a 'low tide' alarm in a kettle, *bain-marie* or double boiler. When the water steams low in the kettle, etc., the action of the water makes the shell bounce lightly up and down."

Kitchen shelves: Sprinkle dry boric acid on the kitchen shelves to discourage cockroaches.

Knives: Wash ivory-handled knives with plenty of soap and water. Then, if possible, expose them to the sun while still wet to whiten them. Rinse with fine salt moistened with lemon juice on a flannel cloth and dry carefully. Never wash the knife blades in water that is too hot or allow them to soak in hot water. The heat expands the steel, and is conducted up to the ivory handle, causing it to crack. When storing carbon steel knives, rub them with lanolin or petroleum jelly to prevent rust.

Lime deposits in glass cooking ware or in a tea kettle: To reduce these deposits, fill with a light vinegar solution and boil for 10 minutes.

Omelette pans: These should never be washed. After use, rub them with salt and a piece of paper towel. Then wipe with a dry cloth. Washing will cause the omelette to stick to the pan the next time it is used, unless the pan is re-seasoned with a little fat melted and rubbed in first.

Ovens:
1. Add 2 tablespoons ammonia (30 ml) to 1¼ cups (1 pt; 600 ml) water. Wash the oven with the solution and leave it to stand overnight. Sponge off the grease with warm water.
2. Sprinkle baking soda (bicarbonate of soda) around the walls and floor of a warm oven. Leave for an hour or so. Wipe clean.

Plate cracks: When a plate cracks, place it in a pan of milk and boil it for 45 minutes. Usually the crack disappears.

Rust in baking pans: To remove rust from the corners of baking pans, dip a raw potato in cleansing powder and scour.

To sharpen kitchen scissors: Cut a piece of sandpaper once or twice with them.

Silver:

1. Before storing silver, gently rub it all over with olive oil. Then pack it away in plastic bags. Kept in this way it needs only to be washed in warm, soapy water before using.
2. Separate stainless steel from silver in the dishwasher to avoid pitting the silver.

The Care and Cleaning of Linens

To make linen colorfast: Soak in a salt and water solution before washing for the first time.

Damask table napkins: Wash them in Ivory Snow, roll in a towel for a few hours and then iron. They should be stiff and glossy without using starch. However, if you prefer them even stiffer, add ½ teaspoon (2.5 ml) of cornstarch (cornflour) to the rinse water.

Pillowcases and hand towels with lace edges: Put the pillowcases and towels, or any other fragile items, into a plain pillowcase, secure the ends with safety pins and put it in the washing machine. In this way the lace will not catch on anything.

STAINS

There are many dry-cleaning products sold in shops. Some clean specific fabrics, others are for general use. Some discolor fabrics, so always test on a small bit of cloth before using a new product. The following are homemade cleaning methods for emergency use. It is a good idea to make a list of these to hang somewhere in the kitchen for easy reference.

General Principles for Cleaning Stains

1. Treat all stains as soon as possible after they have occurred.
2. If you are going to take the fabric to the cleaners, *do not do anything to the stain*. Explain to the cleaner exactly what caused the stain.
3. Before attacking any stain, immediately soak up all excess liquid with layers of absorbent paper towels.

4. Treat the surrounding area as well as the exact spot.
5. Wash out all chemicals thoroughly.
6. If there is no specific remedy, use warm, *not boiling,* water and a pure soap, like Ivory Snow.
7. Test all chemicals in a discreet spot to make sure they do not fade or damage the material.
8. When using benzine or any other volatile chemical, work out of doors or in a well-ventilated room.

Basic Ingredients to Keep in the House for Stains

Benzine (proprietary cleaning fluid)
Boric acid (borax)
Carbon tetrachloride
Carpet cleaner
Denatured alcohol (methylated spirits)
Ivory Snow
Lemons
Linseed oil
Raw potato
Salt
Soda water
Turpentine
White vinegar
Woolite

Two good basic solutions are boric acid (borax) and white vinegar.

Boric acid (borax) solution: 1 tablespoon (15 ml) boric acid (borax) in 1¼ pints (American); 1 pint (English; 600 ml) warm water. Soak for about 10 minutes.

White vinegar solution: 1 tablespoon (15 ml) white vinegar in 1¼ pints (American); 1 pint (English; 600 ml).

A–Z of Stains

Acid: Treat with a weak boric acid (borax) solution: 1 teaspoon (5 ml) to 1¼ cups (1 pt; 600 ml) water. Household ammonia may also be used: 1 part ammonia to 3 or 4 parts of water, but test on a separate piece of fabric, as it may bleach the colors.

Blood: Do *not* use boiling water as this sets the stain. Soak in cold, salted water. Then rinse in warm soapy water. Carpet shampoo is also good.

Chocolate: Sprinkle with powdered boric acid (borax), soak in cold water for 20 minutes, then pour boiling water through the fabric from a great height.

Cocoa, coffee or tea:
1. Sponge the stain with warm water and boric acid (borax): 1¼ cups (1 pt; 600 ml) water to 2 tablespoons (30 ml) boric acid (borax).
2. To remove from fabric: Pour boiling water over the fabric.
3. To remove from cups: Wash with a solution of vinegar and salt.
4. To remove from white linen and cotton material: Use a weak solution of chlorine bleach and water.

Crayon:
1. To remove from painted walls: Clean with lighter fluid.
2. To remove from linoleum: Clean with silver polish.

Dog mess:
1. Urine: Carbonated water (soda water), or a solution of 2 tablespoons (30 ml) ammonia and 1 cup (225 ml) water. Let it stand until bubbling has stopped. Sponge with fresh water.
2. Vomit: Woolite, or use 2½ cups (1 pt; 600 ml) carpet shampoo mixed with 1 egg cup (2 fl oz; 50 ml) white vinegar.

Egg:
1. To remove from plates: (a) Wash off in cold, *not hot,* salt water—1 teaspoon (5 ml) salt to 2½ cups (1 pt; 600 ml) water. (b) Remove egg yolk stains with a grease solvent such as carbon tetrachloride.
2. To remove from silver spoons: Wash in the ordinary manner, then rub with a little fine dry salt and wash again. It is the sulphur in the egg, moistened by saliva, which reacts with the silver and discolors the cutlery.

Fruit:
1. Put salt on to stop the stain from spreading, then soak in a warm boric acid (borax) solution: 1 teaspoon (5 ml) to 2½ cups (1 pt; 600 ml) water, rubbing gently. Then rinse and dry.
2. Soak stain in milk, then stretch fabric over sink and pour boiling water from a 2- to 3-foot height.
3. To remove from table linen, apply powdered starch at once and leave on for a few hours before laundering.
4. To remove fruit or vinegar stains from knives, rub the blades with a raw potato *before* cleaning.

Grass: Sponge well with denatured alcohol (methylated spirits).

Grease:
1. To remove from rugs: Brush baking soda or cornmeal lightly through the pile. Allow to stand overnight, then vacuum. On synthetic rugs, apply thin shellac or denatured alcohol (methylated spirits) to the grease spot.
2. Make a paste of lemon juice and cornmeal, and apply it to the grease stain.
3. To remove salad oil from clothes: Put talcum powder on immediately to avoid spreading and to absorb grease. *Do not rub.* Wash with boric acid (borax) solution (see page 17).
4. To remove grease film from plastic bags: Use powdered water softener only. Avoid suds which leave scum on plastic.

Ice Cream: Sponge at once with warm water and then rinse. If a grease stain remains, use a solvent such as carbon tetrachloride.

Indelible pen or pencil:
1. To remove pencil stains on clothes and fabrics: Use denatured alcohol (methylated spirits). Be careful when using this on rayon, as it will damage certain kinds and should be tested first on a small place where it will not show.
2. For ballpoint pen stains: Sponge area with either sour milk or vinegar and milk. Repeat as necessary.

Ink:
1. To remove ink from fabric: Spray with hair spray before washing.
2. To remove ink from rugs: Drench the stained area with a solution of half water and half white vinegar, taking care that the ink does not splash or spread. *Do not rub.* Instead, absorb the moisture with a terrycloth towel. Part of the ink will come out with each application. Repeat as necessary.
3. Rub the stain with milk, changing the milk until it no longer becomes discolored, then rub the stain with diluted ammonia.

Iodine: Soak affected area in a solution of sodium thiosulphate, ½ level teaspoon (2.5 ml) to 1¼ cups (1 pt; 600 ml) warm water, then wash with warm soap and water and rinse carefully.

Lipstick: This will usually wash out. If not:
1. Use a little carbon tetrachloride or hydrogen peroxide to bleach.
2. Spray the stain with hair spray before laundering.
3. To remove from table napkins: Use rubbing alcohol.

Mildew:
1. Brush off any loose mildew, then rub well with a little ordinary salt, and lastly, sprinkle with powdered French chalk and thoroughly moisten with

clean, cold water. After this, dry slowly in the open air and rinse well. This process may need to be repeated.

2. Rub the spot with a little lemon juice or a little salt and leave it to dry in the hot sun.

3. From fabric: (a) Mix a tablespoon (15 ml) each of starch and softened cake soap with 1 teaspoon (5 ml) of salt and the juice of one lemon. Rub this mixture on both sides of the fabric with a stiff brush and lay the cloth out on the grass until the stain disappears. (b) Rub the stain with strong gin or whisky, cover it with a damp cloth and iron well.

Milk: Wash in soap and water first. If a grease mark still remains, use carbon tetrachloride, benzine or denatured alcohol (methylated spirits).

Nail polish: Sponge with acetone (nail polish remover), testing the material first, then wash in warm, soapy water.

Oil stains: Apply a paste of sugar and water to the stain before laundering.

Red wine: (Use *one* of the following methods)

1. Salt first to stop spreading. Then use boiling water and borax solution.

2. To remove from rugs: Saturate the stain with carbonated water (soda water), then cover with a towel to absorb the moisture.

3. To remove from tablecloths: Either throw on some white wine—the expensive way—or saturate with carbonated water (soda water).

4. If possible, remove immediately from clothes and tablecloths, stretch the soiled area of the material across the sink and pour boiling water through the fabric from at least 2 to 3 feet, the more force the better. If the stain persists, scrub with Fell's Naphtha (naphtha soap).

5. Boil stained portions of fabric in milk before washing.

6. Sponge stains with alcohol before laundering.

7. Rub with salt and lemon juice, then wash in warm soap and water.

8. Treat with a hot solution of boric acid (borax) and water, 2 tablespoons (30 ml) to 2½ cups (1 pt; 600 ml) water. Soak until the water is cool, then wash. If the stain is old and the cloth white, use a chlorine bleach— but not for silk, rayon or wool.

Rust stains from utensils:

1. Stick a rusty knife in a raw onion.

2. Rub the utensil with a cork dipped in olive oil.

3. Rub with lemon juice and salt.

Scorch: To remove from white materials: Make a paste of baking soda (bicarbonate of soda) and water, and spread on the stain. Leave for half an hour or so, then wash.

Shoe polish: Wipe with a rag dipped in turpentine, then with another dipped in denatured alcohol (methylated spirits). Repeat alternately as necessary.

Sugar or syrup: Wash out well in warm water, then rub with ammonia diluted with warm water.

Wax candle grease from tablecloths: Lay blotting paper or quadruple folded Kleenex (face tissue) over and under the stain and iron with a hot iron. The blotting paper or Kleenex (face tissue) will absorb the wax. If a grease mark is left, use a little carbon tetrachloride or benzine.

ODOR KILLERS

1. Put a bayleaf in with *cooking cauliflower* to kill the strong odor.
2. A few grains of ground coffee thrown on a low gas flame will kill the odor of *boiled-over milk, fish, cauliflower, cabbage* and other unpleasant cooking smells.
3. To eliminate unpleasant *cooking odors,* simmer vinegar on top of the stove.
4. Strong odors can be removed from *fingers* with:
   a. A paste of dry mustard and a pinch of damp salt. Then wash with soap and water.
   b. A slice of lemon.
   c. A slice of raw potato.
   d. If you wash your hands immediately with soap and cold water after handling *fish, onion* or *garlic,* the smell won't cling in the first place. Wash in cold water and rub with salt, then rinse again with cold water and wash in the ordinary way with soap.
5. To freshen up the smell in a *kitchen,* use a few drops of oil of peppermint (available in a drugstore or herb shop) on some cotton wool when you wipe down kitchen surfaces.
6. To avoid the smell of *mothballs* in stored clothes or linen while still keeping them fresh, break up a cigar and place it in the bottom of the drawer or chest.
7. To freshen up the *musty smell* in a house which has been locked up for some time, in the fireplace burn carefully dried lavender stems which have been bundled up and tied, or burn dried lavender flowers in a metal container.

8. To remove the taste of *onions* and *garlic* on a chopping board, rub a cut lemon over the surface.

9. *Oniony knives* should be washed first in cold water, then in hot water.

10. Slices of lemon cut through the rind and dipped in salt kill the odor of *onion on the breath*.

11. Fresh *paint:*
    a. A peeled onion left in the room absorbs smell.
    b. If you live in the country, a handful of hay in a bucket does the same job.

12. To eliminate odors in the *refrigerator,* place one of the following inside:
    a. Ground coffee.
    b. Vanilla.
    c. Charcoal.
    d. Baking soda.
    e. A bowl of vinegar.

13. For cleaning out the *refrigerator,* wash inside with a solution of warm water and 1 tablespoon (15 ml) of vinegar.

14. Put a bowl of vinegar and water in the bedroom of any *sick person,* particularly during the summer. This will keep down the musty sickroom smell.

15. To get rid of *tobacco fumes* in a room:
    a. In a corner put a bowl containing 2½ cups (1 pt; 600 ml) of hot water mixed with 2 tablespoons (30 ml) of ammonia. This absorbs the fumes.
    b. If, like me, you cannot bear the smell of ammonia, leave a damp sponge on a plate in the smoke-filled room—this works almost as well.

16. Soaking the *wick of an oil lamp* in vinegar and drying it thoroughly before use will make the lamp burn with a sweeter smell.

HOUSEHOLD PESTS

Flies: When a room becomes infested with flies, heat an old saucepan, close the windows of the room, place the hot pan in the room on two bricks or something similar, and pour 1 cup (8 fl oz; 225 ml) of carbolic acid into the pan. Leave the room and close the door and keep pets and children away. Let it stand for 1 to 2 hours. Then ventilate the room thoroughly. You may have to repeat the process, but in the end it works.

Onion water (see page 10) also helps to keep flies away.

Wasp or hornet stings: Put half a raw onion on the sting—this will draw it out—or saturate a piece of cotton with vinegar or lemon juice and apply to the sting. If stung outside the mouth or on the inner lip, hold the vinegar or lemon juice in your mouth.

THE LINEN CUPBOARD

The position of the linen closet should be very carefully chosen. Under no circumstances should it be on an outside wall, but it should be in the center of the house. Ideally it should be placed near a hot-water tank to facilitate the airing of the linen.

The closet should have wide shelves, preferably slatted, to allow air to circulate and each category of linen, i.e., blankets, single sheets, etc., should have a place of its own. Then, if you label each shelf as well as each piece of linen (indelible ink is good for this) you will have no trouble keeping things in their proper places. If you have a house in the country and often have guests, it is easier to mark sheets and towels for the individual guest rooms—even if you only have one or two spare rooms.

Ideally, blankets should be put in a blanket chest when not in use to prevent moth damage. As there is often a lack of space in a city apartment this cannot always be done, but certainly it should be possible in a country house. Those blankets not in use should be washed and then thoroughly dried and mothballs placed between the folds to prevent moths. Eiderdown quilts when not in use should have mothballs distributed between their folds and should be stored on a top shelf in the linen closet.

The ideal amount of linen to have is three sets of sheets for each bed, four hand towels and face cloths per person, and four bath towels—more if you wish to spend the money. In this way the sheets may be easily rotated. Obviously, the fewer times linen is sent to the laundry the better, as frequent laundering causes wear and fading. We do all our linen at home, both in the city and in country, with a washing machine and drier. In the country, when the weather is fair we dry all our linen outside, and there is nothing to beat the smell of sheets dried in the fresh air. We have a big roller iron to do all the sheets and tablecloths, as well as the napkins, which can then be washed and reused during the weekend. The machines (washer, drier and roller iron) soon pay for themselves as the cost of laundries would otherwise be prohibitive—to say nothing of the cost of replacing lost or damaged items.

This sounds like a lot of work, but I usually do all this myself after a big weekend. After having 10 to 12 guests, I can get all the bed linen, towels and tablecloths washed, dried and ironed in a day and a half, and it is well worth it.

Table linen is usually very expensive to buy. I prefer tablecloths to place mats, both for the dining-room table and the round kitchen table where we eat every day. If you have a dining-room table with leaves to extend it, one tablecloth large enough to cover it when fully extended should be sufficient— two if you are feeling rich. You will also need two tablecloths for when the table is of medium size, and three to four for when it is at its normal or smallest size. They need not all be of expensive fabric; one may be of very good fabric and three of inexpensive cotton. If you use place mats, there are many good ones in woven straw or in plasticized cotton, which is washable and good for everyday use. Then one additional set of good organdy or Egyptian cotton for a dinner party should be enough.

You can never have too many napkins. Even though you may use paper napkins every day, you can also buy very inexpensive printed cotton napkins which make the table a bit gayer. I buy twelve napkins with each tablecloth, so there are always a few spares if one gets lost or ruined. In London we can only seat eight people, including ourselves, but then the extra napkins are used for the bread basket, or to hand around hot plates.

Basic Linen Supplies

Each bedroom in the house should be supplied with:

2 bedcovers for each bed
2 blanket covers for each bed
1 quilt for each bed
2 blankets for each bed
3 sets of sheets for each bed and a total of 12 pillowcases (2 pillows on each bed)

Each child should have:

2 sets of sheets
4 pillowcases

Basic bath supplies:
For each adult or child:

2 hand towels
2 face cloths
2 bath towels

For each bathroom:

2 bath mats

For the kitchen:

2 dozen dish towels (tea towels)
4 terry cloth hand towels
3 roller towels
4 pairs of oven gloves
1 dozen dishcloths

SUPPLYING GUEST BEDROOMS AND BATHROOMS

I like people who come to stay with us in the country to feel as though they are on a short, luxurious holiday. Since everyone we know has either a job, five children, or both, very few of them ordinarily have breakfast in bed, a nap in the afternoon, or servants to cook their food. So when they come to us in North Wales I try to give them a bedroom full of flowers, a comfortable bed with pretty linen, spare toiletries, a pretty breakfast tray—no worries and good food.

The following is a checklist of necessities that I put into each guest bedroom. The items are inexpensive and quick to arrange, but they do make the guest feel as though one has taken the trouble to make his or her stay a happy one.

Bedroom

1. Kleenex and cotton-wool balls on the dressing table or chest of drawers as well as in the bathroom.
2. A pad and pencil on the bedside table.
3. Fresh water, tap or bottled, in a carafe with a glass. These are removed in the morning when the beds are made and replaced in the evening when the bed is turned down. I often do it myself. Many people like bottled mineral water.
4. Fresh fruit on a plate (optional).
5. Lavender bags in the drawers or shelves to add a touch of freshness.
6. Flowers or little bunches of herbs.
7. An ashtray and matches.

Important: Never clutter the top of a dressing table or chest of drawers with useless knick-knacks. Guests need the space for their own cosmetics, jewelry, etc. Also, it is absolutely necessary to have two small lamps with bright lights on the dressing table rather than one large lamp. Women need equal lighting, and bright at that, in order to apply their make-up evenly, otherwise they can look lopsided. Make sure there are enough hangers in the closets. Since women wear trousers and trouser suits a great deal, particularly in the country, you will need more men's hangers to accommodate a couple, and fewer dress hangers.

Bathroom

1. Small cabinet which contains:
   2 new toothbrushes
   toothpaste
   aspirin or the equivalent
   throwaway razors
   antacid tablets
   Tampax
   a small basket with needle and thread, safety pins and scissors

At the end of the weekend I check the cabinet and replace anything that has been used up.

2. Nail brush
3. Clothes brush
4. Mouthwash
5. Bath oil
6. Bath powder
7. Fresh soap. I then collect the soaps at the end of the weekend and the family uses them up.
8. A fresh roll of toilet paper; the half-used rolls are later finished by the family.

THE KITCHEN

If you have the luxury of designing your kitchen, remember to give yourself the greatest possible amount of work space placed, if practicable, next to each of your major pieces of equipment—the stove, the refrigerator and the sink. Choose materials that are easy to care for, with rounded corners, smooth, seamless construction (with few joints for food to fall into), and a stainless, easy-to-clean, heat-resistant surface. Remember, if you have a hard wood-cutting surface built in, that it becomes marred with continued use and retains the odors of strong flavors such as garlic and onions. It is then not possible to use the same surface for pastry-making. A better idea is to have two smaller wooden boards, one for everyday chopping and one kept exclusively for pastry-making. Stainless steel, tile, marble or slate surfaces are easy to clean and also act as quick cooling agents for foods such as melted chocolate or custard bases.

If you are using linoleum as a floor-covering, a marbled effect or a pattern shows fewer spots than a plain color.

If your kitchen is small, but you do have a dining table in it, the table can double as a working surface if you cut a piece of wood to size, like a shallow box lid made to fit over the table top, and cover the underside with protective felt. You will also need a heat-resistant working surface on either side of the stove, where you can put vegetables waiting to be cooked, hot pans, draining bacon and—most important—the serving dish while you pour the food into it.

Standard counter height is 3 feet high (90 cm), but should be adjusted to your own height, otherwise you will suffer from backache and fatigue. To find the correct height, stand with your palms flat on the counter top. You should be able to do this without bending your elbows and without stooping. If you are tall you can raise the height of the base unit by placing blocks of wood under it or, indeed, under table legs. A pull-out board for lap work such as shelling peas or peeling potatoes is also a great help.

Cupboards are available in standard units or can be made to order. But always make sure they are deep enough—from 13 to 14 inches—and high enough—20 inches. I have seen cupboards in which one could put only six dinner plates and two or three glasses, and then only just be able to shut the door. The ideal is to have enough room for at least eight plates and then enough headroom to hang some cups.

Cupboard doors should be easy to open, and should swing out completely to facilitate the removal of dishes, utensils or food as well as to prevent head bumps. If you are short, place the knobs on the lower corners of the wall cupboards. Unless you have a small kitchen and need to conserve space, don't have sliding doors. I find there is always something in the middle, at the point where the doors meet, that you can't get to. Again, unless you need every bit of space in a small kitchen, avoid putting cupboards directly over the refrigerator. You will need both the air circulation around it and the room to clean it. Make sure there are toe indentations in the base cabinets to insure working comfort.

If possible, try to plan cupboards and drawers for each part of the kitchen according to what you do there. For instance, if you have a food processor or mixing unit, you will need an extra deep drawer beneath it or next to it in which to keep the various attachments. An herb shelf should be next to the stove, as should the extra-deep cupboards, for skillets, saucepans, pan lids, casseroles, etc. Or you can have a hanging rack on the wall—or overhead, if your burners are in a center island unit. Next to the stove you can have either jars containing wooden spoons and metal forks and spatulas, or these utensils can be hung on the wall nearby. I find that if one has them in a drawer, one is always shuffling about desperately while something is burning. Knives should be kept either in a slotted shelf hanging on the wall or in a divided drawer. The magnetic knife wall racks often won't hold heavy knives, and they fall, endangering everyone's safety, particularly that of small children. Also, they are a terrific temptation for children to play with, to see how the magnet works. Narrow slots in the base cabinet are extremely useful for storing trays and wooden boards and preventing their continually collapsing on the floor.

The kitchen sink is an important unit, as one spends a great deal of time there. If you have a dishwashing machine, put it next to the sink so that it is easy to rinse the dishes and put them straight in. The garbage (rubbish) compacting unit should be placed here as well. As for the sink itself, my ideal is to have two deep sinks—one for vegetables and washing up, and one for waste and rinsing—with drain boards on either side. This makes it possible to place dirty dishes and vegetables on one, and the drained, washed and rinsed dishes and vegetables on the other. But you may have room for only one sink and one draining board, or two sinks and one draining board.

There should be a glass splash-board or tiles behind the sink high enough to protect the wall. A pull-out rubber hose is extremely convenient for rinsing, and a long swing faucet/tap that mixes hot and cold water is best.

Remember when thinking of the floor of your kitchen that you will spend a great deal of time standing on it. Stone tiles are very pretty but incredibly hard on the feet. Linoleum has the give that you need under your feet.

When choosing cooking utensils, don't practice false economy. Buy what you can afford, but do not buy cheap utensils if you can afford better ones because the cheaper ones will wear out sooner and will need to be replaced a few years later when prices have risen.

Copper is the most expensive metal, but it is also the best heat conductor and is now often combined with stainless steel to improve the speed and uniformity of heat transfer in cooking. Copper utensils are usually lined with tin; the tin lining will eventually need replacing, but the copper itself will last forever. Except for certain tasks like beating egg whites, copper should never come into contact with the food itself because it causes disagreeable chemical reactions. To shine and clean copper utensils, particularly the bottoms of saucepans and frying pans, rub them with salt and a piece of lemon. Some modern copper pans are specially treated, making them easier to clean than traditional ones.

Stainless-steel utensils are made of an alloy of steel, chromium and nickel which doesn't become stained when acid or alkaline foods are cooked in them. They last longer than the comparable aluminum utensils. They do not, however, conduct the heat as evenly as aluminum. Stainless steel utensils with copperclad bottoms are extremely efficient and less expensive than copper utensils.

Aluminum comes in two types: the cast aluminum utensils for which the molten aluminum is poured into casts and molds, and the pressed aluminum, which is formed from sheets of aluminum pressed into shape. The cast aluminum is, again, quite expensive but will last a lifetime, given proper care, and can be used over hot fires and in hot ovens, as well as for slow cooking. The pressed aluminum is easily warped in high heat and dents easily. It heats quickly but also loses heat quickly; therefore it is better used for baking purposes, such as in baking sheets. Aluminum utensils will stain when water is boiled in them or when used for cooking foods containing iron, sulphur or alkalis. Do not use soap or soda solutions in them or water softeners, and *never* cook eggs in them, as the egg discolors the utensil. If you *must* use an aluminum utensil for cooking eggs, wash with a weak solution of vinegar and water boiled up in the pan to remove the discoloration. *Do not cook wine in aluminum* as the metal changes the taste of the wine. To clean aluminum, wash in hot, soapy water, rinse with hot, clear water and dry thoroughly. Use steel wool to brighten the surface.

Earthenware conducts heat slowly and evenly and retains it for a long time. It also makes an attractive dish in which to serve food. Often it can go straight from oven to table. But when buying earthenware, watch out for rough places, discoloration, and cracked or chipped spots. Earthenware is porous beneath the outer glaze and once that glaze is broken, the utensil will absorb moisture, grease and dirt; it then becomes useless. This substance will not endure sudden changes in temperature or hard knocks. Therefore never set a hot dish on a cold surface, such as marble, nor pour boiling water into a cold dish, nor take a dish from the refrigerator and put it in the oven, or vice versa. Like glass, it is not affected by acid or alkali and is easy to clean. Use scouring powder and steel wool or soap and tepid water.

Enamelware is made by dipping steel-based utensils into a liquid porcelain enamel, then drying and firing them. The porcelain enamel, which is the hardest wearing, is first dipped into the dark enamel, then into a second coat of the desired color, and finally into a third coat of acid-resistant enamel.

Never use enamel utensils for waterless cookery as they will crack easily and the chips will enter the food. Never scour enamelware as this removes the surface glaze and the enamel will become darkened. Soak the utensil to loosen foods that are stuck on.

Iron utensils are made of cast iron, which is heavy but durable, and are good, even conductors of heat. They are ideal for long, slow cooking. They are usually lacquered to prevent rusting and require conditioning and seasoning before use. Remove the lacquer by boiling the utensil in a solution of salt and water. Then wash it thoroughly in soapy water, rinse and dry. To season it, thus preventing rust, rub the utensil and lid with unsalted cooking fat or oil and place for several hours in a warm oven. Next, allow the utensil to cool with the fat still on it, then wash again and dry thoroughly. If the utensil shows signs of rust after some use, season it again in the same manner. To remove a heavy coating of grease from an iron utensil, boil it in a strong solution of baking soda (bicarbonate of soda) and water, then wash and dry thoroughly. For day to day use, clean out with paper towels, but do not wash with soap and water.

A–Z of Essential Kitchen Utensils

Aluminum heat diffuser, with handle.

Apple corer.

Baking pans: 2 baking sheets; 2 7-inch cake pans; 1 8.9-inch long loaf pan; 2 8-inch pie pans; 1 8-inch plain flan ring; 1 set of individual muffin pans.

Breadboard, round wooden.

Butcher's steel: for sharpening knives.

Can opener.

Casseroles: enameled heavy cast iron or enameled steel. These can be used in the oven or on top of an electric or gas stove. You will need 2 round casseroles, 3-pint and 5¼-pint size; and 2 oval casseroles, 7-pint and 10-pint size. Plain aluminum casseroles are not good for cooking with wine as the metal affects the taste of the food.

Cheese grater.

Chopping boards, wooden. Keep a separate one for chopping onion or garlic.

Coffee grinder: manual or electric; this can also be used for grinding herbs and spices.

Coffeemaker: I prefer the cafetière plunge method for more than one person. For one person, the Melitta single-cup filter is ideal.

Colander: 8½-inch diameter aluminum or enameled steel with tripod base.

Corkscrew, with bottle opener.

Double boiler: 2-pint aluminum, for delicate sauces and melting chocolate.

Dutch oven, with lid, for roasting.

Egg piercer: to prevent eggs from bursting while boiling.

Electric mixer, stationary or hand held.

Fish kettle: the largest that will fit your stove.

Food processor: for quick chopping, mixing, blending, making pastry dough. Based on the heavy-duty machines used in French professional kitchens, the Cuisinart (Magimix) is more expensive than many of its competitors, but it has a very strong motor. There are now many similar top-loading machines on the market.

Frying pans: Heavy steel with sloping sides and long handles, or copper (which is more expensive), or the compromise of the Cuisinart, steel with copper bottom, which distributes the heat best of all: 7-inch, 10-inch, and 12-inch sizes.

    Enameled steel with white inside, suitable for cooking egg yolks or white wine as it is a nonstaining material. Heavy enough for all types of stoves: 8-inch and 10-inch sizes.

    Oval cast iron for sautéing fish.

Funnel, plastic, for transferring liquids.

Garlic press.

Individual ramekins: 3 for baking eggs, mousses, crèmes brûlées.

Juice extractor.

Kitchen shears: Wilkinson stainless steel for right- and left-handers.

Kitchen utensil set: should include two-pronged fork, slotted spoon, shallow strainer, slotted spatula (fish slicer).

Knives: Carbon-steel knives are the best and sharpest, but must be wiped dry immediately after use. Stainless-steel knives are less expensive, can be left to dry on the dish rack but are less sharp.

    Stainless-steel bread knife with serrated edge; carving knife and fork; Chinese cleaver for chopping; 10¼-inch cook's knife and 8-inch wedge-shaped knife; 6-inch fillet knife; grapefruit knife, also useful as a spatula for filling small mushrooms, tomatoes, etc.; ham knife; meat cleaver; palette knife; paring knife; 10¼-inch slicing knife; curved-blade knife; 4-inch vegetable knife.

Larding knife.

Mandoline: for slicing potatoes, vegetables.

Measuring cup and spoons: with Imperial and metric measures, for liquid and dry ingredients.

Meat thermometer: should have a good sharp spike to penetrate the flesh and an easy-to-read dial or indicator plate.

Metal tongs: for turning and handling.

Mixing bowls: earthenware or pottery, preferably with a lip for easy pouring: 2 large, 1 medium, 2 small.

Mouli-Légumes (or other, similar, hand food mill): for puréeing vegetables and fruits, with three blades for mashing and grating.

Mouli Parsmint: for chopping parsley.

Nutmeg grater: freshly grated is tastier.

Oven gloves: 4 pairs.

Pastry boards: in wood and marble, the larger the better. Keep a separate chopping board for garlic and onions.

Pastry brushes: 2; one to be used for pastry, the other for meat and barbecues. Available flat and round.

Pestle and mortar: porcelain, for pounding and grinding herbs and spices. Porcelain is heavier than wood.

Pie pans (see baking pans).

Potato peeler.

Preserving pan: can also be used for making large quantities of soup.

Roasting pans: aluminum with a rack to lift roasts out of their juices. Flameproof dishes, 2 inches deep, and also good for baking, roasting and gratinéeing.

Rolling pin: wooden and as long as possible, preferably without handles.

Saucepans: It is not worth buying cheap saucepans; they will soon burn out and need repairing. Buy good ones which will last forever if treated properly. Heavy saucepans will distribute heat efficiently so that food does not burn, and can be used on gas or electric stoves: 4½-inch, 7-inch, and 8¼-inch sizes. A deep-fryer with spare basket for blanching. Enameled steel or heavy cast-iron enameled saucepans with long wooden or heatproof plastic handles: 5½-inch milk saucepan (no lid); 6½-inch medium saucepan, with lid; 13½-inch large saucepan, with lid.

Savarin mold: for savory mousses and rum babas.

Scales: either wall-hanging or free-standing. The Teraillon standing scale, which has both Imperial and metric measures and two lucite (perspex) trays for small or large amounts, is excellent. For the precise cook, a scale with individual weights is more accurate—if more expensive.

Skewers: for kebabs and trussing poultry.

Small stainless steel or copper bowl: for whipping egg whites.

Soufflé dishes: 8½-inch, 7-inch, 5¼-inch, and 4½-inch sizes.

Spin-dryer salad basket.

Sponges: at least 4.

Stock pot: earthenware for use in the oven, or enameled steel which can be used either in the oven or on top of the stove.

Strainers: stainless steel wire mesh, 2¾-inch and 7-inch sizes.

Sugar thermometer: for jam and candymaking.

Trussing needles: for poultry or roasts.

Vegetable scrubbing brush.

Wire cooling rack: for cooling cakes, cookies and bread.

Wire whisks: small and large.

Wooden spoons: 4 or 5. I find the ones without bowls most efficient for stirring or scraping, and one flat wooden spatula essential. It is a good idea to set one aside for using *only* when making curry.

Zester: for peeling skin off citrus fruit.

Optional extras: pasta-making machine, potato masher, yogurt maker, electric ice-cream maker.

GENERAL NOTES ON FOOD AND COOKING

STANDARD CULINARY TERMS

This list is not comprehensive, but it includes some unfamiliar words that may crop up in recipes without explanation. A more complete glossary can be found in the pages of *Larousse Gastronomique*.

Aigrettes. sour, piquant; also name given to small cheese fritters.

Aiguille à brider. larding needle used for inserting strips of fat bacon into lean meats or breasts of birds.

Aiguillettes. small strips of cooked meat.

Ail. garlic; *une gousse d'ail*, a clove of garlic; *une pointe d'ail*, a little garlic on the point of a knife.

Aitchbone of beef. the joint which lies immediately under the rump.

Ajoutées. a small garnish served with the vegetable course.

Allumette. literally, a match, but in cooking a small strip, often of potato.

Alum. an acid and astringent flavored salt, composed of double sulphate of potash and alumina. Often used in pickling and sugar-boiling, particularly for spun sugar. One pinch is adequate for 1 pound (450 g) of sugar.

Amandes (*pâte d'*). almond paste consisting of powdered almonds (*douce,* sweet almonds; *pralinées,* burnt almonds), sugar and whites of eggs or water.

Amer, amère. bitter.

Ancienne, à l'. literally, "old style," a garnish consisting of kidney beans, hard-boiled eggs, and braised cabbage leaves.

Arachide. earthnut, peanut, groundnut (England).

Arac; arrack. a liquor distilled from rice, palm juice or sugar cane; principally used in India, Ceylon and Russia.

Aromatiser. to flavor with herbs.

Arroser. to moisten or baste.

Aspic. a clear jelly made from stock used for glazing or decorating.

Assaisonnement. seasoning or condiment.

Au beurre. tossed or sautéed in butter.

Au beurre noir. with black or nut-brown butter.

Au bleu. term applied to fish boiled in salted water, seasoned with vegetables, herbs, and white wine or vinegar.

Au brun. done in brown sauce.

Au four. cooked in the oven.

Au gras. applied to meat served with a rich sauce.

Au gratin. food (frequently coated with sauce) sprinkled with browned crumbs, butter and cheese, served in the dish in which it was cooked (see *gratiner,* page 41).

Au jus. applied to food served in its own juice.

Au maigre. meatless.

Au point. medium rare, as applied to meat.

Bacalao. salt cod, used particularly in Spanish dishes.

Bain-marie. water bath; a large flat open vessel, half filled with hot water, into which are placed smaller pans containing food, such as sauces, stews, etc. A double boiler (double saucepan) may be used in the same way. Dishes such as baked eggs that need to be cooked at very low temperatures can be placed in a pan half filled with water so they do not burn.

Bake blind. to bake a pie shell or other crust shell without its final filling. The pastry shell should be pricked all over with a fork, covered with greaseproof paper, and then filled with dried beans or rice.

Barberry. a small fruit resembling black currants; as it tastes quite acidic, it is not eaten raw, but is used instead for jams, jellies and pickles.

Bard. to cover food with thin slices of pork fat or unsmoked bacon before roasting or braising.

Barquette. a small boat. Applied to dishes prepared in boat-shaped molds.

Basting. keeping meat, fish, etc., moist while cooking by pouring over it juices or fat in the pan.

Batterie de cuisine. a set of cooking utensils.

Bavaroise. a molded custard.

Beignet. fritter.

Beurre fondu. melted butter.

Beurre manié. a 2 to 1 mixture of butter and flour, kneaded together to use as a thickening for sauces, casseroles, etc.

Beurre noir. black butter, i.e., butter heated beyond the *noisette* (see page 43) stage.

Beurrer. to butter or to incorporate butter.

Bigarade. Seville orange, bitter and sour, from which marmalade is made (see Sauce Bigarade, page 259).

Bilberry. also known as blueberry in North America. In Germany, instead of soup, cold cooked bilberries are sometimes served as a first course.

Bind, to. to moisten a mixture with egg, milk or cream, so that it will hold together and not curdle.

Biscotin. a small, hard sweet biscuit.

Biscottes. thin slices of brioche paste, baked, buttered and sugared—often served for tea.

Bisque. name given to a thick, rich fish or shellfish soup.

Blanc. strong white stock. *Au blanc:* cooked in white stock and served in white sauce.

Blancher. 1. To cook in boiling water for a few minutes and then to plunge into cold water to retain color and texture; 2. to whiten or reduce the strong flavor of food by putting it in cold water, then bringing it to the boil.

Blanquettes. a rich stew of veal or fowl, served in white sauce, enriched with egg yolk.

Blondir. to shallow-fry to a light color, using butter, oil or fat.

Bombay duck. known also as bummelo, bumbalo or bumaloe fish. A delicately flavored fish found in the Indian waters. It is salted and cured, then usually served with curry.

Bonne bouche. a small savory mouthful, an hors d'oeuvre.

Boudin. a kind of small French sausage, similar to the English black pudding.

Boudin blanc. white sausage.

Bouillon. a rich, strong, clear stock.

Bouquet garni. a small bag of herbs. On a small square of cheesecloth (muslin) place a pinch of mixed herbs—a clove, 3 to 4 peppercorns, 2 to 3 parsley stalks, a tiny piece each of bay leaf and mace; tie up and add to sauces, soups, stews, etc.

Bourride. a dish strongly flavored with garlic.

Brandade. a Provençal cod dish with garlic, parsley, lemon juice and pepper, beaten up with olive oil. Also stewed haddock.

Brawn. cooked pig's head, similar to Pennsylvania scrapple.

Break flour, to. to stir cold liquid gradually into flour, making a smooth paste.

Brider. to truss with a needle and thread.

Brier. to beat or flatten pastry with a rolling pin.

Brioche. a light yeast dough, or the bread made from that dough.

Broche, à la. grilled or roasted on an open fire.

Brouillé(e). scrambled, as applied to eggs.

Browning. caramel, used as a coloring, made by browning sugar nearly to the burning point, making a thick syrup.

Brunoise. a mixture of vegetables cut into very small dice and cooked in butter or other fat; used in forcemeats, sauces, etc. (see *mirepoix,* p. 43).

Bubble-and-Squeak. a famous English dish, made with slices of cold meat fried together with boiled and minced cabbage and potatoes.

Caille. quail.

Cannelons. small rolls of puff pastry, filled with mince of game, poultry, etc., and baked.

Caper; capre. the unopened flower buds of an orchid-type plant growing wild in Greece and North Africa, but now cultivated in Southern Europe, the best coming from Toulon. Before being exported, they are pickled in salt and vinegar.

Carbonade. stewed or braised meat.

Carré. the rib part of veal, mutton, lamb or pork.

Cartouche. a round piece of greased paper which is placed on top of food while cooking.

Cassolettes. small pastry cases, baked "blind," and filled as desired.

Chapelure. grated bread crumbs.

Charlotte. a sweet preparation which may be of the variety that is served hot (in which slices of bread dipped in butter and baked form a case for fruit), or that is served cold (in which ladyfingers—or sponge fingers—form a case for a cream or cream and fruit mixture set with gelatin).

Chartreuse. a molded preparation of meat, vegetables or fruit, as well as the name of a liqueur.

Chaud-froid. dishes in which chicken, game or meat are masked with a cold sauce and served cold, often garnished with a savory jelly and truffles (see page 242).

Chiffonade. finely shredded green salad plants, or herbs—usually added to soups.

Chinois. wire sieve or strainer, conical in shape, used for sauces.

Citric acid. used in small quantities when making jam or jelly, in particular, and boiled sugar products in general, giving body and thus making the product set, and preventing sugar from getting too moist. Innate in lemon and lime in large quantity, but also available in varying quantities in other acidic fruits such as Seville oranges, currants and sour cherries. It is obtainable commercially as clear crystals or white powder.

Clarify. to purify butter of its milky solids (see page 243), or to clear stock with slightly beaten egg whites (see page 243).

Clouter. to stud something with truffle, bacon or tongue such as poultry, cushions of veal and sweetbreads.

Cocottes. fireproof dishes. Ideally made of copper, but also of glass or porcelain.

Colorer. the addition of something to give a dish color, to pass over or through heat.

Compote. may denote a carefully prepared dish of stewed fruit, or fruit set in sweet jelly, or may denote a game stew, served as an entrée.

Concasser. to chop coarse.

Coquilles. shells; *en coquilles,* small portions of food served in scallop shells.

Cordon. thin line of sauce or thickened gravy surrounding a finished preparation.

Coucher. to arrange the main ingredient on a bed or layer of one of the garnishing elements, such as spinach, noodles, etc.

Coulibiac. a Russian dish which is a kind of fish-cake mixture wrapped up in brioche dough and baked.

Court bouillon. stock, usually composed of white wine, water, pepper, salt, parsley and onions, in which to cook fish.

Crêpes. pancakes.

Crimp. to finish the edge of a double layer of pastry with fluted curves. To slash across at certain distances large fish such as salmon, sea bass or cod to allow heat to penetrate, thus increasing firmness of flesh.

Croquantes. a transparent mixture of various kinds of fruit and boiled sugar.

Croustades. pieces of fried bread, or baked pastry crusts, on which to serve delicate fish, game, ragoûts, minces and meat entrées.

Croûtons. small cubes of bread fried in butter and used as a garnish for soups. Also pieces of sliced bread fried in butter or oil, or toasted and used as a garnish for fish and entrées.

Cuillère. spoon.

Cuire au gras. to cook in fat.

Cuire au maigre. to cook without any fat.

Cuisson. the cooking process; or the liquor in which the ingredients have been cooked.

Cuit(e). cooked.

Dandelion (pissenlit; Lion's Tooth). wild herbs, the young leaves of which are also cultivated for eating raw in salads. They may also be cooked and eaten as a vegetable, like spinach.

Darne. a thick cut from the middle of a large fish, such as salmon or cod.

Daubière. oval-shaped stewpan into which you put poultry or meats that are to be stewed or braised.

Découper. to carve or to cut.

Deglaze (*déglacer*). to heat stock or wine together with the sediment left in the roasting or frying pan so that a gravy is formed. Before adding the liquid all excess fat must be removed.

Degrease (*dégraisser*). to skim off fat from soups, sauces, etc.

Demi-deuil (*en*). a culinary expression used when white meats such as veal, sweetbreads or poultry are larded with black truffles. The term means "half mourning."

Demi-glace. brown sauce, semiclear and glossy.

Dépouiller. to skin, to free fish from skin and bone.

Désosser. to bone.

Diablé. deviled, i.e., cooked with mustard, Worcestershire sauce, cayenne, etc.

Dolma. Turkish dish consisting of chopped meat and rice wrapped in vine leaves and stewed.

Dorer. to glaze, to color golden, to brush beaten egg on an article preparatory to placing in the oven.

Draw. to clean and eviscerate a bird.

Drawn butter (*beurre fondu*). melted butter often served instead of sauce.

Duxelles. preparation containing chopped mushrooms and shallots cooked together in butter (see page 291). Named after the Marquis d'Uxelles, a gourmand and gastronomer who lived at the end of the seventeenth century, and wrote a famous book on French cooking.

Émincer. to cut into thin slices or shred.

En croûte. food which is wrapped in pastry prior to cooking.

En papillote. fish, meat or birds wrapped in waxed paper or foil and then cooked.

Enrich. to add cream, eggs, etc. to a partly prepared dish.

Escaloper. to cut or dice on the bias, slantwise.

Escarole. broad-leaved chicory.

Estouffade. slow cooking in a little water or stock in a covered casserole; braised, stewed or steamed.

Étuver. to stew, cook slowly; to cook with fat, keeping covered and without moistening.

Fagot. like *Bouquet garni* (see page 36), but shaped in a bunch and tied; fresh thyme is used instead of powdered herbs.

Faire revenir. to brown meat or vegetables slightly without actually cooking them; partly fried or tossed in fat.

Faire suer. to cook meat in a covered casserole or claypot with no liquid, so that it cooks in its own juices.

Farci(e). stuffed; forcemeat.

Fariner. to dust or dredge with flour.

Fayol or fayot. a dried French kidney bean.

Fécule. fine potato flour, used for binding soups and sauces.

Filbert (aveline). hazelnut.

Flageolet. dried haricot bean.

Flamber. to singe poultry or game, or to burn off the alcohol in a sauce, as for crêpes suzette.

Flan. an open fruit tart, a French custard tart, or the custard itself.

Fleurons. small shapes (usually crescents) of puff pastry, brushed with egg, baked and used as a garnish.

Fold in. to combine a whisked or whipped mixture with other ingredients, retaining its lightness. Do this with a metal, *not wooden,* spoon, and avoid mixing too much as air bubbles will collapse, resulting in flattening.

Foncer. to line a mold with pastry.

Fondre. to dissolve, to melt, to cook certain vegetables (keeping covered) with little or no liquid.

Forcemeat; farce. finely minced meat, often veal, which is used to stuff meat or birds. Other types of forcemeat are sage and onion, oyster, chestnut and truffle stuffings.

Fouetté. beaten.

Four. oven; *au four,* baked in the oven.

Fourré. coated with sugar or cream. Also applied to stuffed birds.

Frangipane. a substitute for custard consisting of eggs, milk, flour, lemon rind, rum, brandy and vanilla. Used to fill tarts.

Frapper. to chill, put on ice.

Friandines. small patties containing a *salpicon* (see page 46), egged, crumbed and fried.

Fricandeau. braised fillet of veal, invented by Jean de Carême, cook to Pope Leo X.

Fricandelles. small, thin braised steaks of veal or game.

Frisé. curled, e.g., curled chicory or endive.

Friture. this may apply either to a special pan used for deep frying or to the foods cooked by this method.

Fumet. the essence, usually of game or fish, reduced with wine, and added to a dish to increase the flavor.

Galantine. fowl or breast of veal, boned and stuffed with forcemeat and served cold.

Gaufre. wafer or light biscuit.

Gelatin. a transparent substance made by boiling beef bones, cartilage and tendons. It contains protein and has gel-forming properties which melt on warming and set on cooking. There are now a number of synthetic gelatin products on the market.

Glace de viande. meat extract or glaze; stock which is reduced to a syrupy consistency and used to glaze cooked meats for a more appetizing appearance. It is also used to strengthen the taste of soups and sauces.

Glacer. 1. To ice or refrigerate; 2. To give a golden colored skin to heavily buttered sauces by placing them under the grill or in a very hot oven; 3. To brush dishes such as fish or meat with fish or meat glaze to give a brilliant shiny appearance; 4. To prepare food in a sugar syrup.

Glucose. an uncrystallizable sugar produced from dextrine starch and cellulose.

Gluten. a sticky substance found in flour. The albuminous element of the grain which helps to build up the body of the flour. Gluten flour is used a great deal in preparations for diabetics.

Goujons. fillets of sole cut slantwise into small pieces.

Granita, granolata. a type of half-frozen fruit or coffee water ice, served in a glass.

Gras. fat or plump, dressed with rich meat gravy.

Gratiner. to brown the surface of food in a dish under the broiler (grill) or in a hot oven. Dishes cooked in this way are often sprinkled with bread crumbs, butter and grated cheese (see *au gratin,* p. 35).

Grenadine or grandine syrup. syrup made from the pressed juice of the pomegranate combined with sugar.

Gumbo. the Creole corruption of the African word for okra (ladies' fingers) —"*guimbombo,*" it has now become the word for the soup itself. Okra is the annual pod of a tree belonging to the hibiscus family. Native to the West Indies, it is most often used in soups and pickles. Gumbo must be made principally with okra, which thickens it. Then other flavors are added. An example is chicken gumbo which is a thick soup of okra and chicken.

Hacher. to chop.

Hachis. a hash or *rechauffé* of meat.

Hanche. haunch; name applied to the leg and loin of venison, mutton or lamb.

Hominy. derived from the North American Indian term for parched corn, "auhiminea," it is a nourishing farinaceous food made of maize (Indian corn).

Jardinière. a mixture of spring vegetables which are stewed down in their own sauce.

Jarret. shin or knuckle. "*Jarret de veau*," a knuckle of veal.

Jugged. a brown stew of game, often hare, which is cooked by placing the ingredients in a jar with just enough stock or sauce to cover. It is then stewed at an even temperature in a *bain-marie* or in the oven.

Julienne. originally the name of a clear vegetable soup, first made by the well-known French chef Jean Julien in 1785, who left all his money to the poor people of Paris. Has also come to mean any food cut into very fine shreds, as were the vegetables for this soup.

Jus lié. thickened gravy.

Kasha (*kache*). Buckwheat groats. Often used in Slavic countries as a substitute for rice, and as an accompaniment to casseroles.

Kedgeree (*Kishri; kitchri*). originally an Indian dish consisting of rice or lentils, cooked with butter, *dhal* and fish and flavored with fennel, onion and spices. Now mainly known as an English dish consisting of curried rice and fish.

Kirsch or *Kirschwasser*. a liqueur prepared from cherries, used as a flavoring.

Kümmel. a liqueur distilled from caraway and coriander.

Lame. thin slice.

Lanière. slice.

Lard. to introduce small or large pieces of fat bacon with a special needle to enrich meat or game.

Lardons. strips or small dice of larding bacon.

Liaison. the binding or thickening agent used in soups and sauces. This may be egg yolks, cream, *roux*, or *beurre manié*.

Losange. lozenge or diamond shape.

Luting. a paste of flour and water used for covering a joint of venison or spiced beef for baking.

Macédoine. a mixture of vegetables cut in cubes and used as a garnish or as hors d'oeuvre, or of various fruits, frequently set in jelly.

Macerate. to steep in syrup, liquor, brandy, etc.

Maître d'Hôtel sauce. white sauce with parsley. Maître d'Hôtel butter is served on grilled meats, flavored with chopped parsley and seasoned with lemon juice, pepper and salt.

Manié. kneaded; mixed with the hands.

Marbled. veined with fat, as in beef.

Marinate. to steep pieces of meat or fish in a prepared liquid of wine, water, herbs and sometimes garlic, to both tenderize and flavor. Small pieces may be marinated in lemon juice, wine, spirits or oil with herbs.

Marmite. a large earthenware stockpot in which stocks and soups are made. *Petites marmites* are small soup pots in which individual portions may be served. Also a proprietary British yeast extract popular with children of all ages.

Mask (masquer). to cover with a layer of cream or sauce, or savory jelly.

Medaillon. a round slice of meat or fish.

Mie-de-pain. crumbs of bread without crust; fresh white bread crumbs.

Mignonette (pepper). white peppercorns, coarsely ground.

Mijoter. to stew in sauce at a low temperature for a lengthy period.

Mirepoix. more or less large dice of carrots, celery, ham or lean bacon, with melted butter. Used for brown meats, sauces or braised meats (see also *brunoise,* page 37).

Mitonner. to steep and allow to boil during a certain time.

Moisten (mouiller). to cover with liquid (stock, wine, etc.) or to add a specific amount of liquid as directed in the recipe.

Monter. to aerate by whisking or beating egg whites, cream, etc.

Moule. mold; *moule à mangue,* a round tin mold, with a lip 2 inches (5 cm) high. Also a mussel.

Mousse. literally, mossy. A very light mixture of eggs, cream and other ingredients which may be savory, like fish, or sweet, like chocolate—hot, cold or iced.

Mousseline. a lighter mousse.

Muscovado. name give to unrefined sugar.

Napper. synonymous with *mask* (see above). Also used to indicate the point in cooking when a substance has thickened sufficiently to cover a spoon or spatula without flowing.

Navarin. lamb or mutton stew, frequently served in one piece and garnished with turnips.

Neige, battre en. to beat egg whites to a frothy consistency.

Nepaul. an Indian pepper, not so pungent as cayenne, but more so than paprika.

Nesselrode. an iced pudding flavored with chestnuts, invented by Mony, chef to the famous Count Nesselrode. This name applied to any dish indicates the presence of chestnuts.

Nids. nests; savory and sweet preparations sometimes so shaped, with tiny eggs of suitable edible material placed inside them.

Noisettes. literally, nuts. Applies to the the small rounds of lean meat taken from lamb or mutton cutlets.

Noisette, beurre. a butter which has been heated until it acquires a pale brown color and nutty aroma. It is often called simply brown butter.

Normande, à la. the name implies that the flavor of apple is a primary taste in the dish, except when used with reference to fish dishes (see page 94).

Noyau. a liqueur made from peach or other fruit kernels.

Olives. thin slices of raw beef rolled around a little veal forcemeat, tied, and stewed in brown sauce, so named because they resemble a stuffed olive.

Orly, à la. slices of meat or fish coated with a rich batter and fried in deep fat.

Os de moëlle. marrowbone.

Oseille. sorrel, used for soup or as a vegetable. Delicious in salads and in a sauce as an accompaniment to fish.

Pailles. straws, applied to potatoes and to baked strips of cheese pastry.

Panaché(e). striped, mixed with two or more kinds of vegetables or fruits. Also used when referring to frozen dessert creams.

Panade. a paste of flour and water or soaked bread, used in the preparation of forcemeat quenelles and for stuffing.

Paner. to coat with egg and bread crumbs; to cover with bread crumbs.

Panurette. reddish-colored, seasoned, fine bread crumbs, used for coating where a red color is desired.

Papillote, en. paper twisted over certain articles of food for cooking, or food served in paper cases.

Parer. to trim away what is useless or uneatable; *parures,* trimmings

Parfait. a light, rich ice cream; may also be applied to a light mixture of fish, game, etc.

Passer. to pass through a sieve, strainer or tammy cloth. Also means the same as *faire revenir* (see page 40).

Passoire. colander, strainer.

Pastry bag. strong cloth or nylon bag of a conical shape to which various piping tubes are adapted.

Pâte. pastry or dough.

Pâté. 1. Paste, e.g., *pâté d'anchois,* anchovy paste; 2. Raised pie. Patty cases of puff pastry with a rich filling. Diminutive: *petites pâtés.* 3. A seasoned mixture of meats, game, poultry, fish or vegetables cooked in a terrine and usually served cold as an appetizer or picnic dish.

Pâtisserie. a small pastry, also a bakery.

Pâtissier. a pastry cook.

Paupiettes. slices of meat rolled with forcemeat, as in veal birds.

Perdreau. partridge.

Persillade. A mixture of parsley and garlic, chopped fine and used as a garnish. The dish is then *à la persillade.*

Petite marmite. French soup, containing beef and chicken broth (see *marmite,* page 42).

Petites caisses. small, shaped baked pastries with rich savory fillings; or the cases may be made of paper, china or silver.

Pilau, pilaff. an Indian or Turkish dish, prepared from rice, onions, meat and raisins and/or sultanas.

Pincer. to shrink by cooking; to color food in a pan by turning it over in very hot butter; to pinch—to use pastry tweezers to crimp pastry.

Piquer. to stud with small pieces of bacon or truffle, using a larding needle.

Pluche. leaves of aromatic herbs—parsley, tarragon, or chervil divided into tiny pieces, or lettuce or sorrel finely shredded. Used as a garnish.

Poach (pocher). to simmer in liquid between 90°–95° C without allowing to boil.

Poêler. to braise lightly; method of cooking in a closed vessel; to pot roast.

Point. the measurement achieved by inserting the point of a small knife into a finely powdered condiment such as cayenne pepper, and removing it, leaving only a minute quantity on the knife; about half a gram.

Poissonière. fish kettle.

Polenta. a standard Italian dish made of cornmeal (maize meal); similar in taste and appearance to semolina.

Pope's Eye. name given to a small circle of fat found in the center of a leg of lamb or pork. In Scotland, it is the primest rump steak.

Porterhouse steak. a thick steak cut from the middle of the ribs of beef.

Pot-au-feu. an economical but nutritious dish of boiled beef and broth, which is the standard dish of the French, and the origin of beef stock. Brought from Spain by Asmad, chef to King Philip V of France, in 1715.

Poussin. baby chicken.

Praline. a mixture of caramel sugar and browned almonds, pounded and used for flavoring in confectionery.

Printanier. a term implying a collection of early spring vegetables, left whole or cut small, used either in a form of *macédoine* (see page 42) or as a garnish, in clear soups and ragoûts.

Provençale, à la. a dish in which garlic or onion and olive oil have been used.

Prunelle. sloe, wild plum.

Pulled bread. small pieces of bread pulled from a loaf while hot and baked in a moderate oven until they become crisp.

Purée. a smooth pulp obtained by passing materials through a sieve, food processor or blender. The term is also applied to thick soups which have been sieved.

Quadrille. checkered; thin strips of paste laid across tarts to form a kind of net.

Quenelles. forcemeat of different kinds, composed of fish, poultry or meat, eggs, etc., shaped in balls or ovals. Served as an entrée or as a garnish.

Queue. tail; *queue de boeuf,* ox tail; *queues d'écrevisses,* crayfish tails.

Ragoût. a meat stew. A combination of ingredients cooked together over a period of time to give taste to one another.

Raised crust. a pastry used for making meat and other savory pies not requiring a dish. It is usually made with flour mixed into a stiff paste with boiling water and lard.

Raper. to grate or to shred.

Ravigote. a richly flavored green herb sauce, containing vinegar and garlic and served cold.

Ravioli. pasta dough rolled very thin and enclosing a mixture of spinach, cheese, meat, etc., rolled and mixed with sauce.

Réchauffé. literally, rewarmed. Food which has been cooked, and served again.

Reduce. to boil down stocks and sauces to their required consistency and flavor.

Refresh (refrâichir). to place vegetables under cold running water in order to stop the cooking process.

Rémoulade. a cold mayonnaise sauce flavored with chopped pickle, capers, eggs, mustard, parsley, tarragon and chervil.

Renversé(e). turned out, as from a mold onto a dish.

Repassé(e). strained more than once.

Ris de veau. calf's sweetbread.

Rissoler. to give a golden color to; to obtain a crisp or crusty surface by turning the food over in the pan, usually in hot shallow butter or fat.

Rissoles. minced-meat mixture enclosed in thinly rolled pastry, dipped in egg and bread crumbs and fried.

Roux. a preparation of butter and flour, used for thickening soups and sauces. There are three kinds—white, fawn and brown.

Saignant. very rare.

Saisir, faire. to cook meat briskly to seal in the juices.

Salamander. a flat metal grill for gratinéeing. It is made red hot, then applied to the surface of a dish to add color.

Salmis. a rich game stew, made with pot-roasted game.

Salpicon. usually diced chicken, veal or fish, mixed with a rich white sauce, seasoned and flavored with chopped truffles and champignons. Usually used to fill vol-au-vent cases, bouchées, canapés, or to make croquettes or rissoles.

Sangler. to surround a receptacle with ice and salt to freeze the contents—1 part salt, 5 parts chopped ice.

Sarassin. buckwheat.

Saugrené. a French cooking process, where the vegetables are stewed with a little water, butter, salt and herbs.

Saumure. a culinary bath, brine or pickle.

Sauter. to shallow-fry lightly and quickly in hot fat, shaking the pan frequently.

Sauteuse. a shallow, slope-sided saucepan, available in various sizes.

Sautoir. a deep pan for sautéing.

Sauternes. Sauterne, a very sweet, French white wine, used in dessert dishes or as an accompaniment to dessert.

Scald. to bring just to the boiling point.

Score, to. to make incisions crossways on the surface of fish, vegetables or meat to facilitate the process of cooking, thereby improving the flavor.

Sear. to begin cooking over high heat, to seal the juices and brown the meat.

Sec, sèche. dry.

Shin of beef (Jarret de boeuf). the fore portion of a leg of beef which is used for stock and making soups.

Silverside of beef. this cut comes from the top round of beef and is eaten boiled, either salted or fresh.

Singe, to. to pass a plucked bird over a flame in order to burn away any remaining down.

Sloe (prunelle). the fruit of the blackthorn.

Sorbétière. a freezing pan or, now, an electric ice-cream maker.

Soubise. a purée of onions enriched with cream.

Souse. to pickle foods by cooking them in vinegar and spices, allowing them to cool, and soaking them for a period of time.

Spatchcock (poulet à la crapaudine). originally it was a chicken, killed and immediately roasted or broiled (grilled) for a special occasion. Nowadays, it is a young, fat chicken split down the back, flattened, breastbone removed, seasoned, oiled or buttered, and broiled (grilled) or baked.

Suprêmes. term used for fillets of fish and also the best, delicate portions of food.

Sweat. to stew gently in butter without coloring, with added seasoning so that the ingredients cook in their own essences or juices.

Sweetbread (ris). a general name for the pancreas of the calf, lamb or any other animal, used as food.

Tambour. a fine sugar sieve. Also the name of a small dessert biscuit.

Tamis or tammy. a sieve or tammy cloth; *tamis de crin,* a hair sieve; *tamis de fer,* a wire sieve.

Tartare sauce. cold sauce consisting of yolks of eggs, oil, vinegar, mustard, capers, gherkins, usually served with fried fish and cold meats.

Tartaric acid. this is an acid, existing in many fruits, but chiefly in the grape root. It has the same effect on sugar as has citric acid, i.e., keeping it from getting too moist and giving it body, and helping it to set in jam. Available commercially in white powder form.

Tartine. a slice (as of bread and butter). Sometimes used to mean a sandwich.

Timbale. a light mixture of fish, game or poultry cooked or molded in drum-shaped molds.

Tomates concassées. tomatoes skinned, deseeded and coarsely chopped.

Tomates fondues. tomates concassées, gently stewed in butter or oil, with a little chopped shallot, until the moisture has evaporated and the product has become a firm pulp.

Tomber à glace. to reduce a stock to a syrupy consistency, i.e., to make a glaze.

Tournedos. beef fillets, broiled (grilled) or fried quickly.

Tourner. to turn; to give a round shape when peeling or paring. Also, to stir a sauce.

Tourte. a shallow open tart.

Tranche. a slice of meat, fish, melon or cake, etc.; *en tranche,* in slices.

Trancher. to slice or carve.

Tronçons. thick slices or steaks of fish, including the bones, cut from larger fish such as turbot, brill or halibut.

Truss. to tie together in poultry.

Velouté. a velvety smooth foundation white sauce made from fish, chicken, stock, etc. (see page 245). Also applied to cream soups with a similar foundation.

Zest. the outer colored rind of citrus fruits, thinly cut or grated, used as a garnish.

GLOSSARY OF AMERICAN AND BRITISH CULINARY TERMS

American	British
à la mode	served with ice cream
almond paste	marzipan
angel cake	no equivalent
very light, feathery white cake made from special cake flour, not available in Britain	
baking sheet	baking tray
baking soda	bicarbonate of soda
batter	dough or fritter mixture
beet	beetroot
bell pepper	sweet green or red pepper
bing cherry	black morello cherry
biscuit or soda biscuit	scone
blackberry	bramble
blaze	burn with flame

American	British
blender	liquidiser
blood sausage	black pudding
blueberry	bilberry
bok choy, pe-tsai	Chinese cabbage
bouillon cube	stock cube
broiler; to broil	grill; to grill
butter, stick of (packaging measure)	4 ounces (125 g)
candy, to	cook in thick sugar and water syrup
celery root	celeriac
cheese, American	Cheddar
cheese, blue	Roquefort
cherries, candied	glacé cherries
chicken, broiler and fryer	poussin
chicken, stewing	boiling fowl
chicory	Belgian endive
chocolate, semisweet	plain chocolate
chopped fine	minced
cocoa, unsweetened	cocoa powder
collard	spring green
confectioners' sugar	icing sugar
cookies	wide variety of sweet biscuits
cookie dough	biscuit mixture
cornmeal	cornmeal or maizemeal (available in health-food shops)
made by grinding corn (maize); contains no gluten, may be yellow or white	
cornstarch	cornflour
corn syrup	golden syrup (if corn syrup is not available from health-food shops)
liquid from the hydrolysis of cornstarch concentrated to a syrup	
cracker	cream cracker, water biscuit
cream puff	profiterole
cupcake	fairy cake
cut of meat	joint of meat
dessert	a sweet or pudding
double-acting baking powder	baking powder that acts slowly
drawn butter	melted butter
eggplant	aubergine
endive	chicory
escarole	Batavian endive
extract	essence

American	British
flapjack	large pancake
flash freeze	open freeze
flour, all-purpose	plain flour
a blend of hard and soft flour suitable for most things except delicate cakes. It absorbs less water than bread flour.	
flour, bread	strong flour (high in gluten)
flour, buckwheat (ground buck-wheat kernels)	(available only in health-food shops)
flour, cake (very fine-textured flour for making cakes or pastry)	(not available, use self-rising flour)
flour, graham whole wheat containing bran	(sometimes available in health-food shops)
flour, pastry	(not available in England)
softer than bread flour and all-purpose flour, containing less gluten. Can be whole wheat or white.	
flour, potato	farina
French fries	chips
frizzle	pan-fry until edges of food curl
frosting	cake icing
garbanzo	chick pea
gelatin	same (only plain gelatin available)
plain and flavored gelatin sold in envelopes containing 1 level table-spoon (15 ml)	
graham cracker	same (can also use digestive biscuits)
green bean	French bean or bubble bean
green onion or scallion	spring onion
grind, ground	mince, minced
hamburger roll	bread roll
heavy cream	double cream
jelly roll	Swiss roll
kisses	small meringues or plain chocolates in form of a hill with a swirl
kiwi fruit	Chinese gooseberry or kiwi
ladyfinger	sponge finger or boudoir biscuit
light cream	single cream
lima bean	broad bean, nearest equivalent

American	British
maple syrup	same
marguerite	salty biscuit with icing and nuts
molasses	blackstrap molasses or black treacle
thick brown syrup; cane sugar is crystallized from this	
molasses, black	black treacle
oyster plant, vegetable oyster	salsify
pan broil	to cook in a shallow heavy pan with a little fat; excess fat is poured off
pan-fry	sauté
pecan	same (can be found in specialty shops)
pie dough, basic	shortcrust pastry
pie pan	flan tin
pitted	stoned
popsicle	iced lolly
potato chips	crisps
pound	mince fine or beat
preforming	brick freezing
raisin (seedless)	seedless raisin, or sultana, a white raisin
romaine	Cos lettuce
rutabaga	swede
saltine	like a thin cream cracker but salty
scallop squash, patty pan	custard marrow
scampi	Dublin Bay prawns
shortening	(can mean several kinds of fat; lard has the greatest shortening power, butter and margarine have less)
shredded	desiccated
shrimp	prawn
shucked	shelled (referring to oysters or peas)
side bacon	streaky bacon
snap bean	same
spoon bread	soufflé made with cornmeal
spring-form pan	deep cake tin
string bean	French bean
squash (various shapes and sizes)	marrows
sugar, powdered or confectioners'	icing sugar
sugar, superfine granulated	castor sugar
tapioca, pearl	slow-cooking pellet tapioca

American	British
tomato paste	tomato purée
vanilla bean	vanilla pod
waxed paper	greaseproof paper
yeast	same (use 1 level tablespoon or 1
sold in an active form compressed into a cake or dry in packages or envelopes; 1 package of dry is equal to 1 cake of compressed	ounce [25 g] for 1 package or 1 cake)
zucchini	courgettes

TRADITIONAL ACCOMPANIMENTS FOR STANDARD DISHES

Soup:

CLEAR: cheese straws

PURÉES, or any thickened soup without garnish: small croûtons of fried or toasted bread served separately. Cheese straws are often served with vegetable purées.

GAME PURÉES: small forcemeat balls served separately or floating in the soup.

Fish: see page 93.

Meat:

BEEF, ROAST: Yorkshire pudding, hot or cold horseradish sauce, browned potatoes, gravy.

—— boiled (fresh): boiled cabbage, vegetables such as carrots and turnips which have been cooked with the meat, served as a garnish. Parsley sauce.

—— corned (salt): carrots, turnips, and onions. Parsley sauce. Some of the cooking liquid from the meat.

LAMB, ROAST: gravy, mint sauce, mint-flavored new potatoes and peas.

MUTTON, ROAST saddle, leg or loin: red currant jelly, gravy.

—— roast shoulder: onion sauce, baked potatoes.

PORK, ROAST: sage and onion stuffing, applesauce, gravy.

—— baked or pickled: parsnip and carrots. White sauce or mustard sauce.

VEAL, ROAST: thyme and parsley stuffing, grilled bacon rolls, gravy.

Poultry and Game:

CHICKEN OR FOWL, ROAST: grilled or baked bacon rolls. Watercress to garnish. Bread sauce. Thin brown gravy. French fried or roast potatoes, or potatoes lyonnaise. Green salad.

DUCK AND DUCKLING: sage and onion stuffing. Thickened gravy. Apple, cranberry or orange sauce. Orange salad.

GOOSE, ROAST: sage and onion stuffing; prune and orange stuffing; apple and pecan stuffing. Applesauce. Thickened gravy. Sweet and sour cabbage.

GUINEA FOWL, GROUSE, PARTRIDGE, PHEASANT AND QUAIL: as for roast fowl but with bacon rolls omitted, a liver paste or liver stuffing added, and fried bread crumbs.

HARE, ROAST: red currant jelly. Fried savory balls; port wine sauce.

RABBIT: parsley and sage stuffing, fried savory balls, thickened brown gravy. Tomato and piquant sauce.

TURKEY, ROAST: grilled sausages, veal or chestnut stuffing; sausage-meat stuffing. Bacon rolls, bread sauce, cranberry sauce, gravy.

VENISON, ROAST: red currant jelly, sour-cream sauce, gravy.

WILD DUCK OR WIDGEON, ROAST: as above, with orange sauce or orange salad added.

Vegetables:

ARTICHOKES, GLOBE, hot: melted butter, herb and garlic melted butter, hollandaise or piquant sauce.

cold: vinaigrette sauce.

Jerusalem: parsley, béchamel, velouté or tomato sauce.

ASPARAGUS, hot: melted butter or hollandaise sauce.

cold: mayonnaise or vinaigrette.

CAULIFLOWER: white, béchamel or hollandaise sauce.

CELERIAC: béchamel, egg or hollandaise sauce.

CELERY, boiled: white, béchamel or velouté sauce.

braised: brown or piquant sauce or jus lié.

EGGPLANT (aubergines): brown or piquant sauce or tomato sauce.

GREEN PEAS: mint and tiny onions while cooking, then tossed in melted butter.

LIMA BEANS (broad beans): toss in white or parsley sauce, or in melted butter with a minced clove of garlic and minced parsley.

SEA-KALE, hot and cold: as for asparagus.

SPANISH ONIONS, boiled: white or parsley sauce.

roast: browned, thickened gravy.

SQUASH (marrow): béchamel, parsley, brown or piquant sauce.

STRING BEANS (French beans): melted butter and powdered ginger in, which the beans are tossed. Pine nuts or slivered almonds sprinkled on top.

GENERAL COOKING HINTS

Bread

1. To cut fresh bread: Use a heated serrated knife.
2. To freshen stale French bread, rolls or muffins: Place them in a brown paper bag with ½ teaspoon (2.5 ml) water and heat in a low oven.
3. To keep rolls and toast hot for a long time: Place a piece of foil underneath the napkin in the serving basket.

Butter

1. To soften butter quickly, slice it thin into a warm bowl or invert a small heated saucepan over the butter on a plate.
2. A quick method for creaming butter is to add 1 or 2 teaspoons (5 or 10 mls) of hot milk to the mixture.

Cheese (hard)

1. To keep hard cheese fresh and free from mold:
   a. Place the cheese in a plastic bag with ½ teaspoon (2.5 ml) of vinegar, then store it in the refrigerator.
   b. Put 2 lumps of sugar in with the cheese in an airtight container.
2. To use up stale or dried-out cheese: Run it through a meat grinder with a little raw onion and use it as a spread or dip.

Coffee

1. To save on coffee: Bake the used coffee grounds in a baking pan in a 325°F (170° C; Mark 3) oven for half an hour. Then combine them with half the amount of fresh coffee.
2. To use leftover coffee or tea: Freeze the liquid in ice-cube trays, and place the cubes in plastic bags in the freezer. Use these, instead of plain ice, when you serve iced coffee or tea.

Cream and Milk

1. Whipping cream: To make cream whip more easily, put both beater and bowl in the refrigerator to chill first.
2. If a recipe requires sour cream or yogurt and you have only sweet cream in the house, add 2 teaspoons (10 ml) of lemon juice, a pinch of salt, and the result will be the same. The same ingredients can be added to milk for use as sour milk or buttermilk.
3. Before scalding milk, rinse the saucepan in cold water to avoid its becoming coated.

Fires, Oil or Grease

1. Throw a handful of baking soda (bicarbonate of soda) on the pan or burner. It will extinguish the fire immediately.
2. An asbestos fire blanket kept near the stove is a useful precaution.

Gas and Electric Stoves

1. When boiling something, the gas should be turned on so that the flames do not come up the sides of the saucepan. This wastes fuel. Concentrate the flames directly underneath the saucepan, which, incidentally, should have a broad, flat base in order to make fullest use of the heat.
2. Madeleine Kamman in *The Making of a Cook* tells us the trick to cooking on an electric stove: "An electric stove takes more time to heat up and cool off than gas. If you require different degrees of heat within one recipe, put each burner at a different degree of heat, and move the pot from burner to burner."

Gelatin

1. To dissolve gelatin: Moisten it with cold water in the top of a double boiler and heat the water in the lower part very gently, stirring the gelatin occasionally until it has dissolved.
2. To mold croquettes: Soak 1 teaspoon (5 ml) of granulated gelatin in a small amount of cold water for a few minutes, then dissolve it over hot water and add it to the croquette mixture. Put the mixture in the refrigerator to chill. When the gelatin has had time to harden the croquettes will be easier to mold, and they will be far better in consistency, as the gelatin melts with heat and makes the inside creamy.

Leftovers

1. Put leftover salad together with tomato juice or bouillon in a blender for a delicious soup, hot or cold.
2. Use leftover chicken, turkey or goose stuffing to stuff mushrooms, tomatoes or zucchini (courgettes), or add some sausage meat and make delicious patties for breakfast, lunch or a quick supper.
3. Leftover stale cake and cake crumbs can be sprinkled inside a mold for steamed puddings.
4. Use the liquid from canned vegetables in soups, sauces or stews, and for making white sauces.

Sugar Substitutes and Keeping Sugar

1. Rhubarb (or any other stewed fruit): If you add a pinch of salt and a pinch of baking soda (bicarbonate of soda) to the cooking water, you will then need a minimum of sugar. The salt acts as an alkali, neutralizing the acid in the fruit; angelica stalks, cut up and added to the cooking water, will serve the same purpose.
2. Sprinkle salt on grapefruit instead of sugar. It also acts as an alkali, neutralizing the acid in the fruit.
3. To take the bitterness out of coffee and to sweeten it slightly, place 2 or 3 crushed cardamom pods in the coffeepot while brewing the coffee.
4. A few grains of rice in the white sugar or salt shaker absorbs the moisture, keeping the salt or sugar dry.
5. A piece of apple in the brown sugar jar keeps it from drying out and becoming lumpy. Or store brown sugar in a clean can with a plastic lid; add several marshmallows and close tightly.
6. A small carrot, puréed, will sweeten fruit juice without adding sugar.

Water, to Purify

Powdered alum (available from any drugstore) has the property of purifying water. Put 1 teaspoon (5 ml) into 4 gallons (16 l.) of water and stir. After a few hours the water will taste fresh and clean, the alum having precipitated the impure particles to the bottom. You can also buy commercially prepared water purification tablets.

Wine

1. Cooking wine may be preserved by adding a few drops of olive oil to it.
2. Pour leftover wine into a bottle and add 2 or 3 crushed cloves of garlic; you can keep the bottle topped up and use the flavored wine in stews or

soups. Or keep a screw-top jar of dried fruit handy and pour in the remains of red or white wine as it is available. The fruit will soak up the wine to become plump and juicy. Shake the jar occasionally and use the fruit for Christmas cake.

Miscellaneous

1. To give *soup* a richer flavor and color, brown the bones, onions and carrots under the broiler (grill) before adding to the liquid.
2. *Gravy* can be darkened in color by using a bit of caramel, or instant coffee.
3. Rub the *pancake* griddle with salt instead of grease. This will prevent the pancakes from sticking, and it also prevents smoke and odor.
4. *Kitchen scissors* can be used to top and tail gooseberries, to chop parsley, and *always* to snip chives.
5. When mixing *dry mustard powder,* add a few drops of olive oil. This greatly improves the flavor.

COOKING WITH FATS AND OILS

"The healthy action of the digestive process must be provided for by careful attention to various particulars. First of all, the food must be of good quality and properly cooked. The best methods of preparation by cooking are the simplest; such as roasting and baking, broiling (grilling), or boiling. Articles of food which are fried are very apt to be indigestible and hurtful, because the fat used in this method of cooking is infiltrated by heat and made to penetrate through the whole mass of food. Now we know that the fatty substances are not digested in the stomach, as the gastric juice has no action upon them, further than setting them free from the albuminoid substances upon which they may be entangled. This variety of food, together with the starch, is digested below the stomach through the action of the pancreatic and intestinal juices. This is why the saturation of food by fat during cooking should be avoided, as the fat acts as a varnish to the albuminous substances and prevents free access to the latter of the gastric juices, by which alone meat can be digested. In their natural condition fatty substances are simply mixed loosely with the albuminous matters, as butter when taken with bread and vegetables, and the solution of the albuminous matters into the stomach therefore easily sets them free, to pass into the small intestine. But when imbibed, and thoroughly infiltrated through the alimentary substances, they present an obstacle to the access of the watery gastric juices and not only remain undigested themselves, but also interfere with the digestion of the albuminous matters. It is for this reason that all kinds of food in which butter, or other oleaginous matters are used as ingredients, so as to be absorbed into their substances in cooking, are more indigestible than if prepared in a simple manner."

Treatise of Physiology, Dalton

Fats are made up of three types of fatty acids—saturated, monounsaturated and polyunsaturated. These are determined by the amount of room left on the molecule for additional atoms of hydrogen. A fatty acid that has no more room for hydrogen is called saturated; one that can take two or more hydrogen atoms is monounsaturated; and one that has room for four or more additional hydrogen atoms is polyunsaturated. Small amounts of all three kinds of fat are necessary to the proper diet. Some saturated fat is necessary for proper nutrition. Both mono- and polyunsaturates transport fat-soluble vitamins. In addition, some polyunsaturated fatty acids possess special biological properties; these are the essential fatty acids of which linoleic acid is the most important.

Saturated fats do, however, raise blood cholesterol, which eventually clogs the arteries, more effectively than polyunsaturates lower it. Thus a margarine, for example, should contain 2 grams of polyunsaturated liquid vegetable oil to 1 gram of saturated.

Edible vegetable oils are natural products which come from the seeds or the fruit of certain plants. The oils to avoid are coconut oil and palm oil, which, at 53%, are highly saturated. These, together with olive oil, are low in polyunsaturates. Those vegetable oils which have no cholesterol and are relatively low in saturated fatty acids are:

1. Corn oil and sesame oil—14%
2. Cottonseed oil—29%
3. Olive oil—10%
4. Peanut (arachide) oil—10%
5. Safflower (sunflower) oil—11%
6. Soybean oil—15%

The more saturated a fat, the less stable it is—the more susceptible it is to rancidity and overheating, and the lower its melting point. This differentiates between fats (solids) and oils (liquid) at normal temperatures.

The Effect of Heat on Oils

When vegetable oils are heated, their fatty acids undergo chemical changes. At the same time, external indications of this alteration appear: odor, coloring, increased viscosity, sometimes the appearance of foam.

The characteristic sign, which tells one that serious decomposition is beginning, is the "smoke point"—the temperature at which the fat gives off smoke because of unbound free fatty acids which have been insufficiently refined. An oil which has been well refined has a high smoke point. The qualifications required for an oil to be used in high-temperature cooking are:

1. Purity.
2. Good physical characteristics: taste, odor, color.
3. A high smoke point and, thus, a high flash point (the point at which it catches fire).
4. Good heat stability—the oil must not be too saturated.
5. Sufficient fluidity to allow food to drain well.

In *peanut oil,* food may be fried thoroughly to a crisp brown in a short time without being greasy. This oil also has a high smoking point and viscosity, which supports ingredients longer, and is a useful factor in mayonnaise and salad dressing. Polyunsaturated oils do not become saturated when cooked, and are digestible as long as they are not heated to the smoking point for more than 15 minutes. Peanut oil (otherwise known as groundnut or arachide oil), which has a high smoking point at about 428° F (220 ° C), can be used for frying at temperatures up to that level before it begins to smoke and undergo undesirable chemical changes. If the oil reaches flashpoint by mistake, and burns, it is best to throw it away and begin again with fresh oil.

Each time an oil is heated to its smoking point, that smoking point decreases; and with it decrease the cooking and taste qualities of the oil. As most people do not heat peanut oil as high as its smoking point, it can be reused up to 10 or 12 times. You must occasionally strain it, however, to remove particles of food which encourage rancidity and reduce the smoking point.

Peanut oil is liquid at room temperature, tasteless, and virtually colorless. Compared to other seed oils, it contains a high proportion of tocopherols, compounds which are active with vitamin E, and which are also powerful antitoxicants, protecting the oil from rancidity.

Virgin *olive oil,* deriving either from the first pressing of the olives, or that drawn from the top of the settling tank, is the best and most expensive. French olive oil is more delicate in flavor than that from Italy, Spain and Greece, which is more gold-green in color and has a stronger taste of olives.

Olive oil is extracted from the pulp of the fruit which has ripened slowly in the sun for six months. This makes it rich in chlorophyll and vitamins. The oil is protected at all stages of manufacture from contact with light, one of the principal causes of rancidity. It is the most easily digested of all the oils; chemically, it is the oil whose properties are nearest to human fat. It is well-known as beneficial to the liver, and its cholic and cholagocic qualities have earned it a place in the official pharmacopoeia of all major countries, a privilege denied to other fats.

Its disadvantages are that: 1. Pure virgin oil has such a distinctive flavor that for cooking it should be mixed with some refined oil to neutralize the taste; 2. When heated to a high temperature, it contracts a strong taste, probably due to the charring of particles of the flesh of the olive that remain imperceptibly mixed with the oil.

Not all fats are absorbed by humans in equal measure. Research conducted on pancreatic lipase, both living and in vitro, has proved that digestion is total for olive oil, whereas its rate decreases for other oils:

Olive oil—100%
Safflower oil—83%
Peanut (groundnut, arachide) oil—81%
Linseed oil—79%
Sesame seed oil—57%
Poppy seed oil—48%
Corn oil—36%

SLOW AND FAST COOKING: A WORD ON SLOW COOKERS, PRESSURE COOKERS AND MICROWAVE OVENS

Slow Cookers

Slow cookers operate on the old, long, slow-cooking principles of the haybox. In the electric slow cooker, the low temperature is sustained by the heat of the cooker itself; in the case of the haybox, by the heat of the contents of the pan or the casserole. Slow cooking has a double economy: first, you can use the cheapest meat, which will become tender through the long, low-temperature cooking; and second, it saves a great deal of fuel. Because of its insulation it needs only a tiny amount of electricity (the same amount as a 60-watt light bulb on low and 120 watts on high). In addition, slow cooking results in the least possible shrinkage or evaporation of food. And, of course, of great importance is its safety—the cooker can be left on all day, much as you would a lamp.

Busy people can put on the evening meal in the morning before going to work and come home to find it ready. The food will keep so that people can help themselves when they wish. It is, therefore, convenient for large families. The electric slow cooker is also perfect for making stocks, as it allows them to simmer overnight.

The food must be heated first and then put into the already-heated pot (unless cooking from frozen, see page 62). The empty casserole should be preheated on a high setting while the ingredients are being prepared. Meat should be fried in a frying pan to seal in the juices and to help boost the starting temperature. This also browns the meat and improves the appearance of the finished dish. Stock or liquid should be brought to the boil before adding to the slow cooker. Onions and garlic should be browned or softened in a frying pan, then added 10 to 30 minutes after the other ingredients. The slow cooker should be switched to the low setting for the remainder of the cooking period, except when roasting chicken or pork, for which the high setting should be maintained throughout.

The lid should always be left on until the cooking is completed (except to add last-minute ingredients). Steam condensing on the inside of the lid and on the rim of the casserole forms a water seal which keeps the heat in. Lifting off the lid causes considerable heat loss.

Most meat and vegetable recipes require at least six hours on low. Root vegetables and potatoes need longer cooking times than meat. Meats with a high fat content should be trimmed, browned and drained before adding to the slow cooker, as they do not "bake off," as they would in a conventional oven.

All slow cookers can be filled to within one-half inch (15 mm) of the top without fear of their boiling over. They are available from a 2¾ pint (2 pint) size to a 8¾ pint (7 pint) size, the last being the most economical for a family of four if you entertain a great deal or if you have a freezer and can freeze the excess.

Slow cookers are ceramic and won't take sudden temperature changes, therefore they must *never* be put over an open flame. Equally, do not put the hot pot on a cold surface, but rather on a table mat or a wooden chopping board. When washing the pot after use, always use warm water, never cold. Pots with separate heated outer casings may be washed, but never immerse the casing in hot water. Pots with integral heating elements should *never* be immersed. Fill the pot with warm water to soak off any burned-on food. Then scrub lightly with a plastic or nylon scourer.

Basic Rules

1. Use fewer strongly flavored vegetables, such as onions, turnips, or celery, because the slow-cooking method will retain more of their original taste.
2. Frozen meat, fish and poultry *must be thoroughly thawed* before being put into the slow-cooking pot. Or put them into a cold pot, then turn it on to low; it will take longer to cook, but it will make up for the thawing time.
3. Less liquid is needed than in cooking on a stove, ¼ to ½ pint (5 fl oz to 10 fl oz; 125 to 250 ml) is usually sufficient. It can be water, wine, stock or soup, but never milk or cream. These latter liquids should always be added just before serving, otherwise they will curdle.
4. As the flavor of the meat, poultry or fish is retained more than when cooking on a stove, fewer herbs and spices and seasonings are needed. Reduce by half what you would ordinarily use.
5. For the slow-cooking method, the processed cheeses are better. If using hard cheese, grate rather than slice it.
6. The quick-cooking rices are better to use than the raw ones, which tend to give uneven results.
7. When using soup as the liquid ingredient, the best are canned or dehydrated. If you are using the latter, halve the amount of water recommended. Condensed soups need no water. *In all cases,* stir at the end of cooking.
8. Thicken the sauce before serving with plain flour or cornstarch (cornflour).
9. Use whole fresh spices and herbs when possible, since the dried spices tend to develop a stale taste during the long-term cooking. If you must use dried ground herbs, add them during the last hour of cooking.

Pressure Cookers

Pressure cooking is a method which is both economical and quick, with fewer cooking smells and less steam in the kitchen for a shorter period of time. Another advantage of the pressure cooker is that the speed of cooking allows maximum retention of nutrients and flavor. A complete meal can be cooked simultaneously in the dividers within the pressure cooker, as odors are not transferred during steam cooking.

It is the harnessing and control of steam in the pressure cooker, ordinarily lost when cooking in saucepans, that cooks the food. The high rise in temperature and the forcing of the steam through the food softens and tenderizes the food quickly and seals in the vitamins.

Most pressure cookers are supplied with instruction booklets, which not only explain how the appliance should be handled, but also give some idea of the length of time it takes to cook various types of food.

There are three pressures: high (15 pounds), which is used for day-to-day cooking; medium (10 pounds), used to soften fruits for jam, jellies, marmalades, and for bottling vegetables; and low (5 pounds), for steaming mixtures with leavening agents, fruit bottling, and blanching of most vegetables before deep-freezing them.

Microwave Ovens

No one is suggesting that you should get rid of conventional ovens and stoves and just use microwave ovens. There are things, such as browning, that conventional ovens can do better, just as there are certain jobs the microwave does well, more quickly, and using fewer utensils. These include defrosting, reheating, making hot drinks and quick snacks. You can melt chocolate in a bowl in just 1 minute, cook cereal in 2 minutes, and bake potatoes in about 5. If you make your own bread, you can have a loaf on the table in 1 hour. Instead of waiting for the yeast to "prove," you put the dough in the microwave for 15 seconds on full, then rest it for 10 minutes, doing this three or four times until the dough has doubled in size. Vegetables retain their color and vitamins, and have a strong, natural taste when cooked in a microwave oven.

The reason microwave cooking is so quick is that it uses electromagnetic, short-length, high-frequency radio waves. Inside the microwave oven is a magnetron vacuum tube. This converts ordinary household electrical energy into high-frequency microwaves that are either reflected or absorbed by materials. Metals reflect, so cooking utensils must be nonmetallic; glass, pottery, paper and most plastics allow the microwaves to pass through. Dishes are placed on a glass or ceramic shelf to enable the microwaves to reach the food from below; a metal reflector, called the stirrer, built into the top of the oven, distributes the waves evenly. The moisture in the food absorbs the microwaves, causing the molecules to vibrate rapidly, creating friction, which in turn creates heat which cooks the food from within while the oven remains cool. The dishes get warm only through heat transference. Although the stirrer (metal reflector) should insure an even dispersal of microwaves, be sure to keep turning the food during thawing, heating or cooking. Microwaves heat moisture more quickly and therefore you will get certain hot spots.

Because the waves penetrate the food to a depth of about 1½ inches (4 cm) from any surface, top or bottom, the heat is conducted quite quickly, but eventually it does slow up. Therefore with large items such as roasts over 4 pounds (2 kilos), a resting period is needed during the cooking time to allow the heat to penetrate.

When food is thawed or cooked, "standing time" insures good results. This is because, even after the electromagnetic waves have been turned off, the food continues to cook by heat conduction; during the "standing time" the heat will penetrate uniformly, heating right through. This can take 1 to 2 minutes for small amounts of food, or up to 20 minutes for large roasts.

As there is no applied surface heat, food does not brown easily on the outside during short cooking times. A browning dish is needed for this, or you can use a broiler (grill) or conventional oven after the microwave cooking has finished. Any cut of meat over 3 pounds (1½ kilos) will develop some natural browning because of the longer cooking time.

Some people are worried about the dangers of cooking with microwaves. There have been varying reports concerning radiation, which falls into two categories: particle radiation and electromagnetic radiation. There is no particle radiation from a microwave oven. Electromagnetic radiation can be divided into ionizing and nonionizing types. If an organism is exposed to high-frequency rays, a chemical change takes place in the cellular structure. With nonionizing rays there is no chemical change in the organism. Ionizing rays have a cumulative effect while nonionizing rays have no effect but to cause a change in temperature, i.e., heat, so they can be used in cooking. Ionizing rays are rays such as gamma and ultraviolet, while nonionizing rays are radio, TV and microwave.

All the well-known manufacturers have added devices which prevent microwave leakage above an acceptable amount. The primary device is a stainless-steel door which reflects the microwaves. The second is the choke cavity that surrounds the outside of the door and reflects the leaking waves back into the cavity. The third device, the Ferrite, absorbs microwaves on three sides of the door. There is a solid hinge of steel on the fourth side. In addition, there are two or three micro-switches that make it impossible for the oven to cook with the oven door open. If these fail, the crossbar will blow the fuse which will turn off the oven. If by chance someone pushes the "on" button with nothing in the oven, an automatic switch will turn it off in twenty minutes.

The radiation leakage, measured at 2 inches (50 mm) from the door, must never exceed 5 m/w. Most new ovens have a leakage of 0.3 to 0.8 m/w.

A defrost button is a good investment on an oven, as is variable power control. The latter is particularly good for the beginner; it allows more flexibility of cooking time and gives a better texture and flavor to the food. It also allows you to slow down cooking if necessary. On its lowest number, the oven is off more than it is on; on medium to high, it is on more than it is off, and on high it is on the whole time. At the lowest number, for instance, you can keep cooked foods warm for approximately half an hour, melt chocolate, soften butter and prove yeast. At setting 4 you can thaw meat and fish. With a variable power control, you can use cheaper cuts of meat in casseroles.

Many people think that they have to buy new cooking utensils for the microwave oven, but if you look around your kitchen you will find many dishes that are usable, such as china soufflé dishes for baking bread, pottery casseroles, Pyrex and glass. *Do not use metal or gold-rimmed china* (the metal will reflect the rays). Poor quality plastic tends to melt. For roasting, use roasting bags.

One dish worth buying is a ceramic browning dish. Preheat it in the oven, place steaks or chops on it, and it will then sear and brown the food. Many firms recognize the growing popularity of microwave cooking and are making special containers that may be used directly from freezer to oven. Anchor Hocking has a range of microwave cookware that can be used from freezer to microwave oven, or in gas or electric ovens at up to 400° F (200° C; gas mark 6).

Plastic wrap is an essential accessory. Food can be wrapped in it while cooking to retain moisture; small holes pricked in the plastic allow the steam to escape. Paper kitchen towels can also be used. Foil should be used only to protect against overcooking, e.g., for wrapping chicken legs. Remember, foil will reflect the waves. For the same reason, you should not use metal ties on roasting bags.

There are quite a few ovens on the market, and there will be more; the choice depends on the extras you require. The output varies from 600 to 700 watts. One great advantage is that a microwave, unless built in, is entirely portable and can be used anywhere provided there is an electrical source.

CHOOSING AND STORING CANNED AND DRY GOODS

Canned and dried goods should be kept in a cool and dry place. The ideal is to build yourself a larder with an outlet to the outside. Otherwise choose a cupboard well away from the stove or any radiator.

1. Never buy dented cans; the tin lining is probably ruptured and rusting may set in.
2. Avoid storing cans where they could be in danger of being dented.
3. Never buy cans which are rusty or show any signs of leakage.
4. You can tell a "blown" can, in which the contents are deteriorating due to rusting, because the top, bottom, or both will curve slightly outward instead of being flat.

Recommended Storage Time for Canned Goods

Baby food	2 years
Fish in oil (e.g., tuna, sardines in tomato sauce)	5 years
Fruit (except prunes and rhubarb, see below)	1 year
Fruit juice	1 year
Meat (stews, corned beef)	5 years
Milk (*not* evaporated or condensed)	1 year
condensed	4–6 months
evaporated	6–8 months
Milk puddings	1 year
Pasta in sauce (ravioli, etc.)	2 years
Pet food	2 years
Prunes and rhubarb	9 months
Soups	2 years
Vegetables	2 years
Whole meals containing meat and vegetable	2 years

Recommended Storage Time for Unopened Dry Goods

Baking powder	3 months
Baking soda (bicarbonate of soda)	3 months
Cake mixes	6 months
Cereals, breakfast	1 month
Cocoa, drinking chocolate	3 months
Coffee, instant, or ground sealed in a tin	1 year
Cookies and crackers (biscuits)	2 months
Cornstarch (cornflour)	6 months
Cream of tartar	3 months
Custard powder	6 months

Flour, white all-purpose, plain and	
self-rising	6 months
whole-wheat (wholemeal)	6 months
Herbs and spices	6 months in a lightproof container
Dried beans (pulses)	9 months
Milk, skimmed, powdered	6 months
Oatmeal, rolled oats	3 months
Pasta	several years, if good quality
Potato, instant	4 months
Raisins, sultanas, or dried fruit	3 months
Soups and sauces (dehydrated)	2 months
Sugar	2 months
Tea	2 weeks or less
Yeast, dried	6 months

Once you have opened a package, empty it into an airtight container which has been cleaned and dried, even if it held the same kind of food before. Otherwise the stale taste of the earlier product might pervade the fresh product. Always label and date the container. This is particularly true in the case of cornstarch (cornmeal) and rising agents, which lose their thickening and rising powers when stale.

FREEZING

The point of owning a freezer is convenience: buying in bulk or buying specials at the supermarket, and freezing meat, or fruits and vegetables from your own garden. Using a freezer you may have to shop only once a month instead of once a week or more.

A freezer should be used as an extension of your oven: When you are cooking stews, making soups or grinding meat for hamburgers, make more than you need immediately and freeze the rest. It will not take much more fuel or effort, and the time saved later on will be enormous. When the various herbs are in season, freeze them. Even frozen fresh herbs give a better taste than dried ones. Lemon and orange juice should be frozen when these fruits are at their cheapest. Lemon juice, I find, is useful in drinks and in everyday cooking.

The cost of running your freezer will depend upon the efficiency of the machine itself, as well as its position in the house. Obviously, if it is in a hot kitchen, it will use more fuel than if it is in a cool garage or cellar. It also depends upon how often you open the freezer door. Incidentally, if the electricity fails or is turned off at any time, *do not open the freezer at all*. With the power off and the door left shut, food should stay frozen for 10 to 18 hours with no spoilage.

When buying an upright freezer look for one with either removable or adjustable shelves—this will allow for large or cumbersome objects. In general, whether buying an upright, chest or refrigerator/freezer, take into account the *storage volume,* i.e. the usable space, rather than the gross volume, which includes the shelves and bins or baskets. If you are planning to freeze a great deal of fresh food rather than just storing already frozen food, it would be wise to look for a freezer with a fast-freeze switch, although you can also simply turn down the temperature control to its coldest setting. In either case, always turn on the fast-freeze switch or turn down the control two or three hours *before* freezing large amounts of fresh food. Then, when the food is frozen, turn up the setting or turn off the fast-freeze switch.

Defrosting

Defrost the freezer when it is almost empty, just before the new fresh vegetables and fruits come into season. I usually do this in June, or during the year if a one inch thick layer of ice has formed on the inner walls. If the ice is allowed to thicken, the efficiency of the freezer will be reduced. Plan to defrost the freezer at least one day before you start freezing new food as it will take quite a few hours to return to the proper freezing temperature. *Important:* Turn on the fast-freeze switch or turn down the temperature control to its coldest setting two or three hours before defrosting. This will allow the already frozen food to remain frozen longer while removed from the freezer during defrosting. Then go on to:

1. Disconnect the freezer, then remove any remaining food, wrap it in thick layers of newspaper and store in a cool place. Put ice cream into the freezing compartment of your refrigerator. Make a list of frozen foods as you remove them so that they can be put back in the proper order.
2. Place some newspapers on the bottom of the freezer and scrape the frost from the sides with a plastic spatula or special freezer scraper. Never use any sharp implement or you may pierce the freezer lining and the damage will be expensive to repair.
3. Leave the freezer lid or door open. To speed up the process, place a bowl of warm water on the floor of the freezer while you are removing the ice. Sweep out with a clean dustpan and brush. Then, when all the frost has

melted, mop up. Wipe out the entire outside of the freezer with a damp cloth. If there are obstinate food stains, clean them with some baking soda (bicarbonate of soda) and warm water. Again, never use abrasives which would damage the lining.

4. When the freezer is clean and dry, plug it in and place on the lowest temperature for 1 hour with the lid or door closed. Then reload as quickly as possible, replacing the foods in their proper order, having first wiped away any crystals from the packages themselves. If you have a fast-freeze switch, turn it on, otherwise raise the temperature to normal. Close the lid or door, and *do not open it for at least 3 hours.*

5. Be sure to wear freezer gloves or thick leather gloves when doing all this or you will suffer painful frostbite.

6. The entire process ought not to take more than 1½ hours.

Freezing Hints

1. A partially filled freezer accumulates excessive frost and wastes energy. To prevent this, fill the unused space with breads, containers of water and ice cubes.

2. A good method for freezing casseroles without giving up the use of a favorite dish is to line the dish in which you will eventually serve it with heavy-duty aluminum foil. Pour in the cooked food and freeze it in this container. When thoroughly frozen, remove the aluminum-lined contents from the dish, wrap in the foil and place in a plastic freezer bag. Label the bag and indicate what needs to be added when defrosted, i.e., ½ pint (250 ml) cream, garlic, etc. When you serve the casserole, remove the aluminum foil and place the frozen block back into the original casserole to be reheated.

3. Boil-in bags are ideal for freezing stews and cooked meat sauces. The frozen food may then be cooked in the bag in boiling water. To insure a proper seal, if you haven't a proper sealer, place the bag between two layers of newspaper and use an iron at a low setting.

4. It is much more sensible to freeze food and liquids in small quantities. First, you can always defrost several packages more for larger groups, and second, it is easier to thaw small quantities than one huge block.

5. When freezing crêpes, chops, steaks, hamburgers and fish cakes, always put waxed paper or aluminum foil between each item, so that you can peel off as many as you need at one time.

6. Plan meals for weekends to use up frozen food. Have a list of what needs to be removed from the freezer each day in order to give it time to thaw.

Asparagus: Stack in milk or waxed freezer cartons filled with water.

Avocados: Peel, then wash in a solution of 1 tablespoon (15 ml) lemon juice and ½ tablespoon (7.5 ml) sugar for each avocado. Keep protected completely from the air by placing them, covered with a layer of mayonnaise, in an air-tight container. When thawing the avocados, remove the mayonnaise and any discolored portions of the fruit.

Cheese: Freeze cheese when it has reached maturity, particularly Brie. Defrost in the refrigerator, then, when thawed, remove and leave at room temperature for at least 1 hour. If you are buying a whole Brie or Stilton, divide it into portions likely to be consumed within 2 to 3 days, otherwise it will go bad. Hard cheeses such as Gouda, Edam and Cheddar can be frozen in portion-size blocks or grated in 4-ounce (125 g) and 8-ounce (225 g) bags. It is better to add grated cheese for topping cooked dishes, such as casseroles, after reheating them; then place the dish under the broiler (grill) for a minute or two, otherwise the cheese will become oily and stringy.

Crackers and cookies: Broken sweet crackers or cookies can be made into pie crusts. Crush them with a rolling pin and mix with about half their weight in melted butter. Press into a pie plate and freeze. When frozen, remove the shell from the plate and pack carefully in foil, then in a freezer bag.

Eggs: If you have separated yolks or whites left over, freeze the yolks in an ice-cube tray, adding ½ teaspoon (2.5 ml) of salt for every cup (8 fl oz; 225 ml) of yolk. Freeze the whites in waxed freezer cartons. Yolks should be thawed at room temperature for 1 hour, or in a bowl of warm water. Whites can be used straight from the freezer for making meringues, or thawed at room temperature for soufflés. Whole eggs should be broken into a bowl and blended lightly with a fork. Then for every 1 cup (8 oz; 225 ml) of whole egg, stir in ½ teaspoon (2.5 ml) of salt. Pour into containers and freeze.

WHEN DEFROSTED, THESE ARE THE EQUIVALENTS TO FRESH EGGS:

3 tablespoons (45 ml) blended yolks with whites = 1 egg
2 tablespoons (30 ml) egg whites = 1 egg white
1½ tablespoons (37.5 ml) egg yolks = 1 egg yolk

Egg-based mousse cannot be frozen as it develops an unpleasant rubbery consistency.

Egg-based sauces: the oil will separate from the egg yolk, but if an egg yolk is added after thawing, the sauce can be brought back together.

Fruit: Raspberries, blackberries, blueberries, red, white and black currants freeze very well. Buy or pick these when they are ripe. Wash and hull them, then freeze by spreading them out on a cookie sheet (or jelly roll tin) so they do not touch one another. When they have frozen solid, put them in plastic bags in half-pound (225 g) and one-pound (450 g) lots. Seal, label and return to the freezer. They may then be defrosted and used for sauces as well as desserts.

Peaches may be peeled, sliced and frozen in a sugar syrup and kept in plastic containers. Strawberries, mangoes and papayas are so mushy when thawed that they should be puréed (without sugar) and then frozen. Persimmons should be kept at room temperature until they bcome bright red and are just beginning to soften. Then wrap them individually and snugly in aluminum foil and freeze. Allow 45 minutes' thawing time.

Syrup for fruit: Bring 1 cup (8 oz; 225 ml) water and ½ cup (4 oz; 100 ml) sugar to the boil and allow to cool. Add 2 to 3 tablespoons (30 to 40 ml) of lemon juice for tartness.

Leftovers:

POULTRY CARCASSES. If you haven't time to make stock right away, freeze the poultry carcass on an open tray. Then put it in a freezer bag and, with a meat tenderizer, break it into small pieces. Store until you wish to make the stock.

STUFFINGS. Freeze in waxed cartons and use in soups or meat loaves. It is better to freeze stuffing separately from large cuts of meat, as stuffing has a shorter storage life than meat, and also because rolled, stuffed cuts should not be cooked from the frozen state.

PLUM (CHRISTMAS) PUDDING: Slice and place it, as you would crêpes, between sheets of aluminum foil, waxed paper or greaseproof paper. Wrap in aluminum foil and freeze until needed. To serve, fry the slices in butter and serve with brandy or orange butter.

SLICED LEMONS: Remove pits but retain peel; fast-freeze them on a tray, then when they are quite hard pack them in freezer bags or boxes. They will keep for up to one year. Frozen lemon slices can be used for decorating foods or for putting into drinks.

MEAT SAUCES: Those containing wine or vinegar should be packed in plastic or waxed cartons. Do not put them in foil or aluminum containers as the acid acting on the metal may discolor and affect the flavor of the food. Allow all sauces to cool thoroughly and skim off as much fat as possible before freezing.

Nutmeats and coffee beans will keep indefinitely in the freezer.

Raisins, dates, prunes, figs and apricots are easier to grind if they are frozen, and it is easier to grate or "zest" *citrus rind* if it has been frozen.

Rice: Cooked rice can be frozen either in an aluminum container or in a polyurethane bag. If using the latter, remember to separate the grains half-way through freezing by gently squeezing the bag. When completely frozen, seal the bag, allowing ½-inch headspace. Reheat in sealed bag.

Sour cream can be frozen but becomes grainy in texture, so whisk until smooth after defrosting.

Vegetables: Instead of using a lot of little plastic bags for vegetables, blanch them, drain and spread them in a single layer on a baking sheet covered with waxed or greaseproof paper. Put another layer of paper on top of the vegetables and spread more vegetables on top, then another piece of paper and more vegetables until there are four layers. Fast-freeze the vegetables, and when frozen place them in a large plastic bag. Frozen this way the vegetables are separated, so you can take as many or as few as you need. The waxed paper can be reused.

Freezer Storage Life

Bakery:
  Bread
        Uncooked dough: 3 months
        Baked: 2–6 months
  Pastry, cooked
        Baked blind: 3 months
        Baked with fruit: 6 months
        Baked with meat: 2 months
  Pastry, uncooked
        Puff; flaky: 6 months
        Shortcrust: 3 months

Dairy:
  Butter: 6 months
  Cream, whipping: 2 months
  Ice Cream
        Commercial: 1 month
        Homemade: 3 months
  Cheese
        Hard, whole or grated: 6 months
        Soft (Brie, Camembert, Port Salut, Mozzarella): 3 months
        Stilton: 3 months

Fish, raw:
    Salmon: 4 months
    Shellfish: 3 months
    Whitefish: 6 months

Fish, cooked: 2 months

Fruit:
    With sugar: 12 months
    With no sugar and purées: 6 months

Liquids: Soups, stocks and sauces: 2–3 months

Meat, uncooked: (For more detailed information see individual meat sections.)
    Chicken and duck: 12 months
    Goose and turkey: 4–6 months
    Giblets: 3 months
    Venison: 12 months
    Rabbit and hare: 6 months
    Offal: 2–3 months
    Beef: 8 months
    Lamb: 6 months
    Pork: 6 months
    Veal: 6 months
    Smoked and cured meats: 1–2 months
    Sausages: 3 months

Meat, cooked:
    Casseroles and stews: 2 months
    Curries: 2 months
    Meat loaves; pâtés: 1 month
    Roasted meat: 2–4 weeks.

Refreezing

Although refrozen food may not be at its peak of perfection, except for fish, it is in no way unsafe to eat, and its eating qualities will have been only slightly impaired if the food has been handled hygienically and was of a good quality originally. Food which has been thawed covered in the refrigerator is safer to refreeze than that which has been allowed to defrost uncovered in a warm kitchen, as this is the sort of atmosphere that encourages the growth of bacteria.

Unfreezable Foods

Salads: lettuce, chicory (tomatoes may be frozen whole only to be used in casseroles or sauces or as tomato purée).

Fruits: bananas, which turn black. Pears, which lose delicate flavor and texture.

Custards: tend to separate.

Cottage cheese: becomes rubbery.

Fresh milk, light (single) cream and sour cream: separate if frozen.

Fried foods: become tough and dry.

FISH AND SHELLFISH

Both fish and shellfish contain protein of varying qualities, all good. Fat is also present, but in the form of fish oil which has a high proportion of polyunsaturated fatty acid and low amounts of cholesterol. Most have relatively little oil and a higher percentage of protein. This is true of haddock, whiting, cod, shrimp, scallops and lobster. Herring, mackerel and certain freshwater trout have somewhat higher levels of polyunsaturated fatty acids. With the exception of lobsters, which contain only a small amount, neither fish nor shellfish contain any carbohydrates. Generally all freshwater fish, with a few exceptions which will be mentioned later, contain less salt than beef and are rich in the minerals phosphorus, potassium and iron. Saltwater fish contain large amounts of iron, and fish roes and shellfish give up copper, zinc, manganese, cobalt, molybdenum and selenium.

SELECTING FISH

The three main classes of fish are white, oily and shellfish. When buying fish, it is important in white and oily fish that the smell be fresh and salty and the flesh firm, moist, smooth and elastic to the touch, so that when pressure is put on it there is no indentation left by the finger. The gills should be red, the eyes bright and not sunken in the head, the fins firm and the flesh should be well covered with bright scales. Scales that fall off easily indicate a soft condition of the flesh, showing deterioration. Any natural markings on fish, such as are found on plaice, freshwater trout and hake, should be clear and distinct. Any sign of fading indicates staleness. In whitefish the color of the flesh is important. A slight opalescent coloring shows that the condition of the fish was poor when caught. If the fish you buy is not as fresh as it ought to be, washing it in vinegar and water will greatly improve it. Then fry it instead of poaching it.

Remember when buying a large fish that you pay for the whole fish, including the intestines. Therefore, if you need a 6 pound (2.7 kg) fish to cook, buy a 7 pound (3.2 kg) fish, as the intestines and gills weigh between 1 and 1½ pounds (450 and 700 g) according to the size of the fish. Allow 1 pound (450 g) of fish per person when buying a whole fish—before it has been cleaned and scaled. Allow ½ pound (225 g) per person of dressed fish—i.e., fish which has been cleaned, scaled, and the head, tail and fins removed. Allow ⅓ pound (150 g) per person if you are buying fish steaks or fillets.

A fish fillet or steak should have a clean appearance and a firm, moist texture with no leathery traces of yellowing or browning around the edges. Shellfish, when uncooked, should be heavy in weight in proportion to its size, showing that the fish is in good condition. In old shellfish, the flesh shrinks and water creeps into the shell. There should be no barnacles present on the shell, as these are also signs of age. Also, be certain that the tails of fresh lobsters, shrimps and crayfish are tightly curled and will spring back into place when you straighten them. When you bring your fish home, do *not* leave it wrapped in paper or soaking in water. Instead, put it on a plate with a sprinkling of salt and fresh lemon juice, and cover it with a piece of foil. Be sure to place it on a shelf in the refrigerator well away from milk, cream or butter, all of which will absorb the fishy smell.

Anchovy: Has a clear green back when freshly caught, darkening to near black as the fish becomes less fresh. Should have bright silvery sides and a silvery white belly. The average size is 3½ to 5 inches (8.9 to 12.7 cm). To clean and cook: Scale and gut the fish, removing the head, and washing and drying the gut cavity thoroughly.

Atlantic Pollack, Boston Bluefish (Saithe, Coley): Very dark green on the back and upper sides, with dull silvery lower sides and belly. The pinkish flesh turns white when cooked. Usually available at 16 to 30 inches (40.7 to 76.6 cm) and sold as steaks or fillets. It can be baked or fried, but as it tends to be rather a coarse and dry fish, it is better when used for soups or fish pies.

Bass (Black and White, Sea Bass): Has a greenish-gray back with bright silver sides and belly. Can be as large as 2 feet (61 cm), and is sold and cooked either whole or in fillets. To clean and cook: Remove the scales and sharp spines on fins and gills. If you are cooking the fish whole, clean it thoroughly through the gills and remove the eyes. If filleting it, cut off the head and clean it through the belly. It is best stuffed with herbs and garlic, wrapped in foil and baked. But it can also be poached in court bouillon or white wine. Delicious served cold with either Sorrel Hollandaise or Pernod-flavored Mayonnaise (see pages 111–112).

Bluefish (Snapper Blues): Has a blue back with a white belly. As it is a very oily fish, it must be cleaned and gutted as soon as possible after being caught. It should be eaten fresh—some prefer to eat it cold rather than hot, when it has a slightly bitter taste. Bake or broil (grill) the fillets from a fish of 6 to 8 pounds. (2.7 to 3.6 kg). For fish of 10 to 20 pounds (4.5 to 9 kg), it is better to bake them whole over charcoal. When cooked, chill, skin them and serve cold.

Brill: A dull, sandy-brown flatfish belonging to the turbot family, with small darker flecks and lighter spots, and a creamy-white underside. Not as delicate in taste as turbot. Available usually from 11 to 16 inches (27.9 to 40.7 cm) and 1 to 2½ pounds (450 g to 1.1 kg). The flesh should be firm with a yellow tinge. If it has a blue tinge *do not buy it*. Can be cooked whole, preferably baked or poached in court bouillon. Can also be shallow-fried in slices, or broiled (grilled) in fillets as sole is.

Carp: A freshwater fish which these days is usually farmed. It has a brownish-green skin with few or no scales. Available usually at 15 to 20 inches (38.6 to 51 cm) and 2 pounds (900 g). It can be poached, broiled (grilled), or fried if large and filleted. If small, it can be stuffed and baked whole.

Cod (Codfish, Scrod [when 1½ pounds (700 g) or less]): Has a greenish or sandy-brown coloring with darker or lighter mottling on back and sides and a white belly, with white and flaky flesh. Flesh must be rigid, eyes clear and gills red. The head and tail should be small and the fish should be very thick through the shoulder. It may be kept in the refrigerator up to 24 hours. Available usually at 24 to 32 inches (61 to 81.2 cm) and 4 to 14 pounds (1.8 to 6.3 kg). If small, cod is sold whole, but usually it is sold in fillets or steaks. Can be fried, baked, used in pies or poached.

John Dory: Has a yellowish-brown back, with yellow lines and black spots along its sides, and a silver-gray belly. Generally available up to 15 inches (38 cm). Usually sold without the head, as it weighs a great deal and would be very expensive if sold whole. Also sold as fillets. Available mainly in England and France. To clean a whole fish, remove gills, fins and eyes, and clean through the gill openings. Cook as you would sole.

Eel, Common: Has a dark green back with a silver belly. The males grow up to 18 inches (45.7 cm), the females up to 36 inches (91.5 cm). They should be killed when bought and cut into pieces to cook—broil (grill) over charcoal, stew with red wine and mushrooms, use in eel pie, fry or bake. They may be served hot or cold with a variety of sauces.

Eel, Conger: Has a blue-gray back with a light underside. Grows up to 8 feet (2½ m) long. When buying, ask for a thick cut from the head. As it has an extremely strong flavor, this fish is best used in soups.

Flounder (Dab, Fluke, Blackback, Yellowtail): A flat fish, brown in color, with black spots on the eyed side, dull white on the blind side. Is usually 8 to 12 inches (20.3 to 30.5 cm) long, approximately 1 pound (450 g). Generally sold as fillets, but sometimes sold whole when small. To be fried. You need 2 to 4 fillets per person.

Grayling: A small game fish with silver sides and belly, the back ranging from steel blue to silvery green. Best when weighing approximately ¾ pound (350 g). Cook as you would trout.

Haddock (called Scrod when 1½ pounds [700 g] or less): Has a dark grayish-brown back with grayish-silver sides and a white belly. Available usually at 10 to 20 inches (25.4 to 30.5 cm) and 1 to 2 pounds (450 to 900 g). Usually sold filleted and can also be bought smoked. (See page 104 for a delicious soufflé recipe.) Can be cooked as you would cod or hake.

Hake (Whiting, Silver Hake, Frostfish): Has an iron-gray back, silvery sides and a silvery-white belly. Its cousin, the whiting, has a sandy- to greenish-blue back and is a drier-tasting fish. Hake must be eaten fresh, usually as steak or fillets. Poach, steam, bake, grill or fry it. The whiting should be stuffed and baked rather than broiled (grilled), or used in soups.

Halibut: A long, flat fish, with dull greenish-brown coloring on the eyed side and a white blind side. Available up to 6 feet (1 m .83 cm) and from 2 to 90 pounds (900 g to 36.45 kg). It is usually sold in steaks, but when small it is sold whole as chicken halibut. To cook, remove the skin by pouring boiling water on it. Halibut can be broiled (grilled) or fried, baked, steamed or poached.

Herring: Has a deep blue-black back and pearly belly. Usually available at 5 to 10 inches (12.7 to 25.5 cm) and 5 to 12 ounces (150 to 350 g). It must have firm flesh, shiny scales, bright, clear eyes and red gills. If the eyes are red *do not buy*. Herring must be bought and eaten fresh. The roe is a delicacy which may be cooked and eaten on toast or used for pâtés. The fish itself is delicious coated in oatmeal and fried in bacon fat until crisp brown, or stuffed and baked, smoked or soused.

Huss (Dogfish, Flake Rigg): Has a sandy-brown back and small dark spots on the sides, with a cream-colored underside and slightly pink flesh. Available at approximately 25 inches (65 cm) and 2½ pounds (1.1 kg). It must be bought and eaten when very fresh. Best when deep fried in batter or used in soups.

Mackerel (Atlantic Blue, American, Cero, Kingfish): Has a blue-green back with black curved lines, and a paler belly. Available at approximately 9 to 12 inches (22.8 to 30.5 cm) and ½ to 1 pound (225 to 450 g). *It must be bought and eaten very fresh*—on the same day—otherwise it is tasteless and flabby. Mackerel should have firm flesh and clear, protruding eyes with bright red gills. All the blood must be washed away before cooking. To broil (grill), score three times on either side of the backbone to allow heat to permeate. Serve broiled (grilled) with Gooseberry Sauce (see page 256) or mustard butter; also delicious marinated and cooked with onions (see page 108).

Mullet, Gray: Has a dark green or blue-gray back, a gray-white belly, and silver sides striped with gray. Available at 10 inches (25.4 cm) and 1 pound (450 g), and usually sold whole. It must be bought and eaten fresh. You can broil (grill) the smaller fish, but stuff and bake the larger ones. Gray mullet roe is the primary ingredient in authentic taramasalata.

Mullet, Red (Striped): Has a red back shading to pink and then white on the belly. It should have bright, rosy scales. Do not buy if its color is dull. Usually about 8 ounces (225 g). It should be cooked with the liver intact, as this is considered a delicacy. Broil (grill), fry or bake—do not poach or steam.

Perch (Lake Perch, Ringed Perch): Has a greenish-brown back, creamy-white belly and golden-green sides. Usually about 2 pounds (900 g). If freshly caught, skin immediately. If large, stuff and braise in wine, otherwise cook as trout.

Pike: Has a greenish-brown back flecked with lighter golden green, and a yellowish belly. Usually available at 2 to 4 pounds (900 g to 1.8 kg). Young fish are better to eat, as older fish can be coarse and dry. Because they contain a large amount of gelatin, they are particularly good to use in *quenelles* and fish stocks. If cooking whole, discard the roes, stuff and bake or braise.

Pilchards: Adult sardines. They have the general shape of and are cooked like herrings, but their scales are larger and easily detached. Their backs are blue-green, with silvery-white bellies and golden sides. Usually sold at up to 10 inches (25.4 cm). Like herring, they must be *bought and eaten very fresh*. If their eyes are red, they are stale and should not be eaten. To cook, clean them and bake or fry. Treat sardines the same way.

Plaice: A flat fish similar to the summer flounder; brownish-gray on the eyed side, with large, bright red or orange spots. White on the blind side. Approximately 8 to 14 inches (20.3 to 36.7 cm) and 8 ounces (225 g) to 1½ pounds (700 g). Must be bought very fresh, whole or in fillets. Cook as you would sole.

Redfish: Has a bright red back with a rosy belly and dusky gills. Usually 18 inches (46 cm) and 6 pounds (2.7 kg). Usually sold in fillets but also sold whole. Make sure it is not sold to you as sea bream (see below), which it is not. Scale and clean, taking care to remove the sharp spines. Best when eaten stuffed and baked in foil. Also good in soups and stews.

Rockfish or Catfish (Fiddler, Blue Channel): Has a bluish-gray back with darker crossbars, and firm, slightly pink flesh. Should be skinned immediately when landed. Usually sold in fillets. To cook, fry in clarified butter with garlic, braise with vegetables or use in soup.

Salmon: Has a silver-gray back with silver sides and a white belly, and bright pinkish flesh. As it is quite oily, it is also extremely rich. Scotch salmon has a better taste than Canadian salmon. Will grow up to 20 pounds (9 kg). Those at 8 to 10 pounds (3.6 to 4.5 kg) I find have the best taste. Salmon is sold whole or in steaks. The whole fish must be very stiff, with bright scales and red gills. For steaks, the tail piece has a better flavor and more moisture, although it also contains more bones. Salmon will keep in the refrigerator for 48 hours. You can cook it by poaching, but I prefer to bake it wrapped in foil with herbs, lemon, butter and white wine. Skin it after cooking to retain the moisture.

Sea Bream: Has a dull red back, silvery sides and belly, and scarlet fins, and is usually 1½ pounds (700 g). Be careful you are not sold redfish as bream; this usually happens with fillets. To prepare, wash and scale the fish, remove fins, clean through the gills or slit the belly. Best stuffed and baked.

Skate (Ray): A flat fish which has a dark olive-brown top with light brown blotches and darker spots, huge wings and a pale gray belly. The weight ranges from 3 pounds (1.4 kg) to 12 pounds (5 kg). Skate is, usually, best a few days after being caught. The skin should be slimy and the flesh pink and moist. The smaller fish are more delicate and have a better taste than the larger ones, which tend to be tough. Should be sautéed in brown butter with capers.

Smelt: Has smooth, shining, silvery skin. There are many varieties of smelts, the smallest of which are sold as "whitebait." Some think that it smells like cucumber. The average size is from 6 to 8 inches (15 to 20.3 cm). They should be cleaned through the gills and wiped. The whole fish may be eaten, including the head, tail and backbone. You will need two smelts per person. They should be broiled (grilled), pan-fried, or deep-fried in batter.

Snapper: More often found in America than in Britain, the red snapper has firm white flesh not unlike the sea bass. Average size is 2 feet (60 cm), and it is usually sold in steaks.

Sole, Dover: Flat fish, medium to dark brown with patches on the eyed side, creamy on the blind side, with very firm flesh. Dover sole, which originates in the North Sea, is the most expensive white fish; it is at its best 2 to 3 days after being caught, and is sold whole or in fillets. Weighs from 8 ounces (225 g) to 14 ounces (400 g). Usually broiled (grilled), fried whole on the bone, or baked with wine.

Sole, Lemon: A flat fish, brownish to dark brown on the eyed side but paler than the Dover sole, and white on the blind side. Average size is 1½ pounds (700 g), and it is sold whole or in fillets. Broil (grill) or serve the fillets stuffed, in a light cream sauce.

Sprats: With a dark green back shading down to brilliant silver sides, sprats look like young herring. *Whitebait* are the baby sprats or herring, usually 1 inch long, which are eaten whole and ungutted, including the head and tail. Allow 8 ounces (225 g) per person. Delicious dipped in milk, shaken in a bag with some flour, and deep-fried in hot oil until brown and crisp—about 2 minutes. Sprats are 4 to 8 inches (10 to 20.3 cm) long and should be bought very fresh, looking bright and silvery. Cut off the head and tail. If small, they need not be gutted; if large, clean through the gills. Broil (grill) or fry.

Squid: A torpedo-shaped cephalopod with a transparent inner shell or quill, and ten tentacles with suction discs. Usually 3 to 8 inches (7.6 to 20.3 cm) long. Most often sold frozen but sometimes available fresh. Discard the intestines and ink sac. You may want the ink for sauce. Quick-fry small fish; larger squid can be stuffed and stewed.

Trout, Brown: A spotted brown back and white belly, with firm, pale pink flesh. Available from 7 ounces (220 g) to 12 ounces (350 g). Should be eaten very fresh. Cook as you would rainbow trout.

Trout, Rainbow: An olive-green back and greenish-white belly with a pink band on the flank and tiny black spots over the head and body. Size ranges between 7 ounces (220 g) and 12 ounces (350 g). Because they are being farmed, rainbow trout are now available larger and all year round. However, a smaller wild one still tastes better. Clean through the gills or belly. Do not remove the eyes, which should turn white when the fish is cooked. Broil (grill) when very fresh, or bake stuffed.

Trout, Salmon (Sea Trout or Sewin): Dark blue to black on the back, with silvery sides shading down to a white belly. The flesh is pale pinky reddish. These are river trout which have spent one or two seasons in the sea eating seafood so that they combine the best taste of salmon and trout. They have the added advantage of having moister flesh that does not dry out when cooked. Their texture is less dense, their flavor more delicate, and they are less rich and oily than salmon. Usually sold whole, they generally range from 1½ pounds to 4 pounds (700 g to 1.8 kg). Clean and bake them whole in foil, with herbs, butter, lemon and white wine.

Turbot (Greenland Turbot): A flat fish that varies its color to match the sea bed much as a chameleon does, but it is usually dull sandy brown with darker spots and speckles. It must be thick and rigid, and the underside should be a rich cream color. Avoid any that have a bluish-white tint. Turbot has firm white flesh, and can range in weight from 2 pounds (900 g) to 45 pounds (20 kg). It can be kept for 48 hours in the refrigerator. The smaller turbot, up to 2 pounds (900 g), are called *chicken turbot*. They can be bought whole, and serve 2 people. The large fish are usually served as steaks or fillets. Cook as you would sole or bake in foil.

Weakfish (Spotted Sea Trout, White Sea Bass, Corvina): Available from Cape Cod down to North Florida. It has a spotted pale green back and a pale greenish-white belly. The average weight is from 1 to 3 pounds (450 g to 1.4 kg), but can go up to 15 pounds (7 kg). The flesh is white, lean, sweet and finely textured. It should be eaten as soon as possible after being caught to retain its delicate flavor. The alternative is to freeze it immediately upon being caught. The roe is also delicious and makes a very good pâté. Either sauté, broil (grill) or make into chowder.

Witch (Flounder, Torbay Sole): A flat fish, pale brown on the eyed side, with a faint purple tinge, and white on the blind side. Usually around 14 inches (35.5 cm), and sold whole or in fillets; cook as you would sole.

Special Note on Shellfish

Oysters and Clams: When choosing oysters, make sure the shell is difficult to open. If the shell opens immediately on touching, the fish is unfit to eat. The muscles must be sunken, not swollen and standing above the fish.

Mussels: When choosing mussels, do not buy any whose shells are already open. However, after cooking them, discard any whose shells have *not* opened.

Lobster, Shrimp and Crayfish (see page 86)

CLEANING, FILLETING AND STUFFING

Most fish sellers will clean and fillet a fish for you, but if they won't, or, if you have caught the fish yourself, you should know how to do it.

Round Fish

To clean:
Leave on the head and tail. (If you do want to remove the head, make a diagonal stroke with your knife, slanting from the back of the head to the underside of the fish. The gills, located under the flaps behind the head, will come away as well.)

1. Using the back of a knife or a fish scaler, scrape off the scales, working against the grain from the tail toward the head.
2. Next, remove and discard the red gills from the flaps behind the head and then, going in from the head end with a knife, remove the intestines from the belly cavity. Carefully and thoroughly scrape the belly cavity free of all blood. OR
   a. Make a slit two-thirds of the way along the belly starting from below the gills and scrape out the insides, including the black skin. Wash the fish well under running water to remove all traces of blood and any loose scales. Drain thoroughly.

3. Snip off the various fins with a pair of scissors.
   a. Holding the knife diagonally, cut off the bony edges and dorsal fin.

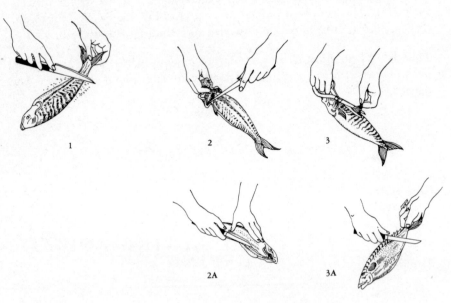

To fillet:
1. Slide the knife along the backbone from the nape to the tail.
2. Roll back one whole side of the flesh leaving the whole backbone on the other side.
3. Cut the whole backbone out, again working from the nape to the tail.
4. Cut into 4 fillets.
5. To remove the skin from the fillet, hold the tail end and slide the knife under the flesh, working toward the head end.

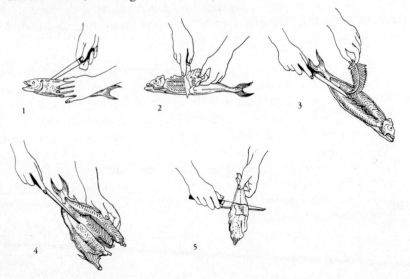

To stuff:

1. Make a large opening in the belly cavity, towards the head.
2. On the upper flap, slide the knife along the rib cage and backbone from the nape to the tail. Then do the same on the lower flap. Remove the rib cage from the flesh.
3. Make an incision at both ends of the backbone. The whole backbone and rib cage should come away.
4. Stuff the cavity.

Flat Fish

To clean and fillet:

1. Hold the fish by its tail and, using the back of a knife or a fish scaler, scrape off the scales, working against the grain.
2. and 3. Cut off the fins and tail with a pair of scissors.
4. Cut off the head with a sharp knife.
5. Press the fish gently and eviscerate it through the cavity left by removing the head. To make sure it is perfectly clean, scrape the cavity with the point of the knife. Wash the fish under running water and pat dry.
6. Place the fish, eyed-side down, on a board and, with its tail end nearest you, slide a sharp knife along the backbone from nape to tail all the way through.

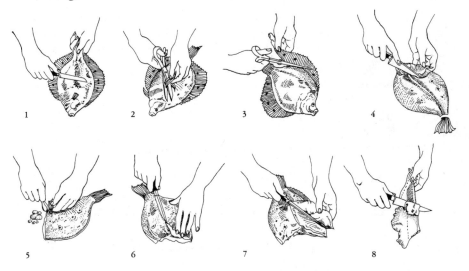

7. Then, lifting the flesh, slide the knife along the rib-cage bone, releasing the fillet. Turn the fish over and release the other side in the same manner.
8. To remove the skin, hold the tail end of the fillet and slide the knife under the flesh towards the tail. You will have 4 fillets.

To stuff:
1. Cut down the backbone to the center of the fillets.
2. Slide the knife along the backbone on each side to release the flesh. Remove the backbone.
3. Stuff the cavity and close the fillets over the cavity.

To Skin a Whole Round or Flat Fish

Hold the fish by the tail; you may need a damp cloth with which to hold the fish firmly. Working from the tail to the head end of the fish, using a sharp pointed knife, slide it between the flesh and the skin.

To Clean Mussels

Place them in cold water to cover and add 2 tablespoons (30 ml) of uncooked Quaker oats (porridge). Leave them for 2 to 3 hours. The mussels will eat the oats and rid themselves of their sand. The oats also make the shells easier to clean. Scrub the shells thoroughly, removing any clinging barnacles. I use a brush with steel or brass bristles for this. Then remove the "beard," sticking out of the shell from one side. Discard any mussels whose shells are cracked, broken or already open.

It is tempting, but can be very dangerous, to collect your own mussels. Be sure to avoid any waters that might be polluted, or beaches located near sewage outfalls. If you are in any doubt, best fight the temptation.

To Clean Lobster and Crayfish

Lay them face down on a board and split them with a large, sharp knife from the head along the back of the middle of the tail. Separate the halves and remove the "sac" from the head and the gray-black thin intestine.

King Prawns (Dublin Bay Prawns)

Remove the intestine in the tail.

FREEZING FISH

Freezing your own fish should be done only if you know the fish is absolutely fresh. Otherwise it is better to buy already frozen fish. Freshly smoked fish may be frozen raw or cooked. Do *not* freeze smoked fish which has already been commercially frozen for distribution purposes and then thawed for sale. Do not keep fish in the freezer longer than 3 to 6 months. It will not go bad, as such, but tends to lose its fresh flavor and texture, and oily fish, in particular, can develop a rancid flavor. One good trick is to thaw frozen fish in milk. This will give it a freshly caught taste. Drain it before cooking and wipe the fish dry.

When thawing a large fish, such as salmon or sea bass, allow 5 to 6 hours per pound (450 g) in a cool larder or refrigerator, and 3 to 4 hours per pound (450 g) at room temperature. Then cook it immediately.

To freeze a large fish, set the freezer at "fast/freeze" for 2 hours before freezing, rub the fish with olive oil to prevent it from drying out, then seal it by dipping it into cold water before open-freezing. Leave until frozen solid. Then remove and dip it in fresh cold water. A thin film of ice will form around the whole fish. Return it immediately to the freezer. Repeat this three times at half-hour intervals. Wrap the fish in heavy-duty aluminum foil and/or heavy-gauge plastic sealed with freezer tape. It is best to freeze only one fish at a time, as it will freeze faster this way.

Fish Freezer Life

Haddock, whole	6 months
fillets	4 months
Herring, whole or filleted	4 months
Mackerel, whole or filleted	4 months
Salmon, whole	6 months
cuts or steaks	4 months
Turbot	4 months
Whitefish, whole, large	6 months
small	4–5 months
Fillets or steaks of other fish	3 months
Smoked fish, whole	8 months
sliced	4 months
Shellfish	2 months

COOKING FISH

In *whitefish,* such as whiting, haddock, plaice, sole, cod and hake, the fat is mostly in the liver and is removed during the cleaning process. The fibers are loosely held together by connective tissue which contains a large quantity of water. During cooking, this connective tissue turns into gelatin as in meat fibers. The high percentage of water dilutes the gelatin so formed, and the fibers readily fall apart. It is for this reason that fish is more easily and quickly cooked and digested than meat.

Boiling is not suitable for cooking whitefish. The weight and movement of the water breaks the fibers and the fish becomes watery and flavorless. Dry methods such as baking, sautéing and frying are more suitable because the high percentage of water in the fish allows it to cook in its own liquid.

Oily fish, such as herring, mackerel and salmon, contain fat, protein, water, mineral matter, and vitamins A and D, with smaller amounts of B and C. The fat is distributed throughout the fibers. When fat is combined with other foods digestibility is retarded, so though the food value of oily fish is greater than that of whitefish, it is not as easily digested. In addition, the fibers of oily fish are constructed in such a way that they are not so easily broken down in cooking. Generally, oily fish have a higher percentage of protein and a lower percentage of water than whitefish. During cooking, the water evaporates and the protein becomes more concentrated; this, combined with the high percentage of fat, yields more calories to the pound. Oily fish should be cooked as soon as possible after catching as their condition deteriorates rapidly.

Shellfish, such as crab, lobster, prawns, shrimp, mussels and clams, again contain protein and fat, but owing to the construction of fibers, they are all difficult to digest. For this reason, vinegar, or a sharp sauce, is often served as an accompaniment. The acid helps to soften the fibers and render them more digestible. The sharpness of the sauce stimulates the flow of the digestive juices. Hard-shelled crabs and lobsters also have a high sodium content, so are not good for salt-free diets. Oysters, however, are easy to digest; they are low in sodium, high in protein, but contain more carbohydrates. In the past when they were quite cheap, they used to be served to the sick, as they were so easily digested. They do, however, deteriorate very quickly when removed from their shells, so they must be eaten at once.

There are a variety of methods by which to cook fish. To some extent the choice is a matter of taste, but some methods work better than others for certain fish. For example, if you marinate a bland-tasting fish in lemon juice or wine, and *then* cook it, the taste is often improved.

Plate Cooking

This is a quick and easy method for cooking small quantities of fish. Put the fish between two enamel or ovenware plates with butter and seasoning. Place in a preheated 325° F (170° C; Mark 3) oven for 6 to 12 minutes, according to the thickness of the fish, or over a pan of simmering water for 15 to 20 minutes.

Braising

Good for whole fish or larger cuts of salmon, salmon trout, trout, carp, pike, brill and turbot.

Butter and line the base of the pan with diced onions, carrots and shallots, which have already been tossed in butter. Add a few parsley stalks. Then place the fish on this bed of vegetables. Moisten with fish stock or white wine, depending on the sauce you will be serving. Cover the fish with buttered greaseproof paper or waxed paper, and make a hole to allow the steam to escape. Bring it to the boil on top of the stove, then place it in a preheated 425° F (220° C; Mark 7) oven for approximately 20 minutes, or at 350° F (180° C; Mark 4) for approximately 30 minutes. When almost done, remove the paper cover and continue cooking, basting frequently, to glaze the fish. Drain well and place the fish on a warm serving dish. Cover. Skim off any excess fat and add the cooking liquid to the chosen fish sauce.

Another braising method is to rub the fish with seasoned flour, brush it with melted butter, and place it in a covered fireproof dish with a small glass of wine and water (or use vinegar or lemon juice and water), a small chopped onion, a sprig of thyme and a bay leaf. Baste it occasionally and cook it in a preheated oven at 350° F (180° C; Mark 4) for approximately 15 to 20 minutes.

Poaching

Recommended for large, firm-fleshed fish such as salmon, sea bass, cod, sole, turbot, brill, halibut and large fillets of other fish.

Whether you are using fish stock or court bouillon, the liquid should be barely shimmering, not even simmering, with no bubbles visible on the surface; the temperature of the liquid should be 180° to 190° F (82° to 88° C). The most important thing is to keep the whole fish from falling apart, so one good trick is to wrap it in cheesecloth (muslin) and tie the ends to the handles of the fish kettle, fireproof dish or shallow pan. Butter the kettle or pan, then add the fish stock, court bouillon, dry white wine, water or even milk. Bring the liquid to the right temperature *before* placing the fish in the pan, or you will lose the delicate flavor of the fish. Then place the wrapped fish in the shimmering liquid, which must completely cover it. Cover with the lid or buttered waxed paper and cook in a preheated oven at 350° F (180° C; Mark 4) for approximately 15 minutes per pound (450 g).

Another method of poaching, good for flat fish or fillets, is to put the fish in a buttered baking pan with mushrooms or tomatoes, a little fish stock or wine and water and bring it gently to a shimmer on top of the stove. Cover with a lid or greaseproof paper and complete the cooking in a preheated moderate oven, 350° F (180° C; Mark 4), basting occasionally. Allow 10 to 12 minutes' cooking time for fillets and 15 minutes per pound (450 g) for a flat fish.

Poaching times may vary according to whether the fish has fine or coarse flesh, whether it is in a solid piece or filleted, whether it is cooked flat or rolled. The fish is cooked when it is opaque all through, or when a little creamy curd appears between the scales, and the flesh parts easily from the bone when the point of a skewer is inserted.

POACHING TIMES FOR FISH

Small, thin fillets, portions of shellfish	3–5 minutes
Smoked fish	5–10 minutes
Medium thick fillets	6–10 minutes
Steaks, cutlets, large pieces (according to thickness)	8–15 minutes
Small whole fish (sole, whiting, plaice)	8–15 minutes
Whole fish (4½ lbs; 2 kg to 6 lbs; 2.7 kg)	15–18 minutes
Larger fish (according to thickness, per lb; 450 g)	5–10 minutes

Au Bleu

A term applied to small fish, such as young pike, small carp, trout and lake trout cooked very briefly to retain the bluish color of the skin. If the fish is to be eaten hot, *it must not be killed until 10 minutes before cooking.* Then it should be taken from the water and killed with a blow on the head, gutted quickly and washed. Do not scale the fish and do not touch it too much so that the external mucosity is not removed. This is what gives the fish its bluish color when cooked. Put the fish into boiling salted water or into court bouillon, until it is just done. If the fish is to be used for a cold dish, the fish must be killed *1 hour* before cooking so that the flesh remains firm.

Steaming

This is particularly good for invalids or for light diets. Wrap the fish in a piece of cheesecloth (muslin) and cook in the top part of a steamer or double boiler, with salt and pepper and a little butter added after cooking.

Baking

There are two ways to bake fish. The first is good for stuffed whole fish cooked in its skin, or for very thick cuts of fish; the second for whole fish such as salmon or sea bass which you want to keep moist.

1. Preheat the oven to 425° F (220° C; Mark 7) if you want a short cooking time, or to 350° F (180° C; Mark 4) for a longer cooking time. Then place the stuffed fish on a heated, greased, foil-lined pan so it will not stick, dab it with knobs of butter or brush it with oil, and place it in the preheated oven. The cooking time will vary according to oven temperature, but you can count on roughly 10 to 30 minutes for the large cuts, 10 to 20 minutes for fillets, and 10 to 15 minutes per pound (450 g) for stuffed whole fish. Baste occasionally while cooking.
2. I prefer the foil-wrapped method, which is very clean and allows the fish to cook in its own juices, giving it much added flavor. Coat the fish in butter or oil and place it on a well-greased sheet of foil big enough to wrap the whole fish. Season it with salt and pepper, tarragon or fennel. Place some lemon slices, butter and herbs in the cavity. Sprinkle lemon juice or white wine over the fish and carefully wrap it with the ends neatly tucked in so that the liquid does not escape. Place it in a preheated moderate oven, 350° F (180° C; Mark 4) on a heated, greased baking tray. Allow 15 to 20 minutes per pound (450 g) for a whole fish.

Broiling (Grilling)

This is a simple method for cooking medium-sized whole fish or cuts of fish, particularly oily fish such as salmon, mackerel, herring and trout. If cooking a whole fish, make small incisions to allow the heat to penetrate. Oily fish need only to be brushed with oil, but fish which dry out quickly should be brushed with oil or melted butter and then dipped into seasoned flour. This will form a crust which will prevent the fish from drying out. Grease and heat the broiler (grill) tray and place the fish about 2 inches (5 cm) from the heat source. A whole small fish takes 3 to 5 minutes on each side, depending upon the size of the fish; cuts of fish take 5 to 6 minutes on each side, and fillets 5 to 10 minutes.

Oven-frying

This is a particularly good way to fry fish if you cannot abide the smell of fish frying.

Put ¼ cup (2 oz; 50 g) butter or margarine in a baking dish and place it in a preheated, very hot—400° F (200° C; Mark 6)—oven. Dip the fish into seasoned flour or in a batter, if you like. Put the fish into the sizzling fat, and cook in the oven until it is golden brown on one side, then turn and brown the other. Thin pieces of fish take approximately 5 minutes per side. Thicker cuts take about 7 to 10 minutes per side.

Shallow or Pan-frying (à la Meunière)

This is useful for cuts of fish, fillets or flat fish, as well as for sole, mackerel, trout, brook trout and smelts. It uses little fat and is easily digestible if the food is properly drained on absorbent paper before serving. Small fish should be fried in 2 to 3 ounces (50 to 75 g) of clarified butter or smoking hot fat. For whole fish, not above 2½ pounds (1 kg), or large fish cut into slices, use half vegetable oil and half clarified butter, as vegetable oil will withstand higher temperatures than butter alone. Dredge the fish in seasoned flour, shake off the excess, and lay it in a large frying pan containing the butter and/or oil. Cook on both sides but do *not* cover the pan as the fish will then steam and become soggy instead of crisp. Do not use batter as the liquid will also make the fish soggy. Cook over a low heat for approximately 12 to 15 minutes on each side, depending on size and thickness, until the fish is golden brown and crisp but not burned. Place the fish on a heated serving dish. Melt a knob of butter in the pan, heat until it is frothy, then add the juice of half a lemon. Pour the lemon butter over the fish and garnish with chopped parsley.

Deep-frying

This method can be used for small whole fish, shellfish, fillets or fish cakes. It is essential to use clean oil; peanut (arachide) oil is the best as it has a high smoking point. Do not wait for the oil to smoke, as it will then burn the fish to a crisp. Instead, throw in a piece of bread; if it browns, the oil is ready. Alternatively use a thermometer. The temperature of the fat must be regulated according to the thickness and weight of the fish. It should be about 370° F (190° C) when frying small fish, which must cook quickly to remain crisp. For thick fish which contain more water, the temperature of the fat should be 345° F (180° C), so that the fish will have a chance to cook thoroughly on the inside without burning on the outside. When deep-frying in quantity, the oil must be allowed to return to the proper temperature after each batch, as the temperature is reduced after the food goes in.

Dipping the fish or shellfish in batter protects it from direct contact with the hot oil and is, in fact, the best method of deep-frying, as the seafood is then virtually steamed in its own juices within the coating. There must be enough oil to cover the fish and quickly seal the coating. To fry shellfish, dip it in salted milk, then in seasoned flour and shake off the surplus. Whitefish should be dipped into seasoned flour, then into beaten egg and bread crumbs. Oily fish is best dipped into seasoned flour and then into matzo meal or oatmeal. Always drain deep-fried fish on absorbent paper and serve immediately.

Fish and Shellfish

Pressure-cooking times at high temperature per pound (450 g) weight.

Crab	7–10 minutes
Oily Fish	5–8 minutes
Salmon	2–3 minutes
Shrimp and Prawns	4–6 minutes
Whitefish	4–6 minutes

Fish Hints

1. To prevent fish from sticking, sprinkle a little salt in the pan before frying.
2. Canned (tinned) shrimp/prawns lose their canned taste if simmered in 2 tablespoons (30 ml) of vinegar and 1 tablespoon (15 ml) of sherry for 15 minutes.
3. It is usually better to use shallots rather than onions for flavoring fish as they have a more subtle taste.
4. The strong smell of fish may be diminished by adding a little vinegar or white wine to the poaching stock or court bouillon.

PRINCIPAL GARNISHES FOR FISH

Americaine: scallops of lobster tails cooked wih tomato sauce (Sauce Americaine), thin slices of truffles, and crescents of pastry (*fleurons*)
Cardinal: scallops of lobster tail, thin slices of truffle, Sauce Cardinal, *fleurons*

Chambord: decorated *quenelles* of fish *farcis,* fluted mushrooms, olive-shaped truffle pieces, scallops of soft roe cooked meunière, cooked crayfish, Sauce Chambord

Chanchat: thick rounds of plain boiled potatoes overlapping on the edge of the serving dish, Sauce Mornay

Commodore: large fish *quenelles* decorated with truffles, crayfish tails, Sauce Normande with crayfish butter

Concalaise: poached oysters, shrimp, Sauce Vin Blanc

Dieppoise: cooked and shelled prawns or shrimp, poached mussels, Sauce Vin Blanc made with the reduced poaching liquid

Doria: olive-shaped cucumber pieces cooked in butter surrounding the fish cooked meunière

Florentine: a bed of buttered leaf spinach, Sauce Mornay

Grand Duc: buttered asparagus tips, shelled crayfish tails, thin slices of truffle, Sauce Mornay

Joinville: salpicon of mushrooms, truffles and shrimp bound together with a Sauce Joinville; the fish topped with thin slices of truffle, shrimp, Sauce Joinville

Marinière: poached mussels, shrimp, Sauce Marinière

Montreuil: spoon-cut balls or olives of plain boiled potato masked with shrimp sauce surrounding dish; fish masked with Sauce Vin Blanc

Nantua: picked crayfish, thin slices of truffle, Sauce Nantua

Niçoise: skinned, pitted, diced tomato stewed in oil with a little garlic; anchovy fillets, pitted black olives, capers and chopped tarragon

Normande: poached oysters and mussels, shrimp; bread-crumbed, deep-fried *goujons;* fluted mushrooms; trussed crayfish, Sauce Normande; E-shaped fried croûtons

Régence: small spoon-shaped *quenelles* of whiting *farci* with crayfish butter, poached oysters; small fluted mushrooms, scallops of soft cooked roe; thin sliced truffles; Sauce Normande with truffle extract

Riche: medallions of cooked crayfish; thin sliced truffles; Sauce Victoria

Trouvillaise: shrimp, poached mussels, fluted mushrooms, shrimp sauce

Tsarine: cucumber olives cooked in butter; fluted mushrooms; fish glazed with Sauce Mornay

Valois: small olive-shaped plain boiled potatoes; scallops of poached soft roe; trussed crayfish and Sauce Valois

Victoria: medallions of cooked crayfish; thin sliced truffles; Sauce Victoria

Walewska: scallops of cooked crayfish or lobster; thin sliced truffles, fish glazed with Sauce Mornay

MARY CHAFIN'S MARINATED FISH

I found this delicious eighteenth-century marinade recipe in Mary Chafin's *Original Country Recipes*. It makes a good first course, and you can use it to marinate a salmon cut into pieces, trout, sole, mackerel, eel, smelts, bream or any other firm fish. I have added modern-day measurements. This recipe serves 4.

4 whole fish or steaks   Oil (I prefer vegetable oil)
Flour

FOR THE MARINADE

½ cup (¼ pt; 125 ml) white wine   A sprig of rosemary
  vinegar   1 bay leaf
½ cup (¼ pt; 125 ml) white wine   Salt and fresh-ground pepper
1 small onion, sliced   2 lemons, sliced
A pinch each of saffron, ground   Onion rings, for garnish
  cloves, and cinnamon

If you are using a whole fish, make gashes in the skin. Dredge the fish in flour and brown it quickly in hot oil. Reduce the heat and cook until the fish is cooked through. Leave it to cool.

Boil all the marinade ingredients together for about 15 minutes. Put aside and allow to cool. Then place the cooked fish in a dish with a lid, pour on the marinade and add half a sliced lemon. Cover and leave for at least 12 hours, turning several times. Drain the fish and serve with the remaining sliced lemon and the onion rings.

Preparation and cooking time: approximately 45 minutes. Marinating time: 12 hours.

SEVICHE

An easier dish to prepare, and one I particularly like to serve as a first course, is Seviche. It is simple and light, particularly good with a heavy main course such as game or a rich meat stew. In Italy and South America it is very popular, and is much like the Japanese sashimi. The acidity of the fresh fruit juices "cooks" the raw fish.

SERVES 6 AS A FIRST COURSE

*1 cup (8 fl oz; 225 ml) fresh lemon
   juice*
*1 cup (8 fl oz; 225 ml) fresh lime
   juice*
*4 teaspoons (20 ml) fresh coriander
   leaves, chopped fine*
*2 pounds (900 g) haddock or any
   firm whitefish, cut into bite-sized
   pieces*

*1 teaspoon (5 ml) fresh ginger,
   grated*
1 teaspoon (5 ml) chili powder
Salt and fresh-ground black pepper
1 clove garlic, crushed
2 tablespoons (30 ml) good olive oil
2 large red onions, sliced thin

In a china or glass bowl mix the fruit juices and 2 teaspoons (10 ml) chopped coriander leaves and place the pieces of fish in it. Put the bowl in the refrigerator, covered, for 3 to 4 hours, turning the fish from time to time so that it becomes completely marinated. The fish will become opaque from the effect of the acidity of the juices. One hour before serving, combine the remaining coriander and all other ingredients except for the onions in another bowl. Drain the fish, discarding the fruit juices, and toss it in the oil and spices. Place some crisp lettuce around the edges of a serving dish, pile the fish into the center, pour on the oil mixture and top with the onion rings.

Preparation time: 30 minutes. Marinating time: 3 to 4 hours.

CRAYFISH SOUP

SERVES 4

1 dozen crayfish
*1½ quarts (2⅓ pints; 1.33 liters)
   water*
½ tablespoon (2.5 ml) salt
*1 teaspoon (5 ml) whole black
   peppercorns*

1 blade mace
¼ cup (2 oz; 50 g) butter
2 tablespoons (1 oz; 25 ml) flour
Juice of ½ lemon
*¼ cup (2 fl oz; 50 ml) light
   (single) cream*

Remove all the meat from the body of the crayfish. Place this on one side. Put the claws and the shells into a mortar, pound them well, and put in a large saucepan with the water. Add salt, peppercorns and the mace; bring the water quickly to the boil. Skim well, cover the saucepan and simmer for 1 hour. Strain the liquid into a large bowl. In another saucepan, melt the butter, add the flour and stir until thoroughly mixed into a *roux*. Add the strained liquid and cook, stirring continually, until the mixture is boiling. Add the crayfish meat and simmer gently for 30 minutes. Pour in the lemon juice and remove the saucepan from the heat. Add the cream, mix thoroughly, pour into heated soup bowls and serve.

Preparation time: approximately 30 minutes. Cooking time: approximately 2 hours.

FISH SOUP

SERVES 4

2 tablespoons (30 ml) butter
½ pound (225 g) hake or whiting, cut into large pieces, but leaving in the bones
½ pound (225 g) cod, cut into large pieces, but leaving in the bones
1 onion, chopped fine
2 tablespoons (30 ml) vegetable oil

2 pounds (2 pints; 900 g) mussels, washed, bearded and cleaned (see page 86)
3¾ pints (3 pints; 1.5 l) water
6 pieces fried bread, broken into pieces
2 to 3 teaspoons (10 to 15 ml) salt
Fresh-ground black pepper

Melt the butter in a saucepan and fry the pieces of fish and the onion lightly until they turn golden. Turn the fish carefully so as not to break it. Remove the pan from the heat and put it aside. In another saucepan, heat the oil and drop in the mussels. Shake them in the oil over low heat to loosen their shells. Take them off the heat, reserve the oil, remove the shells and put the mussels on a plate. Then carefully remove the bones from the fish and return the meat to the saucepan; add the shelled mussels and their oil. Pour in the water and cook for a few minutes. Meanwhile, prepare the fried bread. Season the soup well, then float the fried bread on top. Simmer it for 30 minutes and serve.

Preparation time (including cleaning the mussels): 45 minutes. Cooking time: approximately 1 hour 15 minutes.

MUSSELS IN WHITE WINE SAUCE

SERVES 6 AS A FIRST COURSE

Mussels are cheap and rich in protein, so it is well worth your while to take the time to clean them. You may prepare this dish one or two hours ahead of time up to the point of broiling (grilling) the mussels. This must be done at the last moment. Serve each person 6 mussels, but order more than you require as there are always some that do not open when cooked and must then be discarded. There are approximately 25 mussels in 1 quart (1.5 l), which is 2 pounds (900 g) in weight.

2½ pounds (1.1 kg) mussels, washed, bearded and cleaned (see page 86)
1 onion, chopped fine
2 shallots, chopped fine

2 cloves garlic, chopped fine
1 cup (8 fl oz; 225 ml) dry white wine
Rock salt

FOR THE WHITE WINE SAUCE

1 shallot, chopped fine
1 clove garlic, chopped fine
¼ cup (2 oz; 50 g) unsalted butter
2 tablespoons (30 ml) flour
Reserved mussel liquid

1 pint (¾ pint; 350 ml) milk
2 egg yolks
½ cup (4 fl oz; 125 ml) heavy (double) cream

Preheat the broiler (grill).

Place the mussels, onion, shallots, garlic and wine in a deep kettle or saucepan; bring to the boil and steam until the mussels open. Discard any that have not opened. Drain the mussels, straining and *reserving the liquid*. Discard one half of each mussel shell and place the half with the meat on a bed of rock salt in a heated roasting pan to keep warm.

Prepare the sauce. Place the shallot and garlic in the butter in a saucepan and sauté until they are transparent. Stir in the flour. Add the reserved mussel liquid, then the milk and stir to make the sauce smooth. Reduce the liquid. Beat the egg yolks and cream together in a small bowl, then add to the sauce. Heat the sauce through but *do not allow it to boil*. Transfer the mussels to a serving dish, pour some sauce over each mussel and place them under the broiler (grill) for a few minutes to brown. Serve immediately on individual heated plates.

Preparation time (including cleaning the mussels): approximately 45 minutes. Cooking time: approximately 40 minutes.

TURBOT AND SHRIMP SCALLOPS

SERVES 6 AS A FIRST COURSE

6 scallop shells
Salad oil
½ cup (3 oz; 75 g) fine dry bread
  crumbs
1½ to 2½ pounds (700 g to 1.1 kg)
  turbot fillets, cut into 2½-inch
  (6.3 cm) pieces
Paprika and salt, mixed, for
  dredging

1 cup (8 fl oz; 225 ml) tomato
  sauce (see page 258)
36 raw shrimp (prawns), peeled
¼ cup (2 oz; 50 g) fine-chopped
  tomato
¼ cup (2 oz; 50 g) butter

Preheat oven to 425° F (220° C; Mark 7).

Brush the bottoms of the scallop shells with salad oil and sprinkle with some of the bread crumbs. Roll each piece of turbot in paprika and salt, then dip them into the tomato sauce. Place the fish in the shells and surround it with shrimp (prawns), 6 per shell. Top these with a little chopped tomato, cover with the remaining bread crumbs and dot with butter. Bake until the bread crumbs are brown.

Preparation time: approximately 30 minutes. Cooking time: approximately 15 minutes.

BENGAL FISH CUTLETS

This is a quick and simple dish which originated in British India.

SERVES 2 TO 4 PEOPLE, DEPENDING ON THEIR APPETITES

½ cup (4 oz; 125 g) butter
1 cup (4 oz; 125 g) chopped onions
2 teaspoons (10 ml) coriander seeds,
  roasted and crushed

2 plaice, or any other whitefish,
  filleted
2 teaspoons (10 ml) curry powder

Preheat oven to 450° F (230° C; Mark 8).

Place 3 tablespoons (45 ml) butter, half the onions and 1 teaspoon (5 ml) of the coriander seeds in a fireproof dish. Spread half the remaining butter over the fish fillets and rub them in curry powder. Place them on top of the bed of butter, onions and coriander. Then place the remaining butter, onions and coriander seeds on top of the fish and place it in the oven. When the onions are sizzling and brown, serve the fish and vegetables on a bed of rice or, even better, fried lentils (see below).

Preparation time: 15 minutes. Cooking time: 8 minutes.

FRIED LENTILS

> ¾ *cup (5 oz; 150 g) lentils,*   ½ *cup (4 oz; 125 g) butter*
> *preferably green not orange*

Cook the lentils in fast-boiling salted water to cover for 15 minutes. Drain and place them in a frying pan with the butter, which has been heated to sizzling. Keep frying the lentils and turning them for 15 minutes, or until they are done. Pile them on a dish and place the fish and onions on top.

Cooking time: approximately 30 minutes.

RAJAH FISH CAKES

This is another delicious and unusual Indian dish. You might serve it for brunch on a bed of creamed spinach. It is good for using leftover fish.

SERVES 4 TO 6; MAKES 6 3-INCH (7.6 CM) FISH CAKES

> *1 pound (450 g) cooked whitefish,*   ¼ *cup (2 oz; 50 g) flour*
> *flaked*   *1 teaspoon (5 ml) dry mustard*
> *Juice of 2 lemons*   *A pinch of salt*
> *Paprika and salt, mixed, for*   *1 onion, chopped fine*
> *dredging*   *A good pinch of dried mint*
> ¼ *cup (2 oz; 50 g) chickpea flour*   *2 eggs, beaten*
> *(besan)*   *Vegetable oil for frying*

Marinate the pieces of flaked fish in the lemon juice for 30 minutes, then roll them in the mixture of paprika and salt. In a medium-sized mixing bowl, mix the two flours with the mustard and salt. Add the onion and then the fish. Finally, add the mint. Mix all together with the beaten eggs.

Make 6 3-inch (7.6 cm) cakes. Heat the vegetable oil in a deep saucepan until it reaches 350° F (180° C), or until a small piece of white bread dropped into the oil turns brown in 50 seconds. Drop each cake into the hot oil and fry until very crisp. Serve the cakes on a bed of creamed spinach (see below).

Preparation time: approximately 40 minutes. Cooking time: approximately 15 minutes.

CREAMED SPINACH

2 pounds (900 g) fresh spinach, well
  washed and trimmed
2 cloves garlic, chopped fine
¼ cup (2 oz; 50 g) butter

1 cup (8 fl oz; 225 ml) heavy
  (double) cream
Nutmeg, to taste
Salt and pepper to taste

In a large saucepan filled with boiling salted water, cook the spinach for 5 to 6 minutes or until it is tender. Drain the spinach and refresh it under cold running water until it is cool. Squeeze all the water from the spinach and chop it fine. In a large enamel frying pan, sauté the garlic in the butter until it is golden, then add the spinach and cook over moderately high heat, stirring, until the moisture has evaporated. Add one-third of the cream and simmer the mixture until it is hot and the cream is well reduced. Add the rest of the cream, one half at a time, allowing the first addition to reduce before adding more. Season the spinach with nutmeg, salt and fresh-ground black pepper.

Preparation and cooking time: approximately 1 hour.

EEL WITH MUSHROOMS AND SHALLOTS

SERVES 6

½ tablespoon (15 ml) flour
3 tablespoons (45 ml) olive oil
1 pound (450 g) whole shallots,
  peeled
½ pound (225 g) mushrooms,
  wiped and chopped
1 sprig parsley, minced
1 teaspoon (5 ml) salt
½ teaspoon (2.5 ml) pepper

1¼ cups (10 fl oz; 300 ml) red
  wine
1¼ cups (10 fl oz; 300 ml) fish stock
  or clam juice
2 pounds (900 g) eel, washed,
  cleaned, cut into pieces and
  skinned
1 bay leaf
6 slices fried bread

In a large casserole, cook the flour in the oil until it is about to become brown, then add the shallots. Mix the mushrooms, parsley, salt and pepper together in a bowl and add them to the casserole when the shallots have browned. Pour in the wine and fish stock, then add the pieces of eel and the bay leaf. Cook over low heat for a half hour. Serve the pieces of eel on fried bread, with a border of shallots, and pour the sauce over them.

Preparation time: approximately 30 minutes. Cooking time: approximately 45 minutes.

FISH TOURTE À LA RUSSE

SERVES 4

1 pound (450 g) Rough Puff Pastry (see page 246)

½ pound (225 g) firm whitefish, such as haddock, cod, or hake, cooked and flaked

3 to 4 flat anchovy fillets, chopped

½ cup (4 fl oz; 125 ml) Béchamel Sauce (see page 246)

4 tablespoons (60 ml) butter

3 tablespoons (45 ml) lemon juice

½ pound (225 g) fresh salmon, sliced

4 fillets of sole or whiting

½ cup (4 fl oz; 125 ml) water

1 teaspoon (5 ml) salt

¾ pound (12 oz; 350 g) mushrooms, chopped

8 shrimp (prawns), shelled

1 egg yolk, beaten

Preheat the oven to 350° F (180° C; Mark 4).

Roll out the pastry to ½ inch (1.2 cm) thick, making a large enough round to line an 8-inch (20.3 cm) pie pan with enough left over to fold back over the *tourte* as a covering. Line the pie pan with the pastry. In a bowl, mix the cooked whitefish with the anchovies and ¼ cup (2 fl oz; 50 ml) Béchamel Sauce to bind. Put this mixture in the center of the pastry, leaving a clear edge of pastry to fold over later. In a small sauté pan, melt 2 tablespoons (30 ml) of the butter, add 2 tablespoons (30 ml) lemon juice, the salmon slices and fillets of sole or whiting. Cook the fish for approximately 5 minutes. Remove the pieces with a fish slicer and lay them on top of the whitefish mixture.

In a saucepan, bring the water, salt and remaining lemon juice to the boil. Add the mushrooms and remaining butter and boil rapidly for 4 to 5 minutes. Remove from the heat, drain and cover the fish slices with the mushrooms, the remaining béchamel and the shrimp (prawns). Gather the pastry over the ingredients until it meets on the top. Dampen the edges and press them firmly together. Leave a small opening in the middle to allow the steam to escape, otherwise the pastry will become soggy. Brush the pastry with beaten egg yolk and bake in the preheated oven until it turns a light golden color, approximately 15 to 20 minutes.

Preparation time: 30 minutes. Cooking time: approximately 30 minutes.

STIR-FRIED FLOUNDER

MARINADE

SERVES 6

1 tablespoon (15 ml) peanut oil
1 tablespoon (15 ml) lemon juice

Salt and fresh-ground pepper

6 flounder fillets, cut into ½-inch (1.25-cm) wide strips
Seasoned flour
¼ cup (2 oz; 50 g) butter
4 tablespoons (60 ml) peanut oil
1 pound (450 g) beansprouts
¼ pound (125 g) button mush-rooms, quartered

½ head of lettuce, shredded fine
¼ pound (125 g) shrimp (prawns), peeled
1 tablespoon (15 ml) soy sauce
Lemon wedges

Mix the marinade ingredients together. Put the fish strips into the marinade for 30 minutes. Then drain the fish, toss the pieces in seasoned flour and fry quickly in the butter until brown and cooked. Meanwhile heat the oil in a pan or wok until smoking hot. Stir in the beansprouts and mushrooms and cook, stirring continually, for 2 to 3 minutes. Add the lettuce and shrimp (prawns), then stir in the soy sauce and reheat. Gently fold in the fresh fish; add more seasoning if necessary and serve, garnished with lemon wedges.

Marinating time: 30 minutes. Cooking time: approximately 10 minutes.

HADDOCK AND SORREL SOUFFLÉ

SERVES 8 TO 10

10 ounces (275 g) un- or smoked
   haddock fillets (Finnan Haddie)
1¼ cups (10 fl oz; 275 ml) water
2 tablespoons (30 ml) butter
2 tablespoons (30 ml) flour
¾ cup (5 fl oz; 150 ml) milk
½ pound (225 g) sorrel, shredded
   (spinach may be substituted)

¾ cup (2 oz; 50 g) grated lemon
   peel
Juice of 1 lemon
Salt and pepper
3 egg yolks, beaten
5 egg whites
A pinch of cream of tartar
Butter

Preheat oven to 375° F (190° C; Mark 5).

Put the haddock in a deep frying pan with the water. Cover and simmer for 6 to 8 minutes, or until the fish flakes. Reserve ¾ cup (6 fl oz; 175 ml) of the cooking liquid. Remove the skin from the fillets and flake the fish, using two forks.

Make a white sauce: Melt the butter in a large saucepan, add the flour and milk, and cook, stirring constantly. When the sauce is smooth, add the reserved cooking liquid. Remove the pan from the heat, stir in the flaked haddock, the sorrel, lemon peel and juice. Add salt and pepper to taste (if you are using smoked haddock, do *not* add salt). Allow the mixture to cool, then add the beaten egg yolks. The soufflé can be prepared up to this point 2 to 3 hours in advance.

Place a baking pan in the preheated oven at this point so that the soufflé dish may be put on top of it, giving the instant bottom heat needed to make a soufflé rise properly. Whip the egg whites with a pinch of cream of tartar until they hold their peaks. Then fold them into the soufflé mixture with a metal spoon. Pour the mixture into a 8- to 9-inch (20.3 to 22.8 cm) buttered soufflé dish and place the dish on the baking pan in the oven. Cook for 35 minutes. Serve immediately.

Preparation time: 35 minutes. Cooking time: 35 minutes.

HADDOCK-STUFFED POTATOES

This is a marvelous dish in which to use leftover fish. It makes a good luncheon or supper served with a mixed green salad.

SERVES 4

4 baking potatoes, cooked
¾ pound (325 g) cooked haddock, flaked (other firm whitefish may be used also)

2 tablespoons (30 ml) sour cream or plain yogurt
Fresh-ground pepper and salt

Preheat oven to 350° F (180° C; Mark 4).
Scoop out the flesh of the baked potatoes and mix it thoroughly in a bowl with the rest of the ingredients. Fill the potato skins with the mixture and put in preheated oven until hot.

Cooking time (including baking the potatoes): 2 hours.

HERRINGS À LA CALAISIENNE

SERVES 4

Four 12-ounce (350 g) herrings, backbone and bones removed and roe reserved
3 tablespoons (45 ml) butter or margarine

2 tablespoons (30 ml) shallots, peeled and chopped
¼ cup (2 oz; 50 ml) fine-chopped mushrooms

Preheat oven to 350° F (180° C; Mark 4).
In a bowl, mix the herring roe with 1 tablespoon (15 ml) butter, the shallots and mushrooms. In a frying pan, lightly cook the herring in the remaining butter for 3 to 4 minutes; remove from the pan with a fish slicer and lay them on a board. Stuff each fish with the roe forcemeat, wrap them individually in waxed paper or oiled greaseproof paper, and place them in an ovenproof dish. Bake in the preheated oven for about 10 to 12 minutes, de-

pending upon the size of the fish. When cooked, unwrap, put on a hot dish and serve.

Preparation time: 15 minutes. Cooking time: approximately 15 to 20 minutes.

GAMBAS AL' AJILLO

One of my favorite fish dishes is *Gambas al' Ajillo*. It was taught to me twenty years ago by a very good Spanish friend of mine. I have cooked it ever since for friends who enjoy a lot of garlic and spice in their food. As it is very quick and easy to make, I usually make it for dinner on Friday evenings when we arrive in North Wales after the four-and-a-half-hour drive. This, with a tomato and red onion salad and some cheese to finish, makes a delicious but light supper. As it is a very "hot" dish, one tends to drink a great deal of wine with it, but it must be what we call "plonk"—that is to say a cheap, *rough* wine—to go with all the garlic. In Spain, they substitute the tiny eels, *anguilas,* which look like thin silver spaghetti, for the shrimp. Unfortunately, I have never found these tiny eels outside Spain.

SERVES 2

Good olive oil

4 large cloves garlic, peeled and chopped fine

4 dried chili peppers, chopped, or 1 tablespoon (15 ml) chili powder

1 tablespoon (15 ml) dill weed

1 pound (450 g) shrimp (prawns), peeled and cooked, or frozen or canned

Cover the bottom of a small frying pan with 1 inch of olive oil, add the garlic, chilies, dillweed and finally the shrimp (prawns). Cover the pan and allow the shrimp to simmer for about 6 to 7 minutes. Take 2 small heated earthenware casseroles, the kind in which you might serve onion soup, and, with a slotted spoon, divide the mixture evenly between the two. Then pour the hot oil over it. Serve hot, and for this reason try and find some wooden forks to eat with, as the hot oil will make metal forks burn your mouth.

Preparation time: 10 minutes. Cooking time: 6 to 7 minutes.

BAKED RED MULLET

SERVES 6

½ cup (3 oz; 75 g) dry bread
   crumbs
3 cloves garlic, chopped fine
1 cup (3½ oz; 90 g) chopped
   parsley
1 teaspoon (5 ml) salt
½ teaspoon (2.5 ml) pepper
6 red mullet, cleaned and scales
   removed

½ pound (225 g) whole shallots,
   peeled
2 tablespoons (50 ml) butter or
   margarine
1¼ cups (10 fl oz; 300 ml) white
   wine

Preheat the oven to 375° F (190° C; Mark 5).

In a bowl, mix the bread crumbs, garlic, parsley, salt and pepper, and coat each fish with this mixture. Grease a baking dish and place the mullet into it, surrounded by the whole shallots. Dot with lumps of butter, pour in the wine and bake in the preheated oven for 20 minutes.

Preparation time: approximately 15 minutes. Cooking time: approximately 20 minutes.

FERNANDA'S MARINATED MACKEREL AND ONIONS IN WINE

This is a delicious Portuguese dish taught to me by a great friend and cook.

MARINADE

SERVES 2

½ cup (4 fl oz; 125 ml) white wine
½ cup (4 fl oz; 125 ml) white wine
  vinegar
6 cloves garlic, peeled and crushed
1 bay leaf
1 tablespoon (15 ml) oregano
1 teaspoon (5 ml) ground mace

2 teaspoons (10 ml) ground thyme,
  preferably lemon thyme
1 teaspoon (5 ml) chili powder
2 teaspoons (10 ml) salt
4 teaspoons (20 ml) fresh-ground
  black pepper

2 mackerel, cleaned, heads removed,
  and cut into two or three 2-inch
  (5 cm) pieces
3 large onions, peeled and sliced
  thin

Seasoned flour for dredging
4 tablespoons (60 ml) vegetable oil

Make the marinade with the wine, vinegar, garlic, bay leaf, herbs, chili powder, salt and pepper. Place it in a glass dish or earthenware casserole with cover. Place the mackerel and onions in the marinade, cover, and leave for 2 to 3 days in the refrigerator.

Remove the mackerel from the marinade, drain and reserve the marinade to use in the sauce. Dredge the fish in the seasoned flour, shaking off the excess. Heat the oil in a frying pan large enough to hold the two mackerel lying flat. Fry the mackerel over a moderate flame for about 10 minutes. Then dredge the onions in seasoned flour and add them to the frying pan. When the fish and onions are brown and crisp, remove them to a heated earthenware baking dish and keep hot. Pour the reserved marinade into the frying pan and boil it up until it turns brown, approximately 4 to 5 minutes. Remove from the heat, pour the marinade sauce over the fish and onions, and serve with squares of Fried Semolina (see page 109).

Marinating time: 2 to 3 days. Cooking time: approximately 30 minutes.

FRIED SEMOLINA

SERVES 4

4 pints (2 l) water
2 tablespoons (30 ml) vegetable or
  olive oil

1 clove garlic, crushed
½ pound (8 oz; 225 g) semolina
Oil for frying

Heat the water, oil and garlic until the water is *just* warm with tiny bubbles (if the water is too cold or too hot the semolina will form lumps). Then pour the semolina gradually into the water, stirring constantly, until you have a creamy mixture. Lower the heat, stir occasionally, and cook for 30 minutes. When it is cooked, pour the semolina onto a flat dish so that it forms a cake approximately 1 inch (2.5 cm) high. Cool until it becomes hard. This is best when made either the night before, if serving it for lunch, or in the morning, if serving it for dinner.

When you are ready to serve it, cut into 2-inch (5 cm) squares and fry in oil until it becomes light brown. Serve hot.

Cooking time: 35 minutes plus frying time.

STUFFED WHITING OR HAKE

SERVES 6

2 to 3 pounds (900 g to 1.4 kg)
  whiting or hake
2 to 3 ounces (50 to 75 g) cooked
  ham, chopped fine
2 to 3 cloves garlic, chopped fine
2 to 4 tablespoons (30 to 60 ml)
  fine-chopped parsley
1 hard-boiled egg, chopped fine
A few mussels, cleaned and shelled
  (see page 86)

4 shrimp (prawns), shelled
½ cup (4 oz; 125 g) butter
½ cup (3 oz; 75 g) dry bread
  crumbs
1 egg, beaten
Salt and fresh-ground black pepper
1¼ cups (10 fl oz; 300 ml) fish
  stock or clam juice
6 slices fried bread, cut into triangles

Preheat oven to 375° F (190° C; Mark 5).

Take off the head of the fish and boil it for stock. Scrape off the scales, slit the fish carefully on the abdomen side and remove the bone, but do not damage the skin.

Prepare the stuffing. In a bowl, mix the ham, garlic, parsley, hard-boiled egg, mussels and shrimp (prawns), and then in a frying pan sauté the mixture lightly in 2 tablespoons (30 ml) of butter. In another bowl, add the cooked mixture to the bread crumbs, 2 tablespoons (30 ml) butter and the beaten egg. Season and stuff the fish with this mixture. Sew up the cavity. Grease a baking dish, lay the stuffed fish on it, distribute the remaining butter on top and bake in the preheated oven for 20 to 25 minutes, basting with fish stock or clam juice from time to time. Before serving, remove the thread and decorate the serving dish with triangles of fried bread.

Preparation time: approximately 45 minutes. Cooking time: approximately 1 hour.

SEA BASS WITH SORREL HOLLANDAISE

My family prefers sea bass to salmon, as it is a lighter, less rich fish. With this I make a most delicious Sorrel Hollandaise, which originated because I had so much sorrel in the garden I tried to think of something to make with it other than the delicious sorrel soup which we love. Now I freeze many small bags of shredded sorrel, and add it to the sauce throughout the winter when sea bass is plentiful.

SERVES 8

6 pounds (2.7 kg) sea bass
A sprig of fresh tarragon or 1 teaspoon (5 ml) dried tarragon
Salt and pepper

Juice of 1 lemon
1¾ cups (½ pint; 300 ml) dry white wine

Preheat oven to 325° F (170° C; Mark 3).

Oil a piece of aluminum foil large enough to wrap the sea bass in. Place the sea bass in the center of the paper, put the tarragon, salt and pepper inside the belly cavity. Holding the paper up on all sides, sprinkle the lemon juice and white wine over the fish, fold the ends of the paper over the head and tail, then roll the fish in the rest of the paper to make a package. Place it on the rack of a baking pan and put it in the preheated oven at 20 minutes to the pound plus 20 minutes, i.e., 2 hours 20 minutes for a 6-pound fish.

SORREL HOLLANDAISE SAUCE

*1 cup (8 oz; 225 g) butter at room
    temperature*
*2 tablespoons (30 ml) white wine
    vinegar*
3 tablespoons (45 ml) water
¼ teaspoon (1.5 ml) salt
Fresh-ground pepper

3 egg yolks
Juice of 1 lemon
Salt to taste
Cayenne to taste
*¼ pound (125 g) sorrel, trimmed
    and washed*
2 tablespoons (30 ml) butter

Divide the butter into 12 portions. In a small, heavy saucepan, combine the vinegar and 2 tablespoons (30 ml) of water with the salt and pepper. Cook the mixture over high heat until it is reduced to 1 tablespoon (15 ml). Remove the pan from the heat and add the remaining water. Pour the vinegar mixture into the top of a double boiler, with hot water in the lower pan, and add the egg yolks, stirring briskly with a wire whisk until the mixture is thick and creamy. Set the pan over low heat and beat in the butter, one portion at a time, lifting the pan occasionally to cool the mixture. Make sure that each butter portion has melted before adding more. Continue to beat the sauce until it is thick and firm. Add the lemon juice, salt and cayenne to taste. (Note: If a thicker sauce is required, use 4 egg yolks; if thinner, 2 egg yolks—or thin the sauce by adding 1 or 2 tablespoons [15 to 30 ml] of cream or hot water.) Keep the sauce warm in the double boiler.

In a saucepan soften the sorrel in 2 tablespoons (30 ml) butter for 2 minutes. Then place in a food processor or blender, add the Hollandaise and mix for 10 seconds. Return the Sorrel Hollandaise to the top of the double boiler until needed. If the sauce begins to curdle, add another egg yolk and a tablespoon of hot water and whisk.

Preparation time: 10 minutes. Cooking time: 2 hours, 10 minutes.

SEA BASS ANISETTE

One of my favorite cooking writers is Jane Grigson. Her books are full of marvelous recipes and fascinating information. One of her most delicious ideas is Sea Bass Anisette. The following recipe is from *The International Wine and Food Society's Guide to Fish Cookery.*

SERVES 4
2 pounds (900 g) sea bass fillets

MARINADE

*¼ teaspoon (1.5 ml) chopped
  coriander leaves
¼ teaspoon (1.5 ml) ground mace*

*8 peppercorns, slightly crushed
⅓ cup (6 tablespoons; 90 ml) olive
  oil*

SAUCE

*Pernod-flavored Mayonnaise (see
  below)
3 heads fennel*

*½ cup (4 oz; 120 g) butter
Salt*

Preheat the broiler (grill).

Prepare the marinade. Leave the fish to marinate for 3 hours before cooking it. Prepare the mayonnaise. Slice up the fennel, putting one-third aside. The rest can either be served as a salad with vinaigrette dressing, or it can be blanched in boiling salted water for 10 minutes, then cooked gently in 2 or 3 ounces (50 or 75 g) butter until soft. I think the second way is best, if the fish is being eaten hot.

Butter a broiler (grill) pan, lay the reserved fennel on it, then the fish fillets (dispense with the broiler [grill] rack), which should be cooked under a medium-hot broiler (grill) for 6 to 8 minutes each side. Sprinkle with salt.

Serve the fish immediately with the cooked fennel and the sauce; with new potatoes as well if you like; or leave it to cool and serve it with the fennel salad and the sauce.

PERNOD-FLAVORED MAYONNAISE (also good with sea bream, John Dory, gray mullet and mackerel)

*2 large or 3 small egg yolks
1½ cups (½ pt; 300 ml) salad oil
1 to 2 tablespoons (15 to 30 ml)
  vinegar or lemon juice
Salt, pepper*

*Scant tablespoon sweet-sour
  cucumber, chopped
Scant tablespoon each parsley and
  tarragon, chopped
1 tablespoon (15 ml) Pernod*

Beat the yolks with a teaspoon (5 ml) of vinegar or lemon juice, until they thicken slightly. Add the oil drop by drop, beating all the time, until the mixture turns creamy and heavy. The oil can now be added more rapidly. Correct the seasoning with more vinegar or lemon juice, salt and pepper. Fold the rest of the ingredients into the basic mayonnaise, using the above measurements as a guide only.

POULTRY AND GAME

PLUCKING AND DRESSING POULTRY AND GAME BIRDS

1. The best place to pluck a bird is either into a deep sink, which will contain all the feathers so they do not fly around the kitchen, or, better still, outside in the garden, if you have one, putting the feathers directly into a large plastic rubbish bag. Pluck the feathers after the bird has been hung for the necessary amount of time. Begin by pulling out the feathers at the neck, against the grain, down the back to the breast. There you have to take great care, as the skin is very tender. Make sure it is well plucked by pulling out the pin feathers with a tweezer. Some people become careless in this process, believing that a feather here or there may be singed off. This is a mistake, as it gives the bird the flavor of burned feathers.
2. After all the feathers have been plucked, hold the neck in your left hand and in your right hand hold a long piece of lighted paper or a long taper, but be careful not to get wax on the bird. Quickly singe the bird all over, being careful not to scorch it in any way.
3. Next lay the bird on its back on a table. Cut a slit in the skin at the back of the neck and draw the skinned neck out through it.

4. Chop off the neck at the base, next to the body.
5. Cut off the neck skin, leaving about 2 inches to fold under. This is particularly important for keeping in stuffing or anything else you put in the body cavity.
6. Turn back the remaining neck skin and insert the fingers through the opening, to loosen the entrails as much as possible.
7. Cut a small slit just below the breastbone, insert two fingers if it is a small game bird, or your hand if it is a larger bird. As carefully as possible, pull out the entrails, being particularly careful not to break the gall-bladder, as this will make the bird bitter. Keep the gizzard, heart and liver, discarding all the other organs.
8. Cut off the oil sac or vent at the base of the tail, and carefully wipe out the inside of the bird and the flap of the neck with a clean cloth. **Important:** Do *not* wash the inside of the bird unless you have broken any part of the intestine when cleaning it. If you have, unfortunately, broken the intestine, then wash inside, *but be sure to dry it thoroughly*.
9. Chop off the ends of the claws and the points of the wings.

Exceptions

Turkeys:
1. The sinews must be drawn, otherwise the legs will be inedible. To do this, pass a hook through the leg at the joint between the sinews and the bone. Hold the bird firmly with your left hand and, with your right, pull the hook with all your strength. An easier way is to hang the bird on a hook quite high on the wall, then you can bear down with all your weight.
2. Chop off the feet and the lower legs, leaving only the drumstick.

Snipe, Woodcock and Pigeon: These birds have such tender skins that it is difficult to pluck them. Instead, make a slit in the head and neck, cut slowly down the breast, and gently peel off the skin. The snipe's head remains on the bird and is tucked under the wing when it is trussed. The woodcock's head is tucked under the wing and the beak passed through the thighs, right through the body.

CARVING GAME BIRDS

Small Game Birds

With a sharp knife, cut in half down the side of the breastbone.

Small game bird

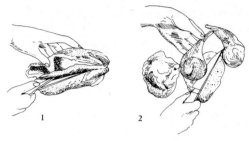

Large Game Birds

1. With large game birds, cut out the backbone with poultry shears.
2. Then cut in half again by severing the legs from the breast.

CHICKEN

Choosing a Chicken

It is very rare these days to see anything but oven-ready chickens, and often even rarer to see fresh chickens—most have already been frozen. However you can still see enough of the animal to make sure that it is the one you want. Check the following signs:

1. The feet should be soft, moist and pliable. The legs should be short, smooth and pliable, with short and sharp claws. The feet of an old bird are hard and rough with larger and blunt claws.
2. The body should be plump, with a white breast and a breastbone that is totally pliable. As the bird ages, the breastbone becomes more brittle.
3. The skin should have a clear color and be free from stains or bruises. If you are buying a frozen bird, make sure there are no signs of freezer burn—discolored patches on the skin.

In England, chickens are not graded by the government as they are in the United States, where you have USDA Grade A for the choicest chickens, and USDA Grade B for good but not the choicest.

Pullets, or baby chickens, weighing from ¾ pound to 1¾ pounds are called *poussins* in France and England. These are delicious roasted, broiled (grilled) or even sautéed.

Spring Chickens weighing from 2½ to 4 pounds are *poulets* in France and England. The broiler/fryer is the nearest to these in the United States.

Fat Fowl ranging from 3½ to 5 pounds, *poulardes* in France and England, are like roasting chickens in the United States. These are plump and young.

The Boiling Fowl or *poule* is the same as a stewing hen. Weighing 4½ pounds and over, it is old and tough. These may be used for boiling, stewing, for casseroles and for stock.

A *Capon* is the same in all countries. It is a cock, chemically emasculated when young to improve its weight and flavor. When sold, it is full-breasted and plump, weighing between 4 and 7 pounds. It is often used at Christmas instead of turkey, and is considerably more succulent. You can prepare it the same way as turkey, using the same stuffings and sauces.

To Truss a Chicken

1. Lay the fowl on the table with the tail toward you and twist the ends of the wings under the back.
2. Thread a trussing needle with strong white twine.
3. Take hold of the thighs firmly with one hand and push the needle through the thighs and body. Draw the string through, and then arrange the legs straight by the sides of the fowl.
4. Pass the needle under the joint of the wing nearest to where it came out of the leg, then through the thick part of the wing.
5. Draw the flap of the neck tightly down and put a stitch through to secure it to the back.
6. Then pass the needle through the thick part of the other wing and out through the joint.
7. Press all the joints down neatly into their places and draw the string tight. Tie the two ends firmly together.
8. Fix the legs in position by passing the needle through a leg just below the first joint (the joint where the claw joins the leg), then through the loose skin on the other side, and through the other leg. Finally pass it through the back, bringing the needle out and then into the back again.
9. Draw the string tight, tie the ends firmly and see that both the bows or knots are on the same side of the fowl, as that makes it easier when the time comes to untie the bird.

To Carve a Chicken

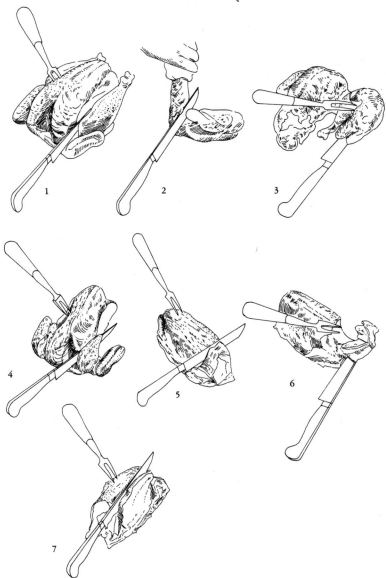

1. Place the chicken on its back on a platter or wooden carving board, with its head diagonally to your left. Insert a fork firmly either across or on the left side of the breastbone and make a clear cut down the leg joint, forcing the leg sharply away from the carcass, exposing the joint, completely severing the drumstick and the thigh in one piece.

2. Cut the thigh: holding the drumstick either with your hand or a fork, make an incision to one side of the bone, cut under at the end, lift it up and cut underneath and between the bone and the meat, thus removing the drumstick entirely from the thigh.

3. Place the knife parallel to the breast and cut through the wing joint.

4. Remove wing joint.

5 and 6. Turn bird sideways and remove the wishbone.

7. Now carve thin slices of the white meat, slicing parallel to the breastbone and beginning halfway up. If carving the whole chicken at once, repeat the same process on the other side. But unless you think that you are going to use it all, do not carve the rest of the chicken until it is needed, as it will dry up.

CHICKEN

These cooking times are for chickens that are fully thawed, at room temperature and stuffed at the neck end only. Add 20 to 30 minutes' cooking time if the body cavity also contains stuffing. The meat thermometer should read 190° F when the bird is thoroughly cooked.

Weight	Number of people served	Time to thaw in refrigerator	Oven temperature	Roasting time	Spit-roasting time	Accompaniments
2 pounds (1 kg)	2–3	28 hours	375° F (190° C; Mark 5)	1 hour	1 hour	Thyme and parsley stuffing; sausages; bread sauce and gravy.
3 pounds (1.4 kg)	4	32 hours	375° F (190° C; Mark 5)	1 hour, 20 minutes	1 hour, 15 minutes	
4 pounds (1.8 kg)	5–6	38 hours	375° F (190° C; Mark 5)	1 hour, 40 minutes	1 hour, 30 minutes	
5 pounds (2 kg)	7–8	44 hours	375° F (190° C; Mark 5)	2 hours	2 hours	
6 pounds (2.7 kg)	8–9	50 hours	350° F (180° C; Mark 4)	2 hours, 15 minutes	2 hours, 30 minutes	
7 pounds (3.2 kg)	10	56 hours	350° F (180° C; Mark 4)	2 hours, 30 minutes	3 hours	
8 pounds (3.6 kg)	12	62 hours	350° F (180° C; Mark 4)	2 hours, 45 minutes	3 hours, 30 minutes	

When spit-roasting a chicken, place a lump of butter and a sprig of herbs in the body cavity. Baste the bird with oil before and during the cooking time, and always place a pan below to catch the juices and drippings.

CURRIED CHICKEN LIVERS

SERVES 2 AS A FIRST COURSE

6 chicken livers, quartered
Salt and pepper
½ cup (3 oz; 75 g) dry bread
   crumbs
1 egg yolk, lightly beaten
2 tablespoons (30 ml) butter or
   margarine

2 tablespoons (30 ml) fine-chopped
   onion
2 tablespoons (30 ml) flour
½ teaspoon (2.5 ml) curry powder
1 pint (16 fl oz; 475 ml) milk

Season the chicken livers and roll them in the bread crumbs. Then dip in the egg yolk and back into the bread crumbs. Melt the butter or margarine in a frying pan and sauté the livers until tender, about 5 minutes. Remove them from the pan and sauté the onions in the same pan, adding more fat if needed. Add the flour, curry powder and milk and cook until the mixture thickens, stirring constantly. Arrange the livers on a heated dish, pour the sauce over them and serve.

Preparation time: 15 minutes. Cooking time: 20 minutes.

CHICKEN LIVERS SAUTÉ FORESTIÈRE
AND MUSHROOMS

SERVES 2 AS A FIRST COURSE

6 chicken livers, halved
Salt and pepper
¼ pound (125 g) mushrooms,
   sliced
¼ cup (2 oz; 50 g) butter or
   margarine

1¼ cups (10 fl oz; 300 ml) Madeira
   Sauce (see page 260)
Chopped parsley

Season the chicken livers and sauté them and the mushrooms in a saucepan in the butter or margarine for about 5 minutes, or until tender. When cooked, cover them with Madeira Sauce and heat through, but do not boil. Sprinkle with parsley and serve.

Preparation and cooking time: 10 to 15 minutes.

CHICKEN LIVER SANDWICH

MAKES 1 SANDWICH OR AN HORS D'OEUVRE FOR 2

4 chicken livers, washed and cooked	*4 drops Tabasco sauce*
2 tablespoons (1 oz; 25 ml) crisp	*Juice of ½ lemon*
bacon, diced	*Salt and pepper to taste*

Mix together in a bowl and spread on rounds of buttered bread.

CHICKEN TYROLIENNE

SERVES 4

One 3½ pound (1.6 kg) spring	*1 whole clove*
chicken, quartered	*4 tablespoons (60 ml) good olive oil*
Salt and pepper	*1 cup (3 oz; 75 g) fresh bread*
1 shallot, chopped fine	*crumbs*
1 tablespoon (15 ml) chopped	*1 lemon, sliced*
parsley	*Sprigs of parsley*
1 teaspoon (5 ml) chopped	*Rémoulade Sauce (see page 253)*
tarragon	

Preheat the broiler (grill).

Lay the quartered chicken in a deep casserole and sprinkle it with salt and pepper. Add the shallot, parsley, tarragon, clove and olive oil. Cover and allow it to stand for 1 hour. Take out the chicken, roll it in bread crumbs and broil (grill) for 20 minutes, or until the pieces are cooked through. Place the chicken on a heated serving dish, garnish with sliced lemon and sprigs of parsley. Serve with Rémoulade Sauce.

Marinating time: 1 hour. Preparation time: 30 minutes. Cooking time: 20 to 30 minutes.

PEPITORIA OF CHICKEN

SERVES 6

One 5-pound (2.3 kg) chicken, cut
   into pieces
4 tablespoons (60 ml) olive oil
1 large onion, chopped fine
1¼ cups (10 fl oz; 300 ml) chicken
   stock
1 cup (8 fl oz; 225 ml) white wine
8 to 10 whole black peppercorns

⅓ cup (2 oz; 50 g) blanched
   almonds
3 to 4 cloves garlic
1 sprig of parsley
2 hard-boiled egg yolks
½ cup (4 fl oz; 125 ml) dry sherry
2 ounces (50 g) chorizo, or any
   other spicy sausage, chopped

In a frying pan, sauté the chicken in 3 tablespoons (45 ml) olive oil until golden. Remove the chicken pieces and put them in a casserole. In the same oil, sauté the onion until it becomes golden, then add it and the oil to the casserole. Cover with stock and simmer for 30 minutes. Add the wine and peppercorns.

In a small frying pan, sauté the almonds and garlic in 1 tablespoon (15 ml) oil until they are golden, then grind them together in a mortar with the parsley and egg yolks until they make a smooth paste. Add the sherry, stir well, and pour the whole mixture into the casserole. Simmer for another 20 minutes. Add the chopped chorizo, heat and serve with potato chips or Jerusalem Artichoke Chips (see page 278).

Preparation time: 30 minutes. Cooking time: approximately 1 hour.

TURKEY

Turkeys may now be bought all year round, but they are in season, fresh, from October to March, and are at their best from November to the end of January. The true original turkey is what we now call the guinea fowl, which was first introduced into Europe from the Guinea Coast of West Africa many, many years ago. In the sixteenth century, Cortez, Mexico's conqueror, sent back the first real turkeys to Henry VIII in England. In those days, the turkey was not as large a bird as it is now, but still bigger than the guinea fowl, though with similar markings. It was, therefore, thought to be a larger version of the same bird. However, in England during that period there was a slang expression, "It's turkey—it's good," because the English believed that anything that was extra-beautiful or extra-delicious *must* come from the vast Turkish Empire. Thus this larger, succulent bird was called a turkey. These days turkey is used a great deal for everyday food, not just on holidays, as it is a high-protein meat with almost no fat or waste. It is available jointed or quartered, or as turkey roll. There is also a delicious spicy garlic and turkey kabanos sausage.

Choosing a Turkey

If you have the chance to choose a fresh turkey, the hen turkey is the better, the male turkey being rather tough even when farmed especially for eating. Only first-year birds should be roasted; second-year ones should be used for stewing. Look for an ample breast, which will feed the most people, smooth black legs with supple feet, and, if a tom, a short spur. The legs of older turkeys have a gray-reddish color, and look very scaly and hard, with hard feet and a long spur. Make sure you ask for the giblets for gravy, and the liver, which is delicious fried with bacon.

To Truss a Turkey

1. Press the legs close to the body and pass the skewer through the leg and body, catching the other leg on the point of the skewer at the other side.
2. Skewer the legs again at the last joint.
3. Twist the wings under the back of the bird, press them well in and skewer firmly.
4. Now put the stuffing, herbs, etc., into the breast through the neck opening, then draw the skin over onto the back and fasten it with a small skewer. If stuffing the breast itself, sew up the tail opening with a needle and thread.
5. Take a long piece of strong string and wind it across the back from skewer to skewer to keep the trussing firm.

To Stuff and Cook the Turkey

There are many experienced cooks who believe that only the neck cavity, *not* the body cavity, should be stuffed. They think that allowing more air to circulate inside results in a moister bird. Instead of stuffing, place an apple, onion or lemon plus a mixture of herbs inside the body cavity to add a subtler flavor. In any case, whether you are stuffing the neck or the body cavity or both, leave some space; do not fill either too tightly, as the stuffing will not have room to expand during the long cooking process. Always stuff the bird just before cooking, never the night before. I make my stuffing the night before and keep it in a bowl covered tightly with plastic wrap. Then on Christmas morning I get up early, preheat the oven (very important), sprinkle the bird inside and out with salt and pepper, stuff the neck cavity, place the herbs, etc., in the body cavity, truss the turkey and brush the whole bird with either pork or bacon fat, or a mixture of honey, lemon and butter.

If you want a bird that is juicy, tender and full of flavor, it must be cooked in a very slow oven—325° F (170° C; Mark 3) for up to 14 pounds, or 300° F (150° C; Mark 2) for over 14 pounds. At this temperature you will not need to cover the bird with foil, and it will need basting only once an hour, so you will be free to get on with your other chores. Put the giblets in the pan with the turkey to make a thick gravy. If you do fill the body cavity with a proper stuffing, then add 20 minutes to the cooking time for up to 10 pounds in weight, and 35 minutes for birds over 10 pounds.

To Carve a Turkey

Turn the bird so that the rump is pointing away from you. Sever the leg as you would a chicken's, as this makes it easier to carve the breast. Then start cutting slices from the breast at the point where it meets the wing bone, working your way up, slice by slice, until you hit the center of the breast-bone. Now repeat the process on the other side. The severed leg joints may be sliced for those who like the dark meat.

Note: Place the plates to the left of the bird, not in front of it, so that you do not have to reach over them to carve. An obvious remark you say, but you have no idea how many people I have seen struggling to carve across a pile of hot plates, especially when the carving is done at the table rather than at the sideboard.

To Thaw a Frozen Turkey

A turkey should be thawed in its bag to prevent its drying out, preferably in a refrigerator or cold larder (40° F; 4° C). Take out the giblets from the body cavity as soon as they are free, to speed up the thawing process. The turkey has thawed completely when the flesh is soft to the touch, all moisture has drained away and there are no signs of ice crystals in the body cavity. Once thawed, it should be kept in a cool place and cooked as soon as possible.

TURKEY

Weight	Number of people served	Time to thaw in refrigerator	Roasting time	Spit-roasting time	Accompaniments
5–6 pounds (2–2.7 kg)	5–7	50 hours	2½ hours	2–3 hours	Gravy made from giblets; bread sauce; chestnut stuffing; sausage-meat stuffing; sage and onion stuffing; sausages; bacon rolls; roast potatoes or roast Jerusalem artichokes.
6–8 pounds (2.7–3.6 kg)	8–10	60 hours	2½–3 hours	3–3½ hours	
8–10 pounds (3.6–4.5 kg)	10–12	66 hours	3–3½ hours	3½–4 hours	
10–12 pounds (4.5–5 kg)	13–15	70 hours	3½–4 hours	4–5 hours	
12–15 pounds (5–6.8 kg)	15–17	74 hours	4½ hours	too big	
15–17 pounds (6.8–7.7 kg)	17–20	78 hours	4½ hours	too big	
17–20 pounds (7.7–9 kg)	20–30	82 hours	4½–5 hours	too big	
20–25 pounds (9–12 kg)	30–40	86 hours	5–6 hours	too big	

These roasting times are for birds with necks stuffed only. If the body cavity is also stuffed, allow 20 minutes extra for birds up to 10 pounds (4.5 kg) in weight and 35 minutes extra for those over 10 pounds.

When the turkey is cooked, the meat thermometer should read 180–185° F.

Oven temperature should be 325° F (170° C; Mark 3) for turkeys up to 14 pounds, and 300° F (150° C; Mark 2) for those over 14 pounds.

The amounts given are for a main meal with enough left over for stews, pies, pâtés and stock.

The following recipe was written in 1789, when it would have taken a long time to prepare, but now we have the food processor which cuts the preparation time to a mere 20 minutes. Ask your butcher to bone the turkey and the chicken or pheasant, but ask him to give you the bones as well.

TO DRESS A TURKEY TO PERFECTION

THE STUFFING

SERVES 10 TO 12

One 3-pound (1.4 kg) chicken or
 pheasant, boned and cut into
 small pieces
1 pound (450 g) ground veal
½ pound (225 g) suet
½ pound (225 g) fresh bread
 crumbs
½ pound (225 g) mushrooms
1 small tin truffles, cut small

A few sweet herbs (thyme, rosemary, oregano)
2 tablespoons (30 ml) fine-chopped
 parsley
2 teaspoons (10 ml) nutmeg
Pepper and salt
½ teaspoon (2.5 ml) mace
Peel of 1 lemon, chopped fine
2 egg yolks, beaten

One 10-pound (4.5 kg) turkey,
 boned but left whole

BASTING MIXTURE

1 cup (8 fl oz; 225 ml) clear honey
¼ cup (2 oz; 5 g) butter

Juice of 1 lemon

Reserved turkey bones
½ pound (225 g) mushrooms,
 chopped

1 truffle, chopped

Preheat the oven to 350° F (180° C; Mark 4).

Mix all stuffing ingredients together in the food processor, adding the egg yolks last. Fill up the turkey with the mixture and truss it (see page 123).

Put the turkey in a roasting pan in the preheated oven and baste it with the basting mixture every 30 minutes for 5 hours. Meanwhile, make a gravy from boiling up the bones, the chopped mushrooms and the truffle.

Preparation time: 20 minutes. Cooking time: 5 hours.

TURKEY LOAF

SERVES 4

½ pound (225 g) cold leftover turkey, chopped fine
1 pound (450 g) lean pork sausage meat
¾ cup (2 oz; 50 g) fresh bread crumbs

½ teaspoon (2.5 ml) salt
¼ teaspoon (1.25 ml) pepper
2 tablespoons (30 ml) chopped parsley
2 eggs, beaten well
1½ cups (½ pt; 300 ml) milk

Preheat oven to 400° F (200° C; Mark 6).

Mix all the ingredients together in a bowl. Turn the mixture into a greased loaf pan, place it in a baking pan half filled with water. Bake for 40 to 45 minutes.

Preparation time: 10 minutes. Cooking time: approximately 45 minutes.

SCALLOPED TURKEY WITH EGG NOODLES

SERVES 4 TO 6

6 ounces (175 g) egg noodles
½ cup (2 oz; 50 g) diced onion
1 tablespoon (15 ml) diced green pepper
2 tablespoons (30 ml) butter or margarine
1 pound (450 g) cold cooked turkey, diced

8 ounces (225 g) fresh or frozen peas, cooked briefly
2½ pints (2 pts; 1 l) turkey cream sauce (see page 128)
1 cup (3 oz; 75 g) buttered bread crumbs

Preheat oven to 350° F (180° C; Mark 4).

Cook the noodles in boiling water for 10 minutes, or until they are tender. Then, in a frying pan, sauté the onion and green pepper in the butter until the vegetables become soft and golden. In a bowl combine the noodles, turkey, and all the vegetables with the cream sauce. Pour the mixture into greased individual ramekins or casseroles, sprinkle with the buttered bread crumbs, and place the dishes in a baking pan half filled with water. Bake in a preheated oven for 25 minutes.

Preparation time: 15 minutes. Cooking time: approximately 40 minutes.

TURKEY CREAM SAUCE

APPROXIMATELY 2½ PINTS (2 PTS; 1 L)

1 tablespoon (15 ml) fine-chopped onion

2 tablespoons (30 ml) butter

2 tablespoons (30 ml) flour

1½ cups (¾ pint; 475 ml) reduced turkey stock

1½ cups (¾ pint; 475 ml) chicken broth

¼ teaspoon (1.25 ml) salt

3 whole white peppercorns

1 bay leaf

1 blade mace or a pinch ground

A pinch of nutmeg

¾ cup (6 fl oz; 175 ml) light (single) cream, scalded

In a saucepan, sauté the onion in butter until it is soft. Add the flour, mix well and cook the *roux* slowly, stirring constantly, until it just starts to turn golden. Add the turkey stock and chicken broth gradually and cook the mixture, stirring vigorously with a wire whisk, until it is thick and smooth. Add the salt, peppercorns, bay leaf, mace and nutmeg. Cook the sauce slowly, stirring frequently, for about 30 minutes, or until it is reduced by one-third. Strain the sauce through a fine sieve, add the hot cream, and mix well.

Preparation time: 15 minutes. Cooking time: approximately 1 hour.

TURKEY DIABLE (for leftover turkey)

Cut the remains of a cold turkey into edible portions, then dip each piece into Sauce Diable (see page 259) and allow to stand for 1 hour. Then broil (grill) slowly, turning once, until the turkey pieces are crisp and brown. Serve with Piquante Sauce (see page 261).

This recipe can also be used for whole cooked turkey legs: Skin the legs, then make a few deep gashes in the fleshy end. Dip them into the Sauce Diable, let them stand for 1 hour, then re-dip in the sauce and broil (grill) them slowly. Brush with a little butter if needed, turning as necessary. Serve with Piquante Sauce.

Marinating time: 1 hour. Cooking time: 10 minutes.

GOOSE

Each year at Christmas we have a goose which my stepdaughter raises on her farm in Wales. Before stuffing it, I remove the marvelous chunks of creamy white fat in the neck and body cavity, melt it down, bottle it and put it in the refrigerator. It is delicious on cooked kasha and other dishes. My stepchildren also swear that it cures bronchitis when rubbed on the chest; however, one must really be ill alone to indulge in such antisocial behavior.

Choosing a Goose

Geese are at their best from September to February, and become too tough to eat after they are one year old. A freshly killed goose has fine pink flesh with creamy white skin. Its feet should be yellow, soft and pliable. As the goose gets older, the feet turn darker and reddish in color, and become dry and stiff.

To Truss a Goose for Roasting

Assuming the goose has been plucked, cut off the neck as close as possible to the back, leaving the skin hanging from the breast long enough to fold over. After drawing, wash and wipe the bird both inside and out, and cut off the feet and the wings at the first joint. Draw the legs up close to the body, and thrust a skewer through one side, fastening the leg securely, and out the other side, holding fast the other leg. When the bird has been stuffed, make a hole in the loose flap of skin and push the rump through to prevent the stuffing from escaping.

To Carve a Goose

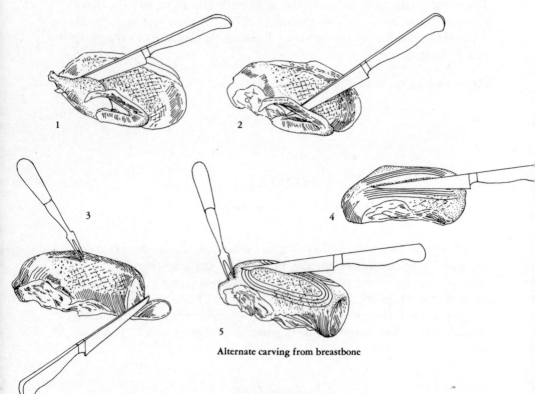

Alternate carving from breastbone

The anatomy of the goose being similar to that of a chicken, one carves both in the same manner, except that the greater size and strength of the goose gives a toughness to the joints, thus calling for the exercise of more force in their separation. Use the point of the carving knife in the joint between the bones, as any attempt to cut through the bone itself will fail. Having sliced the breast in long slices on one side, working your way up until you hit the center of the breastbone, repeat the process on the other side. For those who like dark meat, the severed leg joints may be sliced. I love the wings, particularly the next day when cold, but they are incredibly tough to eat.

GOOSE

Weight	Number of people served	Time to thaw in refrigerator	Roasting time	Accompaniments
6–8 pounds (2.7–3.6 kg)	2–4	60 hours	2½–3½ hours	Red cabbage; Jerusalem Artichoke Chips (see page 278); green beans; orange salad; baked apples stuffed with prunes; Apple and Almond Stuffing (see page 133); giblet gravy
8–12 pounds (3.6–5 kg)	4–7	66–70 hours	3½–4½ hours	
12–14 pounds (5–6.3 kg)	7–10	70–74 hours	4½–5 hours	

Since goose is particularly rich, people eat less of it than they would of turkey. But again, there is less meat on a goose than a turkey.

Preheat the oven to 400° F (200° C; Mark 6) and place the goose in for 10 to 20 minutes depending on its size. Then reduce to 350° F (180° C; Mark 4) for the rest of the cooking time. Make a tent of foil to cover; remove it during the last 30 minutes of cooking.

Cooking time also depends on the breed of goose, as some have more flesh than others. Goose, like duck, is very fatty. Either prick the skin with a fork and allow the fat to drip off while cooking, or baste with the honey, lemon and butter mixture suggested for turkey (see page 126). This will give the skin a texture reminiscent of Chinese duck.

It is not possible to use a meat thermometer here as there is no real flesh on the leg. Use the basic rule of piercing the leg and looking at the juices. If they are yellow or clear rather than pink, then the bird is cooked.

GOOSE JAPONAISE

SERVES 8

2¼ pints (2 pts; 1 l) hot water
1 cup (6 oz; 175 g) brown sugar
1 tablespoon (15 ml) salt
½ teaspoon (2.5 ml) ground
    cinnamon
3 whole cloves
3 sprigs sage, or 2 teaspoons
    (10 ml) dried

1 teaspoon (5 ml) allspice
1 teaspoon (5 ml) fresh-ground
    pepper
One 9 to 10 pound (4.1 to 4.5 kg)
    goose

In a large Dutch oven or casserole, place all the ingredients *except* the goose. Bring them to the boil and cook for 10 minutes. Place the goose in the liquid and cover tightly. Simmer for 2 to 4 hours, allowing 20 minutes per pound and basting occasionally. Remove the pan from the heat and let it stand for 15 minutes before serving. Then remove the goose, slice it and place the slices on a heated serving dish; strain the liquid, removing the fat, and serve the sauce separately.

Cooking time: approximately 3 hours, 45 minutes.

A GOOD POTATO STUFFING FOR A GOOSE

1/4 cup (2 oz; 50 g) butter or
  goose fat
1 onion, chopped fine
3 pounds (1.4 kg) raw potato,
  diced

1 goose liver, chopped fine
1 teaspoon (2.5 ml) fresh-chopped
  sage or 1/2 teaspoon (2.5 ml)
  dried
Salt and pepper

Melt the butter or goose fat in a frying pan and add the onion and potatoes. Cover and toss them over moderate heat for 10 to 15 minutes. Remove from the heat and add the rest of the ingredients. Place the stuffing inside the bird, tie the vent securely, and roast in the usual manner.

Cooking time: approximately 15 minutes.

DEVILED GOOSE

SERVES 8

One 9 to 10 pound (4.1 to 4.5 kg)
  goose
Apple and Almond Stuffing (see
  page 133)
Goose giblets
1 1/4 cups (10 fl oz; 300 ml) red
  wine vinegar

1 teaspoon (5 ml) black pepper
2 tablespoons (30 ml) green
  peppercorn mustard
1 tablespoon (15 ml) salt

Preheat oven to 325° F (170° C; Mark 3).

Put the goose in a pot or casserole and cover with boiling water. Simmer gently for 1 hour. Drain well, wipe dry, and fill the bird with Apple and Almond Stuffing. Then place it on a rack in a baking pan and put it in the preheated oven for approximately 3 hours (allow 20 minutes per pound cooking time). Put the giblets into the pan with the goose. Mix together the rest of the ingredients and use this to baste the goose every 20 minutes.

When the goose has finished cooking, put it on a heated serving dish, remove the giblets and pour off all the fat from the roasting pan, leaving the giblet gravy and devil-sauce juices. Add any remaining devil sauce and scrape off the black bits from the pan. Simmer gently, then pour the sauce into a sauceboat and serve with the goose.

APPLE AND ALMOND STUFFING

3 pounds (1.4 kg) apples, peeled,
cored and cut into small pieces
1 cup (6 oz; 175 g) split almonds

1 cup (5½ oz; 150 g) seedless
raisins

Mix all the ingredients together and fill the body cavity of the goose as full as possible, because during the cooking process the apples will turn to purée and the stuffing will shrink quite a lot. Fasten the vent securely.

Preparation time for goose and stuffing: 30 minutes. Cooking time: approximately 4½ hours.

DUCK

Choosing a Duck

The tests for age are the same as for chickens. Young duck usually have yellow feet which become darker and reddish in color as the bird gets older. The feet should be moist, soft and pliable—they become dry and stiff if the duck is going stale.

Cooking a Duck

Duck are full of fat and are not very economical to buy as there is often more bone than meat. But they can be delicious roasted or braised. When roasting them, prick the skin and allow the fat to run off. The combination

GAME

Game and number of servings	Oven temperature	Roasting time	Season*	Accompaniments
Guinea Fowl (serves 2)	400° F (200° C; Mark 6)	45–60 minutes, depending on size	all year	Thyme and parsley stuffing; sausages; bacon rolls; cranberry sauce; bread sauce and gravy.
Grouse (serves 1–2)	425° F (220° C; Mark 7)	approximately 35 minutes	August 12th–December 10th. At their best from mid September through October.	Game chips; fried bread crumbs; bread sauce; cranberry; red-currant or rowan jelly; giblet gravy.
Partridge (serves 1–2)	400° F (200° C; Mark 6)	approximately 30 minutes	September 1st–February 1st.	As for grouse.
Pheasant (serves 2)	450° F (230° C; Mark 8)	40–50 minutes	October 1st–February 1st. At their best November and December.	As for grouse, plus Jerusalem Artichoke Chips (see page 278)
Snipe (serves 1)	450° F (230° C; Mark 8)	15 minutes	August 12th–January 31st.	Roast on a piece of toast to catch the juices. Same accompaniments as for grouse.
Teal (serves 1)	425° F (220° C; Mark 7)	20–25 minutes	September 1st–January 31st.	Game chips or Jerusalem Artichoke Chips (page 278); orange salad. Strongly flavored gravy, with some Calvados.
Widgeon (serves 2)	450° F (230° C; Mark 8)	20–25 minutes	September 1st–February 20th. Best in October–November.	As for teal.
Mallard (serves 2)	450° F (230° C; Mark 8)	25–35 minutes	September 1st–February 20th.	As for teal.
Quail (serves 1)	450° F (230° C; Mark 8)	15 minutes	all year	Serve on toast with mashed livers, mushrooms and Madeira. Watercress salad.

GAME

Game and number of servings	Oven temperature	Roasting time	Season*	Accompaniments
Wood Pigeon (serves 1)	425° F (220° C; Mark 7)	20–25 minutes	all year	Mushroom sauce and watercress.
Woodcock (serves 1)	425° F (220° C; Mark 7)	15–18 minutes	September 1st–January 31st.	Serve on toast with orange gravy and watercress.
Hare (serves 2–4 depending on size)	350° F (180° C; Mark 4)	1¾ hours–2 hours	August–end of March. At their best October–March.	Fried savory forcemeat balls; red-currant jelly; Port wine sauce; Madeira sauce; gooseberry jelly.
Rabbit (serves 2)	425° F (220° C; Mark 7)	45–55 minutes	all year	Thyme and parsley stuffing; chestnut stuffing; cashew nut stuffing; watercress and thick gravy; red-currant jelly.
Venison (depending on use and cut)	400° F (200° C; Mark 6) for the first 20 minutes, then 350° F (180° C; Mark 4)	2¼–2¾ hours, according to size, or 25 minutes per pound plus 30 minutes	June–January.	Port wine sauce or gravy; red-currant or rowan jelly; orange salad; peas, string beans, or cauliflower—*never* Brussels sprouts or cabbage.

* *Note*: Use only fresh game for roasting. Frozen game is better used in soups, stocks, casseroles and stews.

of lemon, honey and butter painted on the skin and poured into the cavity gives the skin the brown crispness of Chinese duck.

When roasting, preheat the oven to 425° F (220° C; Mark 7) and cook the duck for 20 minutes. Then reduce the heat to 350° F (180° C; Mark 4) and cook a further 20 minutes per pound.

To Carve a Duck

Turn the bird so that the head is pointing toward you, cut through the crackling skin at the point where the left leg fastens to the body, and, with a carving knife or poultry scissors, cut through the ball joint, thus separating the leg from the body. This leaves you free to slice the meat from the breast by starting at the outer edge and working toward the middle of the bird; cut the meat in long slivers along the bone. Having cut the meat from one side, turn the bird around so that the rump points toward you, and repeat the process on the other side.

Wild Duck

Teal: This is a very special wild duck, which, unfortunately, is also very expensive, so it must be reserved for special occasions. One bird serves two people. Its best season is from the end of October to January, reaching full flavor after the first frost.

Widgeon: Widgeon is a wild duck, about a third larger than the teal but smaller than the mallard. Any wild duck recipe may be used for widgeon, with the cooking time adjusted for the size of the bird.

Mallard: This is the most common species of wild duck and the ancestor of many of the domestic ducks. The male is the beautiful one, with a head and neck of emerald green, the back brown and gray shading to black, and white and blue workings on the wings. The female is dark brown and buff. Both the male and female weigh approximately 2½ pounds.

ROAST TEAL

SERVES I

Preheat oven to 425° F (220° C; Mark 7).

Rub teal well with lemon butter, or split a lemon and place it inside the bird; brush it all over with melted butter. Roast in the preheated oven for 20 to 25 minutes, basting frequently, with the giblets cooked in the same pan.

When cooked, put the bird on a heated dish, add some stock or water to the pan, leaving the giblets in the roasting pan and simmering the gravy for 5 minutes. Remove the lemon from inside the bird and serve with the gravy and sliced lemon.

DUCK IN MARMALADE AND HONEY

SERVES 6

1 domestic duck or 3 mallards or 6
teal
4 tablespoons (60 ml) orange
marmalade
4 tablespoons (60 ml) clear honey

1 cup (6 oz; 175 g) dry bread
crumbs
Vegetable oil or melted chicken fat
Goose giblets

Preheat oven to 450° F (230° C; Mark 8).

Place the duck on a roasting rack in a baking pan. Heat the marmalade in a little saucepan until it is nice and runny. Put it through a sieve to remove the bits of peel, then pour it back into the saucepan and add an equal amount of honey. Paint the duck with this mixture and sprinkle it with one quarter of the bread crumbs. Place it in the preheated oven and leave until the bread crumbs begin to brown. Then paint it again with the marmalade mixture and sprinkle with more bread crumbs. Brown again in the oven. Repeat this process twice more; then turn down the oven to 300° F (150° C; Mark 2) and roast the bird for 2 hours. If it is a tame duck you need not baste it; there will be fat enough on the bird. However, if it is a wild duck, brush it all over with vegetable oil or melted chicken fat after the last crumbing, and again every 20 minutes while the bird is cooking. During the last 10 minutes of cooking, turn up the oven heat to 450° F (230° C; Mark 8).

While the bird is cooking, make the Giblet Gravy (see page 163). Then strain the gravy and add it to the marmalade mixture in the pan. Serve the duck with wild rice and an onion, sage, sausage and rusk stuffing which has been made into balls and deep fried until brown.

Preparation time: approximately 15 minutes. Cooking time: approximately 2½ hours.

CHESTNUT DUCK

SERVES 4

1 duck, cut into serving portions
Veal stock to cover
1 pound (450 g) chestnuts, peeled
2 ounces (50 g) mushrooms, sliced

¼ cup (2 fl oz; 50 ml) soy sauce
Salt and fresh-ground black pepper
1 tablespoon (15 ml) ground
  ginger

In a casserole, put the pieces of duck and pour on enough stock just to cover them. Cover the casserole and simmer for 1 hour. Add the rest of the ingredients and cook 20 minutes more and serve.

Preparation time: 30 minutes, including peeling the chestnuts. Cooking time: 1 hour, 20 minutes.

MARINATED WILD DUCK À LAS MANTOUANE

SERVES 2

2 dozen fresh figs, washed, stems
  removed
1¾ cups (14 fl oz; 425 ml) port
  wine
5 tablespoons (2½ oz; 65 ml) sweet
  butter

1 mallard, cleaned and trussed
1½ cups (12 fl oz; 350 ml) rich
  veal stock
A large bunch of watercress

In a deep enamel dish with a close-fitting cover, marinate the fresh figs in port wine for 36 hours.

Preheat oven to 350° F (180° C; Mark 4).

Melt the butter in a large earthenware casserole, add the duck and brown the pieces on all sides. Then baste with the port in which the figs have been marinated and cook over medium heat for 20 to 25 minutes, basting continually until all the wine has been used. Surround the duck with the marinated figs and barely cover with the veal stock. Cover and put in the preheated oven for 30 to 35 minutes. When cooked, remove the bird to a hot serving dish and arrange the figs around it. Remove all fat from the sauce, strain it and pour over the bird, garnished with watercress.

Marinating time: 36 hours. Cooking time: approximately 1 hour, 15 minutes.

WILD OR TAME DUCK SALMI

SERVES 4

¼ cup (2 oz; 50 g) *butter*
1 duck, cut into 8 pieces
2 onions, peeled and sliced thin
Fresh-ground black pepper
2 potatoes, peeled, sliced and
  chopped into neat pieces
8 tablespoons (4 oz; 125 ml) ham,
  chopped

1 large lamb's kidney, washed,
  blanched, trimmed and chopped
Game stock
½ cup (4 fl oz; 125 ml) *sherry or*
  light white wine
Triangles of toast and slices of
  lemon

Melt the butter in a fireproof casserole and fry the pieces of duck for 10 minutes. Remove them to a heated dish. Put the onions in the same casserole, and add the black pepper, then the potatoes, ham, kidney and enough stock to cover. Cook over low heat for 2 hours. Add the sherry or wine and simmer for 15 minutes. Serve with the toast, chopped potatoes and lemon slices.

Note: This could be made in a slow cooker, by frying the duck and onions first, and then placing everything in the slow cooker.

Preparation time: 15 minutes. Cooking time: 2 hours, 30 minutes.

TAMASIN'S WILD DUCK WITH WILD APRICOT AND HAZELNUT STUFFING

SERVES 12

Six 1-pound (450 g) wild ducks
1 pound (450 g) wild apricots,
  soaked overnight, or bottled in
  *syrup**
1 pound (450 g) hazelnuts, chopped
  coarse
A large bunch of parsley, chopped
  fine

1 large or 2 medium onions, chopped
  fine
1½ pounds (700 g) brown bread
  crumbs
Sea salt and black pepper
2 eggs

* Available at specialty food shops.

Preheat oven to 425° F (220° C; Mark 7).

Have the birds split down the middle when you buy them. Clean the insides with a damp cloth. Drain and roughly chop the apricots including the kernels, which will have softened sufficiently. Add the hazelnuts, chopped parsley, onions, brown bread crumbs and seasoning. Then stir in the eggs until the mixture coheres. Fill the halves of the birds, put them back together and tie them securely with string, then pack tightly into two roasting pans. Put in the preheated oven for 45 minutes, if you like rare game; 10 to 15 minutes more for well done. Baste three or four times with pan juices during cooking. No carving is necessary. Serve with roasted potatoes and parsnips.

Preparation time: 15 to 20 minutes. Cooking time: 45 to 60 minutes.

GUINEA FOWL (PINTADE)

The guinea fowl was originally a game bird enjoyed by the ancient Greeks and Romans. It then fell out of fashion for many centuries. It originated on the Guinea coast of West Africa, where it was also known as the Tudor Turkey. The French have known and loved this bird for hundreds of years. For a long time, it outnumbered the chicken for eating 11-1. Considered a delicacy for its succulent flesh and slightly gamy flavor—reminiscent of pheasant but not as strong—it serves as an excellent substitute when game is not in season or is unobtainable. Guinea fowl are available fresh and frozen all year round now that they have become popular in England and America. You will nevertheless have to order them specially from butchers, particularly if you want them fresh. They are more expensive than chicken but a good deal cheaper than pheasants.

When choosing a guinea fowl, look for a plump breast and smooth-skinned feet. They should be young, and, if freshly killed, should be hung for 4 to 5 days in warm weather, longer in cold weather. To roast, truss the guinea fowl as for chicken, and lard it with a thick piece of sliced bacon tied on the breast. Rub the legs with bacon or pork fat, or butter if you prefer, cover with seasoned flour, and sprinkle with black pepper and mace. When cooked, carve into two portions by splitting through the breast and backbones.

GUINEA FOWL À LA SIMLA

SERVES 2

One 3 to 4 pounds (1.4 to 1.8 kg)
    guinea fowl
2 slices (rashers) fat bacon for
    larding
¼ pound (125 g) bacon, diced
1 large carrot, sliced
1 onion stuck with cloves
2 sticks of celery, washed and
    chopped
4 sprigs parsley
Salt and pepper

1¼ cups (½ pt; 300 ml) good
    Brown Stock (see page 247)
2 tablespoons (30 ml) butter
1 onion, diced
½ teaspoon (2.5 ml) curry powder
1 tablespoon (15 ml) flour
1 tablespoon (15 ml) sultanas
¼ cup (2 oz; 50 g) chestnuts,
    peeled, blanched and chopped
8 mushrooms, broiled (grilled)
2 cups (14 oz; 400 g) cooked rice

Preheat oven to 325° F (170° C; Mark 3).

Truss and lard the bird as for roasting (see page 116). Place it in a braising pan with the diced bacon, carrot, onion stuck with cloves, the celery, parsley, salt and pepper to taste and the brown stock. Cover it tightly and cook in the preheated oven for about 2½ hours. When cooked, remove the bird and put it on a heated platter to keep warm. Drain off the cooking liquid and keep it hot, reserving the vegetables for soup or stock.

In a large saucepan, melt the butter and sauté the diced onion. Add the curry powder and flour and mix well. Then add the reserved liquid, a little at a time, stirring constantly, until the sauce becomes thick and creamy. Finally add the sultanas and chestnuts to the sauce.

Cut the bird into 8 pieces and place them in a heated serving dish surrounded by rice; cover with the sauce and top each piece of guinea fowl with a broiled (grilled) mushroom.

Preparation time: approximately 25 minutes. Cooking time: approximately 3 hours.

QUAIL

Quail are now raised for domestic use as well as running wild in the Southern states of America. The ancient Romans thought they brought on epileptic fits, but the ancient Greeks ate them in large quantities. Although they are delicious, you need to eat two to satisfy any appetite, and they are quite a nuisance to eat. They exhibit the usual signs of age. Quail need not be trussed if they are wrapped in vine leaves and bacon and tied with string before roasting. Otherwise, truss as you would any other poultry.

GREEK-STYLE QUAIL

FOR THE RICE

SERVES 6

6 tablespoons (3 oz; 75 ml) butter
2 tablespoons (30 ml) fine-chopped onion
1 cup (7 oz; 200 g) rice, unwashed
3 cups (1¼ pints; 725 ml) veal or chicken stock
2 generous tablespoons (35 ml) pork sausage meat, loosened

2 to 3 tablespoons (30 to 45 ml) fine-shredded lettuce
3 generous tablespoons (50 ml) peas
1 generous tablespoon (20 ml) fine-chopped red pimento

6 plump quail
Lemon juice
Salt and pepper
½ cup (4 oz; 125 g) butter

6 leaves of lettuce, braised
12 tablespoons (6 fl oz; 175 ml) Demi-glace Sauce (see page 143)

Preheat oven to 325° F (170° C; Mark 3).

Prepare the rice. Melt 2 tablespoons (30 ml) butter in a saucepan, and sauté the onions in it for 1 minute. *Do not brown.* To this add the rice and cook, stirring constantly, until it takes on a milky color, then gradually pour in the veal or chicken stock, constantly stirring gently. Cover tightly and set in the preheated oven for 25 minutes *without stirring*. In another saucepan, melt 2 tablespoons (30 ml) butter and add the sausage meat, shredded lettuce, peas and pimento. Cook over a moderate flame for 8 to 10 minutes, stirring constantly. Remove the rice from the oven and transfer it to a casserole, dotting the top with 2 tablespoons (30 ml) butter divided into small bits. Then carefully, stirring very gently so as not to break the grains, add the sausage meat and vegetable mixture. Mix well.

While the rice is cooking, clean the quail and rub them with lemon juice, then with salt and black pepper. Sew and truss them. In an earthenware casserole or a Dutch oven, melt ½ cup (4 oz; 125 g) butter over moderate heat and place the quail in it. Cook, turning often to brown the birds on all sides, for 15 to 20 minutes or until the juice from their thighs runs clear. Put them on a heated platter and keep warm.

Arrange the rice, sausage and vegetable mixture on a hot platter. Make 6 little nests with the back of a spoon and place a small braised lettuce leaf in each one. Arrange the quail on the lettuce leaves. Pour 2 tablespoons (30 ml) Demi-glace Sauce over each bird.

DEMI-GLACE SAUCE

1 cup (8 fl oz; 225 ml) Sauce
Espagnole (see page 249)
½ cup (4 fl oz; 125 ml) dry white
wine
4 tablespoons (60 ml) tomato purée
or paste

1 teaspoon (5 ml) Game Fumet
(see page 165)
Salt and pepper

Place in a saucepan the Sauce Espagnole, wine and tomato purée. Bring it to a rapid boil and reduce it to half its volume over a high flame, then add the Fumet and seasoning.

Preparation time (including the sauce): approximately 30 minutes. Cooking time (including the sauce): 35 minutes.

QUAILS MOUGIN

SERVES 4

¼ cup (2 oz; 50 g) butter
½ cup (2 oz; 50 g) chopped shallots
2 cloves garlic, crushed
1 small bay leaf
2 whole cloves

12 whole peppercorns
4 quails, cleaned and trussed
1¼ pints (1 pt; 600 ml) White
  Wine Sauce (see below)

Preheat the oven to 400° F (200° C; Mark 6).

In a sauté pan, over medium heat, toss the butter, shallots, garlic, bay leaf, cloves and peppercorns. Stir and toss them until the shallots begin to change color, then add the quails and brown them on all sides in this mixture. Remove the quails and pour the mixture into a casserole. Place the quails in the casserole and cover with the White Wine Sauce. Cover tightly, and cook in the preheated oven for 15 minutes, or until the birds are tender. Serve directly from the casserole in which the birds were cooked.

WHITE WINE SAUCE

1¼ cups (½ pt; 300 ml) Béchamel
  Sauce (see page 246)
2 tablespoons (30 ml) onion juice
2 tablespoons (30 ml) Mushroom
  Ketchup (see page 394)

1¼ cups (½ pt; 300 ml) dry white
  wine

Combine all the ingredients and simmer for 5 minutes.

Preparation time: 15 minutes. Cooking time: approximately 40 minutes.

GROUSE

Grouse in the British Isles means the red grouse, which does not seem to live in any other country. Only the young should be roasted, the older ones reserved for casseroles, braising and pâtés. The young can be recognized by the soft, downy plumes on the breast and under the wings, and by their pointed wings and rounded soft spur knob. The spur knob becomes scaly and hard in older birds. No grouse has actual spurs.

Young grouse are usually served whole, one per person. In late September, however, they begin to fatten and become large enough for two people. In this case slit the bird along the top of the breastbone and cut it right through. Then lay the halves on their sides, on the toasts on which they were roasted. All grouse for roasting should be hung 3 to 4 days.

To Truss a Grouse

1. Cut off the first two joints of the wing, leaving only one joint.
2. Press the legs down firmly to the sides, between the side bone and the breast.
3. Pass a skewer through the wing, then through the thigh, through the body, and through the other thigh and wing.
4. Pass a piece of string round each end of the skewer, cross it over the back, bring it up and tie the two legs together with it.
5. Tie a piece of bacon over the breast.

ROAST GROUSE

EACH GROUSE SERVES I TO 2

Preheat the oven to 425° F (220° C; Mark 7).

Tie a piece of bacon over the breast of each grouse and place the grouse on a piece of toast in a roasting pan; roast for 30 to 35 minutes, basting frequently. Five minutes before the end of cooking, remove the bacon from the breast and dredge the grouse lightly in seasoned flour to brown the skin. Serve the birds on their toasts with giblet gravy, bread sauce and fried bread crumbs.

BROILED (GRILLED) GROUSE

SERVES 2

2 young grouse

2 shallots, chopped fine

1 cup (3½ oz; 85 g) fine-chopped
   parsley

1 teaspoon (5 ml) chili powder

½ teaspoon (2.5 ml) salt

2 tablespoons (30 ml) melted butter

1 cup (6 oz; 175 g) fried bread
   crumbs

Preheat the broiler (grill).

Split the grouse down the back, being careful *not* to halve them completely. In a bowl, mix the shallots, parsley, chili powder and salt. Sprinkle
the mixture inside the grouse. Then put them on a skewer, brush them with
melted butter and place them under the preheated broiler (grill), turning
them every 2 minutes, for 5 minutes. Brush them over again with the melted
butter, and put them back under the broiler (grill) for another 3 to 4 minutes,
again turning every 2 minutes. When cooked, serve with fried bread crumbs,
broiled (grilled) mushrooms soaked in butter, and fried potatoes dusted
with paprika.

*Preparation time: approximately 15 minutes. Cooking time: approximately
10 minutes.*

PARTRIDGE (PERDREAU)

The common or gray partridge is considered to be the finest to eat. The rule
for killing young partridge is the same as that applied to grouse, i.e., they
are shot from the 1st of September to the end of December *in the year in
which they were bred*. The young bird has yellow legs, and a dark, well-
pointed, sharp bill. Its first flight feather is pointed at the tip, becoming
rounder as it ages. Its feet turn pale blue-gray with age and in colder climates. This bird is one of the few game birds which should not be hung
more than 3 to 4 days, as it loses its delicate taste if it becomes too high.

To Truss a Partridge

1. Press the legs as much as possible in under the breast, between it and the side bones, in order to make a nice, plump breast.
2. Pass a skewer through the wings and legs to keep them in place. Tie the legs together but do not cross them.
3. Tie a piece of fat bacon across the breast by passing the string around the point and head of the skewer to keep the bacon firmly in place.

To Cook a Partridge

Young birds are too small to cut into more than two portions. Split the bird into two by slicing along one side of the breastbone with a knife. To bring out its best flavor, take a small bunch of vine leaves, doused lightly in brandy, and stuff each half of the breast. Roast as you would a grouse. When cooked, remove and discard the vine leaves. Serve with sauerkraut cooked in champagne.

PARTRIDGES WITH SHALLOTS AND OLIVES

SERVES 6

3 partridges, cleaned and dressed
6 slices (rashers) bacon
3 tablespoons (45 ml) vegetable oil
1 onion, sliced
2 carrots, sliced
2 cloves garlic, peeled and chopped
   fine
1 teaspoon (5 ml) salt

½ teaspoon (2.5 ml) black pepper
1 cup (8 fl oz; 225 ml) red wine
Water to cover
Partridge giblets
½ pound (225 g) whole shallots,
   peeled
2 dozen pitted green olives

Wrap each partridge in 2 slices (rashers) of bacon. In a casserole, brown the birds in 2 tablespoons (30 ml) oil and add the onion, carrots, garlic and seasoning. Then add the wine and water to cover. Simmer for at least 1 hour, longer if the birds are tough. Sauté the giblets in a small frying pan with the remaining butter, chop them, and add to the sauce together with the shallots and the olives. Bring to the boil and simmer for 10 minutes. You may need to add more water if the sauce is getting dry. Remove the partridges and cut them in half. Put them on a heated dish, cut side down, surrounded by the shallots and olives. Strain the sauce, pour it over the birds and serve.

Preparation time: approximately 15 minutes. Cooking time: approximately 1¼ hours.

STUFFED PARTRIDGES

SERVES 4

2 partridges, cleaned and dressed
Salt and pepper
One 20-ounce (575 g) can of grapefruit segments, drained and juice reserved
1 teaspoon (5 ml) chopped mixed herbs (thyme, sage, basil)

1¼ cups (4 oz; 125 g) fresh bread crumbs
2 tablespoons (1 oz; 30 ml) salad oil
4 slices (rashers) bacon
Partridge giblets

Preheat oven to 425° F (220° C; Mark 7).

Dust the partridges inside and out with salt and pepper. In a bowl, combine the grapefruit segments, herbs, ¾ cup (2 oz; 50 g) of the bread crumbs and the salad oil, and stuff the birds with this mixture. Wrap each bird in 2 slices (rashers) of bacon and place them on a rack in a roasting pan. Add the giblets to the pan and roast the birds in the preheated oven for 35 minutes.

When cooked, remove the birds to a heated dish, drain off all the fat from the pan, add the grapefruit juice to the pan juices and stir to form a gravy; boil and strain. Add the remaining fresh bread crumbs to the gravy and serve as sauce for the stuffed birds.

Preparation time: 20 minutes. Cooking time: approximately 50 minutes.

PHEASANT (FAISAN)

The English ringneck, a cross between the Chinese and common pheasant, was introduced into England by the Romans, and into the United States in 1881 from China to Portland, Oregon. The cock is the beautifully colored bird while the hen has a mottled brown plumage. The young hen is, however, plumper and more tender than the cock. As with other birds, the young pheasant is recognized by short, round spurs and soft, supple feet, as well as the soft and downy feathers under the wing and the pointed, long flight feathers.

Pheasants tend to be dry and tasteless, but their flavor is improved by hanging from one to two weeks until the first sign of mortification takes place. The bird should not be allowed to decay, as it then takes on a bitter taste.

To Truss Pheasants

Bring the thighs close under each wing and pass a skewer through the leg, body and out through the other leg. Fasten a string around both ends of the skewer and bring it up around the legs, tying them firmly to the rump.

To Carve Pheasants (see page 115)

The best parts of this bird are the breast and the wings. The drumsticks make better salmi or croquettes than roasted meat.

Put the fork in firmly across the breastbone and cut off even slices, starting from the wing and working up to the center of the breastbone. Repeat this process on the other side; if more meat is needed, cut the thigh.

ROAST PHEASANT

SERVES 4

2 pheasants	4 slices (rashers) bacon
Salt and pepper	Pheasant giblets
Good quality olive oil	Flour, for dredging

Preheat oven to 450° F (230° C; Mark 8).

Sprinkle the birds inside and out with salt and pepper, rub them lightly with olive oil. Truss the pheasants firmly and wrap them in bacon. Place them in a roasting pan together with the giblets and cook for 40 to 45 minutes, according to the size and age of the bird. Ten minutes before the birds are due to be taken out, remove the bacon fat, quickly dredge the birds with flour, and return them to the oven to finish cooking.

Remove all the trussing strings and serve on a bed of watercress, with fried bread crumbs and a rich brown gravy made from the roasted giblets.

Pheasants may also be stuffed before cooking. A particularly delicious stuffing is the Cashew Nut Stuffing below. If using this stuffing, roast the bird in the usual way, but at a slightly lower temperature—425° F (220° C; Mark 7)—and cook for 10 to 15 minutes longer.

Preparation time: approximately 15 minutes. Cooking time: approximately 50 minutes.

CASHEW NUT STUFFING

1 pound (450 g) cashew nuts
1¼ pints (1 pt; 600 ml) game or
  chicken stock
2½ tablespoons (3 oz; 75 ml) fried
  bacon, chopped fine

¼ pound (2 oz; 50 g) butter
Salt and pepper
Sauce Espagnole (see page 249), if
  needed

In a saucepan simmer the cashew nuts in the stock until they are tender. Drain off any surplus stock not absorbed by the nuts. Add the bacon, butter, and salt and pepper to taste. If the nuts absorb all the stock and are a little on the stiff side, add a bit of Sauce Espagnole to make a stuffing of the desired consistency.

Preparation time: 10 minutes. Cooking time: approximately 20 minutes.

PIGEON (SQUAB)

A squab is a young—about 4 weeks old—pigeon. The pigeon must be young to be eaten roasted or baked in pies. Do not use older pigeons in pies, because they must be cooked for a long time to make them tender, and the pie crust will become dry over the long cooking period. Older pigeons can be made into delicious casseroles.

The young bird has small pinkish legs and a downiness under the wings. As it grows older, the legs, as with most game, become larger and darker in color, and the feathers appear more mature. Pigeons should be drawn as soon as they are killed, and should be cooked within 3 to 4 days. When buying a squab, make sure it is small, plump and has light-colored flesh. As their flesh damages very easily, great care must be taken when plucking them. After plucking, singe and clean them, wash well and dry with a clean cloth. Cut off the head close to the body (using the neck to roast with the bird to make the gravy) and the feet at the first joint. Then thread a trussing needle with fine string and run it through both legs and the body, bringing it up around the rump and tying the legs up closely to it.

A slightly larger squab can serve two people. When the bird is cooked, split it in two lengthwise and lay the halves, cut side down, on the dish. To halve the bird the head should be facing you. Point the knife at the vent and draw it along the full length of the breastbone. Then, with a little pressure from both hands, press the knife right through the backbone, and down the center of the bird.

SPICED PIGEONS

SERVES 6

2 to 3 pigeons, cleaned and cut in half

4 tablespoons (60 ml) vegetable oil

Pigeon livers

2 to 3 cloves garlic, chopped

8 to 10 whole peppercorns

1 bay leaf

A pinch of ginger

1 cup (8 fl oz; 225 ml) red wine vinegar

Water

½ cup (2 oz; 50 g) raisins

¼ cup (2 fl oz; 50 ml) port or Madeira

Preheat oven to 350° F (180° C; Mark 4).

In a casserole, brown the pigeons in 3 tablespoons (45 ml) of the oil. In a small frying pan sauté the livers in the remaining oil until just brown. Then remove them and pound them in a mortar, or pass them through a fine grinder. Add the livers to the pigeons in the casserole together with the seasonings and vinegar. Add water to cover. Cover the casserole and place it in the preheated oven for 1 hour or until the pigeons are tender. Meanwhile plump the raisins in the port or Madeira and add them and their liquid to the casserole 30 minutes before the end of cooking.

Preparation time: 30 minutes. Cooking time: approximately 1½ hours.

PIGEON PIE

SERVES 6

3 pigeons
3 ounces (75 g) cooked ham
2 ounces (50 g) bacon
1 pound (450 g) lean pork or veal
3 to 4 gherkins
1 clove garlic, peeled
2 tablespoons (1 oz; 25 ml) parsley

3 eggs
Salt and pepper
1 cup (8 fl oz; 225 ml) brandy
1¼ cups (½ lb; 225 g) flour
1 cup (8 fl oz; 225 ml) milk
½ cup (4 oz; 125 g) butter
¾ teaspoon salt

Preheat oven to 425° F (220° C; Mark 7).

Slit the pigeons along the backbone, turn back the flesh, and remove the backbone and ribs. In a food processor, grind the ham, bacon, pork or veal, the gherkins, garlic, parsley, 1 beaten egg, salt and pepper to taste and the brandy.

Mix 1 egg, the flour, milk, butter and salt in a bowl. Knead thoroughly until the mixture forms a smooth dough; divide and roll it out into two rounds each ¼ inch (0.6 cm) thick. Line a pie dish with half the dough and put in a layer of the ground ingredients. Stuff the pigeons with the rest of the mixture and put them into the pie dish. Cover with the rest of the pastry, crimp the edges and prick a few holes with a fork. Cover the pie with waxed or greaseproof paper, stand it in a pan of boiling water and place it in the preheated oven for 40 minutes. Remove from the pan of water, discard the paper, and brush the dough with the remaining beaten egg. Put the pie back in the oven for a few minutes to set the glaze and serve.

Preparation time: approximately 45 minutes. Cooking time: approximately 45 minutes.

SNIPE (BÉCASSINE)

Snipe are never cleaned before roasting; their entrails are roasted in them and later eaten mixed with pâté de foie gras. The signs of a young snipe are the same as those for most other birds, but in addition, if the bills are moist and the throat muddy, then they have been dead for some time. As they are tiny they need not be carved and you can eat the bones.

To Truss a Snipe

Handle them extremely carefully because of their delicate skin. Peel off the neck and head skin by making a slit from the head down and peeling it away. Do not cut off the head and feet and do not draw the bird. Press the legs quite close to the body, crossing them at the knee joints. Skewer the wings and tuck the head under the left wing. Place a strip of fat bacon over the breast and tie a string around the legs, bill and breast, finishing with a knot at the vent.

ROAST SNIPE

Preheat the oven to 450° F (230° C; Mark 8).

Truss as described above, brush the birds all over with melted butter, and set each one on a slice of buttered toast, well spaced out in a roasting pan. Cook in a preheated oven for 10 to 15 minutes. Snipe should be eaten quite rare.

The entrails should have dripped onto the pieces of toast during the cooking, so serve each snipe on its piece of toast together with some sliced lemon and melted butter. A small amount of good game stock added to the pan juices will make additional gravy. Season and serve with Burgundy.

WOODCOCK (BÉCASSE, BÉCASSEAU)

Woodcock has been described as the queen of the game birds. As they are tiny birds, they are only good when they become fat, and are at their best from October to November. Feel the vent—if it is thin, the bird is not in prime condition. The throat and mouth must be clean, the feet soft and supple.

There is an art to roasting these birds, as the legs must be well-done and the breast underdone. Like snipe, woodcock are not drawn, the intestines being considered the greatest delicacy. So they should be roasted either on a piece of toast or on a piece of paper to catch the entrails. One bird will feed one person.

To Truss Woodcock

Peel the skin off the head and neck by making a slit down the head. Pluck the bird carefully, singe it and cut off the toes, *but do not draw the bird*. Press the wings to its sides and either turn the head under the wing with the long beak pointing forward, or pass the beak through the thighs and through the body. Tie a string round the legs and vent and pass it over the breast.

To Roast a Woodcock

Blanket it with larding pork or bacon slices and put it in a hot oven 400° F (200° C; Mark 6) for 15 to 18 minutes. A woodcock requires high seasoning.

WOODCOCK SOUFFLÉ À LA CZARINA

This soufflé takes quite a bit of time to prepare, as does the Muscovite Sauce. However, it is very much worth it. For those who love game, it is a particularly delicious dish to serve, and totally different from most roast and casseroled game dishes. It may also be made with pheasant, quail, grouse or snipe.

SERVES 4

1 woodcock, plucked, singed and cleaned
Vodka
1 teaspoon (5 ml) allspice
1 juniper berry, ground fine
Salt and pepper
2 generous tablespoons (35 ml) sweet butter
1¼ cups (10 fl oz; 300 ml) rich dry Burgundy

4 sprigs parsley tied with 1 sage leaf and 1 small sprig thyme
1 cup (8 fl oz; 225 ml) good chicken stock
¼ cup (2 oz; 50 g) butter
4 tablespoons (60 ml) flour
5 egg yolks
6 egg whites
A pinch cream of tartar

Preheat oven to 400° F (200° C; Mark 6) and place a baking pan on the rack.

Rub the woodcock inside and out with vodka, then with allspice mixed with the juniper berry and salt and pepper to taste. Now cut the bird into small dice, reserving the intestine, liver and giblets. Discard the gizzard and head. Place the trimmings (all the bones, liver and intestines) in a mortar or a food processor together with 1 generous tablespoon (20 ml) of butter. Process or pound as fine as possible. Turn the mixture into a saucepan and add the wine, herbs and diced woodcock. Set over gentle heat and allow it to come to the boil. Then turn the flame up high and reduce the liquid to almost nothing. Pour in the chicken stock and allow it to simmer for 1 hour. Strain the liquid, reserving both the liquid and the diced woodcock.

In a saucepan melt ¼ cup (2 oz; 50 g) butter slowly; do not allow it to brown. Then add the flour, stirring constantly, until it becomes a smooth paste. Remove the pan from the heat and add the reserved liquid, stirring constantly. Return the pan to the heat and stir for about 1 minute or until the sauce becomes smooth and thick. Then add the diced woodcock. Bring it to the boil, remove it from the heat and rub the mixture through a fine sieve or put it into a food processor until it becomes a fine paste. Transfer the paste to a saucepan, or keep it in the food processor, and add the remaining butter, mixing with a wooden spoon. Next, add 1 egg yolk at a time, working the mixture rapidly after the addition of each egg yolk. Correct the seasoning. Beat the egg whites with the cream of tartar until they hold stiff peaks, and fold them into the mixture with a metal spoon. Turn the mixture into a buttered 8-inch (20.3 cm) soufflé dish and place on top of the baking pan in the preheated oven for 30 minutes. Serve with Muscovite Sauce (see below).

Preparation time: approximately 20 minutes. Cooking time: approximately 2 hours.

MUSCOVITE SAUCE

MAKES 2½ CUPS (1 PINT; 600 ML)

1 pint (16 fl oz; 475 ml) hot Poivrade Sauce (see page 249)
6 tablespoons (3 fl oz; 75 ml) port or Madeira
1 tablespoon (15 ml) crushed juniper berries

3 tablespoons (45 ml) pine nuts, broiled (grilled)
3 tablespoons (45 ml) dried currants, soaked in water

Mix all together. Serve hot.

WOOD PIGEONS (RAMIERS)

Wood pigeons must be hung until tender and then dressed. Again, they must be no more than one year old to be good for roasting; the older ones are fit only for hash. They may be roasted or cooked as any ordinary pigeon.

To Truss

Cut off the head and neck close to the body, and chop off the toes at the first joint. Cross the legs by cutting a slit in the skin of one and passing the other through it. Pass a trussing needle and string through the wings and legs, and bring it out the other side. Pass it back again and bring it out near where it first entered. Tie the two ends of the string firmly together. Tie a piece of bacon around the breast.

RABBIT (LAPIN) AND HARE (LIÈVRE)

The rabbit is distinguished from the hare by its shorter body, ears and feet, and by the absence of black on the ears. There are three types of hare, the common brown hare, and the blue or mountain hare which changes to white in winter and lives principally in Scotland. The Belgian hare again is a larger variety. A young hare, up to six months old, is tender and delicious, whereas older hares are extremely tough. Hare, like pork, must be cooked thoroughly. It is dangerous to eat it if the meat is still red.

The wild rabbit weighs about 2 to 3 pounds, but the domestic animal can grow to over 6 pounds. Some weigh as much as 20 pounds. If you like a slightly gamy flavor, the dark meat of the wild rabbit will appeal to you. On the other hand, there are many who prefer the mild, white meat of the domestic species.

Hares should be hung from the hind legs for 10 to 14 days, longer in cold weather, and should not be paunched for 4 to 5 days after killing. Rabbits, on the other hand, should be killed when they are a year old, about the end of September, and cooked as soon as possible. They do not improve by hanging.

Choosing Rabbits and Hares

Because of the variety of foods eaten by wild rabbits, they tend to have a better flavor than the cabbage and lettuce fed domestic rabbits. To test a rabbit's age, place a slight but firm pressure on the front of the lower jaw. If it snaps at the middle, between the front teeth, the animal is young. If it resists the pressure, however, it is fodder for stewing. Both rabbit and hare have sharp claws and tender ears when young. If the claws are thick and blunt, and the ears tough and hard, you have an old one. There is also the cleft in the lip, known as the hare lip, which is quite narrow in the young, becoming wider as the animal ages. The body of a freshly killed hare or rabbit is stiff; if the body is limp, the animal is stale.

Paunching

1. Cover a bench or table with newspaper.
2. Lay the rabbit or hare on its back, with the hind legs toward you, and slit open the belly with a sharp knife, cutting through the pelt first, laying it open and carefully aside. Then cut the inner skin, being careful not to let the knife go too deep.
3. Remove the intestines, saving the kidneys, heart and liver, and discard the rest.
4. Wipe with a damp, clean cloth but do not wash it yet, or the pelt will become difficult to handle when skinning.

To Skin Hare and Rabbit

1. Cut the skin round the first joint of the hind legs, cutting off the paws completely. Push the hind legs up to the belly, holding tight to the pelt, which should come away easily.
2. Ease the pelt over the rump, snipping the tailbone if it resists normal pressure.
3. Cut off the front paws at the first joint and pull the front legs through the pelt.
4. If you do not want the head, cut it off with the pelt. If you wish to keep it, leave it as it is.
5. Pull off the ears of a rabbit by passing a skewer between the skin and the head and pulling them off in the skin. With hare you leave on the ears.

To Truss Hare and Rabbit

1. Cut the sinews of the hind legs.
2. Bring the forelegs toward the back, flat against the sides, and skewer them or fasten with string.

3. Bring the hind legs forward flat against the front ones and skewer them or fasten with string.
4. All the stumps should be pointing to the middle.
5. Pass a string through the eyeholes and pull the head around to the side, fastening it to the string holding the legs together.
6. With hare, put a piece of buttered paper over the head so that the ears do not burn.

To Carve Roast Hare

1. The head should be pointing away from you.
2. Insert a knife under the shoulder and cut along the backbone down to the rump.
3. Turn the dish sideways and cut moderately thick slices.
4. You could, as an alternative, cut off the shoulders and legs first, and cut the back crosswise into six equal pieces. This can be done only with a young hare, as the bones of older animals become too hard to carve through.
5. The best parts are the back and hind legs.

HARE OR RABBIT PÂTÉ

SERVES 6 TO 8 PEOPLE

1 hare or rabbit, meat removed from bone and sliced

1 calf's foot (pig's trotters can be substituted)

1 large onion, sliced

2 carrots, sliced

1½ cups (12 fl oz; 350 ml) white wine

1 cup (8 fl oz; 225 ml) water

5 (75 g) bacon slices (rashers)

½ pound (225 g) lean pork, chopped fine

½ pound (225 g) veal, chopped fine

6 tablespoons (3 oz; 75 ml) fine-chopped ham

½ teaspoon (2.5 ml) juniper berries, crushed

1 teaspoon (5 ml) thyme

1 teaspoon (5 ml) allspice

1 teaspoon (5 ml) salt

½ teaspoon (2.5 ml) fresh-ground black pepper

Preheat oven to 425° F (220° C; Mark 7).

Crush the bones of the hare or rabbit and place them in a large saucepan with the calf's foot, the onion, carrots, wine and water. Simmer until the meat from the foot falls away from the bone. Remove the meat, pass the rest of the sauce through a fine sieve and keep warm. Line a pâté dish with bacon slices (rashers), reserving a couple to cover the dish.

In a food processor, combine the pork, veal, ham and calf's foot meat. Put the slices of hare or rabbit in the pâté dish, filling in the spaces between with the chopped meat. Season each layer with herbs, spices, salt and pepper. Pour in the sauce, cover with the remaining bacon slices (rashers). Stand the pâté dish in a pan of boiling water and place in the preheated oven for 1½ hours. Remove from the oven and cool with weights pressing down the meat. Serve when cool.

Preparation time: approximately 45 minutes. Cooking time: approximately 2 hours.

EDOUARD DE POMIANE'S LIÈVRE À LA ROYALE

Preparing hare can be a rather gory affair, but the result is delicious. Edouard de Pomiane said about this dish, "In front of each person put a glass of your best Burgundy, a very hot plate, a piece of bread and a spoon. That is all, Lièvre à la Royale is eaten simply with a spoon—and with reverence."

SERVES 3 TO 4 PEOPLE

1 hare
¼ cup (2 oz; 50 g) butter
2 slices (rashers) bacon
20 cloves garlic, peeled and chopped fine
40 shallots, peeled and chopped fine
2 bay leaves
A sprig of thyme or 1 teaspoon dried thyme

2 whole cloves
Salt and pepper
½ glass (6 oz; 175 ml) wine vinegar
1½ bottles of Burgundy
A small glass (2 oz; 50 ml) Cognac

Hang the hare for 4 days. Skin and draw it and use only the saddle and back legs for this dish, reserving the liver, lungs and clots of blood. Melt the butter in a heavy iron or enamel casserole (not aluminum), lay a slice (rasher) of bacon in the bottom and then the saddle and back legs, with the second slice (rasher) of bacon on the top. Add the garlic, shallots, bay leaves, thyme and cloves. Season with salt and pepper, and empty the vinegar and 1 bottle of Burgundy into the casserole. Cook over a low flame for 3 hours. Some of the wine will evaporate. Meanwhile, chop fine the reserved hare's liver, lungs and any clots of blood, and add them to the casserole at the end of the first 3 hours together with the remaining half bottle of Burgundy.

Cook for another 3 hours, after which the meat will have detached itself completely from the bones. Lift these out with two forks. In the bottom of the casserole you will have a savory, shapeless mass. Sprinkle it with the Cognac and warm it for 5 minutes more. Transfer it very carefully to a piping hot dish, and carry it to the table.

Preparation time: 1 hour. Cooking time: approximately 6 hours.

VENISON

Venison is the culinary term for the flesh of all kinds of deer, and some people even call bear venison. Varieties of deer are the roe deer (*chevreuil*), the fallow deer (*daim*), and the red deer (*cerf*) which produces Scotch venison, also known as stag and hind venison.

Stag shooting usually begins in August, ending at the end of September, and the hinds are shot from early October until the end of January. Young deer should not be shot and are no use for eating.

Deer meat must be hung for 14 days in cool weather, but if hung too long it becomes stale; the vein in the neck turns green or yellow instead of blue, and a rancid odor is emitted from under the kidneys. To keep venison, it should be wiped dry and dusted with a mixture of pepper and powdered ginger, then hung end up in a dry, cool, airy place. It should be examined every second day, and dusted with more pepper and ginger after 7 days. The haunch and the saddle are the only cuts which should be roasted—the haunch consisting of the leg and the loin. The best-end of neck can be made into chops, but the rest of the forequarter should be casseroled, stewed or made into game pies.

Choosing Venison

Years ago, a butcher would leave on the hoof to show the age of the venison. If the hoof was small and smooth the meat would be tender; if large and rough, the meat would require a great deal of marinating and long cooking. The meat should be dark and fine grained, the fat firm and thick, clear and white; the more fat the better, since venison tends to be quite dry.

To Carve Venison

To carve the haunch, turn the knuckle end away from you and, with the point of a sharp knife, make a deep cut from the knuckle end to the end of the loin. Then cut long, thin slices from end to end, holding the knife slightly on the slope. *Venison must be carved quickly* as the fat can taste unappetizing if it gets cool too soon. The saddle and leg are carved as you would lamb.

ROAST HAUNCH OF VENISON

SERVES 10 TO 12

5 pounds (2.3 kg) flour sifted with
  4 tablespoons (60 ml) salt
1¼ cups (10 oz; 300 g) lard
2½ pints (2 pts; 1 l) water

7 to 8 pounds (3.2 to 3.9 kg) haunch
of venison, marinated (see page
236)

Preheat oven to 400° F (200° C; Mark 6).

Put the sifted flour and salt into a bowl and rub the lard into it. Mix it together with the water to make a smooth dough. Let it stand for 1 hour. Roll out the dough in an oblong shape to fit the haunch, leaving it no thicker than ¼ inch. Remove the haunch from the marinade and wrap it completely in the paste, taking care to seal all the joinings by moistening the edges with water and pressing them together.

Place in the preheated oven for 20 minutes, then lower the heat to 375° F (190° C; Mark 5) and roast for approximately 2½ hours or until tender. Remove the crust and serve the venison with a good Port Wine Sauce (see below), orange salad and some red currant jelly.

PORT WINE SAUCE

1¼ cups (½ pt; 275 ml) Sauce
  Espagnole (see page 249)

½ cup (4 fl oz; 125 ml) port

Add the port to the Sauce Espagnole and simmer for 10 minutes.

Marinating time: 2 to 4 days.

Preparation time: 1 hour, 30 minutes. Cooking time: approximately 3 hours.

TAMASIN'S CASSEROLE OF VENISON IN ELDERBERRY AND PORT SAUCE

SERVES 8

One 4 pound (1.8 kg) haunch or
saddle of venison, cut into large
bite-sized pieces

MARINADE

1 bottle red wine

12 juniper berries, crushed

1 large onion, sliced

1 cup (8 fl oz; 225 ml) olive oil

2 tablespoons (30 ml) wine vinegar

6 bay leaves

Salt and black pepper

1 pound (450 g) mushrooms

6 cloves garlic

1 large onion

¾ cup (¼ pt; 150 ml) olive oil

A little flour

PORT SAUCE

1 cup (8 oz; 225 g) elderberry jelly

2 tablespoons (1 oz; 25 ml) light
brown sugar

¾ cup (6 fl oz; 200 ml) port

Rind of 1 lemon

A pinch of cinnamon

Place the venison pieces in a large bowl and cover with the mixed marinade ingredients. Leave for at least 2 days—4 days if possible, as venison can be tough—turning every few hours. Then 2½ hours before dinner, slice the mushrooms, garlic and onion, and brown them in the olive oil in a heavy casserole. Strain the marinade into a jug. Add the venison to the browning vegetables and sprinkle with flour, turning to cover evenly. Brown for 5 minutes. Add the marinade, cover and simmer gently for 2 hours or until tender. Ten minutes before serving, put all the sauce ingredients into a pan and boil rapidly until thick, syrupy and reduced. Add this sauce to the casserole at the last moment before serving.

Marinating time: 2 to 4 days. Cooking time: approximately 2½ hours.

BASIC ACCOMPANIMENTS FOR POULTRY AND GAME

GIBLET GRAVY FOR POULTRY

Heart, neck and gizzard of the
  chicken, washed
1 carrot, chopped
1 stalk celery
1 bay leaf

1 whole clove
½ teaspoon (2.5 ml) dried thyme
½ teaspoon (2.5 ml) sage
Salt and pepper
Flour

Put the giblets in a medium-sized saucepan with all the ingredients *except* the flour, and add water to cover. Cover and simmer over low heat for 30 minutes. Strain the giblets and chop the heart and gizzard fine. Reserve the broth and giblets separately. Then strain off the fat at the bottom of the roasting pan leaving only the brown juices. Measure the fat and add an equal quantity of flour, and stir to make a smooth roux. Cook over low heat for 1 minute, then add the giblet broth to the roux, whisking continually (use 2 tablespoons [30 ml] fat plus flour to 1 cup [8 fl oz; 225 ml] broth), and bring it to the boil. Add the chopped giblets, if desired.
Note: For meat roasts, substitute beef broth or wine for giblet broth.

DÉLICES AUX FROMAGES (for game soup)

MAKES 24 LARGE, 48 SMALL BALLS

1 cup (3 oz; 75 g) fresh white
  bread crumbs
1½ tablespoons (20 ml) grated
  Cheddar cheese

1½ tablespoons (20 ml) grated
  Gruyère cheese
3 egg whites, beaten stiff
A pinch of cayenne

Preheat the oven to 350° F (180° C; Mark 4).

In a bowl, mix ½ cup (1½ oz; 35 g) of the bread crumbs with the rest of the ingredients. Shape the mixture into small balls and roll them in the remaining bread crumbs. Put them on a greased jelly-roll pan and bake in the preheated oven for approximately 15 minutes or until they turn light brown. These can be eaten on their own or put into a game consommé.

Preparation time: 20 minutes. Cooking time: approximately 15 minutes.

FORCEMEAT BALLS

This is a recipe I found in a book published in 1841. The forcemeat balls make a game soup or consommé taste something special.

MAKES 2½ DOZEN, ENOUGH FOR 6 TO 8 PEOPLE

4 cups (¾ lb; 350 g) fresh bread crumbs
1 cup (½ lb; 225 g) suet
Peel of 1 lemon
1 teaspoon (5 ml) each lemon thyme, parsley, marjoram and savory, all chopped fine
A pinch of nutmeg
A pinch of mace
A pinch of cayenne
Salt and pepper
1 teaspoon (5 ml) tomato paste (purée)
2 eggs, well beaten
Vegetable oil for frying

In a bowl, mix all the ingredients except the oil, adding the eggs last. With a spoon, form the mixture into small balls. In a deep frying pan, heat the oil to 350° F (180° C), or until a small piece of white bread dropped into the oil browns in 50 seconds. Deep-fry the balls a few at a time until they turn light brown. Drain them on paper towels, and place them on a heated dish in a warm oven, with the door slightly ajar so they do not become soggy from the steam. Just before serving the soup, pop them in.

Preparation time: approximately 15 minutes. Cooking time: approximately 20 to 30 minutes.

GAME FUMET

3 tablespoons (45 ml) fine-chopped
   fat uncooked ham
1 medium-sized onion, chopped fine
2 shallots, chopped fine
A pinch of thyme
1 bay leaf
4 sprigs of parsley

Game carcass and trimmings
2 tablespoons (50 ml) butter
2 tablespoons (50 ml) Madeira
1 cup (8 fl oz; 225 ml) good brown
   sauce (see page 249) or chicken
   or veal stock may be substituted
   (see page 243)

In the bottom of a casserole put the ham, onion, shallots and herbs. On top of this put the game carcass and trimmings and the butter. Heat it slowly and gradually and cook, stirring often, until the mixture is golden. Then pour in the Madeira, and allow it to reduce to almost nothing, stirring continually to prevent scorching. Pour in the brown sauce or stock and allow it to simmer over low heat for 20 to 25 minutes. Strain through a fine sieve. Return the strained liquid to a saucepan and allow it to reduce again to nearly nothing, until it forms a kind of glaze.

A teaspoon of this extract will add game flavor to any sauce. It will keep in a tightly covered jar in the refrigerator almost indefinitely.

Preparation time: 10 minutes. Cooking time: approximately 1 hour.

GOOD GAME SEASONING

MAKES 3 CUPS

2 cups (6 oz; 175 g) fresh bread
   crumbs
1 cup (½ lb; 225 g) suet
1 tablespoon (15 ml) chopped
   parsley
1 tablespoon (15 ml) mixed herbs
   (thyme, sage, basil)

Salt and pepper to taste
1 blade of mace, chopped
Zest of 1 lemon, grated
1 egg, beaten

Mix all the ingredients together and bind with the egg. Either rub on or put inside cavity of game before roasting.

Preparation time: 10 minutes.

CRANBERRY SAUCE WITH HONEY

SERVES 6

> 2 cups (1 lb; 450 g) cranberries   *Honey to taste*
> ⅔ cup (5 fl oz; 150 ml) water

Place the cranberries in a saucepan with the water and cook until the berries burst and are soft. Then strain through a colander and add honey to taste. Serve with game or poultry.

Cooking time: 30 minutes.

MEAT

THE CHEMISTRY OF ANIMALS AND METHODS OF COOKING MEAT

Both meat and game contain skeletal muscle (so called because it is attached to the skeleton and can move about) which consists of bundles of muscle fibers, each of which is shaped like a long sac, the skin of which forms a delicate elastic sheaf. The contents of this sac are semiliquid and contain protein. The muscle fibers are held together with connective tissue in the meshes of which are numerous cells containing fat. If you shred meat and allow it to stand for a while, the fibers of the skeletal muscles and the fat globules break down, and the weight of meat resting upon itself presses out the protein-rich liquid.

The fibers of various types and cuts of animal meats vary in length and nature. Because of this there is a great variety in both the times and methods of cooking different meats such as pork and veal, not to mention different cuts such as rump and shoulder. On the whole, those parts of the animal in which the muscles are used the most, such as the neck, legs and tail, have the longest and most developed muscle fibers, and are naturally coarse. These long-fibered, coarser and cheaper cuts of meat usually require a prolonged and moist method of cooking, such as stewing or braising. These cooking methods turn the connective tissue into gelatin and soften the muscle fibers. Prolonged moist heat causes the gelatin to dissolve and the bundles of fiber to fall apart.

Roasting

The parts with less muscular development, such as fillet, top round (rump) and loin can be cooked by the "dry" method—roasting—which is cooking in a current of air by dry or radiant heat within an oven. This is in reality "baking"; spit-roasting or barbecuing is more like the old method of roasting, which is cooking in a current of air in front of or over an open, extremely hot fire.

By using the "dry" method, the albumen on the surface becomes coagulated as the exterior of the piece of meat is submitted to sudden extreme heat, about 425° F (220° C; Mark 7). This albumen, or coagulated protein, acts as a barrier against the infiltration of liquid from the outside. After a few minutes of brisk heat, the cooking temperature may be lowered to 350° F (180° C, Mark 4), and the meat roasted slowly. The meat is then enclosed in an almost impervious jacket and literally cooks in its own juices, heating up on the inside to a temperature of between 120 to 150 degrees Fahrenheit (48.9° C to 65.6° C), or more if you like your meat well done. This heat is not sufficient to coagulate and harden the interior albumen, but the connective tissue is turned into gelatin and the fat globules are melted. If the oven is too hot the meat will have a slightly shriveled appearance because the fibers will disintegrate and the water contained in them will evaporate. Otherwise the gelatinizing of the muscular fibers and the rendering soluble of the connective tissues which bind these fibers together make the meat more easily digestible and tender. It also creates an agreeable aroma which is increased by the brown sapid substance produced on the outside of the meat during the roasting process.

Roasting may be done on a rack or on a bed of vegetables. Roasting bags actually cause the meat to be steamed, using the moist heat method of cooking rather than the dry roasting method. The outer skin will not become as crisp and brown, even if you open the bag during the last moments of cooking, as it would if the meat were roasted uncovered in an oven. When roasting from frozen, however, it is often better to use a bag or roasting wrap as the meat must cook longer (see page 173).

When lifting the meat from the pan after it has been cooked, use two fish slicers or two perforated spoons. Do not pierce it with a long fork as this will allow the juices to escape.

Broiling (Grilling)

Preheat the broiler (grill) and the broiler (grill) pan to a brisk heat before adding the meat. Otherwise the cold bars will conduct the heat away and prevent rapid coagulation of surface albumen, thus allowing the juices to escape. To prevent the meat from sticking to the broiler (grill) rack, brush the bars lightly with a bland vegetable oil such as corn or safflower. The albumen of the entire surface of the piece of meat, no matter whether it is a steak, chop, cutlet or kidney, should be rapidly coagulated so as to seal in the juice. As the outside coating of coagulated albumen must not be pierced, use flat tongs to turn the meat, never a fork.

If you have a barbecue, make sure the fire extends somewhat beyond the grate, so that the sides of the meat may be acted on by the heat at the same time as the middle part.

Frying—Deep and Shallow

Deep-frying is the process of subjecting food to a high temperature in a bath of hot fat, which at the beginning should be 340° F to 400° F (170° C to 204° C), depending upon the food to be cooked. Precooked food which only needs to be crisped on the outside can take a higher temperature, whereas raw food needs a lower temperature, since the food must be cooked on the inside before it is burned on the outside. To test the temperature of the fat, throw in a piece of bread which should brown instantly. A faint wisp of blue smoke should rise from the oil when it reaches the proper temperature; if there is a great deal of smoke coming from the fat, it is much too hot—turn off the heat immediately and allow it to cool.

The best frying bath is composed of vegetable oil; I prefer peanut (arachide) oil, as it has a very high smoking point, 428° F (220° C). Peanut oil will cook food thoroughly to a crisp brownness in the shortest time. It can also be used a number of times (about 10 to 12) with only an occasional filtering to remove particles of food.

Shallow-frying: Butter can be used for light frying only, and it must be unsalted or clarified, otherwise it burns. One way to prevent butter from burning and raise it to a higher smoking point is to add 2 tablespoons (30 ml) of oil to every 6 tablespoons (90 ml) of butter. The fat must be heated sufficiently so that when the meat is added to the pan the juices will be sealed in.

Never cover foods which are either shallow- or deep-frying and always allow enough space around them, otherwise they will steam rather than fry, and will go limp. For the same reason, if you are not going to eat fried food immediately, as it should be eaten, put the food in the oven to keep hot, but *leave the door open.*

CHOOSING MEAT FOR THE FREEZER

All meats differ in color and texture, the proportion of fat to lean, the size of bones and other details. What they have in common is that their flavor, tenderness and texture vary according to their breed, the pastures on which they were fed—the quality of grass and the sort of soil it grows in— as well as the other foodstuffs upon which they have been fed. Other factors affecting the quality of meat are the season in which the animal was slaughtered, how the meat was hung, as well as how long, and the method by which the meat was stored. The hanging of meat is a most important factor where flavor and texture are concerned. After death there is a stiffening of the muscles known as "rigor mortis," and the meat of a fresh-killed animal is tough. During the hanging process acids are developed, and these acids help in the softening of the connective tissues. The fermentation present in all tissue digests the proteins of the cells and renders the muscles softer and juicier, making the meat more tender.

Natural feeding conditions have been proven to be more nutritious to animals than the intensive animal and poultry farming methods which deprive them of nutrients such as berries, leaves from bushes, seeds and fruit, which they would get in their natural diet. In America, the beef cattle are brought in from the range and then grain-fed for a few months. This gives the meat a coarser grain with more marbling, resulting in a better taste. Through good feeding an excess of fat is stored in the animal's connective tissues between the bundles of muscle fibers. This produces the "marbling" effect which adds to the food value of the meat, as well as making it more tender and flavorful. The USDA Fat Covering ranges from 2 to 5 and is based upon the thickness of the outer fat covering and the marbling as well as the suet (the fat around the kidney). Numbers 3 and 4 are considered Prime Meat, the best coarse-grained meat, which also has the most wastage as it has a very thick outer fat covering. Number 5, because it has the thickest fat covering, is considered by butchers too uneconomical to buy.

The purpose of buying meat for the freezer is that it is more economical to buy in bulk. However, you will lose this advantage if you do not buy intelligently. If you know that you will not use all the cuts of a forequarter or hindquarter, buy in bulk the specific cuts you do use, such as steaks, briskets and legs or shoulders. Another advantage is that you can buy spring lamb in the spring, young calves and pork in the summer when these are cheapest, and use the meat during the rest of the year.

When choosing meat for the freezer, check with your butcher on his facilities. Can he:

a. Cut up the meat;
b. Package it ready for the freezer;
c. Quick-freeze the meat for you;
d. Deliver it.

Give your butcher adequate advance notice so that he can select, age, cut and pack, not to mention quick-freeze the meat. If he does not package meat, then make sure you have the right materials, at home, so that you can proceed as soon as the meat is delivered. Give clear instructions to your butcher in writing as to:

a. Individual weight of braising and stewing packages, weight of roasting cuts, and whether they are to be boned or not.
b. Whether the meat is to be sliced or cubed.
c. Individual weight of ground-meat packages, giving specific instructions such as extra lean, coarse- or fine-ground.
d. Whether some of the ground meat is to be made directly into hamburgers or sausages.
e. Whether you want the bones, and into what lengths they should be cut.
f. If you wish the trimmed fat for rendering, and in what weight packages.

Important:
Secure the date and approximate time of delivery.

1. Clear enough space in the freezer.
2. Turn on the fast-freeze switch one or two hours before delivery.

Do not overload the freezer. Check the instructions on your own freezer for the recommended weight of food to be frozen in a single twenty-four-hour period. One-tenth of the freezer's total capacity is the normal advice.

If a whole forequarter or a whole hindquarter is ordered, it could take several days to freeze it. Either keep the rest of the meat in the refrigerator during this time or, better still, ask your butcher if he can deliver it over the course of a week in the amounts your freezer will take.

Use the fast-freeze compartment in the chest-type freezer or the fast-freezer shelf of upright models.

Trim all excess fat from the meat. It wastes freezer space and shortens the storage life, since it is the fat that turns rancid during a long storage period in the freezer, rather like butter.

Meat must be wrapped or it will "dehydrate" and develop freezer burn. Pack it in moisture- and vapor-proof material, excluding as much air as possible, and seal. Label clearly with details of cut weight and date. One always thinks things will be recognizable, but when frozen, small cuts in particular are very hard to distinguish.

When packaging large, awkward cuts, the bones should be overwrapped with foil to prevent their piercing the wrapping.

Small and evenly shaped cuts can be packed in thick, plastic bags (120 to 150 gauge), or rigid plastic containers.

Use Saran Wrap or plastic sheets to separate small chops, cutlets, steaks or sausages, so that they can be easily separated for cooking while still frozen. Then wrap them in plastic bags.

Pack the meat as closely as possible to the walls of the freezer to insure the rapid freezing that is essential to maintain the fine texture of the meat. Meat that is slow-frozen will lose juices in the freezing process, resulting in the coarsening of the meat and a subsequent loss of flavor. Rapid freezing is rather like searing meat. It quickly seals the outside of the meat, keeping all the juices in, and it also quickly freezes out any possibility of bacteria growing in the meat.

TO THAW AND COOK FROZEN MEAT

All bone-in beef, lamb and pork cuts, as well as unrolled boneless cuts can be successfully roasted from the frozen state, but rolled cuts must be thawed before cooking. This is because both surfaces of the meat *must be thoroughly cooked* to insure that all bacteria have been destroyed. Small cuts of pork on the bone, boiling cuts, meat fillings for pies must be thawed as well. Boiling cuts, if cooked from a frozen state, will suffer weight loss and have a poor flavor. Cubed and minced meat can be cooked from frozen but you must allow extra time in the cooking for the meat to thaw. Meat to be broiled (grilled) and fried can also be cooked from frozen.

Cooking from Frozen

Meat roasted from the frozen state must be slow-cooked at 350° F (180° C; Mark 4). Because the bone is an extremely good heat conductor, bone-in cuts will cook more quickly than those which have been boned, this being particularly true of frozen meat.

Boneless cuts will need about 30 minutes more to cook than bone-in cuts. Place a loose covering of foil over the meat for part of the cooking time to protect the outside from cooking too quickly and burning. Halfway through the estimated cooking time, remove the foil.

When pot-roasting frozen brisket, seal all the outside and cut surfaces to prevent excessive loss of juices: Place in a preheated casserole or Dutch oven on top of the stove for 20 minutes, then when the surfaces are sealed, cover and cook at the temperature given above.

Roasting Bags and Wraps

When roasting frozen cuts of meat, it is better to wrap them in cooking foil or roasting wrap or bags to prevent their drying out during the longer cooking time. By this method, basting is also eliminated and the oven does not get so dirty. Thirty minutes from the end of the calculated cooking time, slit open the covering, insert a meat thermometer, and allow the meat to become brown and crisp.

Roasting bags or wraps should not be used in temperatures over 400° F (200° C; Mark 6). Cooking foil is better at higher temperatures. Read the manufacturer's instructions on the bag before using, as they all vary slightly. In most cases, roasting bags and wraps should be floured and pierced before using.

Meat Thermometers

To insure success when cooking any meat from the frozen state, it is essential to use a meat thermometer. This should be inserted in the center of the meat 30 minutes before the end of the required cooking time. Make sure that the thermometer does *not* touch the bone, as bones conduct heat and will give an inaccurate reading.

A meat thermometer should have a good sharp spike to penetrate the flesh and an easy-to-read dial or indicator plate. Some models have a mercury tube with a metal-covered end, and there may be a skewer to help with the initial penetration of the meat. Others have a dial with an indicator needle. Most types of meat and their cooking temperatures are included on the indicator.

Important:

1. Do not use meat thermometers in covered roasting pans.
2. If a mercury thermometer breaks, it is vital to scoop up and throw away the mercury. But if the thermometer breaks inside the meat, the meat must also be thrown away.

Thawing

Even though it takes longer, slow thawing in a refrigerator is preferable to thawing at room temperature because there is less risk of contamination.

Thawing Time:

	In the refrigerator	Room temperature
Cuts over 3 pounds	4–7 hours per 1 pound (450 g)	2–3 hours per 1 pound (450 g)
Cuts under 3 pounds	3–4 hours per 1 pound (450 g)	1–2 hours per 1 pound (450 g)
1 inch (2.5 cm) thick steaks, chops, undiced stewing steak	5–6 hours	2–4 hours

You can cook thawed meat and then refreeze it, but it must be cooled before freezing. If you are freezing cooked casseroles, be sure that there is plenty of gravy (fat-free) covering the meat, otherwise the meat will dry out.

Pies

These can be cooked before freezing. Do not put a great deal of seasoning in the filling; this should be added while reheating. If uncooked steak and kidney pies are cooked from a frozen state, they will require up to 5 hours steaming time. Other unbaked meat pies baked from the freezer require from 15 to 30 minutes extra cooking time.

Leftover Meat

Small quantities of leftover meat from a roast should be sliced before freezing so that they can be reheated quickly without thawing. Put the slices in a foil tray and pour in sufficient gravy or stock to cover the meat. Cover the tray with its own top or with foil, *not* plastic wrap, carefully sealing the edges. Label with the date, type of meat and how many it will serve; freeze and use within 1 month. Reheat quickly in a hot oven—375° F (190° C; Mark 5)—*before* removing the cover.

BEEF

Buying Beef for the Freezer

Fresh beef should have a fresh, slightly moist appearance, and when cut it should be bright red with a brownish tinge. Actually, all meat is purple-brown when first cut; it is the oxygen in the air that turns it red. If the meat is a dark wine color, it means either that it has been exposed to the air too long, or that it comes from an older animal. Lean beef for roasting should be smooth and velvety in texture, and marbled with small flecks of fat so that it stays moist, well-flavored and tender when cooked. It should be surrounded by a layer of creamy white fat that is firm and dry, almost springy to the touch. If the fat is pale yellow rather than creamy white, it could be due to one of two things:

1. The meat is from a cow rather than a steer, therefore not prime meat.
2. The color could derive from something in the animal's feed which may or may not affect the taste of the meat.

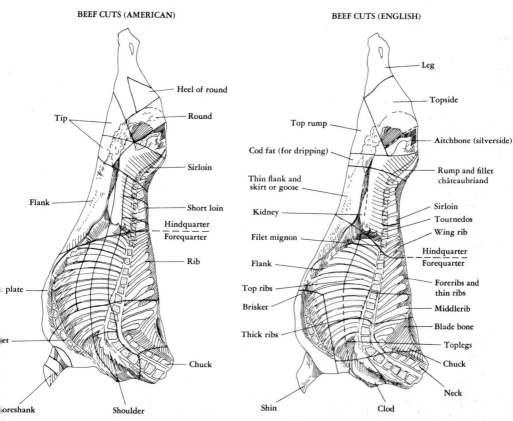

BEEF CUTS (AMERICAN)

Heel of round
Tip
Round
Sirloin
Flank
Short loin
Hindquarter
Forequarter
Rib
plate
Chuck
et
oreshank
Shoulder

BEEF CUTS (ENGLISH)

Leg
Topside
Top rump
Cod fat (for dripping)
Aitchbone (silverside)
Rump and fillet châteaubriand
Thin flank and skirt or goose
Kidney
Sirloin
Tournedos
Wing rib
Filet mignon
Hindquarter
Forequarter
Flank
Foreribs and thin ribs
Top ribs
Middlerib
Brisket
Blade bone
Thick ribs
Toplegs
Chuck
Neck
Shin
Clod

In *prime cuts,* i.e., fillet and sirloin, if there is a large amount of gristle visible just under the outside layer of fat, then the meat probably comes from an older animal and will be tough. In coarser cuts, you will see fibers quite clearly in the meat. These cuts are more suitable for braising and stewing.

Carcass weights and yields: The quality of the meat prepared from a carcass is affected mainly by carcass weight and fatness. Excessive fat is trimmed by the butcher when boning and preparing cuts for retail sale.

A beef carcass consists of two sides. The average weight of a side, including kidney and suet, is 572 pounds (300 pounds in England). The average side can be cut into a forequarter weighing approximately 263 pounds (approximately 145 pounds in England), and a hindquarter weighing approximately 209 pounds (155 pounds in England).

Rough guide for freezer space required:

		Approximate freezer space required
Beef (American)		
Forequarter	263 pounds	12 cu ft
Hindquarter	209 pounds	10½ cu ft
Beef (English)		
Forequarter	145 pounds	4½ cu ft
Hindquarter	155 pounds	5 cu ft

Allow 1½ cu ft for each 30 pounds beef on the bone.
Allow 1 cu ft for each 30 pounds beef boned and trimmed.

The average side of beef will yield:

FOREQUARTER (AMERICAN): Chuck, ribs, foreshank, brisket, short plate.

HINDQUARTER (AMERICAN): Short loin, sirloin, round, flank, tip.

FOREQUARTER (ENGLISH): Neck and clod, chuck and blade, ribs, brisket, shin.

HINDQUARTER (ENGLISH): Sirloin, fillet, top rump, topside, silverside, thin flank, leg.

Other parts of beef and what to do with them:

OXTAIL: Stew

OX TONGUE: Boil fresh

OX LIVER: Stew or braise

OX KIDNEY: Stew, use in pies. Use the surrounding fat for suet (see below). Wrap the kidney and freeze in small amounts; it will keep for 2 months.

SUET: Hard, white fat surrounding the kidneys. Remove paperlike tissue and chop or grate the suet, keeping it well-dredged with flour. Use immediately if using fresh, or freeze and keep up to 2 months.

TRIMMED FAT: Make and freeze dripping from the excess fat. Put 1 cup full of fat in a roasting pan and leave uncovered in a slow oven for 2 to 3 hours, or until all the fat has run out and only crisp scraps remain. Pour the fat through a cheesecloth- (muslin) lined strainer into clean containers. This can be done over a period of time whenever a slow oven is in use.

Freeze the dripping by lining a container with foil, leaving a good overlap so that when it has been frozen solid, it can be removed from the container and wrapped. It should not be kept more than 2 months. The dripping must be clarified before using, otherwise the water and sediment causes splattering. Melt the dripping, then pour into a large bowl half full of warm water. Stir thoroughly to "wash" the fat, then leave it in a cold place until the fat rises to the surface and solidifies into a solid cake. Remove the cake of fat, scrape away the sediment beneath, and wipe it dry with paper towels. Reheat gently to drive off any moisture. It is delicious in meat pies or vegetables; use also in standard shortcrust pastry. Unclarified dripping is delicious on toast, or rubbed into plain or fruit cake to add a spicy flavor.

BONES: You don't have to take the bones with a bulk buy, but you are entitled to them if you want them. They are very good for making stock, but they must be used immediately as they spoil quite quickly, or frozen in small packages to be used as they are needed. Have them cut into small pieces to fit your stock pot.

TO MAKE STOCK: Put the bones, frozen or fresh, into a deep pan and cover with cold water. Bring to the boil slowly, skimming as necessary. For each 2½ cups (1 pt; 600 ml) liquid, add 1 onion and 1 carrot, both peeled and quartered; a bouquet garni; a clove of crushed garlic and a few peppercorns. Cover the pan and simmer very gently on top of the stove, or in a low oven—325° F (160° C; Mark 3)—for at least 2 hours; or pressure cook for 30 minutes. When cold, strain and remove the fat; refrigerate and use immediately or freeze for up to 3 months.

Recommended storage life for beef in the freezer: −18° C (0° F) Storage life is determined by the length of time food can be stored without any change in the quality, taste, color or texture. After the recommended storage time the state of the meat changes very slowly. Buy only as much meat as will be used up within the recommended storage time. If kept somewhat longer, it will do no harm, but the taste and quality will slowly deteriorate. No bacteria can grow in the frozen state, but after the meat has thawed, bacteria will begin to form, so the thawed meat should be treated as though it were fresh and used as quickly as possible.

Large cuts (joints) of beef—approximately 12 months
Steaks and cut-up meat—8 months
Raw ground meat—3 months
Cooked beef pies—3 months
Casseroles containing bacon—3 months
Casseroles without bacon—6 months

To Cook Beef, Fresh or Frozen

Roasting fresh beef:

SIRLOIN, FILLET, RIB (FORERIBS): For the very best flavor, cook it rare by the high temperature method (see below), basting every 20 minutes. It will be brown on the outside and pink in the center. The meat thermometer should register:

125° F   (51° C)—rare
140° F   (60° C)—medium rare
155° F   (67° C)—medium
165° F   (80° C)—well-done

HIGH TEMPERATURE METHOD

On the bone: 20 minutes per pound (450 g) plus 20 minutes, in a preheated oven at 425° F (220° C; Mark 7) for 30 minutes, then decrease heat to 375° F (190° C; Mark 5).

Boned and rolled: 25 minutes per pound (450 g) plus 20 minutes.

MODERATE TEMPERATURE METHOD

On the bone: 35 minutes per pound (450 g) in a preheated oven at 350° F (180° C; Mark 4) for the full cooking time.

Boned and rolled: 40 minutes per pound (450 g) plus 20 minutes.

Roasting frozen beef: When roasting from a frozen state, always use a meat thermometer to check whether the meat has been cooked through.

UNDER 4 POUNDS		Meat thermometer reading
rare to medium	30 minutes per pound (450 g) plus 30 minutes	160° F (71° C)
well-done	35 minutes per pound (450 g) plus 35 minutes	170° F (79° C)
4–6 POUNDS		
rare to medium	35 minutes per pound (450 g) plus 35 minutes	140° F (60° C)
well-done	40 minutes per pound (450 g) plus 40 minutes	150° F (66° C)

Broiling (grilling) or pan-frying fresh beef: Use the top round (rump), sir-loin or fillet, which may be cut into tournedos, filet mignon, châteaubriand, contre filet, porterhouse, T-bone, noisettes or entrecôte.

To broil (grill), trim the surplus fat and brush the meat with butter. Season with pepper and only add the salt just before serving, as it toughens meat cooked in this way. Allow 15 minutes each side for a 1-inch (2.5 cm.) thick steak at medium-well; 8 to 10 minutes medium; and 6 minutes rare.

To pan-fry, trim the fat, then cook in hot vegetable oil or butter. Begin with high heat, then reduce to moderate heat to finish cooking. Season and serve in the pan juices.

Frozen steaks: These are best when broiled (grilled) with a large covering of foil put on toward the end of cooking time to protect the surface of the steak while allowing it to cook through. It can take anywhere from 15 to 20 minutes depending on how you like your steak.

Braising, pot-roasting and stewing, either fresh or frozen: Use round (top-side and silverside), brisket, chuck (neck and clod), shin, tip of sirloin (leg) or flank.

The meat must cook slowly to make it more tender. An electric slow cooker is excellent for this method. Otherwise the meat may be cooked in the oven 325° F (170° C; Mark 3), allowing 2½ hours for cuts up to 3 pounds (1.5 kg) plus an additional 30 minutes per pound (450 g) over this weight. *The meat must not boil* or it will get tough. It may also be cooked on top of the stove over low heat in a heavy, tightly sealed pot. Sear meat in some fat until brown, then season and add vegetables, herbs and spices, beer, wine or cider.

Pressure-cooking times at high temperature per pound (450 g) weight:

Braised	15–20 minutes
Pot-roasted	12–18 minutes
Stewed	15–20 minutes

Microwave oven times for fresh or thawed beef:

	Rare	*Medium*	*Well-done*
On the bone	5½–6½ minutes	6½–7½ minutes	7½–9 minutes
Boned	6–7 minutes	7–8½ minutes	8½–10 minutes

To Carve

Beef sirloin on the bone:
1. With the sharp point of a long knife, free the meat by cutting along the bone.
2. Carve each slice across the grain and remove from the bone.

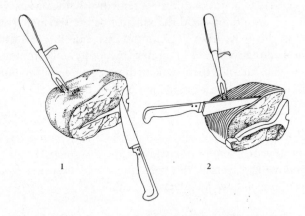

Standing rib roast or wing rib:
1. Remove the chine bone by cutting along the entire length of the back-bone to free the meat; then loosen the meat from the ribs.
2. Slice downwards, toward the ribs; loosen the meat. When you are getting near the end, you will find it easier to lay the meat down flat and carve the rest of the slices horizontally.

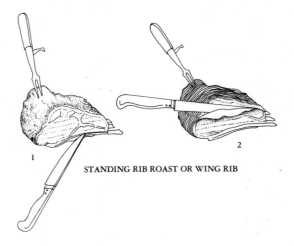

STANDING RIB ROAST OR WING RIB

General Hints

1. *To make meat tender*
   a. If stewing meat is too tough, add a few drops of lemon to the meat; this will break down the tissues, tenderizing and sweetening it as well. This is the same effect it has when put into the cavity of any poultry or game. Another method is to use 1 pint (1¼ pt; 750 ml) of hot tea as the cooking liquid.
   b. To tenderize steak, pierce all around the sides with a skewer to break down the fibers.
2. Brush soy sauce on meat before broiling (grilling) for a rich brown color.
3. For ground-meat dishes: After grinding the meat, pass the herbs and parsley—and bread crumbs, if you are using them—through the same grinder. Use brown bread crumbs for meat dishes.
4. Chop suet the day you buy it, sprinkle it with flour and it will keep very well in the refrigerator for up to one week.

BEEF

Forequarter American	English	Types of meat and ways of butchering	Uses and how to cook
Foreshank (Shin)	Shin	Lean, muscular, with a considerable amount of intermuscular connective tissues. *American:* Shank cross cuts Stewing beef *English:* Small cubes Ground shin	Ideal for meat soups, beef pies, stews, braising. If a bone is included, it makes a rich jellied stock. Cook very slowly for 4 or more hours with water or stock to extract flavor. Ideal for an electric slow cooker.
Chuck	Neck and clod	Lean coarse-grained meat. Cubes Ground	*American:* Beef for stew, chuck short ribs, pot roast or steak. *English:* Hot pots, minces
Shoulder	Back ribs, chuck and blade, top and thick ribs	Medium quality lean meat. Small roasts Thick slices Cubes for casseroles	Excellent for braising; cooks faster than other forequarter meat, but still needs a minimum of 2 hours' slow cooking. Blade roast or steak, crossrib pot roast, pies and casseroles.
Brisket and short plate	Brisket	Coarse-grained belly meat layered with fat in parts. Usually boned, defatted, rolled and cut into joints. Roasts	Slow roast, braise, pot roast or boil. Good for salting, then simmering in water with vegetables, but *do not freeze salted meat.*

Forequarter

American	English	Types of meat and ways of butchering	Uses and how to cook
		Roasts Stewing beef Cubes Ground beef	Fresh brisket, corned beef, skirt steak rolls, short ribs.
Rib	Fore ribs and thin ribs	Prime cut, suitable for roasting, broiling (grilling) or frying. Roasts, on or off the bone Rib steaks	Roast on the bone, or rolled with bone removed. Rib eye (Delmonico), roast or steak.

BEEF

Hindquarter American	English	Types of meat and ways of butchering	Uses and how to cook
Short loin (upper part of sirloin)	Sirloin (including wing rib) Fillet	Prime quality beef should have hardly any discernible gristle. Lean meat should be rich red with slightly brownish tinge. Very tender strip of meat from beneath the sirloin. Roasts—boned and rolled or on the bone, with or without fillet. Individual sirloin steaks—T-bone if on the bone.	Top loin steak, T-bone steak, porterhouse steak, filet mignon, or roast, entrecôte steaks, chateaubriand. Roasting, broiling (grilling), frying. Steak. Roasting, broiling (grilling), frying.
Sirloin Top Butt (if boneless) Short Hip of Beef (with bone)	Rump or Pope's Eye	Prime quality meat from the top of the thigh, excellent flavor. Slices for steaks Roasting cuts	Good for roasting, broiling (grilling), or frying. _American:_ Flat-bone sirloin steak, wedge-bone sirloin steak, boneless sirloin steak. _English:_ End pieces of rump/sirloin are perfect for beef stroganoff or similar dishes.
Round Top Bottom Eye	Topside and Silverside (buttock and round steak)	Very lean, coarse-textured meat. Roasts of required weights Cubed steak Ground beef	Slow roast, pot roast, or boil with vegetables. Braise fresh or salted. Needs very slow and gentle cooking. Perfect for slow cookers. Stews, round steak, top round steak, bottom round roast or steak. Eye of round, heel of round, rolled rump.

Hindquarter		Types of meat and ways of butchering	Uses and how to cook
American	English		
Flank	Thin flank	Coarse-grained belly meat.	Needs slow, moist cooking.
	Goose-skirt	Thin piece of medium-grained meat from behind the flank.	
			American:
		Ground meat	London broil, flank steak, flank steak roll.
		Hamburgers	Good flavor for pies, casseroles.
		Diced for stewing	
			English:
			Stews, casseroles, or ground-beef dishes.
Tip of Sirloin	Top Rump	Inside area of thigh—medium quality lean meat of good flavor.	Tip (top rump) good for slow roasting or braising. Leg should be stewed very slowly.
		Boneless roasts	*American:*
			Tip steak, tip roast, tip kebabs, pot roast.
	Leg	Very good flavor lean, coarse-grained meat.	
			English:
		Small cubes for stewing	Casseroles, pot roast.
		Slices, 1 inch thick	

OXTAIL RAGOÛT

This is the perfect dish to cook in a slow cooker—but the vegetables must be placed *under* the meat, and you will need only half the amount of liquid specified here.

SERVES 6

4 pounds (1.8 kg) oxtail, cut into 2-inch (5 cm) pieces
3 tablespoons (45 ml) peanut oil
3 large carrots, sliced
2 medium onions, sliced
1 parsnip, sliced
1 turnip, sliced
2 sticks celery, sliced
1 bouquet garni, made from 1 bay leaf, 6 black peppercorns, 3 cloves, 1 piece fresh ginger, 1 teaspoon (5 ml) marjoram

Salt to taste
4 cups (1½ pts; 950 ml) beef stock or broth
1½ cups (12 fl oz; 350 ml) dry white wine
1 to 2 tablespoons (15 to 30 ml) Bovril (meat extract)
2 tablespoons (30 ml) fine-chopped parsley

Blanch the pieces of oxtail in boiling water for 2 minutes, drain and refresh them under cold water. Pat dry with kitchen towels. In a deep casserole, heat the peanut oil, then add the oxtail pieces and cook until they become coated with fat. Add the vegetables, bouquet garni, salt and beef stock or broth. Bring to the boil, then reduce to a simmer and add the wine. Simmer the ragoût, covered, for 3 to 4 hours or until the meat is tender.

Preheat oven to 400° F (200° C; Mark 6).

With a slotted spoon, transfer the oxtail pieces to a baking pan large enough to hold them in one layer and roast them in the preheated oven for 10 minutes, or until they have just browned. Reduce the liquid in the casserole to 2 cups (16 fl oz; 475 ml) and strain it through a fine sieve into a bowl.

Allow it to cool.

If you are making the ragoût the night before you are serving it, chill the liquid in the refrigerator overnight. The fat will have solidified on the top and will be easy to remove. The oxtails can be wrapped up in aluminum paper and also kept in the refrigerator overnight.

Return the chilled liquid, fat removed, to the casserole and reheat it over a moderate flame. Add the oxtails and cook until they are heated through. Transfer the oxtails to a heated dish, add 1 to 2 tablespoons (15 to 30 ml) Bovril to the sauce and mix thoroughly. Pour half the sauce over the oxtails and top with parsley. Pour the rest of the sauce into a heated sauceboat. Serve with kasha (buckwheat groats).

Preparation time: approximately 25 minutes. Cooking time: approximately 4½ hours.

POT ROAST

The secret of this pot roast is that *at no time* do you add water. The fat and juices from the meat and the juices from the vegetables will supply the requisite amount of liquid.

SERVES 8

One 4 pound (1.8 kg) brisket
Pepper and salt
2 large or 4 small onions, chopped fine

3 cloves garlic, chopped fine
4 fresh tomatoes, chopped
2 teaspoons (10 ml) ground ginger
1 bay leaf

Preheat oven to 325° F (170° C; Mark 3).

Wipe the meat thoroughly and place it in a very hot iron casserole. Turn frequently over the heat so that the meat becomes dark brown on all sides. Then place it, covered, in the preheated oven for 2 hours, or until the meat begins to become tender. Season with plenty of salt, which will cook into the meat, and some pepper to taste. Put it back into the oven for another half hour, then add the onions, garlic, tomatoes, ginger and bay leaf. Cook for another 4 hours, until the meat is really tender and the vegetables have been reduced to a dark brown pulp. When the meat is thoroughly tender remove it from the pot. Then take off as much fat as possible from the gravy, which will include the vegetables and put the gravy through a food processor or a Mouli Légumes to purée the vegetables. *Do not add any water to the gravy.* Serve with Potato Pancakes (see page 188).

Preparation time: 15 minutes. Cooking time: 6½ hours.

POTATO PANCAKES

SERVES 8

> 2 pounds (1 kg) potatoes, peeled   3 eggs, beaten
>   and grated   3 teaspoons (15 ml) salt
> 1 large onion, peeled and grated   Black pepper
> 4 tablespoons (60 ml) flour   Corn oil for frying

In a mixing bowl, put the potatoes and then stir in the onion, flour, eggs, salt
and pepper to taste. Mix thoroughly, cover, and allow the mixture to stand
for half an hour. Heat the oil to a depth of approximately 1 inch (2½ cm) in
a large but not too deep frying pan. With a large tablespoon, drop a mound
of the potato mixture into the oil and flatten it with the back of a spoon. Fry
for about 4 to 5 minutes, or until the pancake is golden brown and crisp,
turning it over once. Remove and drain on kitchen towels. A few of these
pancakes may be made at one time, in single layers in the oil. Serve with
pot roast or venison.

*Preparation time: approximately 45 minutes. Cooking time: approximately
5 to 10 minutes.*

SEMUR DAGING

An Indonesian friend taught me this unusual dish which she found in Sri
Owen's delightful book, *The Home Book of Indonesian Cooking*. It is ideal
for using up leftover roast beef or pork. If, however, you are starting from
scratch using uncooked meat, buy fillet steak or top round (topside). When
using the latter, cook it a few minutes longer and put the potatoes in a few
minutes after the meat.

You can also cook this dish with pork. Choose a good fillet or use cold
roast pork—but *not* pork with stuffing, because the stuffing will ruin the
taste of the sauce.

SERVES 4

2 tablespoons (30 ml) clarified
    butter
2 shallots, peeled and sliced
1 clove garlic, peeled and crushed
1 pound (450 g) cooked roast beef,
    sliced thin
1 large potato, peeled and sliced
    very thin

1 large tomato, peeled and chopped
2 tablespoons (30 ml) soy sauce
Fresh-ground black pepper
A pinch of grated nutmeg
2 hard-boiled eggs, cut in half
4 scallions (spring onions) chopped
    fine
Fried onions, for garnish

In a frying pan, melt the butter and sauté the shallots and garlic until they
turn golden. Then add the meat and potato slices and sauté for 1 minute.
Mix in the tomato, soy sauce, pepper and nutmeg; cover and cook gently for
a further 5 minutes. Taste. Add the hard-boiled egg halves and cook for another 5 minutes. The scallions (spring onions) should be added just before
serving. Garnish with the slices of fried onion.

*Preparation time: approximately 20 minutes. Cooking time: approximately
15 minutes.*

STEAK WITH GREEN PEPPERS

SERVES 6

2½ pounds (1.1 kg) sirloin steak,
    cut into 2- x 1-inch strips
4 cloves of garlic, minced
2 onions, chopped fine
2 green peppers, sliced thin
½ cup (3 oz; 75 g) chopped
    almonds
Grated rind of 1 lime
1 tablespoon (15 ml) lime juice
½ teaspoon (2.5 ml) each *chili
    powder, ground ginger, turmeric,
    nutmeg*

1 tablespoon (15 ml) soft brown
    sugar
2 tablespoons (30 ml) soy sauce
1 teaspoon (5 ml) salt
¼ pound (4 oz; 125 g) butter or
    margarine
1 cup (8 fl oz; 225 ml) beef
    consommé

Place all the ingredients *except* the butter or margarine and the consommé
in an earthenware or glass dish and marinate the meat for 1 to 2 hours, the
longer the better. Then melt the butter or margarine in a frying pan, add the

meat, marinade and consommé and simmer for 15 to 20 minutes, stirring from time to time, until cooked.

Serve with new potatoes and spring (French) beans or lima (broad) beans, or with rice or kasha instead of potatoes.

Preparation time: 30 minutes. Marinating time: 1 to 2 hours. Cooking time: 15 to 20 minutes.

FILET DE BOEUF POIVRADE

When I was eighteen, and learning to cook for entertaining, I was taught the following recipe. Even then, *filet de boeuf* was a treat, although it was not nearly so expensive as it is today. Make this dish when you really want to pull out all the stops, and, to compensate for the expensiveness of the meat, I would suggest serving a delicious homemade soup to begin the meal and a light fruit dessert to finish.

SERVES 6

2½ pounds (1.1 kg) fillet of beef
Pork fat
Salt

MARINADE

1 cup (8 fl oz; 225 ml) red Burgundy
½ cup (4 fl oz; 125 ml) tarragon vinegar
¼ cup (2 fl oz; 50 ml) Calvados

1 teaspoon (5 ml) dried tarragon
½ teaspoon (2.5 ml) each thyme, ground bay leaves, freshly grated nutmeg, ground cloves
1 medium-sized onion, sliced thin

SAUCE POIVRADE

1½ cups (7 oz; 200 g) carrots, chopped fine
½ cup (2 oz; 50 g) onions, chopped fine
Bouquet garni consisting of 1 bay leaf, 4 sprigs parsley, 1 sprig fresh thyme or ½ teaspoon dried thyme
¼ cup (2 fl oz; 50 ml) olive oil

¼ cup (2 fl oz; 50 ml) tarragon vinegar
Reserved marinade
1½ cups (12 fl oz; 350 ml) brown sauce or stock (see pages 247–249)
6 black peppercorns, crushed
Salt
1½ tablespoons (23 ml) butter

Trim and remove the connective tissue and skin from the whole fillet of beef. Lard it with narrow strips of pork fat. Put the larded roast in an earthenware dish and sprinkle it with *very little salt*. Combine the marinade ingredients in a mixing bowl and pour the marinade over the meat. Then cover the dish with a cloth and marinate the meat in the refrigerator for three days, turning it two or three times a day.

Preheat the oven to 350° F (180° C; Mark 4).

Drain and dry the fillet, reserving the marinade for use in making the sauce. Place the meat on a roasting rack in a pan and roast it for 50 minutes, or 20 minutes per pound for medium rare, 25 minutes per pound for well-done, basting frequently.

MAKE THE SAUCE

In a medium-sized saucepan, cook the carrots, onions and bouquet garni— the latter tied in a piece of cheesecloth (muslin)—in the olive oil, stirring frequently, until the onions turn golden. Drain off any remaining oil, and moisten the mixture with the vinegar and strained marinade from the fillet. Reduce the mixture over a high flame to two thirds its original volume, stirring constantly. Add the brown sauce or stock and simmer gently for 30 minutes. Add the peppercorns and simmer for 10 minutes more. Strain the sauce through a very fine sieve, return it to the heat, bring to the boil and add salt to taste. Just before serving swirl in the butter.

Arrange the roasted fillet on a heated platter. Slice and reshape it, pour part of the Sauce Poivrade over the roast and serve the rest in a sauceboat.

Preparation time: 45 minutes. Marinating time: 3 days. Cooking time: 50 to 70 minutes.

I found the following recipe about twenty years ago. I do not know whose it is, but I have cooked it successfully for years, and am indebted to whose ever idea it was. It is quite time consuming to make, but it is so delicious that it is well worth the effort, and it makes calves liver into a very special dish. Again, as it is quite expensive, try to save money as well as time on the first and last course. If there is any liver left over, you can serve it cold as a pâté.

BAKED WHOLE LIVER

SERVES 6 TO 8

¼ pound (125 g) salt pork, cut into long strips

1 tablespoon (15 ml) brandy

3 tablespoons (45 ml) parsley, chopped fine

Freshly ground black pepper

1 teaspoon (5 ml) ground cinnamon

1 teaspoon (5 ml) ground cloves

3 tablespoons (45 ml) olive oil

Juice of ½ lemon

Salt and pepper

3 pounds (1.4 kg) whole calves liver

2 tablespoons (30 ml) butter

1 onion, chopped fine

1 carrot, chopped fine

Bouquet garni made from 1 bay leaf, 2 sprigs thyme, 3 sprigs parsley

GARNITURE À LA BOURGEOISE

1 pound (450 g) small white onions, glazed in sugar syrup

2 pounds (900 g) carrots, cut in ovals and glazed in sugar syrup

½ cup (4 fl oz; 125 ml) dry white wine

1 egg yolk, beaten

Moisten the salt pork strips with the brandy, then roll the strips in a mixture of the parsley, pepper to taste and ½ teaspoon (2.5 ml) *each* of the cinnamon and cloves. With a larding needle run the seasoned salt pork through the whole calves liver. In a bowl just big enough to hold the liver, combine the olive oil, lemon juice, salt and pepper to taste, and the remaining cinnamon and cloves. Add the liver and marinate, covered, for 4 hours.

Preheat the oven to 350° F (180° C; Mark 4). In a heavy casserole, melt the butter, then add the liver, the marinade, the chopped onion and carrot, and the bouquet garni. Bake the liver in the preheated oven for 45 minutes, basting it often. Then add the Garniture Bourgeoise and bake it for another 15 minutes. Remove the liver to a hot platter and surround it with the garniture. Add the dry white wine to the juice in the casserole, simmer the sauce for 5 minutes and strain it into a small saucepan. Mix a spoonful of the sauce with the beaten egg yolk, then slowly stir the egg mixture into the sauce; reheat it, stirring constantly, until it just begins to thicken, and pour it over the liver.

Preparation time: 30 to 45 minutes. Marinating time: 4 hours. Cooking time: 1 hour 10 minutes.

SPINACH AND MEAT SOUFFLÉ

Adapted from *Kitchen Essays* by Lady Jekyll, it is very good for using up leftovers.

SERVES 4 TO 6

¼ cup (2 oz; 50 g) butter
½ cup (2 oz; 50 g) flour
2 cups (¾ pint; 475 ml) milk
Salt and pepper
A pinch ground nutmeg
1 pound (450 g) cooked beef, ground (minced)
4 ounces (225 g) cooked ham, ground (minced)

1½ pounds (700 g) spinach, cooked and drained
6 eggs, separated
¾ cup (4 oz; 225 g) Parmesan and Gruyère cheese, mixed
Butter
2 tablespoons (30 ml) bread crumbs

Preheat the oven to 425° F (220° C; Mark 7).

In a heavy saucepan, melt the butter, add the flour, stir, and cook the roux over low heat for a few minutes. Add the milk, stirring constantly, for about 5 minutes. Season with salt and pepper to taste, and the nutmeg, remembering that the flavor will be diluted by the egg whites in the soufflé. Stir in the beef, ham and spinach.

In a bowl, beat the egg yolks and add them a little at a time to the mixture; then add the cheese. Beat well. Whisk the egg whites until they are stiff but not dry, and fold a third of them into the mixture with a metal spoon; then fold in the rest. Butter an 8-inch (20.3 cm) soufflé dish and dust it with bread crumbs. Pour the soufflé mixture into the dish and bake in the preheated oven for 40 to 50 minutes. Serve with a thin Béchamel Sauce (see page 246).

Preparation and cooking time: approximately 1 hour.

VEAL

Buying Veal for the Freezer

There are three types of veal sold: Calves which are *milk-fed*, called *plume de veau*, are slaughtered at the age of three months. They have been reared on dry skimmed milk and fatty foods which help to produce white-fleshed, high-quality but extremely expensive veal. This type of veal is usually exported from Holland and France and is available in the United States as well as in Europe. The second type is *bob veal*, young calves slaughtered before they are three weeks old. They are only available in Europe. The meat, apart from the leg, is more suitable for roasts, pie fillings, stews and casseroles than for scallops or cutlets. The third type is *grass-fed* or *nature veal*, which is less tender than the milk-fed veal, but also, according to some, more flavorful. The calves are killed at just under one year old, and have a slightly darker colored flesh. This type of veal is considered to be the very best top-grade meat and is available in both the United States and Europe.

When you buy any veal, make sure that the outside fat, which is very thin, is firm and pinkish-white. The flesh should be soft but firm, fine-grained and moist, varying in color from off-white to very pale pink. Do not buy flabby

VEAL CUTS (AMERICAN)   **VEAL CUTS (ENGLISH)**

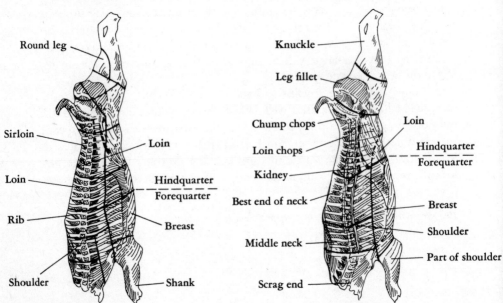

VEAL CUTS (AMERICAN):
Round leg
Sirloin
Loin
Loin
Hindquarter
Forequarter
Rib
Breast
Shoulder
Shank

VEAL CUTS (ENGLISH):
Knuckle
Leg fillet
Chump chops
Loin
Loin chops
Hindquarter
Forequarter
Kidney
Best end of neck
Breast
Middle neck
Shoulder
Scrag end
Part of shoulder

and wet veal, or meat that is dry and brown, or that has a blue tinge or mottled skin. Only the kidneys will be covered in extremely white fat; the bones should be pinkish-white—almost translucent, soft, and large in proportion to the size of the cut.

Unlike beef and lamb, where one buys whole carcasses or sides for freezing, veal is usually bought in specific cuts.

The leg: Contains the best meat on the calf, and is also the largest cut, with a high proportion of meat to bone. The whole leg, after the hind knuckle has been removed, may be roasted on the bone, or the top side, known as the fillet or cushion of veal (usually weighing from 8 to 12 ounces [225 to 350 g]) may be cut off for steaks or escallops and the remainder boned and rolled for smaller roasting cuts. The leg from a nature-fed calf would weigh approximately 50 pounds (20.25 kg); from a milk-fed calf it would vary, but would be much smaller. The hind leg knuckle comes from the lower part of the leg, and can be slow-roasted on the bone or cut into 1½- to 2-inch (3.8 to 5 cm) pieces for osso bucco. The foreleg knuckle is only suitable for boiling or meat pies.

The loin: A prime cut, sold in one piece on the bone to be roasted as a saddle, a loin weighs from 12 to 16 pounds (5 to 6.2 kg); or as half, 5 to 8 pounds (2.3 to 3.6 kg), less the kidneys. It can also be boned, rolled and stuffed. Another way of cooking it is to have single bone portions, perhaps as individual chops which sometimes include the kidney.

Middle neck: This has a high proportion of bone but can be divided into cutlets for braising or stewing. Boned, it can be used as pie veal.

Rib (best-end) chops: This is the prime meat of the central ribs which has been sliced into chops. The last three or four main ribs are very tender and may be broiled (grilled) or fried. They should be chined (removing the very tip of the vertebra) and the ends of the rib bones should be trimmed off and cut about 1 inch (2.5 cm), or they can be boned. You will need two per person.

The breast: A very economical cut, which may be roasted on the bone, or boned, rolled and stuffed, then cut into slices.

The shoulder: Sometimes known in England as the "oyster" of veal after the knuckle has been removed, this can be roasted on the bone, but it is much better when boned, rolled and stuffed. *In a milk-fed calf only,* the meat of the shoulder muscle will be tender enough to make into escallops.

Deep-Freezer Life for Veal

Leg, loin or saddle, shoulder   6 months
Escallops, chops or cutlets   3 months
Kidneys and sweetbreads   2 months

Roasting Times for Veal

	Open roasting	Pot-roasting and braising
	350° F (180° C; Mark 4)	325° F (160° C; Mark 3)
Cuts on the bone	30 minutes per pound (450 g)	35 minutes per pound (450 g)
Boned and rolled cuts	40 minutes per pound (450 g)	45 minutes per pound (450 g)

Pressure-Cooking Times at High Temperature Per Pound (450 g) Weight

Braised   12 minutes
Pot-roasted   12–15 minutes
Stewed   12–15 minutes

Microwave Oven Times

	Medium	Well-done
on the bone	7 minutes	8–9 minutes
boned, rolled	9 minutes	10–11½ minutes

To Carve

Loin of veal:

1. Place the backbone closest to your right hand (or the hand holding the knife) and carve along the bone, with the grain of the meat.

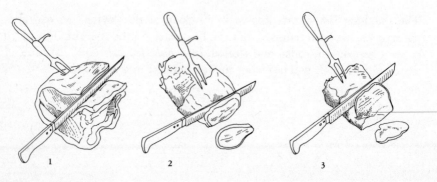

1   2   3

2. Turn the backbone around so that it is at the fork end, and carve from the chump end, again with the grain. These will be in small slices.

3. In order to remove all the meat from the bone, turn the loin over and carve small slices, at an angle to the bone.

ROULETTEN OF VEAL or Veal Birds

SERVES 6

6 veal escallops, pounded thin (pork escallops may also be used)
1 teaspoon (5 ml) salt
½ teaspoon (2.5 ml) black pepper
6 slices prosciutto or Parma ham
1 cup (3 oz; 75 g) fresh bread crumbs
3 shallots, chopped fine
2 teaspoons (10 ml) fine-chopped capers

1 teaspoon (5 ml) grated lemon rind
2 teaspoons (10 ml) fine-chopped fresh basil or rosemary, or 1 teaspoon (5 ml) dried basil or rosemary
1 egg yolk
3 tablespoons (45 ml) butter

Preheat the oven to 375° F (190° C; Mark 5).

Rub each escallop with salt and pepper, lay 1 slice of prosciutto on top of each escallop, and put them aside while you make the stuffing. In a bowl, mix the bread crumbs, shallots, capers, lemon rind, herbs and egg yolk, until they form a thick paste. Form the mixture into 6 cone shapes and place each cone on top of the prosciutto in the middle of each escallop. Roll up the escallops and tie them with string.

In an ovenproof dish melt 1 tablespoon (15 ml) of butter, place the veal rolls in the dish, cut up the remaining butter and distribute it over the veal. Place the dish in the preheated oven for 40 to 50 minutes or until the meat is tender. Serve with creamed spinach (see page 101) and glazed carrots.

Preparation time: 30 minutes. Cooking time: 40 to 50 minutes.

HERBED VEAL CHOPS

SERVES 6

1½ ounces (37 g) butter
*1½ tablespoons (22 ml) vegetable
  oil*
6 large veal chops
Salt and fresh-ground black pepper
2 garlic cloves, peeled and chopped
*3 tablespoons (45 ml) shallots or
  scallions (spring onions), chopped
  fine*

*¾ cup (6 fl oz; 175 ml) dry white
  wine*
1 teaspoon (5 ml) basil
1 teaspoon (5 ml) thyme
¾ cup (6 fl oz; 175 ml) beef stock
*1 tablespoon (½ oz; 15 ml)
  softened butter*
*2 tablespoons (30 ml) chopped
  fresh basil or parsley*

Preheat oven to 325° F (160° C, Mark 3).

Heat the butter and oil in a large heavy frying pan and add the chops—you may have to do this in two stages if all the chops do not fit into the pan. Brown the chops on each side for 3 to 4 minutes, then place them in an enamel casserole. Do not use aluminum because of the wine to be added. Season with salt and pepper and place in a very low oven to keep warm. In the same frying pan, sauté the garlic and shallots or scallions (spring onions) for a minute or two. You may have to add a little more fat if the other has become black. Add the wine and herbs and simmer for another few minutes, scraping up the burnt bits on the bottom of the pan. Pour this mixture over the veal chops in the casserole and bake in the preheated oven for 15 to 20 minutes, turning and basting the chops once or twice. When they are cooked, place the chops on a heated serving dish, and add the stock to the liquid in the casserole. Place it over high heat so that the liquid reduces and thickens, then remove it from the heat, whisk in the softened butter and pour the sauce over the veal chops. Sprinkle some chopped fresh basil or parsley over the meat and serve.

*Preparation time: approximately 10 minutes. Cooking time: approximately
25 minutes.*

VEAU POÊLÉ À L'ORANGE AVEC COINTREAU

Adapted from *Good Cooking* by Marshall Cavendish

SERVES 6

¼ cup (2 oz; 50 g) butter
2 tablespoons (30 ml) olive oil
3 pounds (1.4 kg) shoulder of veal,
  boned, rolled and tied
½ pound (225 g) carrots, chopped
2 medium-sized onions, peeled and
  sliced
Salt and fresh-ground black pepper
¾ cup (3 oz; 75 g) whole blanched
  almonds

2 tablespoons (1½ oz; 30 ml) flour
1 tablespoon (15 ml) French
  mustard
Juice and grated zest of 1 orange
3 tablespoons (45 ml) Cointreau
½ cup (4 fl oz; 125 ml) heavy
  (double) cream
Watercress or parsley, for garnish

Preheat the oven to 325° F (170° C; Mark 3).

In a large heavy casserole melt half the butter and half the oil over low heat until the fat becomes hot. Then add the veal and brown it on all sides. This seals in the juices. Remove the meat to a warm plate, and add the vegetables to the casserole. Stir once, cover and simmer over low heat for 5 minutes. Rub the salt and pepper into the veal and return it to the casserole, placing it on top of the vegetables. Add water to come two-thirds of the way up the vegetables. Cover the casserole with a tight-fitting lid. If your lid is not tight enough, cover the casserole first with foil, making it tight around the edges, then fit the lid on top of that. Place in the center of the preheated oven and cook for about 2 hours, or 40 minutes per pound (450 g).

In another frying pan melt the remaining oil, add a little salt and brown the almonds for 1 or 2 minutes, then drain on paper towels.

When the meat is cooked, allow it to rest for 5 minutes, then slice it in thick pieces and place them on a heated serving dish to keep warm. Cook the liquid in the casserole over high heat until it has reduced by half. Then strain the liquid into a jug.

In a small saucepan, melt the remaining butter. Add the flour, stirring continuously, to make a *roux*, then gradually add the strained liquid. Next add the mustard, then the orange juice and zest and the Cointreau. Taste for seasoning, then stir in the cream but *do not allow it to boil*. Pour a small amount of sauce over the meat, sprinkle the nuts over the top, add the watercress or parsley, and serve remaining sauce in a sauceboat.

LAMB

Buying Lamb for the Freezer

In America, there are three top grades of lamb: USDA Prime; Choice or Good; and two varieties: spring lamb, approximately 4 months old, and winter wonder lamb, between 9 and 12 months old. The advantage of buying either a whole lamb or half a lamb is that you can order it cut to your own particular needs. If you require more individual portions, both the loin and the rib can be cut into chops (cutlets). If you buy a large lamb, both the leg and shoulder can be divided into two cuts (joints) each.

Weight range of whole carcass:
American: Kentucky and California—25 to 30 pounds (11.3 to 13.5 kg)
English lamb: 28 to 45 pounds (12.6 to 20.3 kg)
New Zealand lamb: 17½ to 35 pounds (8 to 16 kg)

In England, New Zealand lamb is the best value. It first appears in January as "spring lamb," and is then plentiful until the summer. English lamb's peak season is usually between August and November, the price dropping as supplies increase. New Zealand lamb is shipped to England frozen, so when buying it for the freezer make sure you ask the butcher to *keep* it frozen. Clearly, he will not, therefore, be able to bone the shoulder, and you will have to do that when it is thawed and ready for use. Either take it back to the butcher at that point or do it yourself. New Zealand carcasses are graded by weight and by the proportion of lean to fat to bone. Those sold retail vary in weight from 17½ to 35 pounds (8 to 16 kg). Butchers stock whichever grade is most popular with their customers. In North Wales, from June until September, we can buy the new Welsh mountain lamb, which is the most tender and flavorful of all.

Unless you can use every bit of a whole or a half of a lamb, it is cheaper to buy single-cut packs—such as all legs, all shoulders or all chops (cutlets)—at a special rate for quantity. Another way of economizing is to leave the most expensive cuts, i.e., the legs and loin, and to order fore-end of lamb, which is 2 forequarters consisting of:

1. 2 shoulders
2. rib (best end of neck)
3. 2 breasts
4. chuck (middle neck) and neck and shank (scrag).

Choosing lamb: In order to insure succulent, well-flavored meat, the carcass should have a thin covering of fell, but avoid a carcass which is very large and very fat. Legs and shoulders should have a "plump" look and a thin covering of fat, plus the fell, which is an outer layer of paperlike, pliable skin. The fat itself should be firm and white but not brittle, and the cut flesh should be pink with a fine grain. The knuckle bones should be bluish, indicating a young animal. As lamb ages, passes its first birthday and becomes mutton, the flesh becomes redder, the fat faintly yellowish, and the bones spongy and red inside. Crumbly yellow fat means that the animal is too old and has been stored too long.

In America and England, the shoulder is cut as a separate joint. In Scotland, the shoulder is not cut separately; the entire forequarter is boned out, rolled and then cut into smaller joints.

LAMB CUTS (AMERICAN)   LAMB CUTS (ENGLISH)

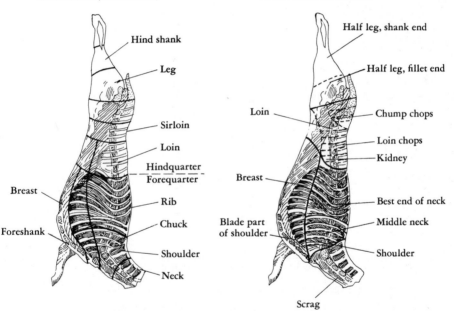

How lamb is sold: It is usually left on the bone and cut into joints.

1. *Whole carcass* with two of each cut, usually 28 to 45 pounds but can be larger.
2. *Sides* with one of each cut.
3. *Hindquarter* with leg and loin (expensive).
4. *Forequarter* with shoulder, neck, rib and breast (less expensive).
5. *Individual cuts and portions*—shoulders, legs, loin chops, rib chops (best end cutlets).

Freezer space needed: For every 35 pounds of lamb on the bone, allow 1½ cubic feet in the freezer.

Deep-freezer life:

Lamb: large joints   8 months
           chops, noisettes   6 months
           cubed for stews   4 months

Offal: hearts, kidneys, liver   2 months

To Cook Frozen Lamb

ON THE BONE: 450° F (230° C; Mark 8) for 20 minutes in hot fat to seal, then cover and reduce to 350° F (180° C; Mark 4) and cook as indicated below.

UNDER 4 POUNDS		Meat Thermometer Reading
rare to medium	30 minutes per pound (450 g) plus 30 minutes	170° F (79° C)
well-done	35 minutes per pound (450 g) plus 35 minutes	180° F (82° C)
4–8 POUNDS		
medium	35 minutes per pound (450 g) plus 35 minutes	160° F (71° C)
well-done	40 minutes per pound (450 g) plus 40 minutes	190° F (88° C)

BONED: Add 30 minutes to the times given above.

LOIN CHOPS (DEPENDING ON THICKNESS)
Broil (grill): 15–20 minutes on high heat, then lower heat to cook through
Pan-fry: 15–25 minutes on high heat, then lower heat to cook through
Bake: 350° F (180° C; Mark 4) for 1¼–1½ hours in a preheated oven

RIB CHOPS (BEST-END CUTLETS; DEPENDING ON THICKNESS)
Broil (grill): 10–15 minutes
Pan-fry: 15 minutes

NOISETTES OF LAMB
Broil (grill): 20 minutes
Pan-fry: 30 minutes

To Cook Fresh Lamb

Low temperature roasting times, based on cuts at room temperature and an oven temperature of 350° F (180° C; Mark 4).

Cut	Medium-Rare	Well-Done
	meat thermometer 170° F (77° C)	meat thermometer 180° F (80° C)
Leg, on the bone	25 minutes per pound (450 g) plus 20 minutes	35 minutes per pound (450 g) plus 20 minutes
boned	30 minutes per pound (450 g) plus 20 minutes	40 minutes per pound (450 g) plus 20 minutes
Shoulder, on the bone	30 minutes per pound (450 g) plus 20 minutes	40 minutes per pound (450 g) plus 20 minutes
boned and rolled	40 minutes per pound (450 g) plus 20 minutes	45 minutes per pound (450 g) plus 20 minutes
Loin	25 minutes per pound (450 g) plus 20 minutes	35 minutes per pound (450 g) plus 20 minutes
Saddle	20 minutes per pound (450 g) plus 20 minutes	25 minutes per pound (450 g) plus 20 minutes
Rib (best end of neck)	45 minutes per pound (450 g) plus 20 minutes	50 minutes per pound (450 g) plus 20 minutes

Braising, pot-roasting, stewing:

1. Use neck (scrag end), shoulder, breast, leg. Cook in the same way as beef (see page 179).
2. Allow 30 minutes per pound (450 g) for young, tender cuts, but double the time for cheaper cuts and allow even longer for mutton.

Broiling (grilling) and pan-frying

Use loin (chump), rib (neck), shoulder (middle neck).

Broil (grill) in the same way as beef (see page 179).

1-inch (2.5 cm) thick chops:
medium rare—8 minutes
medium—15 minutes
well-done—20 minutes.

Important: The broiler (grill) must be preheated.

To pan-fry, use oil or butter, or mix the two fats and cook until just brown.

Pressure-cooking times at high temperature per pound (450 g) weight:

Pot-roasted	10–15 minutes
Stewed	10 minutes
Liver and kidneys	7 minutes

Microwave oven times per pound (450 g) weight:

At room temperature	9 minutes
From refrigerator	10–11 minutes

To Carve

Leg of lamb:

1. Place the leg with the knuckle on your left and the rounded side up. Put the fork in near the knuckle and hold the leg while you make a cut, at a slight angle, right through to the bone.
2. Make a second cut to the left of the first one and remove the thin slice. Then, slanting the knife so that the slices are as long as possible, keep slicing on either side of the original cut until you have removed all the meat possible from that side.
3. Turn the leg over, hold the knuckle with your hand and make vertical slices until you have removed all the meat underneath the leg bone.

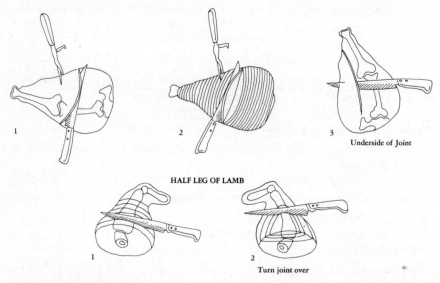

1   2   3

Underside of Joint

HALF LEG OF LAMB

1   2

Turn joint over

Shoulder of lamb:

1. As you would with a leg, make a cut in the center of the shoulder straight through to the bone. Make another cut right next to it to create a slice about ¼ inch thick.

SHOULDER

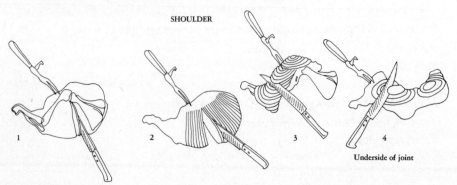

1   2   3   4

Underside of joint

HALF SHOULDER LAMB

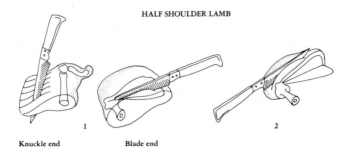

Knuckle end   Blade end

2. Continue slicing on either side of the original cut until you have removed all the meat from that side.
3. Cut off all the meat you can from the shank bone.
4. Turn the shoulder over and cut small slices from underneath the bone.

Rack or Saddle of lamb:
1. Put the fork into the left side of the saddle and make a cut down the center, along to the backbone.
2. Hold the right-hand section of meat with the fork and slide the knife under the meat to free it from the bone. Then make a second cut to the right of the backbone. This will completely free the section.
3. Holding the knife slightly at a slant, slice all the meat from this section. Repeat the same process with the left-hand section. Turn the saddle over and slice from the other side.
4. Reassemble the saddle incorporating slices from the best sections, i.e., the top, and the underneath part.

RACK/SADDLE OF LAMB

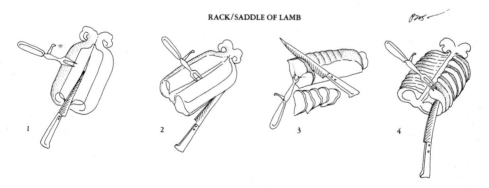

LAMB

Forequarter American	English	Types of meat and ways of butchering	Uses and how to cook
Neck and shank	Scrag	*American:* neck slices	Good for slow braising in hotpots and stews.
		English: cut into chops	
Chuck of lamb	Middle neck	Rather bony inexpensive cut with rich flavor.	Braise; slow, moist cooking for stews. Make stock from bones.
Shoulder and Foreshank	Shoulder	Sweet succulent meat for roasting.	
		American:	
		Square shoulder	Roast
		Precarved shoulder, trimmed, cut into chops and tied back into original shape	Roast
		Cushion shoulder—the one to stuff	Roast
		Rolled shoulder—boned and rolled	Roast
		Boneless blade chops (Saratoga)	Pan-fry, broil (grill), pan-broil.
		Cubes for kebabs, etc.	Stews, casseroles, curries and pies.
		English:	
		Large roast	Roast
		Small roast—large shoulder can be divided into the blade and the knuckle end, providing 2 joints	Roast
		Boneless roast—ask butcher to bone out the shoulder, roll and tie it. Eliminates carving problem.	Good for spit-roasting where a compact shape is essential.
		Boned shoulder, ground or cubed.	Ideal for kebabs, casseroles, curries, and pies. Perfect for moussaka or hamburgers.

Forequarter American	English	Types of meat and ways of butchering	Uses and how to cook
Rib	Best End of Neck	*American:*	
		Rib Roast or rack	Roast
		Crown Roast—rib roast bent and tied in circle, i.e. crown of lamb.	Roast
		Frenched rib chops	Broil (grill), pan-fry
		Rib chops	Broil (grill), pan-fry
		English:	
		Best end—good roast for small family as is, or boned, stuffed and rolled.	Roast
		Crown of lamb or guard of honor—trimmed and tied *pair* of best ends.	Roast
		Noisettes—boned out, rolled, tied, and cut in 5 to 6 "nuts," each 1-1½ inches thick. Must use a *large* best end for this, not worth doing with a small one.	Broil (grill), pan-fry
		Cutlets	Broil (grill), pan-fry
Breast	Breast	*American:*	
		Single breast	Roast, braise
		Boned and rolled breast	Roast, braise
		Stuffed breast—boned	Roast, braise
		Stuffed chops	Broil (grill), pan-fry
		Riblets—individual	Bake, braise
		Spareribs	Bake, braise
		English:	
		Two narrow breasts—best boned and rolled with stuffing sandwiched between them.	Slow roasting
		Single, boned and rolled stuffed breast—ask the butcher to cut *wide* breasts, which will mean shorter shanks on the loin joint.	Slow roasting
		Lamb Riblets—cut-up breast	Slow roasting

LAMB

Hindquarter American	English	Types of meat and ways of butchering	Uses and how to cook
Loin	Loin	*American:*	
		Loin	Roast
		Saddle or double loin	Roast
		Rolled, double loin	Roast
		Loin, kidney or English chops	Broil (grill), pan-broil, pan-fry
		English:	
		Saddle roast—the two loins still joined across the back for a special roast.	Roast
		Small roast—single loin	Roast
		Boneless roast—bone the loin with a sharp knife for stuffing and rolling.	Roast
		Chops—loin can be divided between the rib bones into 4 to 6 chops plus 2 bonier chump chops from the end next to the leg.	Broil (grill), pan-broil, pan-fry
Leg with sirloin	Leg	*American:*	
		Full or French-style leg, including sirloin.	Roast
		French style—sirloin cut off	Roast
		Sirloin half of leg	Roast
		Center leg	Roast
		Shank half of leg	Roast
		Boneless leg rolled	Roast
		Leg chop (steak)	Broil (grill), pan-broil, pan-fry
		Hind shank—whole, ground or cubed lamb.	Braise
			Broil (grill), pan-fry, pan-broil lamb patties or cubed steak
		English:	
		Whole—small leg, with bone in, or boned, stuffed	Roasted or spit-roasted with bone in / Roasted boned and stuffed
		Halved—a large leg can be halved, providing a fillet and a shank end (knuckle end).	Fillet to be roasted. Shank or kunckle end to be braised.

SWEET AND SOUR LAMB

SERVES 6 TO 8

1 medium-sized onion, chopped
1 tablespoon (15 ml) olive or
  vegetable oil
2 cloves garlic, peeled and crushed
1 green chili, seeds removed and
  sliced
1 teaspoon (5 ml) ground
  coriander
1 teaspoon (5 ml) ground ginger
One 3 to 3½ pound (1½ kg) leg
  of lamb, cut into bite-sized pieces

1 tablespoon (15 ml) white wine
  vinegar
Juice of ½ lemon
1 tablespoon (15 ml) brown sugar
1 tablespoon (15 ml) soy sauce
Salt
1 small bunch chives, snipped fine

In a frying pan, sauté the onion in the oil until it becomes transparent, then add the garlic, chili, coriander, ginger and, finally, the meat. Mix them thoroughly, cover and simmer for 10 minutes, then add the vinegar, lemon juice, sugar and soy sauce. Taste before adding the salt, as soy sauce has some salt in it. Simmer for a further 20 minutes, adding a little water if necessary. Just before serving, sprinkle the lamb with chopped chives. Serve with plain rice.

Preparation time: approximately 10 minutes. Cooking time: approximately 30 minutes.

CURRIED SHOULDER OF LAMB

SERVES 4

2 pounds (1 kilo) boned shoulder
  of lamb, cut into 1-inch cubes
5 tablespoons (75 ml) clarified
  butter (see page 243)
2 medium onions, chopped
2 garlic cloves, chopped fine
1¼ teaspoon (6.5 ml) ground
  ginger
1 teaspoon (5 ml) turmeric
½ teaspoon (2.5 ml) ground
  cardamom

2 teaspoons (10 ml) cumin seed,
  roasted and crushed
2 tablespoons (30 ml) fresh
  coriander leaves, chopped
A pinch of cinnamon
½ cup (4 fl oz; 125 ml) water
¼ cup (2 fl oz; 50 ml) Tomato
  Sauce (see page 258)
1 cup (8 fl oz; 225 ml) plain yogurt

In a small frying pan, melt 3 tablespoons (45 ml) clarified butter and brown the meat in it. Then remove the browned meat with a slotted spoon and place it in a casserole dish. Melt 2 more tablespoons (30 ml) clarified butter in the same frying pan in which you browned the meat, and sauté the chopped onion until it has turned soft and golden. Add to this the chopped garlic, herbs and spices and cook the mixture for 5 minutes, stirring constantly. Add the water and simmer until the whole mixture has the consistency of a paste. Pour this paste over the meat in the casserole and add the tomato sauce. Cook the curry, covered, over low heat for 1 hour or, until the meat is tender. You may have to add some more liquid—lamb stock, water or tomato sauce—during this period. When the meat is cooked add the yogurt and simmer for a few minutes, but do not allow it to boil. Serve with Lemon or Lime Rice (see page 211) or kasha (buckwheat groats).

Preparation time: approximately 20 minutes. Cooking time: approximately 1 hour 35 minutes.

LEMON OR LIME RICE (NIMBO BHAAT)

SERVES 6

2 tablespoons (30 ml) cashew nuts
½ cup (4 fl oz; 125 ml) cold water
1 cup (7 oz; 200 g) rice
1½ cups (12 fl oz; 375 ml) hot
  water
½ teaspoon (2.5 ml) turmeric
2 tablespoons (30 ml) clarified
  butter or oil
½ teaspoon (2.5 ml) mustard seeds
3 teaspoons (15 ml) mild curry
  powder

2 to 3 fresh green chilies, seeds
  removed, chopped
2 teaspoons (10 ml) salt
½ a fresh coconut, grated
Juice of 1 lime or lemon
1 tablespoon (15 ml) fresh
  coriander leaves
½ cup (4 fl oz; 125 ml) coconut
  milk

Soak the cashew nuts in the cold water for 1 hour and drain. Soak the rice in water to cover for 5 minutes. Drain and add the hot water and turmeric. Simmer for approximately 15 to 20 minutes, or until tender. Add a drop or two of oil or clarified butter just before the rice is done.

Heat the remaining clarified butter or oil in a deep saucepan and fry the cashew nuts, the mustard seeds, curry powder and green chilies for 3 to 4 minutes. Add the cooked rice and salt and stir for another 2 to 3 minutes. Then add the grated coconut, lime or lemon juice, coriander leaves and coconut milk. Cook covered, over low heat for 10 to 15 minutes, or until all the liquid has been absorbed. If the rice is damp, place a folded cloth over the pan, and cover with a lid for 5 to 7 minutes. This helps to absorb the excess moisture and make the rice fluffy.

Preparation time: (soaking) 1 hour. Cooking time: approximately 50 minutes.

PORK

Buying Pork for the Freezer

Pork is in season all year round but it is at its cheapest during the summer months because people tend to eat leaner meats during the hot weather.

The flesh of young animals is smooth and firm with pale pink meat containing some marbling, extremely white fat as an outer covering and almost no gristle. The skin is light-colored and supple, the bones small, pink and delicate. The skin darkens and coarsens, as does the meat itself, as the pig ages; the bone turns off-white and the fat becomes oily and flabby. These older pigs tend to be used mainly for bacon. Don't buy pork that is very fat, dark-colored and coarse even if it is cheaper.

If you can use all the cuts it is more economical to buy a complete side. However, if you cannot, it is better to ask your butcher to quote you the price for a forequarter only, leaving out the expensive leg and loin.

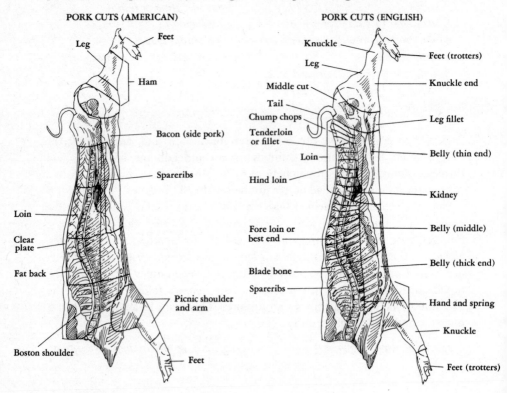

PORK CUTS (AMERICAN)

Feet
Leg
Ham
Bacon (side pork)
Spareribs
Loin
Clear plate
Fat back
Picnic shoulder and arm
Boston shoulder
Feet

PORK CUTS (ENGLISH)

Knuckle
Leg
Feet (trotters)
Middle cut
Knuckle end
Tail
Chump chops
Leg fillet
Tenderloin or fillet
Loin
Belly (thin end)
Hind loin
Kidney
Fore loin or best end
Belly (middle)
Belly (thick end)
Blade bone
Spareribs
Hand and spring
Knuckle
Feet (trotters)

A forequarter yields:

1. A fore loin for chops.
2. A thick end of the belly for roasting whole or grinding.
3. The blade and spareribs for roasting.
4. The hock and arm picnic (hand and spring) for pies and slow roasting.

Pork for freezing should be freshly killed and the carcass thoroughly cured.

Do *not* freeze brined or salt pork, as it has an extremely short storage life. Do *not* freeze stuffed joints.

Pork freezer life:

Large roasts or cuts	6 months
Chops	4 months
Fat pork (e.g. belly)	3 months

Cooking Pork

It is dangerous to taste pork before it is fully cooked.

The natural flavor of pork develops fully as a result of slow and thorough cooking. It is essential too to kill the parasites causing trichinosis, a lethal disease. Therefore the internal temperature of cooked pork, measured by a meat thermometer, should read a minimum of 325° F (170° C) and a maximum of 360° F (185° C).

Although rich in flavor, pork needs the addition of herbs and spices to bring out its flavor. If frozen, it must, of course, be thawed before marinating. The following make particularly good seasonings for pork: garlic, rosemary, fennel, thyme, sage, bay leaves, ginger, peppercorns, caraway seeds, chopped chives, curry powder, juniper berries and mustard.

I also prefer to marinate it before roasting or baking to remove the very porky taste. The pork will have a much better flavor if you braise it in a tomato or fruit sauce rather than in water. Fruit sauces with a tang, sweet and sour sauces or fruit stuffings make the cheaper cuts delicious.

Pork chops should be at least ¾ inch (1.9 cm) thick, those to be stuffed 1½ inches (3.8 cm) thick. Cook them by braising or baking rather than broiling (grilling) or pan-frying (sautéing), to prevent them from becoming dry and tough.

The hock, arm picnic (hand and spring) and belly improve tremendously by being soaked in brine for several days, then simmered gently in water. Brining can be done at home if you have a really cold storage place, a large crock and a means of keeping the meat submerged in the brine. On the whole, however, it is better to ask your butcher to do it for you.

For good crisp crackling, the outer skin of the pork should be scored fine, which will also make the roast easier and more economical to carve. Frozen crackling is as good as fresh; score it in the frozen state rather than in the soft thawed state. Just before roasting, brush the skin with vegetable oil or melted lard, rub it generously with salt and lightly with fresh-ground pepper mixed with sage and dry mustard. This will insure a brown and crisp crackling. Place the pork, rind uppermost, on a rack in a roasting pan, and place in a preheated oven. Do not baste pork. There is so much outside fat that it will seep to the meat below and keep it moist. Do not cover it with aluminum, or the crackling will not crisp.

Roasting frozen pork: Small cuts of pork on the bone can be cooked from either the frozen or thawed state. Timing is more difficult to judge when cooking frozen pork; therefore, it is essential to use a meat thermometer. Approximately 30 minutes before the end of the cooking time, insert the thermometer into the thickest part of the meat. Be sure not to allow it to touch the bone, which conducts heat, and which will give you an inaccurate reading. Cover the meat with foil to prevent spitting for the first half of the cooking time, but remove the foil halfway through to crisp the crackling.

Roasting time for frozen pork:

ON THE BONE: 25 minutes per pound (450 g) plus 25 minutes, in a pre-heated oven at 425° F (220° C; Mark 7) for first 20 minutes, then decrease heat to 325° F (170° C; Mark 3).

OFF THE BONE: 45 minutes per pound (450 g) plus 45 minutes, in a pre-heated oven at 350° F (180° C; Mark 4).
Meat thermometer should register 190° F (88° C) when thoroughly cooked.

Roasting thawed or fresh pork: To thaw, leave the meat in an *unopened* package in the refrigerator, allowing 4 to 6 hours per pound, or at room temperature allowing 2 to 3 hours per pound. When completely thawed cook exactly as you would fresh pork. Boned and rolled joints and joints for stuffing should be thoroughly thawed before cooking. It is also preferable, though not essential, to thaw meat to be braised or boiled.

Roasting times for thawed or fresh pork: Start in a preheated 425° F (220° C; Mark 7) oven for the first 20 minutes to seal in the juices. Then turn the heat to 375° F (190° C; Mark 5) and cook as follows:

	Minutes per pound (450 g)
SMALL JOINTS under 2½ pounds (1.1 kg)	55
BELLY	40
LEG	
Whole ham (10–14 pounds) (4.5–6.3 kg)	25
Whole boneless ham (7–10 pounds) (3.2–4.5 kg)	35
Half ham (5–7 pounds) (2.3–3.2 kg)	30–35

LOIN

Center-cut loin roast (3–5 pounds) (1.4–2.3 kg)	30
Sirloin and blade loin (3–4 pounds) (1.4–1.8 kg)	40
Half loin roast (5–7 pounds) (2.3–3.2 kg)	35
Rolled loin roast (3–5 pounds) (1.4–3.2 kg)	40–45
Whole loin roast (8½–14 pounds) (3.9–6.3 kg)	40

SHOULDER

Blade (2–3 pounds) (900 g–1.4 kg)	55
Boston Butt (4–6 pounds) (1.8–2.7 kg)	40
Rolled Boston Butt (3–4 pounds) (1.4–1.8 kg)	45–50
Fresh Picnic (5–8 pounds) (2.3–3.6 kg)	30
Cushion-style Picnic (3–5 pounds) (1.4–3.2 kg)	35
Rolled-fresh Picnic (3–5 pounds) (1.4–3.2 kg)	40
Arm Roast (3–5 pounds) (1.4–3.2 kg)	35–40

SPARERIBS	45

COOKING STUFFED PORK on the bone—weigh *after* stuffing. Allow 30 minutes per pound (450 g) plus 30 minutes.

BONED, ROLLED AND STUFFED PORK: Allow 35 minutes per pound (450 g) plus 35 minutes.

Broiling (grilling) and pan-frying:

Fresh or thawed pork chops	12–15 minutes
Frozen pork chops—depends on thickness	18–24 minutes

Baking, fresh or thawed: 350° F (180° C; Mark 4) in a preheated oven for 1¼ to 1½ hours.

Pressure-cooking times at high temperature per pound (450 g) weight:

Boiled	18–20 minutes
Braised	12 minutes
Pot-roasted	12–15 minutes
Stewed	12–15 minutes

Carving Pork

Pork loin:

1. Put a fork into the crackling to hold the loin steady and, with a sharp, pointed knife, carefully ease the meat away from the chine bone.
2. Turn the loin so that the crackling is facing diagonally to the left of you and carve downwards through the crackling in thin slices.

PORK LOIN

Picnic shoulder (hand and spring):

1. Holding the fork with your left hand, carve downwards in thin slices from both the lean and fat end until you reach the center bone.
2. Turn over the shoulder and slice away all the meat from underneath.

HAND AND SPRING

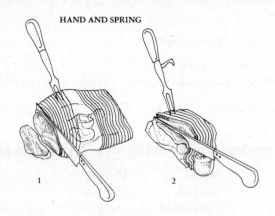

Shoulder of pork:

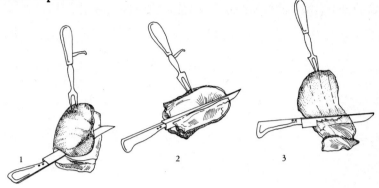

1. The crackling should be facing up. To make carving easier, remove some of it and reserve to serve, chopped up, with the meat.
2. Carve in thin slices from one side until you reach the blade bone, then turn the shoulder around and carve from the other side of the bone.
3. Turn the shoulder over and carve the underside crosswise in thin downward slices towards the wide end.

Whole Leg (Ham)

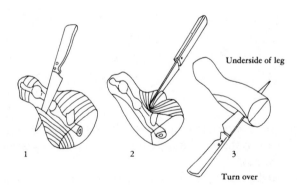

Fillet end of leg of pork:

1. and 2. Carve thin slices downwards at an angle across the leg. Work

across the leg towards the thick end.

3. Turn the leg over and start carving from the other end.

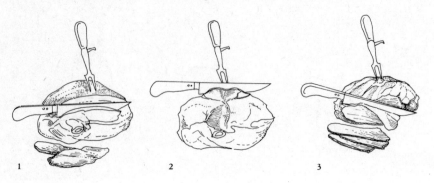

Knuckle end of leg of pork:

1. and 2. Start at the wide end. Carve thin slices downwards and along the bone.

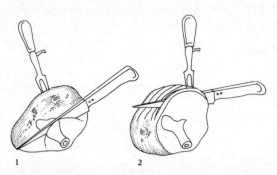

Large country-style sausages, frozen, are best baked or broiled (grilled) when cooked from frozen, as they tend to split if pan-fried when frozen.

Broil (grill): 10 minutes

Bake in a preheated oven at 350° F (180° C; Mark 4) for 1 to 1½ hours.

Turn occasionally during cooking.

Link sausage (chipolatas) can be pan-fried as well as broiled (grilled) and baked from frozen.

Pan-fry: 12–15 minutes

Broil (grill): 12–15 minutes

Bake in a preheated oven at 375° F (190° C; Mark 5) for 45 minutes.

Bacon and Gammon

Bacon is the brine-cured meat taken from either the *middle* or *forequarters* of a specially bred lean pig. Gammon comes from the *hind legs*. The main difference between ham and gammon is that gammon is a small joint cut from the carcass *after* the whole side has been brine-cured, whereas the ham is the whole hind leg removed from the carcass at the *fresh pork* stage, then brine-cured and smoked *individually* for special flavoring. Gammon is available only in England.

The lean flesh of bacon should be firm, deep pink or bright red, with firm, white fat. If the flesh is very dark or dry, it has been exposed to the air too long. Green or yellow stains with soft grayish fat means the meat is of poor quality.

The color of the rind depends on whether the bacon has been smoked or cured only in brine. If cured only in brine, the rind is off-white, while the rind of smoked bacon is a yellow or pale tan color. Bacon cuts are usually sold already boned, whereas gammon is left on the bone unless you ask the butcher to bone it.

Bacon in America: Comes from the belly after the spareribs have been peeled off.

SLAB BACON is a cured and smoked side of pork. Cheaper than pre-sliced bacon, some think it has a better flavor.

SLICED BACON is slab bacon, trimmed of its rind, sliced and packaged.
Regular sliced—the best all-purpose bacon.
Thick-sliced—particularly good for barding poultry or game.
Thin-sliced—I prefer this for eating on its own.

COUNTRY-CURED OR COUNTRY-STYLE is more expensive than ordinary slab bacon. Dry-cured, heavily smoked and salty, it is available in slabs or sliced. This is taken from the same pigs as the Virginia and Smithfield hams.

IRISH BACON is more expensive than regular sliced bacon. Taken from the whole belly, this is very much like country-cured bacon. It contains "streaky," which is like the regular sliced bacon, whole belly and the lean eye of the loin back bacon, which is used in Canadian bacon. Irish bacon is heavily salted and smoked.

CANADIAN BACON is equivalent to English back bacon. It comes from the boneless, lean eye of loin which is brine-cured and smoked. The taste resembles ham more than bacon. In England this is considered the best cut and is the most expensive bacon. Available in slices.

Bacon and gammon in England:

UNSMOKED BACON OR GAMMON (green or pale) is milder in flavor and paler in color than smoked.

MODERN SWEET-BRINE CURE results in an extra mild-flavored bacon.

SMOKED BACON (smoking done after the *initial* brine-curing) is dark in color and has a very strong flavor.

BACON SLICES:
Streaky is the fattiest and cheapest cut.
The middle, back and oyster, in that order, are leaner and more expensive. All three are available either green, sweet-cured, or smoked, very thinly sliced to a maximum of about ⅛ of an inch (3 mm) thick. All come from the lean eye of the loin.

BACON CHOPS are the back and shoulder cuts, usually sweet-cured and mildly flavored. Available from ¼ to ½ inch (6 to 12 mm) in thickness.

GAMMON is available green (unsmoked) or smoked. The smoked slice of the middle cut is the best for broiling (grilling). An average portion weighs about 4 to 5 ounces (125 to 150 g) and is about ¼ inch (6 mm) thick, but it can be cut thicker if required.

Storing and Freezing

Gammon should be unwrapped as soon as you get it home. Put it on a plate and cover it loosely with plastic wrap or foil. Stored in the coldest part of the refrigerator, directly under the frozen-food compartment, it will keep for 3 days. If buying bacon or gammon to freeze—wrap, freeze and store no longer than the time stated below. The drying action of freezing is intensified by the salt used in curing, and the meat becomes dehydrated and hard.

Bacon freezer life:

Slabs or slices specially packed for the deep freezer	5 months
Ordinary vacuum-packed slabs or slices	2–3 months
Home-packed slabs, smoked	2 months
Home-packed slabs, unsmoked	1½ months
Home-packed slices, smoked	1½ months
Home-packed slices, unsmoked	1 month

Roasting Slab Bacon (Bacon Joints)

	Minutes per pound (450 g)	Oven temperature
Whole gammon on the bone	20 minutes	325° F (160° C; Mark 3)
Gammon slabs (joints)		
Up to 3 pounds (1.4 kg)	30 minutes	350° F (180° C; Mark 4)
Up to 6 pounds (2.7 kg)	25 minutes	
Over 6 pounds (2.7 kg)	20 minutes	

All slab bacon

Up to 3 pounds (1.4 kg)	35 minutes	350° F (180° C; Mark 4)
Up to 6 pounds (2.7 kg)	30 minutes	
Over 6 pounds (2.7 kg)	25 minutes	

Carving Gammon

1. Starting at the "slipper area," carve thin slices until you reach the bone; then cut off the knuckle.
2. Cut out the aitchbone by carving off the corner of the meat.
3. With the knuckle facing you, carve thin slices off the middle section.
4. Roll the joint over and carve slices from the underside.
5. Continue doing this, turning the bone around until you get all the meat.

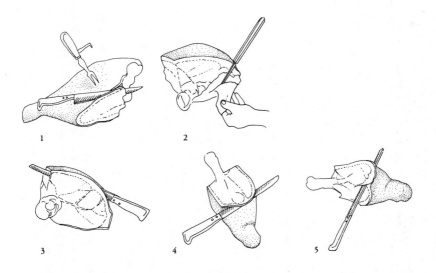

Cooking Hints

1. To stop bacon spattering during frying, sprinkle salt in the cold frying pan before using.
2. To clarify bacon drippings, pour the cooled liquid into a can containing cold water. The burned portion will drop to the bottom of the can. Chill for easy removal of the drippings.

PORK

American	English	Types of meat and ways of butchering	Uses and how to cook
Head	Head		
Jowl		Sweet, tender, fairly lean meat.	Can be used broiled (grilled) as the base for scrapple (American) or brawn (English). Also in Southern American cookbooks, there are special recipes for cooking smoked jowl, considered to be a great delicacy.
Shoulder	Shoulder	*American*: a moderately priced cut	
		Boston butt or Boston shoulder; cut from the upper shoulder. Also available boned and rolled.	Roast, braise
		Fresh picnic or picnic shoulder—lower part of the shoulder, containing some shank; less tender than Boston butt.	Skin *must* be removed before cooking.
		Cushion-style picnic—boned but not rolled	Roast, braise
		Rolled fresh picnic—boned and rolled	Good for stuffing—roast, braise
		Arm Roast —the top part of the picnic without the shank.	Roast, braise
		From this cut one also gets pork cubes or ground pork for link sausages.	Roast, braise, casserole
		Country-style spareribs—shoulder is butterflied, like English spareribs.	Bake
		English:	
		Whole shoulder—can be divided into 2–3 joints, or it can be boned, rolled and cut into smaller joints.	Roast
		Blade—an oyster-shaped blade cut from the loin-end makes a compact small joint (2–3 lbs.) (900–1.4 kg), often boned and stuffed.	Roast

PORK (continued)

American	English	Types of meat and ways of butchering	Uses and how to cook
		Spare rib (different from American spareribs)—can be cooked whole, or divided into rib cutlets. Also sometimes called neck cutlet—more economical than loin or chump chops.	Roasted whole. Ribs to be grilled, baked or barbecued with barbecue or sweet-and-sour sauce.
		Minced shoulder meat.	Ideal for pâtés. Make homemade sausage by mixing 1 pound (450 g) shoulder pork with ½ pound (225 g) minced hard back fat and adding salt, spices and herbs.
		Cubed shoulder meat.	Pork pies or kebabs.
Hock and Pig's feet (can also include the Arm picnic)	Hand and Spring	American: Fresh and smoked hock (trotters)	Boil whole (2 medium trotters per person); fry; broil (grill); jelly; cut into pieces for casseroles and stews.
		Pickled pig's feet	
		English: Front leg of the pig, a large inexpensive cut of rather coarse meat. Can be divided in two parts.	Slow roast Braise Braise with vegetables and herbs
		Hand—the large part used as is or boned and stuffed, or cut up for casseroles. A good lean piece for pickling and spicing. Shank end—good for casseroles.	
Belly	Belly	The long cut from the underside of the rib is interleaved with fat. A good, versatile cut.	
		American: The spareribs are peeled off the belly, which is used as sliced bacon or as fresh belly, or salted as salt pork.	
		Spareribs or Chinese spareribs—belly bones with little meat attached. In England you must specify that you want American or Chinese spareribs, otherwise you will get English spareribs (Country-style ribs) which are taken from the shoulder and they do not taste as good.	Bake, broil (grill), braise, pan-broil, pan-fry
		Salt pork	Bake, broil (grill), pan-broil, pan-fry, braise
		Sliced bacon	Bake, broil (grill), pan-fry, pan-broil

PORK (continued)

American	English	Types of meat and ways of butchering	Uses and how to cook
		English: The thicker and leaner end is good as a roasting cut when split horizontally through the middle and stuffed.	Roast or braise
		The Streaky End—can be treated as a roast or sliced as streaky bacon.	
		Minced (ground) 1-inch (2.5 cm) cubes.	For use in pâtés. Freeze in small quantities for this use or to use for *rillettes*, the French hors d'oeuvre. Needs careful preparation and long, slow cooking. (See Jane Grigson's *The Art of Making Sausages, Pâtés and Other Charcuterie*.)
Loin	Loin	Most expensive cut of pork. The whole loin will divide into two or three. Easy to carve if the chine bone is removed.	
		American:	
		Blade loin—has shoulder blade but no tenderloin.	Roast
		Center loin—the preferred loin as it contains a high proportion of tenderloin.	Roast
		Crown—very expensive, made by removing backbone from one or two half loins and shaping them into a circle. *Small crowns* have 10–14 ribs; *large crowns* have 24 ribs or more— 2 ribs per person.	Roast
		Sirloin—second-best cut, includes some tenderloin.	
		Tenderloin, whole or in slices. Extremely expensive, tender and boneless. The equivalent to beef fillet. Each slice is tiny, so allow 2–3 slices per person.	Roast or braise whole tenderloin. Pan-fry or broil (grill) slices
		Chops	Braise, broil (grill), pan-fry chops.
		blade loin roast—1 per person.	
		1. Blade chop—moderate in size and price. Chop from the	

American	English	Types of meat and ways of butchering	Uses and how to cook
		2. Rib chop—smallish in size; moderate to expensive. From the rib end of the center loin, usually cut 1-rib thick —1–2 per person.	
		3. Butterfly chop—a double-rib chop, made by removing the rib bone, cutting the meat almost in half horizontally and opening it out flat. Fairly expensive. Must usually be ordered in advance.	
		4. Loin chop—choicest and most expensive pork chop; cut from the heart of the center loin, usually 1-rib thick with a knob of tenderloin—1–2 per person.	
		5. Top loin chop—fairly expensive. Loin chop with tenderloin removed—2 per person.	
		6. Sirloin chop—moderately expensive. From the sirloin with a bit of tenderloin.	
		Canadian-style bacon	
		Fat back	
		English:	
		Whole loin. Can be completely boned, rolled and tied to make compact roasts. This is economical and can be served cold. The English prefer the skin to be left on for crackling. In France, they remove the skin and use it to enrich casseroles. They also use the thin, hard-back fat, immediately beneath the skin, for larding lean meat and for lining pâté dishes.	Roast, spit roast
		Tenderloin or fillet. A long boneless strip of meat found beneath the loin in *large* pigs; often left attached to the loin, but can be detached and is excellent, fine-grained meat with little or no fat.	Kebabs, pan-fry. Sliced across the grain, it can be beaten flat and treated like miniature veal escallops.

American	English	Types of meat and ways of butchering	Uses and how to cook
Leg (Ham)	Leg (Ham)	Prime, lean meat, good for smoking	
		American:	
		Hams—fresh and smoked	
		Fresh	
		1. Boneless leg	Roast
		2. Sliced cooked boiled ham	
		3. Ham steaks (pork cutlets)—taken from the butt portion. 1 leg steak serves 2.	
		Smoked	
		1. Boneless smoked ham	Bake
		2. Center smoked ham slice	Broil (grill), pan-broil, pan-fry
		3. Butt portion	Bake, braise
		4. Shank portion	Bake, braise
		English:	
		Whole leg—good for a large group of people. Can be boned and stuffed.	Roast, bake
		Fillet—the meaty end. If not used whole, it can be cut into thin slices, then beaten even thinner to make escallops.	Roast, bake, pan-fry
		Knuckle-end—improved if boned and stuffed with prune or apricot stuffing.	Braise
		A really large leg can be divided into 3 pieces, including a mid-leg cut.	

PORK CHOPS À LA MILANAISE

SERVES 6

6 pork chops, trimmed and
  flattened
Salt and fresh-ground pepper
Flour
1 cup (3 oz; 75 g) fine white bread
  crumbs
2 egg yolks, beaten
4 tablespoons (60 ml) clarified
  butter (see page 243)
½ pound (8 oz; 225 g) elbow
  macaroni

½ pound (8 oz; 225 g) mushrooms,
  sliced
4 tablespoons (60 ml) vegetable oil
¼ pound (4 oz; 125 g) cooked
  ham, cut into thin strips
¼ pound (4 oz; 125 g) smoked
  tongue, cut into thin strips
½ cup (1½ oz; 32 g) grated
  Parmesan cheese
2 cups (16 fl oz; 475 ml) Tomato
  Sauce (see page 258)

Season the pork chops with salt and pepper, sprinkle with flour, then dredge in a mixture of bread crumbs and beaten egg yolk. In a frying pan large enough to hold all the chops, melt the butter and fry the pork chops slowly over a low flame for 20 to 30 minutes until they are well-cooked through. Turn once during the cooking.

Approximately 15 minutes before the pork chops are finished cooking, fill a medium-sized saucepan with water, add 1 teaspoon (5 ml) salt and bring to the boil. Then add the macaroni and cook for approximately 10 minutes or until the macaroni is just cooked. Meanwhile, sauté the sliced mushrooms in the oil for 5 minutes. Drain the cooked macaroni into a colander, then pour it into a bowl. Add the cooked mushrooms, the strips of ham and tongue, the cheese and ¼ cup (2 fl oz; 50 ml) of the tomato sauce. Mix it together and pile the macaroni mixture into the center of a hot serving dish. Place the pork chops around it. Serve the remaining tomato sauce separately.

Preparation time: approximately 30 minutes. Cooking time: approximately 20 minutes.

PORK ESCALLOPS WITH FENNEL

SERVES 6

½ cup (4 oz; 125 g) butter
1 large or 2 small heads Florentine
  fennel, sliced thin, and reserving
  green feathered leaves, chopped
2 shallots or small onions, peeled
  and chopped fine
1 tablespoon (15 ml) flour
Salt and fresh-ground black pepper
  to taste

6 pork escallops (from the fillet),
  each weighing approximately
  4 oz (125 g)
5 tablespoons (75 ml) red wine
1¼ cups (½ pint, 300 ml) plain
  yogurt

In a medium-sized frying pan melt ¼ cup (2 oz; 50 g) butter and gently fry the fennel together with the shallots or onions for approximately 10 minutes, stirring continuously, until the onion is golden but not burnt, and the fennel is tender. Mix the flour with salt and pepper on a large plate, then toss each escallop in the seasoned flour. Shake off the excess flour. Melt the remaining butter in a large frying pan and sauté the escallops until they are tender and *thoroughly cooked,* approximately 15 minutes. Remove them from the pan and place them on a heated serving dish to keep warm.

Add the cooked fennel and shallots to the pan in which the escallops were cooked; add the wine and cook rapidly for 2 to 3 minutes. Remove from the heat and stir in the yogurt and salt and pepper to taste. Return to a very low heat and reheat until very hot *but not boiling.* Pour the sauce over the pork escallops and sprinkle with the reserved chopped fennel leaves.

Preparation time: 20 minutes. Cooking time: approximately 30 minutes.

FERNANDA'S BAKED MARINATED PORK LOIN

SERVES 6

1 medium-sized onion, sliced thin
3 garlic cloves, crushed
1 tablespoon (15 ml) salt
1 tablespoon (15 ml) fresh-ground black pepper
6 dashes Tabasco sauce
A pinch of turmeric
¼ teaspoon (1.25 ml) ground cumin

½ teaspoon (7.5 ml) chili powder
1 bay leaf
1 cup (8 fl oz; 225 ml) red wine
½ cup (4 fl oz; 125 ml) red wine vinegar
3 pounds (1.4 kg) Pork Loin on the bone and scored

In a medium-sized ovenproof earthenware or enamel casserole, mix all the ingredients and add the pork loin. Do not use an aluminum dish as it will make the wine and vinegar turn to acid, which makes you ill. Marinate for 4 days, turning the pork twice a day. Left in a cool place, the wine and vinegar will preserve the pork for a long time.

Preheat the oven to 350° F (180° C; Mark 4).

Place the pork in its marinade in the preheated oven and bake for 2½ hours. Serve with new potatoes in their skins. Parboil the potatoes, then, 20 minutes before the end of the pork cooking time, place the potatoes in the casserole around the pork and roast them, turning once.

Lamb and chicken are also delicious cooked and marinated in this manner.

Marinating time: 4 days. Cooking time: 2½ hours.

FERNANDA'S PORTUGUESE MIXED BEANS AND CHORIZO

This is a good inexpensive dish to serve for a buffet. It is better if made the night before and reheated the next day, but it must be kept in the refrigerator, otherwise the beans will turn.

SERVES 16 TO 18

1 pound (450 g) kidney beans
1 pound (450 g) butter beans
1 pound (450 g) black-eyed peas
6 garlic cloves, crushed
5 tablespoons (85 ml) olive oil
6 large onions, sliced
½ teaspoon (2.5 ml) ground
*   coriander*
1 teaspoon (5 ml) ground basil
1 teaspoon (5 ml) ground oregano
1 teaspoon (5 ml) ground thyme

½ teaspoon (2.5 ml) turmeric
½ teaspoon (2.5 ml) chili pepper
Two 14-ounce (400 g) cans of
*   Italian plum tomatoes*
1 pound (450 g) smoked bacon in
*   one piece, cut into ½-inch*
*   (1.2 cm) pieces*
2 pounds (1 kilo) chorizo sausage,
*   sliced into ⅓-inch (1.2 cm)*
*   rounds*
½ cup (4 fl oz; 125 ml) red wine

Place the kidney beans in one saucepan, the butter beans in another, the black-eyed peas in a third, making sure they will have room to expand when the water has been added. Pour boiling water to cover into each saucepan and leave the beans to soak for 3 hours, adding more water if needed. Drain into 3 separate colanders. The beans must be cooked separately as each type takes a different length of time. In each of three saucepans crush 1 clove of garlic, add 1 tablespoon (15 ml) olive oil. Fill the pans with cold water and bring to the boil. Add the beans, cover and cook until tender, from 20 to 30 minutes. When cooked, drain the beans into one colander, as at this point they may be mixed together.

In a large casserole or pot put 2 tablespoons (30 ml) of olive oil, add the remaining garlic and the onions and cook over low heat until the onions become soft and golden. Add the tomatoes with their juice and simmer, covered, until the tomatoes become pulpy and the mixture is thick and dark red in color. Add the herbs and spices, then the bacon and chorizo. You needn't add salt as the bacon will have enough in it. Cook for 20 minutes, then add the wine and the beans and simmer for 10 minutes.

Note: when stirring the mixture use a metal spoon; a wooden one will break up the beans.

Preparation time: approximately 3½ hours, including soaking the beans.
Cooking time: 1 hour 20 minutes.

STUFFINGS AND MARINADES

STUFFING HINTS

Specific stuffing recipes are included with individual meat and poultry dishes in previous chapters. This chapter is meant to give you a more general sense of what a stuffing is made of, so that you can devise your own variations.

Bread stuffing can be made from white bread, but to give it more flavor you might substitute cornbread, rye or pumpernickel. Fresh bread crumbs make the best stuffing, but even then the bread should be one day old so that the crumbs have a bit of body but do not taste stale. You can make bread crumbs in a blender (liquidizer) or food processor or simply break the bread up with your hands.

Packaged stuffings are also usable, but these must be moistened, preferably with butter or margarine, chicken or beef broth, milk, light (single) cream, well-beaten eggs or heated wine. Fresh bread crumbs may then be added to the moistened packaged ingredients in order to enhance flavor and give added bulk. You will need roughly ½ to ¾ cup (4 to 6 fl oz; 125 to 175 ml) of liquid per 2 cups (6 oz; 175 g) of bread crumbs.

If you are adding vegetables to the stuffing, they should be chopped or diced. Adding vegetables such as mushrooms, celery, green pepper, chestnuts, water chestnuts or onion will give taste and texture to the stuffing.

Herbs also add more flavoring and seasoning to stuffings. If you are using a mild herbal combination, allow 2 tablespoons (30 ml) of each chopped herb if fresh, or 1 tablespoon (15 ml) of the dried herb per cup (3 oz; 75 g) of bread crumbs. But if you are using a strong herbal combination, use 1 tablespoon (15 ml) of each chopped herb if fresh, or ½ teaspoon (2.5 ml) of dried herb per cup (3 oz; 75 g) of fresh bread crumbs.

Meat stuffings are a very good way to use up leftover meat, game and poultry, as the meat for the stuffing must already have been cooked. Chop or julienne the meat and add the vegetables or herbs as you would for bread stuffings, i.e., 2 parts meat to 1 part seasoning.

The following herb–meat combinations are particularly good:
Beef—thyme, marjoram, coriander, oregano, sage, rosemary and mace.
Chicken—combine parsley and thyme.
Fish—fennel.
Lamb—combine rosemarry, thyme and garlic. Or use savory, dill, marjoram, tarragon, basil and chives.
Pork—sage.

Fruit stuffings using apples, oranges, lemons or prunes are particularly good for poultry such as duck or goose, as well as for game birds. The acid in the fruit helps to cut down the fat in the bird. It is important to cut the fruit into large pieces so that it will not become too soft and mushy during the cooking process, and *never* add liquid as the fruit has its own.

The best meats to stuff are boned shoulder or breast of lamb or veal; rolled flank steak or various thin cuts of beef and veal; a crown roast of lamb or pork; and thick lamb or pork chops with pockets cut inside. If you are not stuffing food within a closed cavity, add it halfway through the cooking time instead of at the beginning.

Some particular points to remember about using stuffings are:

1. Always stuff meat and poultry before cooking, except in the special circumstances mentioned above.
2. The stuffing can be prepared the night before and stored separately. This is particularly convenient if stuffing a turkey or goose, since they take so long to cook.
3. Never place warm stuffing in meat or poultry; always cool it first.
4. Never fill the cavity more than three-quarters full, as stuffing expands when it cooks.

5. Brown in a frying pan all raw pork or sausage meat before using it in a stuffing, then remove all excess liquefied fat.
6. Stuffings are cooked when they reach an internal temperature of 325° F (170° C).

MARINADES

Larousse Gastronomique, the Bible of cooking, defines a marinade as "A seasoned liquid, cooked or uncooked, in which foodstuffs, notably meat and fish, are steeped." Marinating is one way of introducing a variety of tastes into meat and fish; the combination of liquids and highly flavored herbs and spices in which meat, game or fish is left to soak not only adds these interesting flavors but also, through the acidity in the wine, lemon juice or vinegar, tenderizes and preserves it. Meats are more quickly marinated when soaked in a cooked marinade.

The length of time one should marinate depends on the individual foodstuffs, the type and size of the meat, the temperature of the meat and the room, and the time of the year. In winter a piece of game or meat may be left as long as 5 to 6 days, whereas in the summer, from 24 to 48 hours is really the maximum you can safely allow it to steep. If the meat is to marinate for a long time, especially in the summer, add ½ teaspoon (2.5 ml) boric acid per 2 quarts (2.5 l) marinade. In the summer the marinade should be boiled every 2 days and in winter every 4 to 5 days. Freshen after each boiling with 6 fl oz (175 ml) of the same wine used in the original marinade and 3 fl oz (75 ml) vinegar. If you leave something like venison in a marinade too long, it tends to become so impregnated that the cooked venison will retain a sour taste. Most recipes will indicate the length of time for the marinating process.

The basic ingredients for marinades include red or white wine; red wine vinegar; herbs and spices such as black peppercorns, juniper berries, coriander seeds, cumin seeds and ground cumin, rosemary, thyme (particularly serpolet, the wild thyme), bay leaf and parsley. Many vegetables may also be included: parsnips, onions, garlic, leeks, shallots and celery. The cook can use creativity by experimenting with different combinations to impart strong or subtle tastes—in particular to foods which begin with rather indifferent tastes.

There are two basic kinds of marinades: the "Light Marinade," which is usually used for small game, fish and meat. It may be very simple, consisting only of a little lemon juice and vinegar mixed with a little oil, and some spices and seasonings. Other additions such as red wine, French dressing, fruit juices, spicy sauces and sour cream are also used. The "Ordinary Marinade" may be made cold, but more often it is hot, and is used for the same small game, fish and meat as the Light Marinade. The ingredients are the same, and are prepared in the same way, except that they are heated up, nearly cooked, cooled, then poured cold over the game, fish or meat to be marinated. The reason for cooking is to precipitate more rapidly the essences, aromas and extracts from the ingredients, which in turn produce a stronger effect and taste. This type of marinade should be kept in a cool place.

Marinade for Large Game or Large Pieces of Meat

This should *not* be used for fish. It would normally be applied to venison, wild boar or bear, and may be used either hot or cold depending upon the requirements of the specific recipe. Additional aromatic herbs such as rosemary, sweet basil, salt, mace and sage are added to the original recipe for light marinade. The instructions are the same as well, but the proportions of the ingredients should be increased according to the size of the game or piece of meat. If the meat or game is going to marinate for several days, reduce the amount of vinegar in proportion to the other liquids. If it will marinate only for a period of hours, then the vinegar should be in equal proportion. Keep the meat or game in the marinade in a cool place in a covered dish, or cover it with cheesecloth (muslin).

LIGHT MARINADE

FOR SMALL GAME, FISH, MEATS

1 small lemon, sliced thin	*2 small bay leaves*
1 small raw carrot, sliced thin	*3 whole cloves, slightly bruised*
1 tablespoon (15 ml) vinegar	*1 large sprig parsley*
1 tablespoon (15 ml) olive oil	*12 peppercorns, slightly crushed*
1 sprig thyme	*Salt to taste*

Place all the ingredients in a flat-bottomed dish, preferably earthenware, large enough to take the meat, fish or game in one layer. Add the food to be marinated, stir gently once in a while and turn often. The marinade must completely cover the meat or the air will decompose the exposed parts. Keep in a cool place.

LAMB AND BEEF MARINADE

1¼ cups (10 fl oz; 300 ml) fresh
orange juice
½ cup (4 fl oz; 125 ml) sherry
1 tablespoon (15 ml) lemon juice
2 tablespoons (30 ml) Worcestershire sauce

½ teaspoon (2.5 ml) rosemary (for
lamb), or basil (for beef)
1 garlic clove, crushed

Combine all marinade ingredients and soak meat for 2 to 3 hours, or overnight.

FISH MARINADE

¼ cup (2 fl oz; 50 ml) fresh lemon
juice
1 teaspoon (5 ml) fine-chopped
onion
¼ teaspoon (1.25 ml) crushed
fresh garlic

1 teaspoon (5 ml) Worcestershire
sauce
Salt and fresh-ground black pepper

Heat marinade ingredients to the boiling point, pour over the fish and let
stand for 1 to 2 hours. Broil (grill) fish, brushing from time to time with
marinade.

MARINADE FOR VENISON

ENOUGH FOR $2\frac{1}{2}$ POUNDS (1 KG)

2 cups (16 fl oz; 475 ml) Burgundy
or other red wine

$\frac{1}{4}$ cup (2 fl oz; 50 ml) cider
vinegar

2 juniper berries, cut in half

1 teaspoon (5 ml) salt

$\frac{1}{4}$ teaspoon (1.25 ml) whole black
pepper

1 medium bay leaf

$\frac{1}{2}$ medium onion, sliced thin

$\frac{1}{2}$ small carrot, sliced

2 tablespoons (30 ml) sugar

2 whole cloves

Mix all the ingredients in a shallow dish and place the venison in it for 3
days, turning from time to time.

SAUCES

Sauces should be used to supply additional flavor and richness to foods, to hold certain ingredients together and to improve the appearance of a dish when served.

Flour-based sauces are made from a mixture of fat and flour cooked together, and stirred constantly to prevent burning until the mixture is free of lumps and absolutely smooth. A short cooking time will produce a white *roux,* which is used as the base for a white sauce; a longer period of cooking will produce a brown *roux* to be used as a base for brown sauces.

WHITE SAUCE

If you are making a white sauce, you should use as your fat either butter or margarine, which have a light flavor. The fat melts and mixes with the starch, cooking without discoloration. The liquid is then added *gradually*—stock is best for savory sauces, milk for others—and brought to the boiling point. Stir constantly to prevent lumps, as the starch gelatinizes during cooking and absorbs the liquid. If the starch is not stirred, it is only held in suspension for a certain time and eventually absorbs the liquid unevenly. The longer you cook the sauce, the better the flavor, but in order to prevent evaporation, it is a good idea to cook it in a double boiler or *bain-marie*. Other ingredients such as vegetables may be added either before or after the liquid has come to the boil, but the sauce must not be allowed to boil after egg yolks have been added, otherwise the sauce will curdle. Wine may be added either during cooking or just before serving.

BROWN SAUCE

When making brown sauce, drippings or clarified butter are often used as the fat. Margarine should not be used because when cooked for any length of time it produces a sediment which burns, giving a speckled appearance to the sauce. Color is given to the *roux* by the frying and eventual browning of the flour. The fat and flour are fried together, but while being fried they must be kept in constant motion to prevent uneven browning or the flour burning. In fact, the *roux* should be a café au lait color; if the color becomes darker, it means that it has burned too much and will have a bitter taste. Whereas with white sauce you add the liquid gradually, with brown sauce the starch in the flour has become soluble during the browning process so the liquid, either stock or water, can be added all at once. When the boiling point is reached, the liquid will have been absorbed by the flour, and you should have an even, smooth sauce. If you wish to add vegetables, they can either be fried with the fat and flour, or they may be added *after* the liquid has reached the boil, then simmered in the sauce.

One very important point: Brown sauce needs to be cooked for a long time with constant skimming. Once the cooked starch is unable to hold all the fat, the surplus fat rises to the top during cooking and must be removed, otherwise the sauce will be too greasy. If the sauce is too thin, it means the flour was cooked too long before the stock was added. Wine may be added either during cooking or just prior to serving.

These two sauces serve as the base for an endless variety of others which are formed by the addition of specific ingredients. Following is a list of the main sauces in each category:

White	*Brown*
Aurore	Bigarade
Béarnaise	Bordelaise

White	*Brown*
Béchamel	Chasseur
Bretonne	Demi-glace
Cardinal	Diable
Chivry	Espagnole
Joinville	Financière
Mornay	Genevoise
Nantua	Grand-veneur
Normande	Hussard
Smitane	Italienne
Soubise	Madère
Suprême	Moscovite
Velouté	Périgueux
Vin Blanc	Piquante
	Poivrade
	Portugaise
	Régence
	Robert
	Venaison

EGG FOUNDATION SAUCES

This class of sauce includes custards as well as hollandaise, béarnaise, mayonnaise, mousseline, valois, choron, rémoulade, ravigote and tartare. Here the main thickening ingredient is the egg. Therefore, if you overcook it the result will be a disaster, as any further heat beyond the boiling point results in a curdled sauce. Eggs contain a large percentage of albumen, which sets when heat is applied and holds only a certain proportion of liquid; a hollandaise owes its thickness to the coagulation of the heated egg, which absorbs and holds the melted fat and vinegar. If exposed to either extreme or prolonged heat, the albumen hardens and shrinks, liberating the liquid and resulting in a thin watery sauce with curds of overcooked albumen. If you add a starchy substance such as flour or arrowroot this curdling is not so noticeable, as the starch will absorb the liquid and thus bind the sauce. It is the added cornstarch (cornflour) that allows you to boil a custard, for example, but even so you must stir it constantly in order to keep the albumen in motion and insure a smooth sauce. If a hollandaise sauce curdles, mix 1 egg yolk with a little melted butter. Stir this into the sauce, then add a little hot water.

To make a mayonnaise sauce, olive oil is added slowly while the eggs are being beaten to form an emulsion. If, however, the oil is added too quickly, the film of oil holding the egg in suspension breaks and liberates the egg, resulting, once more, in a curdled sauce. If the mayonnaise does curdle, take a fresh egg and beat it into the curdled mixture, then add 1 cup (8 fl oz; 225 ml) olive oil to compensate for the extra yolk. Alternatively, add a little iced water or a small sliver of ice to a clean, cold mixing bowl and beat while adding the curdled mixture.

BUTTER FOUNDATION SAUCES

The basis of these sauces is creamed butter. During the beating, friction melts the fat slightly and the fat globules are broken up. When the additional ingredients have been added the sauce is allowed to solidify once more before serving. Among this type of sauce is maître d'hôtel butter, brown butter, beurre noir (see page 269), clarified butter (see page 243), butter fermière, Indian butter (see page 268), pimento butter and many others. Hard sauce or brandy butter is a sweet butter-foundation sauce which is used as an accompaniment to plum puddings (Christmas puddings) and other rich desserts. The butter and sugar are creamed together and chopped nuts and brandy are added. In the process of creaming, air is beaten into the butter and sugar, and the mixture becomes light and fluffy.

CHAUD-FROID SAUCES

These sauces, as the name indicates, are made by combining a hot sauce, which has cooled, with a cold one. The result is a sauce used as a coating for cold meat or fish, which prevents it from drying out. The hot sauce has either a white or brown *roux* foundation (such as *béchamel, velouté* or *espagnole* sauce) and the cold sauce is usually an aspic. After the two sauces have been mixed, they are passed through a sieve to incorporate them and achieve the desired thickness. If the resulting sauce is too thin, not enough gelatin has been used, or too much water has been added to the jelly. If the sauce is too thick, the problem is the opposite. The foundation *roux* must itself be smooth, otherwise you will get a lumpy *chaud-froid* sauce.

The amount of *chaud-froid* sauce to make obviously depends upon what you want to coat. This is also true of aspic. The usual proportions are ½ cup (¼ pt; 150 ml) of aspic, 1 teaspoon (5 ml) gelatin and 1¾ cups (14 fl oz; 425 ml) *velouté* or *demi-glace* sauce. When you have made the *demi-glace* or *velouté* sauce, soak the gelatin in the aspic in a small saucepan for 5 minutes. Place the pan over low heat and stir until the aspic looks clear. *Do not allow the aspic to boil*—the gelatin will become rubbery. Warm the white or brown sauce slightly if it has become cool. Then pour in the aspic in a steady stream, constantly stirring the sauce. Allow the sauce to cool to the point where the mixture will coat the back of a wooden spoon. Use at this point to coat whatever meat or fish you are using; 2½ cups (1 pt; 600 ml) of *chaud-froid* sauce will coat 1 medium chicken, 1 small turkey, 1 medium boned turkey, 1 medium boned chicken, 5 to 6 small chicken or turkey pieces, or 6 medium cutlets.

CHAUD-FROID SAUCE (brown)

MAKES 2½ CUPS (1 PINT; 600 ML)

1¾ cups (14 fl oz; 425 ml) Demi-glace Sauce (see page 143)
1 cup (8 fl oz; 225 ml) clear brown stock (see page 247)

1 envelope (1 oz; 25 g) unflavored gelatin
2 tablespoons (30 ml) Madeira, port or sherry

Put the *demi-glace* sauce and half the brown stock in a thick-bottomed saucepan, and boil it down over strong heat, stirring with a wooden spoon. Soften the gelatin in the remaining brown stock and add it, a little at a time, to the sauce. Boil down the mixture until it coats the back of a wooden spoon. Remove it from the heat and stir it until it becomes cold. Add the Madeira, port or sherry. Pour it over the meat *before* it sets. Then place in the refrigerator.

CHAUD-FROID SAUCE (white)

MAKES 2½ CUPS (1 PINT; 600 ML)

1¾ cups (14 fl oz; 425 ml) Velouté
Sauce (see page 245)

½ cup (4 fl oz; 225 ml) Mushroom
Fumet (see page 260)

1 envelope (1 oz; 25 g) unflavored
gelatin

2 cups (16 fl oz; 475 ml) chicken,
veal or fish stock (see pages 243–
244)

¾ cup (6 fl oz; 200 ml) heavy
(double) cream

2 tablespoons (30 ml) Madeira,
port or sherry (optional)

Put the *velouté* sauce and mushroom fumet in a thick-bottomed saucepan and boil down the sauce. Soften the gelatin in the chicken, veal or fish stock, and add it to the *velouté* sauce, a little at a time, stirring constantly. Then add the cream. Boil down the sauce until it coats the back of a wooden spoon. Strain the sauce and whisk it until it becomes quite cool, then add the wine if desired.

Mayonnaise can also be turned into a coating sauce (*mayonnaise collée*); you will need to add more gelatin to the ordinary amount of aspic, otherwise it will not set. Make 1½ cups (12 fl oz; 350 ml) of mayonnaise, add to this ½ cup (¼ pt; 150 ml) of aspic plus 1 teaspoon (5 ml) gelatin. Dissolve the added gelatin in the aspic and whisk it into the mayonnaise; use the *mayonnaise collée* at just the point of setting. This sauce may also be used as a base for vegetable or fish mousse: Stir in the chopped ingredients, pour the mixture into a mold and allow it to set.

To Coat

Always remove the skin of game, poultry or fish before coating, otherwise the finished appearance will be spoiled. Aside from fish, which must be coated on a serving dish because of its delicate consistency, place the food to be coated on a wire rack with a plate underneath it to catch the dripping sauce. To decorate small pieces, pour the sauce in a thin stream onto the center of the food. It will run down all the sides. Stop as soon as the piece of meat or poultry is covered. Then you can decorate it as you wish (see page 243). For whole birds, skewer the bird underneath through the wire rack so that the handle of the skewer comes up under one of the crisscrosses of the rack. Then you can tilt the bird to coat its sides; and it won't move. In order to avoid uneven patches and "start-and-stop" lines, it is important to coat in a continuous stream. Start by pouring down the center, back down one side then down the other side, tilting the bird so that the sauce goes underneath to coat the legs. Decorate.

Decoration

This can be done with aspic, chopped or in cut-out shapes; cucumber skin; tomato skin; hard-boiled egg yolks; olives; canned pimento; tarragon leaves, or anything else you fancy. The pieces can be sliced or cut into any shape.

To Clarify Butter

In a heavy saucepan, melt butter over low heat. Allow the butter to rest for 2 to 3 minutes away from the heat and skim the froth off the top. Pour the clear butter carefully through a cheesecloth (muslin)-lined sieve into a small bowl, leaving the milky solids in the bottom of the saucepan. One cup (8 oz; 224 g) butter yields about ¾ cup (6 fl oz; 175 ml) clarified butter.

To Clarify Stock

For each 3¼ cups of stock (1½ pts; 900 ml), use 1 egg white, slightly beaten, and 1 egg shell, crushed. Skim all fat from the stock, add the beaten whites and crushed shells, and bring the liquid to the boil, stirring constantly. Simmer the stock for 15 minutes, remove it from the heat and allow it to stand for 5 minutes. Skim off the froth and strain the stock through several thicknesses of cheesecloth (muslin) or a linen napkin. The liquid should be a good strong color and absolutely clear.

WHITE OR CHICKEN STOCK FOR SAUCES

MAKES 6 CUPS (2½ PTS; 1.5 L)

1 pound (450 g) veal bones	*2 onions, peeled and quartered*
1 pound (450 g) chicken bones	*2 leeks, cut into chunks*
2 quarts (2.5 l) water	*Bouquet garni (4 sprigs of parsley,*
1 teaspoon (5 ml) salt	*1 stalk of celery with leaves, 1*
1 carrot, cut into chunks	*sprig of thyme, 1 bay leaf)*

Parboil the bones for a few minutes, just long enough for the first scum to rise to the surface. Drain the bones, cover them with the 2 quarts (2.5 l) water and add the rest of the ingredients. Bring the water to the boil, skim off the fat and simmer the stock for 3 hours. Remove the fat and strain the stock. It can be stored in the refrigerator for up to 1 week or frozen indefinitely. The best method for freezing is to pour the stock into ice-cube trays with the dividers in. Then freeze the stock in cubes. One ice-cube tray usually holds 1 cup (8 fl oz; 225 ml) of stock.

FISH STOCK

MAKES 3 CUPS (1½ PTS; 900 ML)
- *1 pound (450 g) bones and trimmings from any whitefish, chopped*
- *1 cup (5 oz; 150 g) sliced onions*
- *6 sprigs parsley*
- *2 tablespoons (30 ml) lemon juice*
- *½ teaspoon (2.5 ml) salt*
- *3½ cups (1½ pts; 900 ml) water*
- *½ cup (4 fl oz; 125 ml) dry white wine*

Put the fish bones and trimmings, onions, parsley, lemon juice and salt in a heavy, well-buttered saucepan and steam, covered, over moderately high heat for 5 minutes. Add the water and white wine and bring the liquid to the boil. Reduce the heat and skim the froth that rises to the surface. Simmer the stock for 25 minutes and strain it, pressing the solids so as to obtain all the liquid. Allow the stock to cool, then chill it. This stock may also be frozen, using same method as for white stock (see page 243). It may also be greatly reduced by boiling to make a fish fumet, with the addition of some white wine, and used in some special white or brown sauces.

VIN BLANC SAUCE FOR FISH

MAKES 2 CUPS (16 FL OZ; 475 ML)
- *½ cup (4 fl oz; 125 ml) dry white wine*
- *½ cup (4 fl oz; 125 ml) Fish Stock (see above)*
- *1 cup (8 fl oz; 225 ml) Velouté Sauce (see page 245), made with fish stock*
- *Salt and pepper to taste*
- *Heavy (double) cream*
- *2 tablespoons (30 ml) butter*
- *A few drops lemon juice*

In a saucepan, combine the white wine and Fish Stock and cook the mixture over high heat until it is reduced by half. Add the Velouté Sauce and salt and pepper to taste. Thin to the desired consistency with cream, add the butter and lemon juice and strain the sauce.

VELOUTÉ SAUCE

MAKES 2 CUPS (16 FL OZ; 475 ML)

1 tablespoon (15 ml) minced onion
3 tablespoons (45 ml) butter
2 tablespoons (30 ml) flour
2 cups (16 fl oz; 475 ml) white or
  chicken stock, or fish stock,
  scalded

¼ teaspoon (1.25 ml) salt
White pepper to taste

In a saucepan, sauté the onion in the butter until it is soft. Add flour, mixing well, and cook the *roux*, stirring, over low heat for 3 minutes. Remove the pan from the heat and pour in the stock, stirring vigorously with a whisk until the mixture is thick and smooth. Add salt and pepper to taste and simmer the sauce for 10 minutes. Strain it through a fine sieve and cover it until needed with a buttered round of waxed paper.

BASIC COURT BOUILLON

MAKES 6 CUPS (2½ PTS; 1.5 L)

½ cup (2½ oz; 75 g) chopped
  onions
½ cup (2½ oz; 75 g) chopped
  carrots
½ cup (2½ oz; 75 g) chopped
  celery
2 tablespoons (30 ml) butter
8 cups (2½ pints; 1.5 l) water

½ cup (4 fl oz; 125 ml) white
  wine vinegar
½ cup (4 fl oz; 125 ml) dry white
  wine
1 tablespoon (15 ml) salt
½ teaspoon (2.5 ml) white pepper
Bouquet garni (1 sprig of parsley,
  1 bay leaf, 1 sprig of thyme)

In a saucepan, cook the onions, carrots and celery in the butter, covered, until the vegetables have softened. Add the rest of the ingredients and bring the liquid to the boil. Reduce the heat, simmer for 25 minutes and allow the mixture to cool. Put the sauce in the refrigerator overnight, then remove solidified fat and freeze or use at once.

BASIC WHITE OR BÉCHAMEL SAUCE

MAKES APPROXIMATELY 2 CUPS (16 FL OZ; 475 ML)

1 tablespoon (15 ml) fine-chopped onion
2 tablespoons (30 ml) butter
2 tablespoons (30 ml) flour
3 cups (1¼ pts; 750 ml) milk, scalded

¼ teaspoon (1.25 ml) salt
3 white peppercorns
A sprig of parsley
A pinch of nutmeg

In a saucepan, sauté the onion in the butter until it is soft. Add the flour, mix well, and cook the *roux* slowly, stirring constantly, until it just starts to turn golden. Add the milk gradually and cook the mixture, stirring vigorously with a wire whisk, until it is thick and smooth. Add the salt, peppercorns, parsley and nutmeg. Cook the sauce slowly, stirring frequently, for about 30 minutes, or until it is reduced by one-third. Strain the *béchamel* through a fine sieve.

MORNAY SAUCE

Particularly good with egg and cheese.

MAKES APPROXIMATELY 3 CUPS (1¼ PTS; 750 ML)

1 tablespoon (15 ml) fine-chopped onion
¼ cup (2 oz; 50 g) butter
2 tablespoons (30 ml) flour
3 cups (1¼ pts; 750 ml) milk, scalded
¼ teaspoon (1.25 ml) salt
3 white peppercorns

A sprig of parsley
A pinch of nutmeg
3 egg yolks, lightly beaten
1 tablespoon (15 ml) light (single) cream, heated
2 tablespoons (30 ml) grated Parmesan cheese

In a saucepan, sauté the onion in half the butter until it is soft. Add the flour, mix well, and cook the *roux* slowly, stirring constantly, until it just starts to turn golden. Gradually add the milk and cook the mixture, stirring vigorously with a wire whisk, until it is thick and smooth. Add salt, peppercorns, parsley and nutmeg. Cook the sauce slowly, stirring frequently, for about 30 minutes, or until it is reduced by one-third. Strain the sauce through a fine sieve. Mix the egg yolks with the hot cream and combine them with the sauce. Cook the sauce, stirring constantly, until it just reaches the boiling point. Add the remaining butter and the grated cheese.

AURORA SAUCE

MAKES APPROXIMATELY 2 CUPS (16 FL OZ; 475 ML)

1½ cups (12 fl oz; 350 ml) Fish Velouté (see page 245)

½ cup (4 fl oz; 125 ml) Tomato Sauce (see page 258) or tomato paste (purée)

¼ cup (2 fl oz; 60 g) butter

In a large saucepan, mix the *velouté* and tomato sauce. Bring to the boiling point. Remove from the heat and whisk in the butter.

The following brown sauces and stocks will keep refrigerated for several days and will last longer if they are brought to the boil every 3 days, cooled and stored in airtight jars. They also freeze well for up to 3 months.

BROWN STOCK

MAKES APPROXIMATELY 8 CUPS (3½ PTS; 1.5 L)

2 pounds (900 g) meaty beef bones, cracked into small pieces

2 pounds (900 g) meaty veal bones, cracked into small pieces

2 onions, cubed

1 carrot, cubed

3 quarts (5 pts; 3 l) water

1½ teaspoons (7.5 ml) salt

A pinch of thyme

Bouquet garni (4 sprigs parsley, 2 stalks celery, 1 small bay leaf)

Preheat oven to 375° F (190° C; Mark 5).

Spread the meat bones, onions and carrot in a flat pan. Brown the bones and vegetables well on all sides in the preheated oven. Transfer them to a large saucepan and add the water, salt, thyme and bouquet garni. Bring the water slowly to the boil, skimming the fat from the surface when necessary. Cook the stock slowly for at least 4 hours or until it is reduced by about half. Strain through a fine sieve or cheesecloth (muslin).

PHEASANT STOCK

MAKES APPROXIMATELY 6 CUPS (2½ PTS; 1.2 L)

Giblets, trimmings and feet of 2 or
   3 small pheasant
A few whole peppercorns
1½ teaspoons (7.5 ml) salt
8 cups (2½ pts; 1.5 l) water
3 small leeks

2 stalks celery
1 medium onion stuck with a few
   cloves
½ bay leaf
A pinch of thyme

Blanch and skin the pheasant feet. Add them, along with the other pheasant parts and the salt and peppercorns, to the water. Bring to the boil and simmer for 1 hour, skimming frequently. Add the leeks, celery, onion, bay leaf and thyme and continue to simmer the stock for 1 hour or longer. Strain through a fine sieve and cool.

GAME STOCK

MAKES APPROXIMATELY 8 TO 10 CUPS (3½ TO 4 PTS; 1.5 TO 2.4 L)

Bones and any remaining meat
   from roast venison, pheasant,
   partridge or rabbit
1¼ cups (8 oz; 225 g) coarse-
   chopped onions
1 cup (5 oz; 150 g) coarse-chopped
   celery
1 cup (5 oz; 150 g) coarse-chopped
   carrots

¼ pound (5 oz; 150 g) salt pork,
   blanched and cut into pieces
1 teaspoon (5 ml) salt
A few grinds of black pepper
Bouquet garni (6 sprigs parsley, 1
   bay leaf, 1 clove, ½ teaspoon
   [2.5 ml] juniper berries)
12 cups (4 pts; 2.4 l) water

Put all the ingredients into a large soup kettle. Bring the stock to the boil over high heat. Lower the heat, simmer the stock for 2½ hours, skimming the surface every 15 minutes, and strain it.

POIVRADE (PEPPER) SAUCE

Suitable for all game.

MAKES APPROXIMATELY 2½ CUPS (1 PT; 600 ML)

1 cup (5 oz; 150 g) chopped onion
1 cup (5 oz; 150 g) chopped carrots
¼ cup (2 oz; 50 g) butter
2 tablespoons (30 ml) vegetable oil
1 pound (450 g) stewing beef, cubed, or
1 pound (450 g) poultry giblets
3 tablespoons (45 ml) flour

1½ cups (12 fl oz; 360 ml) hot brown stock (see page 247)
1 tablespoon (15 ml) tomato paste (purée)
Bouquet garni (4 sprigs parsley, ½ bay leaf, ¼ teaspoon thyme, 2 bruised juniper berries)
4 peppercorns, crushed

In a deep, heavy saucepan, sauté the onion and carrots in the butter and oil until they are lightly browned. Remove the vegetables with a slotted spoon and reserve them. In the fat in the pan, brown the stewing beef or giblets. Remove the meat cubes or giblets with a slotted spoon and reserve them. Add the flour to the fat remaining in the pan and cook the *roux* over low heat, stirring until it is lightly browned. Add the hot brown stock and cook the sauce, stirring, for approximately 5 minutes or until it is thickened. Return the vegetables and meat or giblets to the saucepan and add the tomato paste (purée) and bouquet garni. Simmer the sauce, covered, skimming it occasionally, for 3 to 4 hours. Add the peppercorns, cook the sauce for 10 minutes more, strain and discard the solids.

SAUCE ESPAGNOLE OR BROWN SAUCE

This is used as a base for various sauces, so you should always try to keep a quantity in the freezer.

MAKES APPROXIMATELY 4 CUPS (1½ PTS; 900 ML)

½ cup (4 oz; 125 g) beef, veal or
  pork drippings
2 medium-sized onions, chopped
  coarse
1 small carrot, chopped coarse
½ cup (2 oz; 60 g) flour
9 cups (3 pts; 1.8 l) hot brown
  stock (see page 247)

3 sprigs parsley
1 stalk celery
1 small bay leaf
1 clove garlic, crushed
A pinch of thyme
5 tablespoons (75 ml) tomato sauce
  (see page 258) or tomato paste
  (purée)

Melt the drippings in a heavy saucepan. Add the onions and carrot and cook
until the onions start to turn golden, shaking the pan to insure even cooking. Add the flour and cook the mixture, stirring, until the flour, carrot and
onions are a rich brown. Add 3 cups (1¼ pts; 750 ml) hot brown stock, the
parsley, celery, bay leaf, garlic and thyme, and cook the mixture, stirring
frequently, until it thickens. Add 3 more cups (1¼ pts; 750 ml) stock and
simmer the sauce slowly, stirring occasionally, for 1 to 1½ hours, or until it
is reduced to about 3 cups (1¼ pts; 750 ml). As it cooks, skim off the fat
that rises to the surface. Add the tomato sauce or paste (purée), cook for a
few minutes more and strain through a fine sieve. Add 3 more cups (1¼
pts; 750 ml) stock and continue to cook the sauce slowly for about 1 hour,
skimming the surface from time to time, until it is reduced to about 4 cups
(1½ pts; 900 ml). Strain the sauce and let it cool.

HOLLANDAISE SAUCE

Serve with fish, vegetables and eggs.

MAKES APPROXIMATELY 2 CUPS (16 FL OZ; 475 ML)

1 cup (8 oz; 225 g) butter
2 tablespoons (30 ml) white wine
  vinegar
2 tablespoons (30 ml) water
¼ teaspoon (1.25 ml) salt
Fresh-ground white pepper

1 tablespoon (15 ml) cold water
3 egg yolks
Lemon juice to taste
Salt to taste
Cayenne to taste

Have the butter, divided into 12 parts, at room temperature. In a small,
heavy saucepan combine the white wine vinegar and the water with the

salt and a few grinds of pepper and cook over high heat until reduced to 1 tablespoon (15 ml). Remove the pan from the heat and add 1 tablespoon (15 ml) cold water. Add the egg yolks and stir briskly with a wire whisk until thick and creamy. Set the pan over low heat and beat in the butter, one part at a time, lifting the pan occasionally to cool the mixture. Make sure that each part of the butter is completely melted before adding more. Continue to beat the sauce until it is thick and firm. Add lemon juice, salt and cayenne to taste.

Keep the sauce warm over a shallow pan of warm water until needed. It may be refrigerated for a few days and reheated over hot water, beating constantly. Add a few teaspoons cream while reheating if the sauce is too thick.

Note: If a thicker sauce is desired, use 4 egg yolks, or thin it by adding 1 to 2 tablespoons (15 to 30 ml) cream or hot water.

MOUSSELINE SAUCE

MAKES 1¼ CUPS (10 FL OZ; 300 ML)
Into 1 cup (8 fl oz; 225 ml) Hollandaise Sauce (see page 250), fold 2 to 4 tablespoons (30 to 60 ml) whipped cream. Serve at once with vegetables, eggs or poached fish. Or spread over a fish or asparagus dish and put under a broiler (grill) to brown.

MALTESE SAUCE

MAKES 1¼ CUPS (10 FL OZ; 300 ML)
To 1 cup (8 fl oz; 225 ml) Hollandaise Sauce (see page 250), add 2 to 3 tablespoons (30 to 45 ml) orange juice and fine-grated orange zest to taste. Use a blood orange or add 1 to 2 drops red food coloring. Serve with asparagus or broccoli.

BÉARNAISE SAUCE

Delicious with steak or eggs.

MAKES APPROXIMATELY 2 CUPS (16 FL OZ; 475 ML)

1 cup (8 fl oz; 225 g) butter

3 sprigs tarragon, chopped fine

2 teaspoons (10 ml) fine-chopped chervil

2 shallots, chopped fine

4 crushed peppercorns

4 tablespoons (60 ml) tarragon vinegar

4 tablespoons (60 ml) white wine

1 tablespoon (15 ml) cold water

3 egg yolks

Salt to taste

Cayenne to taste

1 teaspoon (5 ml) fine-chopped tarragon

1 teaspoon (5 ml) fine-chopped chervil

Have the butter, divided into 12 parts, at room temperature. In a small, heavy saucepan combine the tarragon, chervil and shallots, the peppercorns, vinegar and white wine. Cook the mixture over high heat until all but 1 tablespoon (15 ml) of the liquid has evaporated. Add the cold water and strain, if desired. Add the egg yolks and stir the mixture briskly with a wire whisk until it is thick and creamy. Set the pan over low heat and beat in the butter, one part at a time, lifting the pan occasionally to cool the mixture. Make sure that each part of the butter is completely melted before adding more. Continue to beat the sauce until it is thick and firm. Season it with salt and cayenne to taste and add the remaining tarragon and chervil.

CHORON SAUCE

Serve with broiled (grilled) meats and fish.

MAKES 1¼ CUPS (16 FL OZ; 475 ML)

To 1 cup (8 fl oz; 225 ml) Béarnaise Sauce (see above), add 4 tablespoons (60 ml) thick tomato paste (purée).

MAYONNAISE

MAKES APPROXIMATELY 2 CUPS (16 FL OZ; 475 ML)

4 egg yolks
2 teaspoons (10 ml) warm water
1 teaspoon (5 ml) Dijon mustard
Juice of 1 lemon

1 teaspoon (5 ml) salt
A pinch of pepper
1 teaspoon (5 ml) vinegar
1½ cups (12 fl oz; 350 ml) olive oil

Combine all the ingredients except the oil. Add the oil, a few drops at a time, beating constantly with a whisk until the sauce begins to thicken. Then continue adding oil in a thin stream, beating steadily, until all is absorbed.

MAYONNAISE VERTE

Serve with cold fish.

MAKES 2¼ CUPS (18 FL OZ; 550 ML)

To 2 cups (16 fl oz; 475 ml) stiff mayonnaise (see above) add 2 tablespoons (30 ml) fine-chopped parsley, 1 tablespoon (15 ml) *each* chopped chives and tarragon, and 1 teaspoon (5 ml) *each* of chopped dill and chervil. Mix the sauce well, and let it stand for at least 2 hours before serving.

RÉMOULADE SAUCE

Use for fish, shellfish, and egg salads, for beef fondue.

MAKES 2 CUPS (16 FL OZ; 475 ML)

To 2 cups (16 fl oz; 475 ml) mayonnaise, add ½ cup (2½ oz; 65 g) sour pickle and 2 tablespoons (30 ml) capers, both well-drained and chopped fine; 3 hard-boiled eggs, chopped fine, and 1 tablespoon (15 ml) each of Dijon mustard and mixed chopped parsley, tarragon and chervil.

SAUCE GRIBICHE

Serve with hot fish, cold meats and cold vegetables.

MAKES 2½ CUPS (1 PT; 600 ML)

3 hard-boiled eggs
½ teaspoon (2.5 ml) salt
1 teaspoon (5 ml) dry English
  mustard
Fresh-ground pepper
1½ cups (12 fl oz; 350 ml) olive oil
½ cup (4 fl oz; 125 ml) vinegar

4 tablespoons (60 ml) fine-chopped
  sour pickles or gherkins
1 tablespoon (15 ml) capers
1 tablespoon (15 ml) chopped
  parsley, chervil, tarragon and
  chives, mixed

Mash the egg yolks in a bowl and add the salt, mustard and pepper. Add the olive oil and vinegar alternately, little by little, beating vigorously after each addition and adding the vinegar whenever the mixture begins to get too thick. Chop the hard-boiled egg whites and add them with the pickles, capers and herbs to the sauce. Mix well.

GREEN PEPPERCORN MAYONNAISE

For beef fondue or cold meats.

MAKES 1 CUP (8 FL OZ; 225 ML)

2 tablespoons (30 ml) freeze-dried
  green peppercorns
1 tablespoon (15 ml) coriander seed
2 tablespoons (30 ml) roasted
  cumin seed

1 cup (8 fl oz; 225 ml) mayonnaise
  (see page 253)
3 tablespoons (45 ml) green
  peppercorn mustard
Salt and fresh-ground black pepper

Put the green peppercorns, coriander seed and roasted cumin seed in a mortar and pestle and crush them together. In a small mixing bowl mix the mayonnaise and mustard, then add the crushed spices and salt and pepper to taste. Serve.

AIOLI SAUCE

MAKES I CUP (8 FL OZ; 225 ML)

*1 thick slice of white bread, crusts
    removed*
3 tablespoons (45 ml) milk
4 to 6 cloves garlic
¼ teaspoon (1.25 ml) salt

2 egg yolks
1 cup (8 fl oz; 225 ml) olive oil
Juice of 1 lemon
Salt and fresh-ground black pepper

Crumble the bread into a bowl, stir in the milk and let the bread soak for 10 minutes, then squeeze out the milk. Crush the garlic cloves thoroughly in a mortar and pound in the salt. In a bowl, blend the garlic and salt with the egg yolks. Add a few drops of the olive oil, beating vigorously with a whisk or an electric mixer at low speed. Continue adding oil, a little at a time, until about 2 tablespoons (30 ml) have been added. Then add the rest of the oil in a thin, steady stream, beating constantly. If the mixture seems too thick, beat in ½ tablespoon (2.5 ml) or more of water. Finish the sauce with the lemon juice and season it with salt and fresh-ground black pepper to taste. If the sauce separates, rebind the emulsion by beating it again while adding 1 egg yolk.

BEURRE BLANC

For steamed and poached fish.

SERVES 6 TO 8

*2 tablespoons (30 ml) shallots,
    peeled and chopped fine*
*10 tablespoons (5 fl oz; 150 ml)
    white wine*

1 pound (450 g) butter, diced
*2 teaspoons (10 ml) white wine
    vinegar*
Salt and fresh-ground black pepper

In a heavy-based saucepan combine the shallots and white wine over medium heat. Bring to a simmer, and cook for approximately 30 minutes or until the liquid is reduced to 1 tablespoon (15 ml). Transfer this liquid to a *bain-marie* or the top of a double boiler, over low heat. The water in the lower saucepan should remain hot. Gradually whisk in the butter, adding a few pieces at a time, until all is absorbed and the mixture is white and slightly foamy. Add the vinegar, salt and pepper to taste and serve immediately.

GOOSEBERRY SAUCE

Serve with duck, goose and fish.

MAKES APPROXIMATELY 1½ CUPS (12 FL OZ; 350 ML)

1 pound (450 g) green gooseberries
1 tablespoon (15 ml) vinegar
A pinch of salt
1 ounce (15 g) butter
½ cup (4 fl oz; 125 ml) heavy
   (double) cream
Pepper
Ground ginger

Boil the gooseberries in enough water and vinegar to cover; add salt. When tender, put the mixture through a sieve, heat up the pulp, add the butter and cream with pepper and ginger to taste. Can be frozen.

BREAD SAUCE

Serve with poultry and game.

MAKES APPROXIMATELY 2 CUPS (16 FL OZ; 475 ML)

2 onions
4 cloves
1 blade mace
1 sprig parsley
1¼ cups (10 fl oz; 300 ml) milk
½ cup (4 fl oz; 125 ml) heavy
   (double) cream
¼ cup (2 oz; 50 g) butter
1 cup (3 oz; 75 g) fine fresh bread
   crumbs
Pepper and salt

Stick each onion with 2 cloves. In a little water, boil down the onions with the mace and parsley. Strain, and then chop the onions fine. Return them to the saucepan and add the milk, cream and butter. Stir well and when at boiling point, put in the bread crumbs to thicken well. Add pepper and salt to taste and serve very hot. Do not allow the sauce to stand too long before serving.

HORSERADISH CREAM

MAKES APPROXIMATELY I CUP (8 FL OZ; 225 ML)

3 tablespoons (45 ml) grated horseradish
1½ teaspoons (7.5 ml) French mustard
3 tablespoons (45 ml) light (single) cream or milk

A pinch of salt
3 teaspoons (15 ml) superfine granulated (castor) sugar
3 to 6 tablespoons (45 to 90 ml) white wine vinegar

Mix all ingredients well, bring to the boil and cool.

SUSSEX SAUCE

Adapted from a nineteenth-century recipe—serve with sea and fresh-water fish.

MAKES APPROXIMATELY 2 CUPS (16 FL OZ; 475 ML)

3 tablespoons (45 ml) water
2 tablespoons (30 ml) wine vinegar
1 large onion, sliced
5 cloves
2 blades mace or 2 tablespoons (30 ml) ground mace

4 eggs
1 teaspoon (5 ml) anchovy paste (essence)
1¼ cups (10 fl oz; 300 ml) heavy (double) cream
1 teaspoon (5 ml) French mustard

In a saucepan, boil the water, vinegar, onion, cloves and mace rapidly for 1 minute. Beat the eggs and anchovy paste into the cream, and add to the mixture. Place over low heat, stirring constantly, until it thickens, but do not allow it to boil. Add the mustard, mix thoroughly and serve.

TOMATO SAUCE

MAKES 1 CUP (8 FL OZ; 225 ML)

4 tablespoons (60 ml) olive oil   *¼ teaspoon (1.25 ml) thyme*
1 medium onion, chopped fine   *1 clove*
2 shallots, chopped fine   *Salt and fresh-ground pepper*
1 clove garlic, chopped fine   *1 tablespoon (15 ml) sugar*
6 tomatoes, chopped coarse   *Ground cumin seed*
1 bay leaf

In a heavy saucepan, heat the olive oil and add the onion, shallots and garlic. Cover the pan and cook over very low heat for about 15 minutes, or until they are soft but not browned. Add the tomatoes, bay leaf, thyme, clove, salt and pepper to taste, and simmer the sauce over low heat for about 20 minutes. Put the sauce through a fine sieve and add the sugar and cumin seed to taste. Heat the sauce slowly.

STANDARD SAUCES AND THEIR INGREDIENTS

Admiral, à l'. A butter-based sauce for boiled fish.

Aïoli. A heavily garlicked Mediterranean sauce made with a mayonnaise base. Used with *crudités,* fish and some meats. (See page 255.)

Albert. Horseradish sauce with cream, butter, bread crumbs, mustard and vinegar. Used with beef.

Allemande. Velouté Sauce with egg. (See page 289.)

Anchovy. Usually a basic sauce or *roux,* flavored with wine, to which fresh or salted anchovies are added.

Aurora. Béchamel Sauce to which tomato has been added. (See page 247.)

Bâtarde. Béchamel Sauce with added eggs.

Bavaroise. Wine vinegar, butter and horseradish, seasoned, flavored with nutmeg. Served with fish and shellfish.

Béarnaise. French herbs, shallots, white wine and egg yolks. (See page 252.)

Béchamel. Basic white sauce. (See page 246.)

Bercy. Velouté Sauce (see page 245) flavored with fish *fumet,* chopped shallots, parsley, white wine and butter.

Beurre blanc. Butter sauce, flavored with shallots and white wine.

Bigarade. Reduced duck gravy flavored with orange and lemon juice, julienne of orange rind, and thickened with arrowroot or duck's liver.

Bolognese. An Italian sauce made with ground beef and mixed, diced mushrooms and tomatoes, flavored with herbs and white wine. Used for pasta.

Bordelaise. Red wine sauce, mixed with Demi-glace (see page 143) and flavored with shallots, parsley, mignonette pepper and herbs. Serve with broiled (grilled) meat.

Bourguignonne. Chopped shallots, parsley, bay leaves and mushroom trimmings cooked in red wine, then strained and thickened with *beurre manié* (see page 36). Serve with meat.

Bread Sauce. An onion stuck with cloves and simmered in milk, then parsley, lemon, bread crumbs and seasoning are added. (See page 256.)

Brown Butter Sauce. The butter is cooked until it bubbles, then various herbs, capers and lemon juice are added. Serve with fish, cabbage, broccoli, asparagus and broiled (grilled) meat. (See page 269.)

Chantilly. Sauce Suprême (Velouté Sauce [see page 245] mixed with cream) to which thick cream is added. Serve with eggs, poultry, sweetbreads and brains.

Chasseur. A white wine sauce with ground mushrooms, chopped shallots, butter, chopped parsley and a meat glaze (see page 143). Serve with meat, chicken, rabbit and game.

Chaud-froid (brown). Demi-glace Sauce (see below) with aspic or gelatin, flavored with truffles and Madeira. Use to coat cold meats. (See page 241.)

Chaud-froid (white). Velouté Sauce set with aspic or gelatin. Serve with eggs, white meat and fish. (See page 242.)

Chivry Sauce. Velouté Sauce (see page 245) with white wine and cream added and flavored with chopped mixed herbs, spinach and butter. Serve with eggs and poultry.

Choron. Béarnaise Sauce with added tomato sauce or paste (purée). (See page 252.)

Demi-glace. A basic Espagnole Sauce reduced with meat stock until one-tenth its original volume and finished off with white wine. (See page 143.)

Diable. Meat stock and tomato paste (purée) flavored with chopped shallots, mignonette pepper, white wine and cayenne. Serve with meat.

Diplomat. Sauce Normande (see page 261) with lobster and brandy. Serve with fish dishes and garnish with diced lobster meat and chopped truffles.

Espagnole. Basic brown sauce. (See page 249.)

Financière. Madeira Sauce flavored with truffles and chicken livers.

Génoise. Fish stock, red wine and mixed diced vegetables, flavored with butter, pepper and herbs, then strained and finished with butter and anchovy essences.

Gooseberry. Purée of gooseberries with added cream. (See page 256.)

Grand Veneur. Poivrade Sauce (see page 249) with venison gravy, mixed with red currant jelly and cream. Serve with game.

Green peppercorn mayonnaise. Mayonnaise with green peppercorn mustard, crushed coriander seeds and green peppercorns. (See page 254.)

Gribiche. Chopped gherkins and capers mixed into a sauce made from pounded hard-boiled egg yolks, seasoning, oil and vinegar, and garnished with strips of hard-boiled egg white. Serve with cold fish and shellfish. (See page 254.)

Hollandaise. A butter sauce made with egg yolks, fresh white pepper, lemon juice and a lot of butter. Serve with fish, eggs and vegetables. (See page 250.)

Horseradish Cream. Grated horseradish, French mustard and cream. (See page 257.)

Joinville. Sauce Normande with fine chopped shrimp, crayfish and truffles added. Serve with shellfish.

Lyonnaise. Onions cooked in butter, white wine and vinegar, mixed with a Demi-glace and strained. Serve with braised meats, ragoûts and leftovers.

Madeira. A concentrated Sauce Espagnole (see page 249) to which stock, Madeira, gravy and butter are added. Serve with braised or roast meat.

Maltese. Hollandaise Sauce with added orange juice and zest. (See page 250.)

Marinière. Bercy Sauce to which mussel liquor, egg yolks, butter and mignonette pepper are added. Serve with fish dishes.

Matelote. Fish stock, red wine, mushrooms and demi-glace mixed and sieved. Serve with fish.

Mayonnaise. A cold sauce made with egg yolks, olive oil, wine vinegar and seasoning. Serve with cold chicken, fish, eggs and salad. (See page 253.)

Mayonnaise Verte. Mayonnaise with added herbs. (See page 253.)

Mint. Chopped mint, lightly sweetened and seasoned, with a touch of vinegar. Serve with lamb.

Mornay. Béchamel Sauce mixed with butter and grated Parmesan cheese, or Gruyère. (See page 246.)

Mousseline. Hollandaise Sauce with added whipped cream. Serve with fish, asparagus, broccoli or cauliflower. (See page 251.)

Moutarde. Hollandaise Sauce heavily flavored with mustard.

Mushroom fumet. Liquid in which mushrooms have been cooked, boiled down to a quarter of its original volume.

Nantua. Fish velouté with white wine and Cognac added, with ground cray-fish, butter, tomatoes and seasoning mixed in. Serve with shellfish.

Noisette. Hollandaise Sauce with browned butter added, or hazelnut browned butter on its own.

Normande. Velouté Sauce, fish fumet (see page 244), mushroom stock, mussel or oyster liquid, egg yolks and cream. If you add truffles soaked in Madeira, or poached oysters, it is then called *Laquipière.* There are many variations of this sauce.

Parsley. Butter sauce with chopped parsley. Serve with fish.

Périgueux. Demi-glace blended with Madeira and diced truffles.

Piquante. Brown Sauce flavored with white wine, shallots and capers, then sieved and garnished with gherkins and chopped herbs and seasoned with fresh-ground black pepper.

Poivrade. Brown stock with added tomato paste and black peppercorns. (See page 249.)

Poulette. Béchamel Sauce with shallots, mushrooms, egg yolks and cream.

Provençale. Usually tomatoes, veal stock, shallots, garlic, olive oil and seasoning. Serve with eggs, fish, chicken and vegetables.

Ravigote. The cold sauce is a mayonnaise with capers and hard-boiled eggs, anchovy paste, onions, shallots and herbs. Serve with eggs, fish and shellfish. The hot sauce is a Velouté Sauce, white wine, wine vinegar, butter, chopped chives, chervil and tarragon. Serve with eggs, fish, variety meats (offal) and lamb.

Reform. Demi-glace and Poivrade sauces in equal amounts, garnished with julienne of egg whites, gherkins, mushrooms, truffle and tongue.

Rémoulade. Mayonnaise with mustard, garnished with capers, parsley, gherkins or sour pickles, chervil and tarragon, and a touch of anchovy paste (essence) if desired. Serve with fried or broiled (grilled) fish, shellfish and egg salads. (See page 253.)

Robert. Brown Sauce (see page 249) to which are added onions cooked in white wine and seasoned with mustard and pepper. Serve with meats.

Soubise. Béchamel Sauce (see page 246) mixed with an onion purée and grated fresh nutmeg. Serve with roast pork, eggs, chicken or lamb.

Suprême. A Velouté mixed with cream.

Sussex. An egg, mustard and cream sauce with added seasonings. (See page 257.)

Tartare. Mayonnaise made with hard-boiled egg yolks and garnished with capers, chives and onions. Sometimes gherkins are also added. Serve with fish, cold chicken and other cold meats.

Tomato Sauce. (See page 258.)

Valois. Hollandaise Sauce (see page 250) to which is added a tiny bit of beef extract or beef stock. Serve with eggs and broiled (grilled) chicken.

Velouté. A flour-based white sauce with added stock. (See page 245.)

Victoria. Lobster Sauce with diced mushrooms and butter. Serve over cheese or fish soufflés.

Vin Blanc. Fish Velouté, thinned with fish stock, thickened with egg yolks and finished with butter. (See page 245.)

VEGETABLES

Vegetables are divided into five groups:

Tubers, Roots and Bulbs: Beets, carrots, celery root or celeriac, fennel, parsnips, radishes, rutabagas (swedes), salsify or oyster plant, turnips, Jerusalem and Japanese artichokes, potatoes, onions.

Stalks and Stems: Asparagus, cardoons, celery.

Leaves: Brussels sprouts, cabbage (red and green), Scotch kale, kohlrabi, chicory, broccoli, cauliflower, spinach, sorrel, spring greens, leeks, lettuce, endive, watercress.

Pod Vegetables: All sorts of beans, peas, lentils, chilies or sweet peppers, okra (ladies' fingers).

Fungi: Mushrooms and truffles.

In addition, some foods that we generally think of as vegetables are really

Fruits: Eggplants (aubergines), chestnuts, cucumbers, squash (marrows), pumpkin, tomatoes.

COOKING VEGETABLES

There are some basic rules to remember about cooking vegetables:

1. Green beans should always be plunged into boiling salted water and cooked with the *lid off.*
2. Root vegetables should be put into cold water and boiled with the lid on. Whenever possible, peel vegetables after they have been cooked. This preserves both the food value and the taste.
3. Sauces for vegetables should include the vegetable "cuisson," the water in which the vegetable was cooked, instead of plain water.
4. Use olive or vegetable oil for frying, and butter for sauces.
5. Always use *freshly ground pepper,* whether black or white, to give flavor to vegetables (or their sauces). You might combine black, white and mignonette pepper with a dash of cayenne to taste, and grind it all together in a peppermill.

Roots and Tubers

The chief purpose of roots and tubers is to supply nourishment to the plant. They contain a large percentage of water and store nourishment in the form of starch and many mineral salts. They contain practically no protein or fat. Their fibers are formed of a woody substance known as cellulose, which must be softened before the digestible substance in the vegetable can be extracted. The older the vegetable, the coarser the cellulose becomes. Thus winter carrots and turnips take much longer to cook than the younger spring roots.

Potatoes are different—the cell walls in the new potato are ripe, but they still have a very hard, close texture. Rapid boiling is required to soften these walls. The heat then penetrates to the starch inside. In the old potato, the cell walls have stretched to accommodate the increasing size of the grains of starch. If old potatoes are boiled too rapidly, the cellulose breaks down, the starch bursts and the potato falls to pieces.

Green Vegetables

Except for peas, green vegetables contain almost no starch and no fat. They do contain many mineral salts which give them great nutritional value. In addition, they supply the body with undigestible waste matter known as "roughage," which is formed by the bulk of the vegetable. Green vegetables contain much water and also absorb water in cooking; this, together with the cellulose not digested by the body, adds to the general bulk and helps the food along the alimentary canal, so preventing constipation. Green vegetables are generally rich in vitamins, but the vitamin C can be destroyed unless they are cooked carefully and quickly.

Vegetables that grow near to the ground require special washing. The best method is to place them in a colander and allow cold water to run through them; this removes any clinging earth. Then soak them in a bowl of cold water with lemon juice or vinegar added. The acid removes any insects, carrying them to the bottom of the bowl. Lift the vegetables out, leaving the sediment behind.

When peeling green vegetables, try to remove as few of the outside layers as possible as they contain the most flavor and nutrition. When storing, exclude light and air to retard deterioration. Wrap in foil or plastic wrap and refrigerate.

Methods of Cooking

Boiling: Prolonged boiling is suitable for tubers and root vegetables. The high percentage of cellulose contained in these vegetables is softened by long and rapid boiling. Green vegetables, however, must be either blanched quickly in rapidly boiling, salted water, or—as in the case of spinach—cooked in their own juices. If subjected to prolonged boiling, the mineral salts in green vegetables will be dissolved and the vegetable become watery. When green vegetables are cooked in water, small amounts of volatile acids are produced, and unless these are removed by evaporation or neutralized by alkali, the cooked vegetable has a brownish or faded color. However, if you add an alkali, such as baking soda, to preserve the color it immediately destroys the vitamin C, as does high temperature. Vitamin A can withstand high temperature if no oxygen is present and, therefore, pressure cooking is feasible. Vitamin B will withstand any ordinary cooking temperature for a considerable period.

The amount of water that green vegetables contain (from 70 to 90%) should be sufficient for them to cook in, but owing to the large percentage of cellulose (or fiber) that they also contain, it is necessary to add a small quantity of any liquid to start the cooking. This, which can be milk, stock or water, softens the cellulose and assists in the extraction of the natural liquids. Vegetables are good fat absorbers, and either butter or margarine can also be added at the beginning of the cooking time to enhance flavor. A piece of butter the size of a walnut is sufficient for 4 leeks.

Green vegetables should be cooked in one layer, not piled up. Choose a thick saucepan, casserole or Pyrex dish. A thick or earthenware utensil retains a more regular and even heat than a thin utensil like enamel. As there is only a small quantity of liquid added, it is absolutely essential to prevent evaporation, thus the possible burning of the vegetables. As casserole and saucepan lids are rarely tight-fitting, a good trick is to put some cold water in a soup plate, place this on top of the casserole or saucepan, and cover the plate with the lid. As the steam from the cooking rises, it touches the plate containing the cold water, which causes it to condense and fall back as moisture onto the vegetables.

Vegetables should be sliced before cooking to allow the heat to penetrate easily. This is particularly essential with old vegetables whose cellulose is coarse. Add butter if you wish, and sufficient liquid to start the cooking. To 3 to 4 carrots, add 2 tablespoons water. Once the heat penetrates through the vegetables, their own liquid will come out and increase the quantity for cooking. Once the liquid has come to a boil, the cooking should be gradual, over low heat, and the pan should be shaken from time to time to prevent the vegetables from sticking. When they are tender, remove the lid and allow the superfluous liquid to evaporate before serving.

Blanching: Bring the water to a fast boil over maximum heat. Blanch the vegetable in this, then lower the heat and cook slowly for the necessary length of time. I always undercook so that they retain a certain crunchiness. Also, after blanching, the vegetables may be roasted or sautéed and still keep their color and flavor. You can blanch a vegetable in the morning and finish the cooking later—sautéing, roasting, glazing or puréeing as desired. Root vegetables and potatoes may also be boiled or parboiled, then sautéed in hot butter until golden and tossed with fresh herbs and freshly ground black pepper.

After blanching, always refresh vegetables immediately by running them quickly under cold water, or plunging them straight into deep cold water for 2 to 3 minutes, or long enough to cool them. This abruptly halts their cooking; thus they don't lose any of their color, flavor, texture or nutrients as they can do if left to cool by themselves.

Steaming: Steamed vegetables do not come into contact with the water. Thus they retain a crunchier texture and do not suffer any loss of flavor or vitamins. They are cooked by the vapor rising from the boiling water beneath them. To obtain the maximum amount of steam, water must be kept at boiling point. A steamer—adaptable enough to fit more than one size pan—is the best and cheapest utensil. The lid must fit tightly and the steamer must fit the pan well, otherwise there won't be enough trapped steam to cook the food. Half again as much time should be allowed to cook vegetables by steam as by boiling, e.g., boiling artichokes—60 minutes; steaming—1½ hours.

Roasting: Most vegetables require moist heat to soften the cellulose; therefore, roasting is usually not satisfactory. However, potatoes and Jerusalem artichokes with their high percentage of water, can be roasted satisfactorily.

Broiled (Grilled): The only vegetables that can be broiled (grilled) are tomatoes, which contain a very small percentage of cellulose.

Pressure-Cooking times at high temperature per pound (450 g) weight:

Artichoke, globe	4–10 minutes
Artichoke, Jerusalem	4– 5 minutes
Asparagus	1– 3 minutes
Beans, broad	2– 4 minutes
Beans, runner	2– 5 minutes
Beans, string (French)	1– 2 minutes
Beans, soy (dried)	30 minutes
Beans, soy (fresh)	1– 2 minutes
Beet (Beetroot)	10–15 minutes
Broccoli	2– 4 minutes
Brussels sprouts	2– 4 minutes
Cabbage	2– 4 minutes
Carrots	2– 4 minutes
Cauliflower	4 minutes
Celeriac	3– 4 minutes
Celery	3– 4 minutes
Chicory	4– 6 minutes
Eggplant (aubergine)	1– 2 minutes
Leeks	4– 6 minutes
Mushrooms	3– 4 minutes
Pulse, dried	20–30 minutes
Spinach	1 minute
Spring greens	4 minutes
Squash (marrow)	4 minutes
Sweet corn	1– 5 minutes
Tomatoes	1 minute
Turnips	4– 5 minutes
Zucchini (courgette)	1– 4 minutes
Rice:	
Long grain	5 minutes
Short grain	4 minutes

BUTTERS AND SAUCES

The following butters are delicious used as flavorings for vegetables. They give added taste and color when used on their own or as an addition to other sauces. The most usable and deliciously special of all is *Ravigote Butter*. But the herbs used in it *must be fresh* in order to obtain the true flavor.

3 sprigs each of marjoram, tarragon,   parsley, oregano and chives
1 tablespoon (15 ml) chopped   shallots

8 tablespoons (125 ml) butter, at   room temperature

Blanch the herbs and shallots in boiling water for 5 minutes, then drain, pound in a mortar and rub through a sieve; cream the butter and blanched herbs and shallots thoroughly, by hand or in a food processor. When thoroughly mixed, shape the batter into a roll or square, wrap it in aluminum foil and place in the refrigerator. Then remove as needed, make into little walnut-sized pats, and top the finished vegetable.

CAPER BUTTER

Use the above herbs, but add 1 tablespoon (15 ml) capers pounded in a mortar and pestle with 1 or 2 spinach leaves or a sprig of watercress for color. This is a sharp-flavored butter which gives an added taste to string beans and cauliflower.

MINT BUTTER

Pound 6 sprigs of mint in a mortar and pestle and process with the butter, as above. Bright green in color, this is delicious with peas and lima beans.

INDIAN BUTTER

Use 1 pinch of curry powder per ¼ pound (125 g) butter. The color will be brown—a good addition to cauliflower or broccoli topped with toasted bread crumbs.

PIMENTO BUTTER

Parboil 1 sweet red bell pepper, rub through a sieve, and cream with ¼ pound (125 g) butter by hand or in a food processor.

CHERVIL BUTTER

Pale green in color and delicate in flavor. Make it as you would Ravigote
butter. It is particularly good on salsify.

BLACK BUTTER SAUCE (BEURRE NOIR)

Particularly good served with asparagus, and sometimes even with globe
artichokes.

¼ cup (2 oz; 50 g) butter   1 tablespoon (15 ml) malt vinegar
1 tablespoon (15 ml) parsley,
    washed, dried and chopped
    coarse

Melt the butter in a small saucepan over low heat, allowing it to turn a
rich, golden brown, but *never black*, otherwise it will burn. Add the parsley
and continually shake the pan until the parsley is crisp. Then pour the
butter into a *hot* sauceboat. Add the malt vinegar to the pan in which the
parsley has fried, stir well, boiling it once, and pour into the hot sauceboat
with butter and parsley. Mix well. The sauceboat must be kept hot, otherwise the sauce will be inedible, as the butter will congeal.

VEGETABLE AND FRUIT HINTS

Vegetables

1. Put a dry sponge in the vegetable or crisper drawer of the refrigerator to
   absorb moisture.
2. To crisp celery, place it in a bowl of cold water and add a slice of raw
   potato. Let it stand in the refrigerator for a few hours.
3. To crisp lettuce, place it in a bowl of cold water, add the juice of 1 lemon
   per head of lettuce and let it stand in a cool place or in the refrigerator.
   An old-fashioned method was to add a piece of coal; the minerals released therefrom perked up the lettuce.
4. To flavor pot roasts and stews, combine onion, garlic and carrots in a
   blender with a small amount of water. This makes a quick stock.
5. Bake potatoes with a small skewer inserted. The skewer conducts the

heat to the inside, thereby cooking them from the inside as well as the outside and shortening the cooking time.

6. **Onions:** Blanching onions for 3 to 5 minutes will change their chemistry and reduce their pungency, and the chance of indigestion. If they are to be fried, slice them and place in a sieve, then pour boiling water over them, pat dry and fry. Onions taste sweet when fried because the sugar contained in the onion caramelizes.

The reason we cry when peeling onions is that they contain a chemical called allyl isothiocynate which causes the tears. The eyes are particularly sensitive to it, so they protect themselves by flooding with tears to wash away the chemical.

HOW TO CHOP AN ONION FINE: Do not cut off root—it holds the onion together, making it much easier to cut.
a. Remove *skin,* cut off *top,* then cut onion in half from top to root, put cut side down on board, root end to your left.
b. Slice it vertically, lengthwise, almost but not quite to the root.
c. Slice it horizontally, starting at the bottom and working up to the top—but still not through the root.
d. Cut it across, downward, into dice, starting at the right-hand cut.

TO AVOID CRYING:
a. Remove the stem last, as this reduces the juices.
b. Peel under very cold or ice water.
c. Refrigerate the onion before peeling and cutting. This chills the juices which cause the tears.

TO MAKE ONION JUICE: Cut a slice from the root end of the onion, then either grate it or squeeze it on a lemon squeezer *especially kept for this purpose.*

7. To insure that cold string beans retain their bright-green color, plunge them into boiling salted water. Cook them over high heat with no lid on the pan, and be careful not to overcook them. Drain and transfer them to cold water, changing the water often until the beans are cold.
8. To peel chestnuts: Bake them for 20 minutes in a preheated oven at 400° F (200° C; Mark 6). Both the outside shell and the inside skin will come off easily.

9. Artichokes:

TO PREPARE A GLOBE ARTICHOKE:

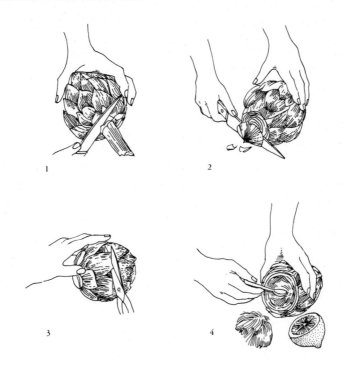

a. Cut off the stalk with a sharp knife and pull off the two lower rows of leaves as well as any bruised outer leaves.

b. Lay the artichoke on its side and slice off the top third. Rub all the cut edges and the base with a piece of lemon.

c. With kitchen scissors, trim ¼ inch off the points of the remaining leaves and rub the cut edges with lemon.

d. To remove the choke, spread the top leaves apart and pull out the prickly leaves surrounding the choke. With a teaspoon, scrape out the choke. Squeeze lemon juice into the center. If you are going to boil the artichokes, press the leaves back together. If you are going to stuff them, leave the leaves apart.

Note: The lemon juice prevents discoloration of the exposed base and edges. Never cook artichokes in aluminum or iron saucepans, as they turn the vegetable gray.

TO EAT AN ARTICHOKE: Pull off a leaf with your fingers, beginning with the lower leaves, and dip the base of the leaf into melted butter or sauce.

Scrape off the tender pulp with your teeth and discard the leaf. Continue
like this until you have reached the last rows of leaves. If the choke has
not been removed, you will reach a pointed cap of thin leaves with purple tips. Pull all these out together. Then scrape off the hairy choke by
sliding a knife under it and carefully scraping away a quarter at a time.
You then have reached the heart, which is delicious and meaty. Cut up
the pieces with a knife and fork and eat.

TO PREPARE ARTICHOKE BOTTOMS:

For uncooked bottoms: Bend back the lower leaves until they snap off.
Remove all the outer leaves until you reach the inner leaves which bend
inward. Pull these out or, placing the artichoke on its side, cut off the
inner leaves and choke just above the heart. Slice off the stalk and,
rotating the base of the artichoke against the knife blade, trim off all
the lower leaf bases.
For cooked bottoms: Boil the artichoke and remove leaves and choke in
the ordinary way.

10. When cooking vegetables such as cauliflower, Jerusalem artichokes and
    sea kale (i.e., white vegetables), put two lumps of sugar in the water.
    This will keep them white.
11. Beets will peel easily if you dip them into cold water right after they
    have finished boiling. Then rub off the skins.
12. Cook fresh peas without water by lining the saucepan and covering the
    peas with lettuce leaves. The moisture in the lettuce will steam them.
13. To keep boiled potatoes white, add a teaspoon of lemon juice or vinegar
    to the cooking water.

Fruits

1. Fruits such as avocado, tomato, etc., will ripen faster if placed in a paper
   bag or in newspaper, and then stored in a drawer or closed cupboard. Remove the stem of the avocado before putting it in the bag.
2. To obtain the most juice from limes, lemons and oranges, heat them in
   hot water for several minutes before squeezing.
3. Before peeling oranges, cover them with boiling water and allow them to
   stand for 5 minutes. The whole bitter membrane can then be removed
   more easily.
4. To make frozen orange juice taste fresh, add the juice of a lemon.
5. To unstick dried dates, figs or raisins, place them in a low oven for a few
   minutes.

SERVING QUANTITIES

Artichokes, globe—1 per person

Artichokes, Jerusalem—1 pound (450 g) for 4 people

Asparagus—6 to 8 stalks per person

Beans, green—1½ pounds (700 g) for 4 people

Beans, lima (broad beans)—1 pound (450 g) for 4 people

Beets—3-4 small beets per person

Broccoli—1 large head for 4 people

Brussels sprouts—1½ pounds (700 g) for 4 people

Cabbage—1 large cabbage for 4 people

Carrots—1½ pounds (700 g) for 4 people

Cauliflower—1 large head for 4 people

Celeriac—1 pound (450 g) for 4 people

Celery—1 large head for 3 people

Sweet corn—1 to 2 ears per person

Cucumber—1 large cucumber for 2 people

Endive, Belgian—1 to 2 heads per person

Greens (dandelion leaves, corn salad or lamb's lettuce, lettuce, sorrel, spinach, etc.)—1 pound (450 g) per person

Leeks—3 to 4 per person

Lettuce—1 medium lettuce per person

Mushrooms—1½ pounds (700 g) for 4 people

Onions—1 pound (450 g) for 4 to 5 people

Parsnips—1 pound (450 g) for 4 people

Peas—1½ pounds (700 g) unshelled peas per person; ½ pound (225 g) shelled

Peppers, sweet—1 medium per person

Potatoes—½ pound (225 g) per person

Salsify or sconozera (oyster plant)—10 to 12 roots for 4 people

Squash, acorn—1 for 2 people

Squash, summer (vegetable marrow)—1 medium squash for 2 people

Tomatoes—1½ pounds (700 g) for 3 to 4 people

Turnips—1 pound (450 g) for 2 to 3 people

VEGETABLE RECIPES

I've chosen to include the following recipes because they are some I've found to be particularly successful. Some of them are taken from books written by my favorite cooking writers, some of whom are also good friends.

Artichoke, Globe

In the *Receipt Book of Joseph Cooper* (1654), cook to Charles I, only the hearts of the globe artichokes were used. In one recipe for a "raised pie," he suggests a mixture of boiled artichoke hearts, dates, hard-boiled yolks of eggs and a sauce made with marrow from bones and lemon juice, seasoned with salt, sugar, ginger, cinnamon and nutmeg. Another recipe is for "resoles" made by mixing equal quantities of boiled hearts, rubbed through a fine sieve, with marrow from bones and seasoning them with salt, nutmeg, ginger, orange flower or rosewater, and either baking or frying the rissoles. In the eighteenth century, in the *Receipt Book of Vincent La Chapelle, Chief Cook to the Prince of Orange* (1744), the author suggests serving the hearts with truffles, mushrooms, scallions (spring onions) and parsley, flavored with lemon juice.

The most famous recipe of all is *Artichauts à la Barigoule* from Provence. Jane Grigson in her *Vegetable Book* has the best recipe for this. It must have originated in Vincent La Chapelle's book, which describes a recipe in which you take out all the chokes after the artichokes are cooked and then fill the interstices with small pieces of bacon, chopped sweet herbs and green onions (spring onions).

ARTICHAUTS À LA BARIGOULE

Start by preparing 6 artichoke cups. If you are in a hurry cook them before you start on the stuffing, but it makes a better dish if you stuff them raw and leave them to simmer gently for a long time. The other ingredients are:

175 grams (6 oz) mushrooms, chopped
100 grams (3 to 4 oz) green streaky bacon, chopped (see Author's Note *below)*
Butter
Chopped fresh parsley and chives
3 tablespoons bread crumbs
Salt, pepper

Oil
2 large onions, sliced
1 large carrot, sliced
1 small clove garlic, chopped fine
Pinch savory (pebre d'ase)
200 milliliters (7 fl oz) dry white wine
6 long strips of pork fat, cut very thin (optional)

Fry the mushrooms and bacon in butter until lightly browned. Mix in the herbs and bread crumbs and season. Stuff the artichoke cups. Tie the fat strips over each one with thread, if you are using them—they are not essential—and brown all over in oil. Put 2 tablespoons oil into a large pot that will take all the artichokes in one layer. Put the onion, carrot and garlic in a bed on top, with seasoning and savory. Pour over the wine, plus enough water to bring the liquid level slightly above the vegetables. Put in the artichokes. Cover and simmer until they are tender—about 1½ hours, if they started raw. If they were already cooked, simmer a little more vigorously for about ½ hour.

The liquor can be thickened slightly, if you like, with flour, cornflour or potato flour but do not make it too gluey. I think it is better to reduce the cooking liquid slightly if it is on the watery side, rather than to make starchy additions.

Author's Note: An acceptable American substitute for green streaky bacon is an equivalent amount of lean pork belly.

For instructions on how to prepare artichoke cups, see page 271.

To prepare the artichoke cups: approximately 20 minutes. Cooking time: approximately 2½ hours.

ARTICHOKE BOTTOMS STUFFED AND FRIED

FORCEMEAT

SERVES 6 AS A FIRST COURSE

5 ounces (150 g) crabmeat, picked over and flaked (chicken or veal may be substituted)

4 tablespoons (2 oz; 50 ml) onion, chopped fine

¼ pound (4 oz; 125 g) mushrooms, chopped fine

1 sprig fresh thyme or ½ teaspoon dried thyme

2 sprigs fresh coriander leaves, chopped

Salt and fresh-ground black pepper

¼ cup (2 oz; 50 g) butter

A pinch of cayenne

2 egg yolks, beaten

1 whole egg

12 artichoke bottoms, prepared as on page 272

1 cup (8 fl oz; 225 ml) beef stock

1 egg yolk, beaten

1 cup (5 oz; 150 g) dried bread crumbs

Olive oil or vegetable oil

6 rounds of fried bread

Make the forcemeat: In a bowl, mix the crabmeat, onion, mushroom, thyme, coriander, salt and pepper. Melt the butter in a small frying pan and fry the mixture until it is soft and golden. Then turn it back into the bowl and allow it to cool. Add the cayenne and the eggs and mix thoroughly.

In an enamel saucepan, braise the artichoke bottoms in the stock until they are just soft, but still firm. Remove them to a plate. With a spoon, stuff each bottom with the forcemeat and put 1 bottom stuck upside down on top of another, brushing the edges with egg yolk. You will have 6 double bottoms. Mix the bread crumbs in the leftover egg yolk and dip each double bottom into the mixture. In a deep frying pan heat the oil until it is 360° F (184° C), or until a piece of bread turns brown in 30 seconds. Quickly fry each double bottom until the bread crumbs turn golden, remove with a slotted spoon and serve on a round of fried bread.

Preparation and cooking time: approximately 1 hour.

Artichoke, Jerusalem

Peeling Jerusalem artichokes can be a terrible trial. I find the easiest method is to prepare them as you would beets: Parboil them and then, wearing rubber gloves, rub off the skins. Anything which does not come off may be cleaned with a peeler or knife.

JERUSALEM ARTICHOKE PIE

SERVES 5 TO 6

3 tablespoons (45 ml) butter or
  margarine
1 large onion, sliced thin
1 pound (450 g) Jerusalem
  artichokes, cooked, peeled,
  washed and sliced
1 cup (3 oz; 75 g) grated Cheddar
  cheese

3 sprigs fresh coriander leaves,
  chopped fine
Salt and pepper
1 tablespoon (15 ml) Marmite or
  yeast extract

Preheat the oven to 350° F (180° C; Mark 4).

In a small frying pan, melt 1 tablespoon (15 ml) of the butter or margarine and sauté the sliced onion until it turns golden. Fill an earthenware casserole or ovenproof dish with alternate layers of artichoke, onions, cheese and coriander leaves. Add salt, pepper and Marmite, dot the top with the remaining butter, and bake in the oven for 10 minutes or until the top is browned. Serve in the dish in which it was cooked.

Preparation time: 30 minutes. Cooking time: 30 minutes.

JERUSALEM ARTICHOKE FRITTERS

MAKES APPROXIMATELY 18 FRITTERS

1/4 cup (2 fl oz; 50 ml) olive oil
2 tablespoons (30 ml) red wine
  vinegar
1 tablespoon (15 ml) chopped fresh
  coriander leaves
1 teaspoon (5 ml) crushed roasted
  cumin seed

3 very large Jerusalem artichokes,
  cooked, peeled, washed and cut
  into slices
1 cup (3 oz; 75 g) grated Parmesan
  cheese
Vegetable oil for deep-frying

BATTER

*1 cup (5 oz; 150 g) chick-pea flour
  (besan)
1 tablespoon (15 ml) salt
1 teaspoon (5 ml) ground
  coriander*

*1 teaspoon (5 ml) ground cumin
½ teaspoon (2.5 ml) cayenne
½ to ¾ cup (4 to 6 fl oz; 125 to 175
  ml) water*

In a glass dish or bowl, make a marinade of the olive oil, vinegar, coriander leaves and cumin seed. Steep the sliced artichoke for 1 hour in this mixture. Meanwhile make the batter: Sift all the dry ingredients into a mixing bowl. Add enough water to make a smooth batter, stirring constantly. Set it aside, covered, for 30 minutes. Then remove the artichokes from their marinade, dry them on paper towels and sprinkle them with cheese.

When you are ready to make the fritters, heat the vegetable oil in a deep frying pan to approximately 360° F (184° C). Then dip each artichoke slice into the batter and deep-fry in the oil until it turns a golden brown. Depending upon the size of your frying pan, a number of slices may go in at the same time. When cooked, drain them on paper towels and serve in a hot dish. They would be delicious served with hot chicken, turkey or goose, or with cold meat.

Preparation time (including marinating time): 1½ hours. Cooking time: 30 minutes.

JERUSALEM ARTICHOKE CHIPS

SERVES 4

*1 pound (450 g) Jerusalem
  artichokes, cleaned and peeled*

*Vegetable oil
Salt and pepper*

On the thin slicer of a food processor or a mandoline, slice the artichokes as you would for potato chips. Put them into cold water for a few minutes, then dry them with a clean cloth. Heat oil in a deep frying pan with a basket until it reaches a temperature of 360° F (184° C). Put the artichoke slices in the basket and fry in the oil until they turn a light brown. When cooked, remove them and put them into a low oven on a dish with paper towels to drain and dry; leave the door slightly ajar. Sprinkle them with salt and pepper. Serve with poultry or game.

Preparation time: 15 minutes. Cooking time: 20 minutes.

JERUSALEM ARTICHOKE AND CHESTNUT SOUP

SERVES 6

1 pound (450 g) Jerusalem
  artichokes, unpeeled
2 medium onions, chopped fine
1 cup (8 fl oz; 225 ml) chicken
  stock
1 pound (450 g) chestnuts, peeled

Salt and pepper
¼ cup (2 fl oz; 50 ml) pale dry
  sherry
1½ cups (12 fl oz; 375 ml) milk
2 sprigs fresh coriander, chopped

Cut the artichokes into small pieces *but do not peel them.* In a saucepan, boil the artichokes and onions in the stock for 45 minutes. Meanwhile, in another saucepan, boil the chestnuts in water to cover for 45 minutes. When cooked, the artichokes should be almost disintegrated and the chestnuts quite soft. Drain the artichokes and onion, reserving the stock, and drain the chestnuts. Combine the nuts and vegetables in a blender or food processor and purée. Then force the mixture through a wire sieve into a bowl and add salt and pepper to taste and the sherry. Add the reserved stock to this and 1 cup (8 fl oz; 250 ml) milk. If the soup is still too thick, add more milk. Correct the seasoning, reheat but do *not* boil. Serve in heated soup bowls and top with coriander leaves.

Preparation time: 45 minutes. Cooking time: 45 minutes.

Beans

SAVORY FRENCH BEANS

SERVES 4

1 pound (450 g) string (French)
  beans, topped and tailed
1 tablespoon (15 ml) water or stock
2½ tablespoons (38 ml) butter

A pinch of salt
1 tablespoon (15 ml) lemon juice
1 teaspoon (5 ml) grated nutmeg
1 tablespoon (15 ml) pine nuts

Place the beans in a pan with 1 tablespoon (15 ml) of stock or water, 1 tablespoon (15 ml) butter and the salt. Cover, bring to a boil, then lower heat and simmer for 4 to 5 minutes, shaking the pan from time to time—the beans should still be crunchy. When cooked, put them in another pan with the lemon juice, the remaining butter, nutmeg and pine nuts. Stir the beans in this mixture, heat and, just before serving, grate a little more fresh nutmeg over the beans.

Preparation and cooking time: approximately 40 minutes.

SWEET AND SOUR BEANS

Good with roast pork or boiled ham.

SERVES 3 TO 4

1 pound (450 g) string beans (French or runner beans), cleaned and sliced
Salt
4 slices (rashers) bacon

1 tablespoon (15 ml) white wine vinegar
1 tablespoon (15 ml) soft brown sugar

Place the prepared beans in a pan of lightly salted boiling water; cover and simmer for about 7 minutes. Meanwhile, slice the bacon crosswise into narrow strips. *Fry without any extra fat* until the bacon bits are crisp. Lift them out with a slotted spoon and keep warm. Stir the vinegar and sugar into the bacon fat, add the drained beans and stir to coat them evenly with the sweet and sour mixture. Spoon the beans and liquid into a dish, and sprinkle with the bacon pieces.

Preparation time: 20 minutes. Cooking time: 15 minutes.

BROAD BEANS IN THE TOURAINE STYLE
FÈVES À LA TOURANGELLE

(from Jane Grigson's *Vegetable Book*)

2½ *kilos (5 lbs) broad beans (see*
  Author's Note *below*)
Bouquet of parsley and tarragon
20 *small new onions (very large*
  scallions [spring onions] do
  well)
100 grams (3 to 4 oz) butter

150 grams (5 oz) lean bacon,
  chopped
2 *egg yolks*
Sprig of chervil
3 *tablespoons cream*
Chopped parsley and savory

Shell and cook the broad beans with the bouquet of parsley and tarragon and a few of the better pods. Brown the onions lightly in the butter, then add the bacon. When it begins to color, lower the heat, cover the pan and leave to finish the cooking. When the beans are ready, skin the largest ones unless the outer skins are tender. Discard pods and bouquet. Beat up 150 ml (¼ pt) of the strained bean cooking liquor with the egg yolks.

Add the beans to the cooked onions, stirring them well together. Check the seasoning. Stir the egg mixture into the pan with the chervil, and keep the heat very low, so that the sauce thickens to double (heavy) cream consistency. Stir in the cream. Check the seasoning again and fish out the chervil. Turn into a warm serving dish and scatter with chopped parsley and savory. Serve immediately with wholemeal (whole wheat) bread, unless you have good light bread in the French style.

Author's Note: The American lima bean may be substituted for the broad bean.

Preparation time: 30 minutes. Cooking time: approximately 30 minutes.

LIMA (BROAD) BEAN SOUP

MAKES 1½ PINTS (900 ML)—SERVES 6

¼ pound (4 oz; 125 g) cooked lima beans (broad beans)—or string beans (French beans) may be substituted
1 tablespoon (15 ml) cooked shallot
¼ cup (2 fl oz; 50 ml) milk

2 tablespoons (30 ml) butter
1 egg yolk
1 tablespoon (15 ml) fine-chopped parsley
Salt and pepper
More milk, if needed

Make a purée of the cooked beans and shallot in a blender or food processor. Put back on the heat and add the milk and 1 tablespoon (15 ml) butter. When almost but not quite boiling, add the egg yolk, the remaining butter, the parsley, salt and pepper. The soup must not boil after the egg has been added or it will curdle. If too thick, add a little more milk.

Preparation time: 15 minutes. Cooking time: approximately 15 minutes.

Beets

CREAMED BEETS (BEETROOT)

SERVES 4

4 large beets (beetroot) cooked thoroughly
4 large onions, grated
¼ cup (2 oz; 50 g) softened butter
1 egg yolk
2 tablespoons (30 ml) butter
1 teaspoon (5 ml) cream

1½ teaspoons (7.5 ml) lemon juice
Salt to taste
Milk
Fine-chopped parsley
Hard-boiled egg, chopped fine

Preheat the oven to 350° F (180° C; Mark 4)

Rub the beets (beetroot) through a sieve or place in a food processor for 3 seconds. Place the beets and onion in a bowl with the softened butter. Mix well. Then put the beet and onion mixture into a baking dish and bake in the preheated oven for 40 minutes. In the meantime make a sauce of the egg yolk, butter, cream, lemon juice and a little salt. Heat it *slowly,* do not allow it to boil or the egg will curdle. If the sauce is too thick, add a little milk. When beet and onion mixture is cooked, remove the dish from the oven, mix in the sauce and serve in a china quiche or flan dish topped with chopped parsley and egg.

Preparation time: 30 minutes. Cooking time: 40 minutes.

Curly Kale

Curly Kale is richer in salts, proteins and carbohydrates than any other member of the Brassica family, Brussels sprouts being second. It contains vitamins A and C. If grown on good ground, it will provide tender young leaves to use in salads when lettuce is rare and expensive. Cook as you would any cabbage.

CURLY KALE AND CHESTNUT PIE

SERVES 4

1 clove garlic, chopped
A sprig of thyme
1 bunch of curly kale, washed but left whole
½ pound (225 g) cooked chestnuts, rubbed through a sieve, or substitute canned (tinned) chestnuts

4 tomatoes, sliced
Salt and pepper
1 cup (3 oz; 75 g) fresh bread crumbs
¼ cup (2 oz; 50 g) butter

Preheat the oven to 400° F (200° C; Mark 6).

Put 1 cup (8 fl oz; 225 ml) water in a saucepan with the chopped garlic, the thyme and the kale leaves. Steam the kale until it is tender but still crisp. Drain it but do not throw away the cooking liquid. Chop the kale coarsely. In a buttered ovenproof dish, make alternate layers of the kale, chestnuts and tomatoes. Season to taste, cover with the bread crumbs and dot with butter. Cook in the preheated oven for 10 to 15 minutes, until the bread crumbs are golden and the dish has been heated through.

Preparation time: 15 minutes if using canned chestnuts; 45 minutes if using fresh. Cooking time: approximately 30 minutes.

Cabbage

Many people dislike cabbage because they are used to having it at school, and even at home, boiled to death. Cabbage, either raw or cooked, contains vitamins A, B and C. Contrary to belief, it is more digestible eaten raw, preferably grated, than cooked. Grated cabbage, either green or red, is delicious combined with grated onion, but first cut out the coarse stalk in the middle.

To cook cabbage, put 1 chopped garlic clove, 1 teaspoon (5 ml) caraway seeds, a sprig of thyme and the quartered cabbage into ½ cup (4 fl oz; 120 ml) water. Steam until the cabbage is tender but crunchy.

COLCANNON

SERVES 4 TO 6 PEOPLE

2 tablespoons (30 ml) butter
1 large onion, chopped
3 large potatoes, cooked and mashed

1 green cabbage, cooked and then chopped
Salt and pepper

This Irish dish can be either baked or fried. I prefer the latter. Melt the butter in a large frying pan and sauté the onion in it until golden. Then add the mashed potatoes and cooked cabbage, add salt and pepper to taste. Mix the vegetables and press the mixture flat like a pancake. Allow the underside to brown, then cover the frying pan with a plate and turn it over so that the vegetables are on the plate, browned side uppermost. Slide this back into the frying pan and allow the underside to brown. Serve with steak or roast lamb.

Preparation time: 20 minutes. Cooking time: 15 minutes for precooking cabbage and potatoes, plus 10 minutes to fry.

RED CABBAGE

SERVES 6 TO 8 PEOPLE

2 tablespoons (1 oz; 30 ml) butter
1 head red cabbage, shredded thin
1¼ cups (½ pt; 300 ml) beef stock
2 tablespoons (30 ml) red wine
   vinegar
8 bacon rinds, tied together, or
   substitute a small piece of salt
   pork

1 teaspoon (5 ml) sugar
1 tablespoon (15 ml) marmalade
Salt and pepper

Melt the butter in a large saucepan and add the cabbage. Pour in 1 cup (8 fl oz; 240 ml) of the stock and the vinegar and bacon rinds. Cook for 3 hours over low heat. Then add the rest of the stock, the sugar, marmalade and salt and pepper. Continue to cook until the cabbage has absorbed most of the liquid. Remove the bacon rinds and serve. Good with pheasant, goose and pot roast.

Cooking time: approximately 3½ hours.

STIR-FRY CABBAGE AND SHREDDED PORK

"Cabbage with shredded pork is a hearty dish, particularly good in winter," say Craig Claiborne and Virginia Lee, in *The Chinese Cookbook*. It may be made in advance and reheated, or kept warm over very low heat.

SERVES 8 OR MORE

1½ pounds celery cabbage
1 12-ounce can bamboo shoots
½ pound lean pork
2 tablespoons dark soy sauce
8 tablespoons peanut, vegetable or
   corn oil

Salt to taste
1 teaspoon sugar
½ teaspoon monosodium glutamate, or to taste (optional)

1. Separate the leaves of the cabbage and cut one leaf at a time into thirds. Pile the thirds, one on top of the other, and slice lengthwise (the direction in which the leaf grew) into fine shreds about 2 inches long.

2. Drain the bamboo shoots, drop the pieces into boiling water, and simmer for about 5 minutes. This will remove the canned flavor. Drain and cool. Thinly slice the bamboo shoots, then cut the slices into thin strips the same length as the cabbage. There should be 1 cup loosely packed.

3. Thinly slice the pork and then cut the slices into fine shreds the same length as the cabbage and bamboo shoots. Place the pork in a bowl and add the soy sauce, stirring to coat the pieces.

4. Line a mixing bowl with a sieve or colander.

5. Heat half the oil in a wok or skillet, and when it is almost smoking add the pork, stirring quickly to cook. When the meat starts to brown, about 2 minutes, drain it in the sieve. Reserve both the pork and juices that drain from it.

6. Wipe out the pan and add the remaining oil. Add the bamboo shoots and cook, stirring, about 30 seconds. Add the cabbage and cook, stirring almost constantly, until the cabbage is quite wilted. Add the pork juices, the salt, sugar and monosodium glutamate. Continue cooking and stirring for 3 to 4 minutes. Cover and cook 3 minutes longer, or until the cabbage is tender. Add the pork and toss quickly until hot and well blended, about 2 minutes. Turn into a heatproof casserole and cover. Keep warm over a very low fire until ready to serve.

Preparation time: approximately 40 minutes. Cooking time: approximately 20 minutes.

Cardoons

Cardoons, of the same genus as the globe artichoke, grow in height to three or four feet. The stalks and the thick rib of the leaf are the parts that are eaten.

CARDOONS HOLLANDAISE

SERVES 6

4 pounds (1.8 kg) trimmed cardoons
Juice of ½ lemon
Salt
¼ cup (2 oz; 50 g) butter or margarine

1¼ cups (1 pt; 300 ml) chicken stock
2 teaspoons (10 ml) chopped parsley or chervil

Cut any prickles from the outer leaves and blanch the cardoons in acidulated salted water for 15 minutes. Drain and remove them from the liquid. Cut away the prickles from the softer inner leaves and stalk to remove any stringy bits. Cut the cardoons into 3-inch (7.5 cm) lengths. In a saucepan, melt the butter, add the stock and parsley or chervil, and the cardoons. Cover and simmer for another 20 to 25 minutes. Serve in an earthenware dish topped with Hollandaise Sauce (see page 250).

Or they can be cooked as above, then put into an earthenware dish with alternate layers of white sauce thickened with grated Parmesan cheese. Dot the top with butter and more grated Parmesan cheese and bake in a preheated oven at 425° F (220° C; Mark 7) until the top has turned golden brown.

Preparation time: 30 minutes. Cooking time: 30 minutes.

Carrots

CURRIED CARROTS

SERVES 4

1 large onion, sliced
1 tablespoon (15 ml) chopped ham
1 sweet green pepper, chopped
1 teaspoon (5 ml) turmeric
A pinch of cayenne
1¼ cups (10 fl oz; 275 ml) milk

Salt to taste
1½ pounds (700 g) young carrots,
* sliced ½ inch (1.2 cm) thick*
Juice of half a lemon or lime
1 tablespoon (15 ml) light (single)
* cream*

Put all the ingredients except the lemon juice and cream into an enamel casserole. Simmer gently for 30 minutes, or until the carrots are tender. At the last moment, add the lemon or lime juice and the cream. Serve at once.

Preparation time: 15 minutes. Cooking time: 30 minutes.

SWADISH CARROTS

SWEDISH CARROTS

SERVES 6

10 tablespoons (5 oz; 155 ml) butter
1 dozen large carrots, cleaned and
  julienned
1 cup (4 oz; 125 g) confectioners'
  (icing) sugar
Fresh grated nutmeg, to taste

Salt and pepper to taste
1½ cups (10 fl oz; 275 ml) white
  wine vinegar
A dash of paprika or mignonette
  pepper (see page 43)

In a deep saucepan, melt 8 tablespoons (120 ml) of the butter and stir in the carrots, sugar, nutmeg, salt and pepper, and the white wine vinegar. Simmer gently for approximately 1 hour, stirring the mixture from time to time with a wooden spoon. When the carrots are cooked, most of the liquid should have evaporated. Drain the carrots and, in the same pan, melt the remaining butter, add the paprika or mignonette pepper. Return the carrots to the pan and toss them in the butter. Serve hot.

Preparation time: 15 minutes. Cooking time: 1¼ hours.

Cauliflower

Can be cooked in almost any way, but steam rather than boil it in order to retain the proper flavor. One way of keeping the head white is to cook it in milk.

CAULIFLOWER SPRIGS

SERVES 4

1 head of cauliflower
Milk
2 egg yolks, beaten
1 cup (6 oz; 175 g) fine bread
  crumbs, browned

2 cups (6 oz; 175 g) grated Gruyère
  cheese

Preheat the oven to 400° F (200° C; Mark 6).

In a saucepan, steam the cauliflower in a small amount of milk until tender but still crunchy. Drain it in a colander. Carefully break it into separate sprigs of flowerets. Dip each piece into the beaten egg yolk and then into the browned bread crumbs and grated cheese. Arrange the pieces in one layer in a large, flat pan and put them into the preheated oven until they brown. Serve neatly piled on a dish.

Cooking time: 20 minutes.

Celeriac

FRIED CELERIAC

SERVES 4

1 pound (450 g) celeriac, washed and trimmed
1 cup (8 fl oz; 225 ml) Sauce Allemande (see below)
2 cups (12 oz; 350 g) dried bread crumbs, or crushed vermicelli

2 egg yolks, beaten
Olive oil
A small bunch of fried parsley
8 slices of lemon

In a saucepan, boil the celeriac in salted water, until it is *tender but firm.* Peel and cut into thickish slices. Dip each slice into the Sauce Allemande and leave them on a plate to cool. When the celeriac is completely cold, sprinkle it thickly with bread crumbs or crushed vermicelli, brush with beaten egg and roll again in the bread crumbs or crushed vermicelli. Heat 2 inches (5 cm) of oil in a deep frying pan and fry the celeriac until it turns golden brown. Serve piled high on a dish covered with a folded napkin and garnish with fried parsley and lemon slices.

SAUCE ALLEMANDE

5 egg yolks, beaten
½ cup (4 fl oz; 125 ml) Velouté Sauce (see page 245)
A pinch of grated fresh nutmeg
¼ cup (2 fl oz; 50 ml) Mushroom Catsup (see page 394), or reduced mushroom cooking liquid

1 tablespoon (½ oz; 12 ml) butter
Fresh-ground black pepper

In a mixing bowl, add the beaten eggs to the Velouté Sauce, then pour into a flat, heavy-bottomed pan and simmer for 15 minutes, stirring continually so that the eggs combine thoroughly with the Velouté Sauce and the sauce becomes thick enough to cling to a spatula. Then mix in all the remaining ingredients. Keep the sauce hot in a *bain-marie* or double boiler, the surface of the sauce dabbed with butter. This sauce may be served with vegetables or fish.

Preparation time: 30 minutes. Cooking time: 45 minutes.

Fennel

FENNEL IN ANCHOVIES WITH VINEGAR SAUCE

SERVES 4

3 tablespoons (45 ml) olive oil
3 to 4 anchovy fillets, rinsed and
  minced
4 bulbs Florentine fennel,
  trimmed and quartered
Pepper

¼ teaspoon (1.25 ml) powdered
  mustard
¾ cup (6 fl oz; 175 ml) white wine
  vinegar
Tabasco (optional)

Heat the olive oil in a frying pan and mash the minced anchovies into this. Take the pieces of fennel and cook them slowly in this mixture. Sprinkle them with pepper. Dissolve the mustard in the vinegar and add it to the fennel. Cover the pan and continue to cook over moderate heat until the fennel is tender, about 15 to 20 minutes. If you like a sharpish taste, add a few drops of Tabasco.

Preparation time: approximately 15 minutes. Cooking time: approximately 30 minutes.

Mushrooms

To prepare mushrooms for cooking, trim off the tip and lightly scrape the stalk, or, for certain dishes, remove the stalk completely. Wipe the mushroom cap with a damp cloth and dry. *Never allow mushrooms to stand in water or to be washed in warm or hot water, or they will lose their flavor and become limp.* If they are good, fresh, white mushrooms, I rarely peel them.

However, if you prefer to peel them, do so only just before cooking, peeling as one would an apple; hold the mushroom in the left hand and turn it, peeling with a small knife in the right hand. In this way there will be no marks left by the knife and you will have a smooth mushroom. Never throw away the stalks or peelings; they can be used in soups or stews.

To retain their full flavor, mushrooms should always be cooked in a small quantity of liquid. If you are adding mushrooms to a sauce, soup or stew, do so just before serving the dish. If they cook too long they become tough and lose their flavor.

DUXELLES

This can be used for stuffings, garnishes, sauces etc.

MAKES APPROXIMATELY ½ LB (225 G)

2 tablespoons (30 ml) butter
2 tablespoons (30 ml) vegetable oil
1 tablespoon (15 ml) fine-chopped onion
1 tablespoon (15 ml) fine-chopped shallots

½ pound (8 oz; 225 g) mushrooms, stalks and peelings chopped fine
Salt and pepper
A pinch of chopped parsley

Melt the butter with the oil in a saucepan and add the onion and shallots. Squeeze the mushrooms in a cloth to extract as much moisture as possible, then add them to the saucepan. Mix all the ingredients thoroughly and cook until all the moisture has completely evaporated from the mushrooms. Season with salt and pepper, add the parsley, mix together and pour into an earthenware terrine. Cover with buttered paper or put into a jar with a tight-fitting lid. It will keep for several weeks in the refrigerator. Use when required.

If you want to use this mixture to stuff tomatoes or cucumbers, to every 8 tablespoons (125 ml) of Duxelles add 4 tablespoons (60 ml) of soft bread with crusts removed, soaked in milk, dried in a saucepan over a high flame, and allowed to stand until it cools.

DUXELLES STUFFING À LA BONNE FEMME

Use this to stuff meat, poultry and vegetables.

Add an equal amount of sausage meat to the cooked Duxelles and either cook both together or use uncooked, according to the dish it is intended for. However, it is always preferable to partially cook this mixture when it is to be used to stuff a bird.

DUXELLES SAUCE

MAKES APPROXIMATELY 1½ PINTS (900 ML)

1 teaspoon (5 ml) butter
2 tablespoons (30 ml) vegetable oil
2 tablespoons (30 ml) fine-chopped onion
1 shallot, chopped fine
1½ tablespoons (22 ml) fine-chopped mushrooms
Salt and fresh ground pepper
A pinch of nutmeg

6 tablespoons (90 ml) white wine
1¼ pints (1 pint; 600 ml) good chicken stock
1 tablespoon (15 ml) tomato paste (purée)
3 tablespoons (45 ml) butter
1 tablespoon (15 ml) flour
1 teaspoon (5 ml) fine-chopped parsley

In a small, heavy saucepan, heat the butter and oil. When hot, add the onion and shallot and cook until they are a light golden color. Then add the mushrooms, season with salt and pepper and nutmeg. Stir the mixture for 5 to 6 minutes, then add the white wine, stock and tomato paste (purée). Mix 1 tablespoon (15 ml) of the butter with the tablespoon of flour. Add; this will thicken the mixture. Stir, and simmer gently for 15 to 20 minutes. Just before serving, add the remaining butter, divided into small pieces, and the parsley.

Preparation and cooking time: approximately 40 minutes.

MUSHROOMS PULAO

SERVES 4

1 cup (8 oz; 225 g) butter or
  margarine
2 small onions, peeled and sliced
1 cup (7 oz; 200 g) uncooked rice
Salt and fresh-ground pepper
2 small sticks cinnamon
3 cardamom seeds

1 to 2 bay leaves
2 tablespoons (50 ml) chopped
  almonds
¾ pound (12 oz; 350 g) small
  mushrooms, cooked (see below)
A pinch of saffron or turmeric

Preheat the oven to 325° F (170° C; Mark 3).

In a large saucepan melt ¼ cup (2 oz; 50 g) of the butter or margarine and sauté the onions until they turn a golden brown. Add the rice and the remaining butter or margarine and cook the rice, stirring frequently, until it has absorbed the fat. Season to taste with salt and pepper, then add the spices, bay leaf and the almonds and barely cover the mixture with boiling water. Put the lid on the saucepan and simmer very gently until the rice is tender. When cooked, drain the rice into a large bowl and mix with the cooked mushrooms. Sprinkle the mixture with saffron or turmeric and bake in the preheated oven for 5 minutes, so that the moisture will evaporate from the rice.

TO COOK MUSHROOMS

In a saucepan bring ½ cup (4 fl oz; 125 ml) water, 1 teaspoon (5 ml) salt and 2 tablespoons (30 ml) lemon juice to the boil; add the mushrooms and 2 tablespoons (30 ml) butter. Boil rapidly for 4 to 5 minutes. Remove the saucepan from the heat and drain the mushrooms.

Preparation and cooking time: approximately 30 minutes.

MUSHROOMS AND ZUCCHINI (COURGETTES)

SERVES 4

*1 pound (450 g) zucchini
(courgettes), scrubbed, trimmed
and cut into 1-inch (2.5 cm)
rounds
2 tablespoons (30 ml) snipped dill
1 garlic clove, minced
½ pound (225 g) mushrooms,
sliced
Juice and zest of 1 lime*

*4 tablespoons (60 ml) butter
1 tablespoon (15 ml) flour
3 tablespoons (45 ml) reserved
cooking liquid
1 cup (8 oz; 225 ml) sour cream
Salt and pepper to taste
1½ tablespoons (23 ml) dried bread
crumbs*

Preheat the oven to 400° F (200° C; Mark 6).

Cook the zucchini, 1 tablespoon (15 ml) of the dill, and the garlic in boiling water for 4 to 5 minutes, or until just tender. Drain it through a sieve over a bowl, reserving the liquid. In a large frying pan, sauté the mushrooms, lime juice and zest in 3 tablespoons (45 ml) butter for about 3 minutes. Mix together the flour and 3 tablespoons (45 ml) reserved cooking liquid. Stir this into the mushrooms and cook for 3 minutes more. To this add the zucchini, sour cream, remaining dill, and salt and pepper to taste and cook, stirring, for 5 minutes. Transfer the mixture to a buttered casserole, sprinkle with dried bread crumbs and dot with the remaining butter. Bake in preheated oven for 10 minutes.

Preparation time: approximately 30 minutes. Cooking time: approximately 30 minutes.

SAYUR BAYEM

Adapted from *Indonesian Food and Cookery* by Sri Owen.

This Indonesian dish is particularly delicious, especially if the spinach is fresh and young. It can be made with either corn on the cob or sweet potatoes.

SERVES 6

2 young ears of corn or ¼ pound
   (120 g) sweet potatoes
2 shallots, sliced fine
½ green chili, sliced fine, or a pinch
   of chili powder
1½ cups (12 fl oz; 350 ml) water

A pinch of ground ginger
Salt
1 bay leaf
1 pound (450 g) young spinach
   leaves, washed and chopped
   coarse

Cut each ear of corn into three pieces (or peel and cut the sweet potatoes into small cubes). Put the shallots and chili into a saucepan with 1 cup (8 fl oz; 240 ml) water. Add the spices and seasoning and bring to the boil. When the water boils, put in the corn or sweet potatoes, cover the pan, and simmer for 15 minutes. Uncover, add the chopped spinach and another ½ cup (4 fl oz; 125 ml) water. Taste and add more salt if necessary. Cook until the spinach is tender; this will take about 5 to 7 minutes. Serve hot.

Preparation time: 15 to 20 minutes. Cooking time: approximately 30 minutes.

HERBS AND SPICES

ORIGINS, CULTIVATION AND USES

Allspice: (pimento, Jamaican pepper). Named because their small brown berries combine the flavors of cinnamon, cloves, nutmeg and juniper berries. Their appearance is similar to that of black peppercorns, but they are smoother and larger. Use whole berries in meat marinades and pot roasts; add to the liquid for poaching fish. Can be ground over pork chops, casseroles, pâtés, stews and potted meat. Also used in steamed puddings and fruitcakes; for flavoring slices of lemon for tea; to flavor spinach and carrots.

Angelica: Believed to have been native to Syria but has spread to many cool European countries. It is found in large amounts in Scotland, Lapland and Iceland and is said to have come to England in about 1568. American angelica or masterwort grows throughout the eastern United States. The juice of the fresh root of the American plant is acrid and said to be poisonous. The root itself has a strong odor and a warm aromatic flavor but is thought to be inferior in taste to the continental type. Both have the same medicinal qualities. The volatile oil in the root is used as a digestive, in the bath to stimulate the skin, as a diuretic tea to cleanse the blood and in herb pillows to induce calmness.

In cooking, the leaf stalks are candied and used for decorating cakes and pastry; for this they should be cut in April. The stalks may also be added instead of sugar when stewing rhubarb to take away the bitter flavor, but remove them before serving. The same is true for rhubarb jam. Mrs. M. Grieve in *A Modern Herbal* gives another good recipe for candying the leaves:

> Choose young stems, cut them into suitable lengths, then boil until tender. When this stage is reached, remove from the water and strip off the outer skin, then return to the water and simmer slowly until the whole has become very green. Dry the stems and weigh them, allowing one pound of white sugar to every pound of Angelica. The boiled stalks should be laid in an earthenware pan and the sugar sprinkled over them, allowing the whole to stand for a couple of days: then boil all together. When well boiled, remove from the fire and turn into a colander to drain off superfluous syrup. Take a little more sugar and boil to a syrup again, then throw in the Angelica, and allow it to remain for a few minutes, and finally spread on plates in a cool oven to dry.

Angelica is a perennial and likes heavy, damp conditions in which it will grow to over 6 feet high. Sow seeds in August and transplant to 18 inches apart before winter. Or divide the roots in spring and autumn.

To candy, pick young shoots and soak at once in strong brine for 10 minutes, then rinse and dry. Boil for 7 minutes, then scrape off the outer skin. To 1 pint (1¼ pt; 725 ml) boiling water add 1 tablespoon (½ oz; 15 ml) sugar, boil and pour back hot onto the angelica. Repeat this each day for 5 days. Finally, boil the angelica in the last syrup for 2 minutes, let stand for 2 more days, take out and dry in a cool oven.

Anise: Native to Egypt, Crete, Greece and Asia Minor. It was cultivated by the ancient Egyptians, then in the Middle Ages its cultivation spread to Central Europe. A dainty white flowering annual, the cultivated plant is considerably larger than the wild one. It is grown commercially in southern Russia, Bulgaria, Germany, Malta, Spain, North Africa and Greece. Recently India and South America have started to grow it commercially.

The extracted oil of the seeds of the anise plant can be used medicinally for bad coughs and digestion. Smeared on mousetraps, it is better bait than cheese.

The extracted oil is used in Germany for flavoring cakes and soups, in France, Spain, Italy and South America in the preparation of cordial liqueurs.

Sow seeds in dry, light soil on a warm, sunny border early in April. When they come up, thin plants and keep them clean from weeds. Allow 1 foot between each plant. Seeds may also be sown in pots in greenhouses and the plants removed to a warm site in May.

Arrowroot: Indigenous to the West Indian islands and possibly Central America, it grows in Bengal, Java, the Philippines, Mauritius, Natal and West Africa. The name is a corruption of the Aru-root of the Aruac Indians of South America, and is derived from the fact that the plant is said to be an antidote to arrow poison. It is a herbaceous perennial, reaching 6 feet high and bearing creamy flowers.

The starch is extracted from the rootlike underground stem of the plant when not more than one year old; it is odorless and tasteless and keeps well if quite dry. The powder creaks slightly when rubbed. It is the most digestible starch food and has been used as a basic part of convalescents' diets for many generations. Added to milk, it renders the milk digestible to patients for whom milk might be too heavy. For this reason, it is also useful in the latter stages of infant feeding. Very effective in stopping diarrhea.

Balm (sweet balm or lemon balm): Originally native to southern Europe but now cultivated in many places. The name is an abbreviation of the word "balsam," from which it derives its honeyed sweetness. The leaves emit a fragrant lemon odor when bruised. Used medicinally as an infusion for colds, it makes one perspire and so get rid of the fever.

It can also be added as lemon flavoring to soups and stews, herb sauces, sauces and marinades for fish and mushroom dishes; for salads and salad dressing, mayonnaise and egg dishes; good in all fruit cups, wine cups, milk dishes and milkshakes.

CLARET CUP

1 bottle red wine	*1 orange, cut in half*
1 pint (1¼ pt; 725 ml) seltzer water	*½ cucumber, sliced thick*
A small bunch balm	*1 liqueur glass Cognac*
A small bunch borage	*2 tablespoons (30 ml) sugar*

PROCESS

"Place these ingredients in a covered jug well immersed in rough ice, stir all together with a silver spoon, and when all the cup has been iced for about one hour, strain or decant it free from the herbs, etc." (from Francatelli's *Cook's Guide*).

The root is a perennial. The plant grows 2 to 3 feet high but dies down in winter. Sow the seeds, or plant cuttings in April/May, or divide the roots in spring or autumn, but not later than October so the offshoots may be established before the frost comes. Plant the roots 2 feet apart, with 3 or 4 buds to each. Keep them free from weeds, cut off the decayed stalks in the autumn and stir the ground between the roots. Balm is a vigorous grower so it must be well cut back or it will soon take over the herb garden.

Basil: Bush and sweet or common are both natives of India where basil is considered a sacred plant and cherished in every Hindu house because of its disinfectant value. Every religious Hindu is buried with a leaf of basil on his chest, in the belief that it is his passport to Paradise. It has a strong aromatic scent much like cloves. One type was found in 1789 in the West Indies and was used for chest trouble and dysentery. It is an essential oil which has been used for mild nervous disorders and some sorts of rheumatism.

Both bush and sweet basil are used in cooking. The French prefer the sweet basil (and I agree). The aromatic, volatile oil is used for flavoring soups, in particular turtle soup. It is also especially good in ragoûts and sauces. I cannot eat tomatoes without it, or, for that matter, a tomato dish. It increases in flavor when cooked. Add it to eggs, cheese and fish dishes. The famous English Fetter Lane sausage had basil as an essential ingredient. It can also be sprinkled over vegetables such as asparagus, eggplant (aubergine), carrots, mushrooms, spinach and rice. Also used in marinades for beef, liver, veal, lamb, pork and to flavor those meats on their own.

Francatelli's *Cook's Guide* gives the recipes for his well-known "Aromatic Seasoning" which I have adapted into modern English:

2 tablespoons (30 ml) freshly grated nutmeg

2 tablespoons (30 ml) ground mace

4 tablespoons (60 ml) cloves

4 tablespoons (60 ml) black peppercorns

2 tablespoons (30 ml) dried bay leaves

4 tablespoons (60 ml) fresh winter savory

1 tablespoon (15 ml) cayenne pepper

1 tablespoon (15 ml) grated lemon peel

2 cloves garlic, crushed

6 tablespoons (90 ml) fresh basil

6 tablespoons (90 ml) fresh marjoram

6 tablespoons (90 ml) fresh thyme

Pulverize all the ingredients with a mortar and pestle or in an electric coffee grinder and sift through a wire sieve. Put away in a dry, corked bottle for use.

Basil flourishes in rich soil and in the heat. In hot countries it can be grown in the garden. I find it best to grow several plants in a series of separate pots, so that when I have used up the leaves from one plant, I can go on to the next plant, allowing the first to grow new leaves. In this way, I usually have fresh basil until January.

One way of preserving basil until the next crop comes in is to put a layer of basil leaves in a jar, then some coarse sea salt, some more basil leaves, some salt, and so on until the jar is full. Then fill the jar with olive oil to cover; all winter you can take out the leaves, blot them on kitchen paper and use them in stews, salad dressings, etc. When they have been used up, the oil, which is impregnated with the basil, is delicious to use in cooking or in salad dressing.

If sowing outdoors, sow seeds in a frame or greenhouse in March and transplant to a warm, sheltered position in the garden in May or June.

Bay leaves: The sweet bay, which is the true laurel tree, grows to 25 feet in Britain, but in warmer climates it can grow as high as 60 feet. It is an evergreen, aromatic shrublike tree, the branches of which are covered with smooth, waxy, long oval pointed leaves.

Oil of bay is used externally for sprains, bruises, etc., and sometimes for earaches. In cooking, the leaf is an essential ingredient of bouquet garni. Use it in marinades for all meats, when roasting chicken and duck, in fish stock and court bouillon, rice dishes, tomato sauce, chicken, vegetable soups and meat stews. Always use it sparingly—half a leaf—as it has a very strong bitter taste which can take over and overpower other herbs.

The bay can be grown in tubs and is quite hardy. As it grows slowly, it should either be bought as a small shrub or cultivated by taking the cuttings of half-ripened shoots. The leaves can be picked all year round, but if using them dry, pick them early in the morning and place in thin layers on trays, not in the sun which causes them to fade, but in a warm, shady place. Or hang bunches, upside down, in the kitchen where they will dry well. Then place them in glass jars, as they exude oil continuously.

Bergamot: A plant indigenous to North America. The Oswego Indians used the plant as a tea, thus Oswego tea, for which the dried red flowers are used. It has a soothing and relaxing effect. I often drink it after driving the 4½- to 5-hour trip to our house in North Wales.

The plant is a perennial, needing rich, moist soil; near running water is ideal. It needs sun but does best in a slightly shaded position. Propagate by division and by cuttings. After two years, change its position into fresh soil.

Borage: Borage has beautiful blue flowers. When they appear, the young leaves, which have a cucumberlike flavor, should be picked. The old leaves are too prickly. Young leaves can be used as a hot herb tea and for people on salt-free diets, as it has a somewhat salty flavor. They can also be used chopped in salads, or in wine or fruit cups, or cooked like spinach (half spinach to half borage). Use it with cabbage, green pea and bean soups and stews.

It is an annual plant flourishing in ordinary soil which reseeds itself and which, if you are not careful, will take over the garden. Sow the seeds from late March to May.

Burnet salad: The leaves, which contain tannin, have a nutty, cucumber-like taste. The flowers are deep crimson. It is delicious in salads almost all the year round, as it is the last herb to die down in winter. Good in soup with other herbs—add it at the beginning of cooking—and for flavoring wine and fruit drinks. It is a perennial, common in dry pastures and by the roadside, liking especially chalk and limestone. It resows itself every year, or you can divide the roots in the autumn.

Cardamom: The aromatic pale green or black fibrous pods of an Indian flowering plant belonging to the ginger family. They have a sweet flavor with a touch of lemon. The Vikings discovered cardamom, and now it is used in almost all Danish pastry. The Indians, particularly in the north, use it as a basic ingredient in their cooking, and sometimes they suck the seeds as sweets to neutralize the smell of garlic. They and the Arabs often use cardamom seeds in coffee, and even in jasmine tea. I always use it to take the bitterness out of the very strong coffee which I prefer—there is then no need to use sugar. It also gives a mellow taste to tea and cocoa. Use crushed cardamom seeds infused in syrup for fruit compotes and salads or use ground cardamom in fruit pie fillings. Melon wedges are delicious sprinkled with ground cardamom. Also put it into chilled buttermilk or a plain yogurt milkshake. Also delicious cooked with game.

Cayenne: Cayenne derives its name from the Greek "to bite" because of the pungent properties of the fruits and seeds. It was introduced into England from India in 1548. It is ground from the dried pods of chili peppers, which are also sold fresh, dried or toasted. Chilies stimulate the appetite and cause sweating, thus cooling the body. This is why both the fresh green and the dried chili are used in making curries and many other Indian dishes. Delicious when used whole in jambalaya, chicken casserole and Gambas al Ajillo (see page 106). Put a pinch of cayenne in cheese pastries, soufflés, or fondues. Use in fish pâté, seafood dishes and in hollandaise sauce.

Celery: Although celery is technically a vegetable, its dried leaves or seeds, added near the end of cooking, improve soups, stocks, stuffings and stews. Celery salt also improves the flavor of tomato juice.

Chamomile:

ROMAN CHAMOMILE. An evergreen which was grown in medieval gardens for paths, lawns and "edging." When stepped upon, it gives out a delicious fragrance.

THE TRUE CHAMOMILE. The herb used in chamomile tea which aids the digestion. In France it is often drunk after heavy meals because it acts as a cleansing agent with a disinfectant and antispasmodic effect. Also useful in a facial steam bath as a cleanser, or on cotton for inflamed eyelids, or as a hair rinse for blonde hair. It can also be used as an infusion to soothe the pain of a toothache.

True chamomile is an annual, but it seeds itself quite easily. The Roman chamomile is propagated by division of roots and cuttings in April. It looks particularly pretty placed in between flagstones.

Chervil: Brought to France by the Romans, and used extensively throughout France and Central Europe in cooking. It has a slightly sweet flavor and is sometimes used as an alternative to parsley. Delicious with fish dishes—particularly crab—and raw vegetables, vegetable soups and vinaigrette sauces. Always add the chervil last thing, as its delicate flavor must be fresh. Very good in egg dishes, particularly omelettes, or with cream cheese. Sprinkle it on roast beef, lamb, veal. Use it on vegetables such as eggplant (aubergine), spinach, tomatoes, peas and all beans. Pour chervil butter over veal and fish.

Chervil can be sown at any time of year, but it must have the full winter sun and a half-shaded position in the summer. It does not require particularly rich soil but it must be well-drained. If chervil is sown monthly from January onward, you can harvest from May onward. Sow where the plants are to mature, then thin out when 2 to 3 inches high by pinching off at the ground. Keep cutting it back, weed continuously and keep the soil moist, otherwise the plant will flower and destroy the flavor of the leaves. Pick leaves from the outside of the plant, as with parsley. Best when fresh—drying, if not done with expertise, will destroy the flavor.

Chives: Grown since ancient Roman and Greek times, this plant has since traveled across the world to England and North America. Milder than the onion, chives contain iron, pectin, small quantities of sulphur and pungent volatile oils. These have the effect of stimulating the appetite and, therefore, food given to convalescents is often liberally sprinkled with chives.

Use chive butter for broiled (grilled) meat or fish. Add chives to mashed potatoes, mayonnaise or omelettes. Use it in fish or meat croquettes, mixed in with sausage meat, in French dressing, or in white and tomato sauces.

Chives grow wild or can be cultivated and are a hardy perennial. The grasslike leaves are the part used in cooking. They should always be snipped with scissors, rather than cut with a knife, so that they will break evenly. Once chives are planted they need only to be cut back—a natural process as they are used. They produce purple flowers, which can also be used in salads.

In general, they can be used fresh or freeze-dried as a substitute for small amounts of onion. Grow from seeds or by dividing the clumps of roots in the autumn. Leave several of the small bulbs together and place them 1 foot apart. The roots should be divided at least every third year. Cut the leaves up to four times during the season and they will become more tender.

Cinnamon: A sweet aromatic spice which is powerfully antiseptic and numbing, it is also capable of destroying bacteria—which makes it useful in hot countries. In India it is used whole, broken into 2-inch pieces, to flavor rice and lentil dishes, or ground in *garam masala,* a mixture of spices used as a basic ingredient in Indian cooking. An essential ingredient for baked apples, mulled wine and sangria, and in making orange liqueur, it is delicious with sugar on toast, in hot chocolate and in Irish coffee. Can be used in couscous, roast pork, *pasta e fagioli,* Christmas pudding and fruitcakes.

Cloves: The clove is the dried flower bud of a type of myrtle tree. Dark brown in color, with a strong aromatic flavor, cloves can be used either whole or ground. Use whole cloves stuck in a crisscross pattern over a baked ham, in whole onions to make bread sauce and with game. In India they are used to flavor rice dishes, broiled (grilled) or roasted fish, roast chicken or lamb; or they may be stuck into a lemon for mulled wine. Ground cloves are used in baking gingerbread and fruitcakes; in Indian cooking they are added to *garam masala* (see above). Like cinnamon, cloves are antiseptic and numbing. Some people chew them to destroy the odor of garlic or to soothe a sore throat.

Coriander: An annual plant indigenous to southern Europe, it was brought by the Romans into Britain. Fresh coriander resembles Italian parsley in leaf formation, but whereas parsley has stalks, coriander has roots and a distinct honey aroma. The leaves are particularly good ground in Jerusalem Artichoke and Chestnut Soup (see page 279), as well as in most meat stews and casseroles. Combined with ground roasted cumin seeds, the coriander leaf is delicious when added to plain yogurt. Pounded together with ginger and garlic, it is a good base for lamb and chicken curry. The dried coriander seeds, when pulverized together with black pepper and pressed into beef, give a special pungent taste to cold roasts. Use the pulverized seeds in marinades for meat and game, and always in curries and sauerkraut. Coriander is used by Peruvians in most of their dishes.

Coriander likes warm, dry soil. Sow in mild, dry weather. Dry the seeds by hanging the plant upside down in the kitchen and placing a paper bag over the head of the bunch to catch falling seeds.

Cumin: The fruit of a small annual herbaceous plant, cumin has a warm, powerful aroma with a spicy pungent flavor. In the Middle Ages it was one of the commonest spices of European growth. Indigenous to upper Egypt, in early times it was cultivated in Arabia, India and China and the countries bordering the Mediterranean. Cumin belongs to the same family as caraway, coriander and aniseed. In Malta they distinguish between hot cumin and anise, which they call sweet cumin. The odor resembles caraway but is not as agreeable. The dried seeds are used in every kind of curry, whole or ground, and in bread. Roasted, the seeds can be munched to aid digestion and are delicious when added to yogurt.

Dandelion: Dandelions can be used in salads or added to spinach purées, and tea made from them is good for liver and gallstone complaints.

Dill: Native to the Mediterranean and southern Russia, it grows wild in Spain and along the Italian coast. It has been used as a drug from the earliest of times to aid digestion and to cure hiccoughs. As a mild soporific, it can be used to calm babies. The name is derived from the Norse word "dilla," to lull.

Dill closely resembles fennel in appearance and has yellow flowers and feathery leaves. Use the *leaves* added to tomato and cucumber soups and salads, in sauces, in fish dishes, and in brine with pickling spices for cucumber or tomato pickle. The leaves are also good with yogurt and delicate vegetables. The *whole seed* (which is sharper than the leaf) can be used on lamb chops and in stews, herb butters, salad dressings, and in veal goulash and rice dishes. Sprinkle it on broiled (grilled) or boiled fish, and on beets, cabbage, cauliflower, sauerkraut and turnips. The French also use dill seed for flavoring cakes and pastries. Dill weed and yogurt make a delicious sauce for steamed whole turnips.

It is a hardy annual which is easy to grow, requiring no special kind of soil. The seeds must be sown as flat as possible and then should be slightly pressed into the soil. Sow dill from April until June in successive plantings. In some climates it is possible to continue sowing into July. Kept well watered, it will grow quickly. Plant in a sheltered position. *Do not plant near fennel* as the two will cross-polinate and you will have neither one nor the other.

Fennel: Generally considered indigenous to the Mediterranean coast, whence it spread eastward to India, it grows wild in most parts of Europe. Wherever Italians have moved to live, fennel has followed. It is related to and resembles dill, with yellow flowers and feathery leaves. The fennel seed has a strongly aromatic scent which is sweeter and less pungent than the dill seed. It is used as an ingredient in "gripe" water for babies.

The taste resembles aniseed more than dill, but fennel should never be planted near dill as they will cross-polinate, resulting in an indistinct herb. Fennel leaves are delicious used in fish soups or on broiled (grilled) or poached fish, especially oily fish such as trout, salmon, herring and mackerel. Also used in pâtés, or as fennel sauce for meat or creamed chicken. The root of Florence fennel can be used as a vegetable, braised or in salads. Fennel is good used with shellfish, pork or sauerkraut, and in biscuits and apple pie.

It flourishes in limestone soils and chalky districts and tends to seed itself. Easily propagated by seed, it is sown early in April in ordinary soil, and likes plenty of sun and not too much water.

Fenugreek: An annual herb with brownish seeds, similar in taste and odor to lovage and celery, it is cultivated in India, Africa, Egypt, Morocco and sometimes in England. One of the spices used in curries, but also used medicinally for diabetes; where quinine is not available it can prevent fevers. It is also sometimes used as a substitute for cod's liver. The pulverized seeds are put into things such as jams and marinades.

Garlic: According to Pliny, garlic and onion were invoked as deities by the Egyptians when taking an oath. Garlic was consumed in great quantities by the Greeks and Romans, but even then the smell was disapproved of—in Greece people who ate it were not allowed to enter the temples of Cybele.

Garlic was thought to have blood-cleansing and antiseptic qualities—lowering the blood pressure and helping to prevent colds. A good method for incorporating it into dishes and making it more digestible is to pound it in a mortar with some salt, working it into a paste. Add the paste to rice dishes, stews, casseroles or bean dishes, but use it sparingly. Garlic wine is also useful in cooking (see page 56).

For cultivation, the soil should be prepared as for onions. Garlic flourishes best in rich, moist, sandy soil, but will also grow in loam or clay soil. Dig some lime into the soil, and press firmly. Divide the bulbs into cloves, but leave out the middle clove which is not so good. With the point of a dibber, plant the cloves so that the top is just showing above the soil; leave 6 inches between the plants and 1 foot between the rows. Garlic should be planted in a sunny spot, kept thoroughly free from weeds and the soil gathered up around the roots from time to time. If planted in February or March, it should be ready for lifting in August or, if there has been a wet and cold summer, possibly mid-September. We plant ours in November in Wales, giving it a longer time to get itself rooted before the wet winter.

Ginger: Taken from the rootlike subterranean stem of a tropical bamboolike plant, it can be bought fresh, dried or powdered, candied or crystallized. Bruised fresh ginger, which is milder than dried ginger, is delicious when infused into marmalades and chutneys; it is wrapped in cheesecloth (muslin) while cooking, then removed before the product is put into jars. Ground ginger is used in baking, such as gingerbreads and cakes—particularly in Christmas (plum) puddings. It gives a special taste when sprinkled over carrots and string (French) beans, as well as over melon. I use it in chicken curry as well as in most oriental dishes. It can also be used instead of salt by those on salt-free diets.

Horseradish: Some authorities think horseradish is indigenous to the eastern parts of Europe, from the Caspian, through Russia and Poland, to Finland. Both the roots and leaves were used as medicines in the Middle Ages, and as condiments in Denmark and Germany. It is now used for lung trouble and coughs. It is thought that scraped horseradish, applied to chilblains and secured with a light bandage, will help to cure them. When infused in wine, the root will stimulate the nervous system, causing perspiration and thus reducing fevers. Also, if eaten frequently during the day, it helps rid one of the cough following influenza.

Horseradish has been adopted by the British, who use it, grated and mixed with lemon and whipped cream, as a sauce for roast beef. Grated and mixed with sour apples or sour cream, it is delicious with smoked meat, ham and sausages. Grated horseradish is also used in dips for shellfish or in cream with river trout, cod or carp. Use the young leaves in salads.

Take cuttings ½ inch thick and 9 inches long; plant in March, remove and replant in the autumn. A hardy perennial, once it is established horseradish is almost impossible to rout. It also has a nasty tendency to take over and run rampant. When planting, put in plenty of manure deep down in the soil.

Hyssop: An aromatic, evergreen bushy herb with deep blue flowers growing 1 to 2 feet high, it is native to southern Europe. Hyssop contains volatile oils and tannins which attract bees and butterflies. It is an ingredient in Chartreuse liqueur and has a slightly bitter, minty taste which is delicious when the young leaves are used in salads or added, chopped, to meat and game, soups and stews. It is also used to make a tea for coughs and bronchial troubles. The leaves, stems and flowers are distilled to provide an essential oil which is used in perfume.

Juniper berries: The Juniper is a small shrub, 4 to 6 feet high, found throughout the northern hemisphere, particularly where bands of lime occur. It was considered to be a magic shrub throughout the Middle Ages.

If you burn a juniper twig or branch and wave it around the room, the strong aromatic scent pervades the room and is believed to act as a disinfectant. Juniper berry tea is particularly good for liver and slight kidney conditions, but *not for inflamed kidneys.* Crush 12 to 18 berries per cup of water, bring to the boil and boil for 15 minutes. If taken every morning, a tea made from the young sprouts will help to protect one from infection. The berries are delicious when pulverized together with coriander and pressed into a steak; or the same combination can be used in a mustard mayonnaise for Beef Fondue. Three or four berries can be used in place of 1 small bay leaf. Added to the liquid used for cooking grouse and wild duck, the berries will take away the gamy taste which some people dislike. Add the berries also to meat pickled in brine and when cooking cabbage. They are delicious used in marinades for game and game dishes, as well as in sauerkraut.

Juniper berries take two to three years to mature, starting green, then ripening to blue and black when they are ready for picking. Then they are dried on trays until they shrivel up.

To cultivate, buy *Juniper communis,* which is the only variety suitable for culinary and medicinal purposes. The berries are produced only by female flowers, and since female and male flowers occur on different bushes you will need to buy both. April to May is the flowering period; the berries are harvested in the autumn. The leaves and shoots can be collected at any time of the year.

Lovage: Garden lovage is one of the cultivated Old English herbs, but it is also native to the Mediterranean region, growing wild in the mountainous districts of the south of France, in northern Greece and in the Balkans.

As an addition to your bath or taken as a tea, it will improve circulation and stimulate the kidneys. It is also helpful in heart conditions and will act as a deodorant.

The lovage leaf, with its special yeast flavor, is used a great deal in Europe as an addition to soups, casseroles and stews; in mixed vegetables, salads and marinades, fish sauces, cabbage, roots, sauerkraut and mayonnaise. You can rub poultry or game with the leaves before roasting and, like garlic, you can rub the salad bowl with it. Whole seeds can be used in beef, lamb, mutton, hare or venison stew, but remove the seeds before serving. The stems can be candied like angelica.

Lovage is an immensely tall and spreading perennial with greenish-yellow flowers. It is easy to grow. Propagation is by division of roots in early spring or by seeds sown in late summer when they ripen, and then transplanted either in the autumn or early spring.

Mace: The mace blades are the orangish spiky tendrils which lie around the shell of the nutmeg. Mace is milder but not as delicate as nutmeg. The blades are used for infusing—for *béchamel* or bread sauce, or in marinades for poached fish. Ground, it is delicious in fish pies. Sift together three times 1 cup (8 oz; 225 g) salt, 1 level tablespoon (15 ml) ground white pepper and 1 teaspoon (5 ml) ground mace. Store the seasoning in a screw-top jar and use for seasoning sauces, casseroles and soups. Also delicious in yogurt mixtures. Use mace in lemon and honey cakes, fruit tarts, egg and cheese dishes.

Marigolds: Came originally from India. The florets and leaves of the common deep-orange flowered variety are of medicinal value. The florets must be dried quickly in the shade in a good current of warm air, spread out on sheets of paper without touching each other, or they become discolored. Some people think that if you rub the flower on a bee or wasp sting it will stop the pain and swelling. A water distilled from the flower is good for sore or inflamed eyes. The petals can be used in place of saffron for giving color to rice, etc. Crushed petals give a sweet-salt flavor to fish, venison and chicken. French Marigolds in the greenhouse, or as a border in an herb garden, will keep away white fly.

Wild marjoram: It is also known as oregano, which can be cultivated as a perennial, and is used in Italian, Spanish and Mexican cooking.

Wild marjoram contains thymol, a powerful antiseptic used either internally or externally. It has an ancient medical and mystical reputation. The Greeks and Romans crowned young couples with marjoram, and they thought that if marjoram grew on a grave it brought great happiness in the afterlife. Found chiefly in chalky soils, the whole plant has a strong, fragrant, balsamic odor and a warm, bitterish aromatic taste, all of which are preserved when the herb is dried. It grows best in a warm, sunny spot.

Pot marjoram: A hardy perennial, propagated by seeds in April, by division of roots in the autumn, or by offsets—slipping rooted pieces off the plants, planting them with a trowel or dibber, and watering them well. Pot marjoram prefers a warm place and dry, light soil.

Sweet marjoram: The seeds should be sown in a cold frame in March and transplanted to a warm bed in May. It is a strong herb and should therefore be used sparingly. It can be used in forcemeats instead of or in addition to thyme; in salads, particularly tomato salads; in tomato sauces and also to flavor vinegar and egg dishes. Rub on strongly flavored meats such as pork and lamb, or add to potato and bean dishes and stuffed vegetables.

Mint: Mints should be planted away from other herbs in the garden, and each bed of mint should be contained within metal strips, as it tends to spread. Propagate by dividing the creeping roots in February or by taking cuttings in the summer. The soil should be well dug and given a moderate dressing of well-rooted compost or manure in the spring.

Culinary mints are:

SPEARMINT. A common garden mint, the oil of which is taken to make spearmint chewing gum. The herb is delicious sprinkled on melon, or the leaves used whole to flavor iced tea.

BOWLES MINT. It has round woolly leaves and is the best mint to use in mint sauce and on new potatoes. Its delicious, fresh flavor is good on carrots, peas, string beans and zucchini (courgettes).

EAU DE COLOGNE MINT. Has a fragrant lemon flavor and smell. Useful in drinks, in potpourri or on baked or broiled (grilled) fish. It is also a deterrent to flies.

VARIEGATED APPLEMINT. Combines the flavor of apples and mint in one plant. Used a great deal in the United States as the British use Bowles Mint (see above).

BLACK PEPPERMINT. Makes a delicious, refreshing and digestive tea. Also good added to jams, jellies, fruit juices and lentil soup.

Mustard seed: Both the black and white mustards are wild herbs in Britain, but are cultivated as well for their seeds, which are used both medicinally and to flavor foods.

White mustard is an annual plant with large yellow leaves and spreading, roundish pods, each containing 4 to 6 globular seeds, yellow both inside and out. Black mustard has smaller flowers with smooth, erect, flattened pods, each containing 10 to 12 dark reddish-brown or black seeds, which are collected when ripe and dried.

Both varieties grow throughout southwestern Europe and are cultivated in England, Holland, Italy and Germany for their seeds. Both are included in pickling spices and to make a delicious mustard (see page 395). Medicinally, they are used against colds and headaches, and for sore feet.

Nutmeg: The seed of the nutmeg tree, which has a warm, aromatic and slightly sweet flavor. If taken in large doses it becomes an emetic and a narcotic, but in small doses it is a good digestive and has a soporific effect. Therefore, it is very good in hot milk, taken just before bedtime. Ground nutmeg is obtainable, but it soon loses its flavor. It is most effective if kept whole and grated as needed. Often used in Europe, together with salt and pepper, for seasoning vegetables; delicious sprinkled over cooked cabbage, Brussels sprouts, spinach, cauliflower or in mashed potatoes. Good with all egg and cheese dishes. In India it is used to flavor candies (sweets). Use in baking cakes and breads.

Paprika: The dried and ground flesh of the sweet pepper, it ranges from sweet to hot in quality, also giving color as a garnish to many dishes. Sprinkled over fried or broiled (grilled) chicken, it gives a crispness and appetizing color. It is an essential ingredient in goulash.

Parsley:

CURLY-LEAVED PARSLEY. Parsley was grown in ancient times and often mentioned by Pliny. The Greeks used to crown their heroes with a wreath of parsley, and also placed it on the tombs of the dead. It was said to have sprung from the blood of a Greek hero, Archenorous, the forerunner of death.

The seeds of the Triple Moss curled variety are used in making Apiol, a drug which helps to cure malaria, and parsley leaves, infused for tea, are used extensively as a diuretic and for kidney complaints.

Its culinary uses are many—the leaves, finely chopped, are delicious when sprinkled over vegetables or used as flavoring in soups, casseroles and stews, as well as in forcemeats for meat, game and poultry. It is an essential ingredient of "gremolata"—chopped garlic, ground lemon peel and a quantity of minced parsley. Use it in parsley sauce; fried in hot oil it is delicious with fish.

Parsley takes 5 to 6 weeks to germinate. The seeds like a moist, part-shady position. Sow throughout the summer in drills, in rich, well-worked soil. The roots must be allowed to go down deep. Loam or clay soil is best. If you have sandy soil, fork in heavy loam or clay and plenty of manure. In the second year, cut off the flower stems when they appear. Put another sowing in. It should be well watered and kept free from weeds.

Always pick parsley from the outside of the plant so as to encourage regrowth. It can be easily dried by picking it in dry weather, putting it in a low oven—200° F (90° C)—with the door open for ventilation. When brittle, rub the parsley between your hands, pick out the stalks and store in an airtight container.

HAMBURG PARSLEY. Its wild habitat is said to be Sardinia, Turkey, Algeria and Lebanon; it was brought to England in 1548. The leaves contain vitamins A, B and C, and a considerable quantity of minerals, particularly iron. The roots contain a high proportion of vitamin C. If taken every day, it is a natural way to absorb these vitamins, particularly during winter. It also stimulates the digestive glands and so aids digestion. The root may be sliced and made into potatolike chips (crisps) or fritters.

Pepper: Black peppercorns are dried, unripe pepper berries with the skin or husk, and white peppercorns are dried, ripe berries with the skin or husks removed. White pepper is hot and fiery, the black more aromatic. In southern India, peppercorns growing on vines are as common as beans in the west. Pepper should always be used freshly ground, to stimulate the gastric juices. Whole peppercorns keep their flavor a long time, while ground pepper quickly loses its pungency.

Whole black peppers can be used in goulash and other stews. Crushed, they can be used together with crushed coriander on steak. Freshly ground pepper can be used in salads, pasta, soups, egg dishes and some vegetables— I use it on almost everything, and particularly in Poivrade Sauce and Piperade.

Poppy seeds: Derived from the white opium poppy, which is indigenous to Asia Minor and is cultivated in Europe and Turkey, Persia, India and China. Poppy seeds are used in "chapatties," an Indian bread. Sometimes they are used as a substitute for sesame seeds. Poppy seeds are delicious when lightly toasted, and they add texture to bread.

Rosemary: The ancient Romans and Greeks thought rosemary strengthened the memory and, therefore, it became the emblem of fidelity for lovers and was entwined in bridal wreaths.

Some people believe that it stimulates hair growth and prevents premature baldness. An infusion of the leaves and flowers, combined with borax and used when cold, prevents dandruff. Rosemary boiled with lovage and juniper makes a good diuretic tea. Use it with care, as the flavor is strong. It is used as an ingredient in eau de cologne.

Good with roasts of lamb, veal and pork; in meat marinades and with strongly flavored fish, such as eel and halibut. Put it inside chicken, duck, pheasant and quail, or mix with cottage and cream cheese.

Rosemary grows best in light, sandy and rather dry soil, preferably overlying chalk, as it needs lime. Put it in a sheltered position looking south with a great deal of sunlight. It is a perennial evergreen shrub with small, pale-blue flowers which grows to between 5 and 6 feet high. It can be propagated by seeds, cuttings, division of roots and layering. The easiest way is to take the cuttings in February or March, at the end of May, or in June, after the plant has flowered. It must be dried and stored carefully, otherwise it takes on a musty flavor.

Rocket, garden: Native to Italy where it is known as rugola or arugola, it is also found throughout central Europe and the Mediterranean region. The mature leaves are very acrid in taste but delicious in salads when young. They must be gathered before their white flowers have appeared. A biennial plant which is easy to grow, the seeds should be sown in May or June in drills 6 inches apart. It prefers sunlight and warm, sandy soil.

Saffron: Very expensive, but you need use only a little at a time because it is very pungent. Saffron is used in chicken, shellfish and, particularly, risotto dishes. In England it is used to make saffron bread and cakes.

I use it as well in duck and turkey dishes, and a little added to cream cheese gives it a good color and a lovely taste. Infuse the saffron in 2 tablespoons (30 ml) boiling water for 5 minutes, then add to whatever dish you wish—it gives a pretty yellow color.

Sage: An evergreen shrub native to the northern shores of the Mediterranean but now cultivated everywhere. A good border plant that will grow anywhere. Replant shoots from old plants every 4 years. Sage doesn't need any special soil preparation but grows best in light, dry, chalky soil in a sunny position. The annual seeds are sown in April and the crop cut in September or October.

Broad-leaved sage is the best for drying. A perennial, it is propagated only by division of plants, layerings or cuttings, and cannot be grown from seed.

Narrow-leaved sage is the best for using fresh in cooking. Cut off the blue flowers.

Sage is used with onion in stuffings and forcemeats for roast pork, veal and game. Use it on liver and fatty fish such as eel, or in meat pies, cheese spreads, omelettes, cream soups and meat stews.

Savories:

SUMMER SAVORY. An annual, small evergreen subshrub, stronger than winter savory in flavor. It is grown from seeds sown in a sunny spot in fairly rich soil in April, then thinned in May to 1 plant every 6 inches. The soil must *not* contain fresh manure or compost.

WINTER SAVORY. A hardy perennial subshrub, it grows best in poor, light soil, preferably chalky, well-drained and in full sun. Sow in August or the beginning of September, or propagate from the cuttings of side shoots stuck in cold frames in April.

Both species of savory are grown near beehives for their fragrance, which the bees transfer to their honey. The Romans used a vinegar, flavored with savory and other aromatic herbs, as an addition to mint sauce with lamb. Savory can be added to vegetable juices, egg and cheese dishes, bean and pea soups, fish chowders, or used in horseradish and barbecue sauces, stuffings for poultry, and in all bean, sauerkraut and mushroom dishes.

French sorrel: Native to the south of France, Italy, Switzerland and Germany, the plant is glaucous with oblong, fleshy and succulent leaves. It grows abundantly, and if the leaves are culled back continuously you will get many cuttings during the summer.

Fresh or dried leaves are used in a diuretic infusion and as a treatment for kidney stones. It is also believed to have blood-cleansing properties.

Sorrel can be shredded, then made into a purée and used as a base for soup, or combined with spinach purée in a soup. It is also delicious shredded raw over salads to give a sharp, lemony flavor. It can be chopped fine to use in omelettes, to make a quiche with leeks and to flavor fish dishes.

It is best propagated from seeds sown in drills 6 inches apart from March to May, and later thinned when the plants are 1 to 2 inches high. The roots may also be divided in the spring or autumn. Sorrel grows best in light, rich soil in a sheltered, preferably shady position. Harvest in 3 to 4 months when four or five leaves have appeared. If you cut back the first leaves, the second and successive cuttings will be more tender, which is useful for cooking.

Tarragon: An easily cultivated perennial, the French tarragon has more flavor than the Russian, although the latter is more resistant to weather conditions. It is easy to propagate by division of roots in March or April, or by cuttings taken in the spring or in late summer. Some young plants should be raised annually. Tarragon likes dry, warm soil and the roots should be protected in the winter, otherwise the cold and wet will kill them.

Tarragon may be used as a salt substitute for salt-free diets. It is used in béarnaise, hollandaise and mousseline sauces. The chopped leaves are delicious in French dressing and in green salads. Use in herb bouquets and fines-herbes mixtures, in marinades for meat, in fish soups, or in omelettes and other egg dishes. Sprinkle it on chicken, veal, spinach, zucchini (courgettes), asparagus and artichokes.

Thymes:

GARDEN THYME. Perennial.

LEMON THYME. Perennial.

WILD THYME OR SERPOLET.

Thyme is native to the Mediterranean and was used by the ancient Greeks for fumigation purposes and as an antiseptic. They also used it as an emblem of activity, bravery and energy, according to Lady Northcote in *The Herb Garden*. The honey from the bees of Mount Hymettus near Athens is particularly delicious because they feed on the flowers of the wild thyme.

Strongly aromatic, thyme stimulates the appetite and aids digestion. For catarrh and coughs, make a tisane of thyme: 2 tablespoons (30 ml) thyme to 1¼ cups (1 pt; 600 ml) boiling water, sweetened with honey.

Thymol, the volatile oil of thyme, is used to medicate gauze and wool for medical dressings, and the distilled oil of thyme can be used as a liniment or bath oil. It is a powerful antiseptic for both internal and external use, and can also be used as a local anesthetic and a deodorant. It can be applied like carbolic, with less irritation and a stronger germicidal action.

Thyme is an integral ingredient of bouquet garni, and one of the many herbs used in Benedictine liqueur.

It helps digest fats and is therefore used efficiently with fatty meats. Rub on beef, lamb, veal, fat pork and oily fish before broiling (grilling), roasting or braising. As it is very strong and pungent, it must be used with discretion. Add it to stews and thick soups, such as split pea and bean; use it to flavor vegetables such as beans, beets, carrots, potatoes, mushrooms and tomatoes; and in herb sauces.

A French friend of mine makes a delicious herbal mixture which can be added to roasts and all meat dishes. It is best to use fresh herbs, but dry ones can be almost as good: Mix together 7 tablespoons (105 ml) garden thyme, 3 tablespoons (45 ml) wild thyme, 3 tablespoons (45 ml) rosemary and 1 large bay leaf, and grind them with a mortar and pestle or in an electric coffee grinder. Pack the mixture in airtight jars.

Thyme likes a well-drained, dry, sunny position, preferably in chalky soil. Rock gardens are a good place for it. Propagate either from seed, by division of an old plant or from cuttings taken in April or May. A thyme bed should be replaced every 3 to 4 years, otherwise the plant becomes woody and straggly. Keep the bed well watered and free from weeds.

Turmeric: Turmeric, with lilylike leaves and yellow flowers, grows in Southeast Asia and belongs to the ginger family. But there the resemblance ends. It doesn't taste like ginger. The dried tubers are ground to a fine powder which gives an instant yellow staining effect to risottos and curries. It can sometimes be used as a substitute for saffron, but the color and taste of turmeric are stronger. It gives celery rémoulade, homemade mayonnaise and mustard an extra bit of color.

HERBAL HINTS

1. *To dry fresh herbs:* Pick early in the morning before the sun has baked them. Wash, then dry thoroughly by patting with paper towels, and spread on a baking sheet. Leave in a 250° F (130° C; Mark ½) oven until completely dry or place on a screen in a warm room. Alternatively,

they can be tied in a bunch and hung upside down to dry in the kitchen. When the herbs have dried and become crisp, either leave them whole or crush them and store in airtight jars.

2. *A sprig of rosemary*, the branch part, can be used as a skewer for kebabs, holding the cubes of lamb, onions and pepper. The flavor of the herb will then impregnate the meat while it is cooking. A sprig of rosemary can also be used as a brush for barbecue sauce or marinades when cooking lamb and chicken. Rosemary oil rubbed on the scalp encourages hair growth, and a good rinse for brunettes can be made from fresh or dried rosemary, sage, nettles (which give the hair body), and catnip, which invigorates and encourages hair growth.

3. *Make an herb bouquet:* Combine a pinch to ½ teaspoon (2 ml) of each of the herbs needed. Tie the mixture in cheesecloth (muslin) to facilitate later removal, and add to soups, stews, etc. It is cheaper than buying commercial bouquet garni, and you have your own choice of herbs.

Mixtures for bouquet garni:

a. *Beef*—marjoram, savory, basil, thyme, parsley, oregano
b. *Lamb*—marjoram, rosemary, savory, dill, mint
c. *Pork*—allspice, cinnamon stick, fresh ginger, rosemary, thyme
d. *Poultry*—tarragon, basil, chives, savory
e. *Eggs*—tarragon, basil, chives, savory
f. *Vegetables*—basil, savory, chives, thyme, marjoram, parsley
g. *Soups and stews*—parsley, thyme, basil, marjoram, rosemary, savory

4. *A mixture of nettles, parsley and catnip removes dandruff.*

5. *Herbal mixtures for the bath:* Place the herbs in a cheesecloth (muslin) bag and tie so that the bag hangs under the hot water faucet (tap) with the water running through it.
A relaxing and invigorating bath mixture—lovage, rosemary, peppermint and lemon balm.
A relaxing and sleepmaking bath mixture—elderflowers, chamomile, basil and lavender.
A spring bath mixture—dandelion, daisy, cowslip, nettles and angelica leaves.

6. *To chop mint:* Wash and dry the mint. Cut off the leaves with a kitchen scissors, then sprinkle the leaves with sugar before chopping.

7. *To chop parsley:* Pinch the tufts of parsley tightly between the thumb and first two fingers of the left hand, then cut across with your scissors. This method is much quicker than chopping on a board, and there will be no board to clean afterward.

8. When cooking with herbs, use twice as much fresh as its dried counter-

part. Date jars of dried herbs at the time of purchase, as some dried herbs last only 4 to 6 months.

9. Allspice berries, which grind like black pepper, may be used as a substitute for cloves or cinnamon.

10. To give a lot of spice, and to brown toasted cheese or cheese toppings, sprinkle some paprika on top.

11. To make freshly ground ginger without the tedious peeling and chopping, grind fresh gingerroot in an electric coffee grinder for 2 or 3 seconds.

SALADS

"It takes four people to make a successful salad: a spendthrift to throw in the oil, a miser to drop in the vinegar, a lawyer to administer the seasoning, and a madman to stir the whole together." An old Spanish proverb.

1. Always use fresh, clean, crisp vegetables or fruits.
2. On a hot day, place the salad in the refrigerator before serving it, to insure its looking crisp.
3. Make sure the salad is dried well before adding the dressing. The new salad spinners are ideal for this.
4. It is better to pull apart lettuce, romaine, chicory and endive than to cut or slice it.
5. *Never* swamp the salad with dressing. A thin coating is ideal.
6. If you wish a taste of garlic and/or onion, but not an overpowering aroma, rub the salad bowl with either before adding the salt. Another method is to place the garlic or onion in the salad dressing for 15 minutes before serving, then remove it.
7. When making a dressing, always mix the seasonings with the vinegar before adding the salad oil. The oil coats the herbs, thus trapping their flavor.
8. Keep an oil-based salad dressing from separating by adding the juice of 1 lemon or a coddled egg.

9. A sugar cube in the olive oil will keep it from becoming rancid.
10. Mayonnaise is not as rich if you make it with half peanut (groundnut) and half olive oil.
11. The dressing should be added to the salad only at the last minute.

Salad oil is beneficial as it tends to prevent the fermentation in the stomach caused by raw vegetables.

Vegetables such as beans, dried beans (haricots), peas and all pulses should be boiled, drained and thoroughly cooled before using them in salads. Then a little onion and a lot of parsley should be added. The vegetables may be eaten just like that, or mixed with lettuce, endive, etc. Other vegetables that are delicious used in salads are asparagus, globe artichokes, boiled beets, celery, cucumber, cauliflower, dandelions, radishes, salsify and tomatoes. Nasturtium leaves and flowers, and marigolds, have a pleasant flavor and add a nice touch to vegetable salads.

FENNEL SALAD

Serve with white fish such as turbot, cod, halibut or hake.

SERVES 4

1 bulb Florentine fennel, inner leaves only, shredded
½ head Chinese cabbage (bok choy), shredded fine

1 hard-boiled egg, chopped
Shredded zest of 1 fresh lemon
Pickled walnut, to taste

Pile up the fennel leaves and Chinese cabbage in the center of your salad bowl and garnish with the egg, lemon zest and pickled walnut. Use a simple French dressing.

GAME SALAD

A particularly good way to use up leftovers.

SERVES 4

1 pound (450 g) pheasant, partridge
or grouse meat, sliced thin,
almost shaved
½ head Romaine lettuce
1 mustard green (mustard and
cress) plant and 1 bunch of
watercress, or 2 bunches of
watercress

1½ teaspoons (7.5 ml) mixed
thyme, rosemary and oregano

THE DRESSING

3 tablespoons (45 ml) green tomato
or mango chutney
4 tablespoons (60 ml) sesame oil
2 tablespoons (30 ml) spiced
vinegar

1 tablespoon (15 ml) red currant
jelly

Make alternate layers of the game with lettuce, mustard greens (and cress) or watercress and the mixed salad herbs, arranged in a bowl. Mix all the dressing ingredients together. Pour on the dressing and serve.

CUCUMBER SALAD

SERVES 4

1 cucumber, sliced thin
½ small onion, chopped fine
Salt and fresh-ground black pepper
A pinch of superfine granulated
(castor) sugar

Lemon and dill dressing (see
below)

Place the slices of cucumber and onion on a plate with a sprinkling of salt, and cover with another plate. Let stand for 30 minutes to "weep," then drain the "tears" away and put the cucumbers and onions in a salad bowl. Dredge with salt, pepper and a pinch of sugar. Pour on the lemon and dill dressing.

LEMON AND DILL DRESSING

Salt and fresh-ground black pepper
1 teaspoon (5 ml) chopped fresh dill, or 1½ teaspoons (7.5 ml) freeze-dried dillweed
1 teaspoon (5 ml) Dijon mustard

⅔ cup (5 fl oz; 150 ml) safflower oil
⅓ cup (2½ fl oz; 65 ml) lemon juice

Mix all the ingredients well.

INDIAN SALAD

SERVES 6 TO 8

1 head curly chicory, washed and dried
1 head lettuce, washed and dried
3 tablespoons (45 ml) mango chutney
¼ teaspoon (1.5 ml) allspice
2 tablespoons (50 ml) red wine vinegar

2 tablespoons (50 ml) red wine
2 hard-boiled eggs, sliced thin
One 3½-ounce (92 g) can (tin) of shrimp
6 slices of lemon

Pull the chicory and lettuce into bite-sized pieces. In a bowl, combine the chutney, allspice, vinegar and wine. Arrange the chicory and lettuce in a mound in a salad bowl. Around it place a ring of egg slices, shrimp and lemon slices. Pour on the dressing and serve with brown bread and butter.

JERUSALEM ARTICHOKE SALAD

SERVES 6

1 tablespoon (15 ml) flour
1 tablespoon (15 ml) white wine vinegar
1 pound (450 g) Jerusalem artichokes, peeled and washed

Salt and pepper
½ cup (2 oz; 50 g) chopped onion
2 sprigs fresh coriander leaves, chopped fine

FRENCH DRESSING

⅔ cup (7 fl oz; 200 ml) safflower oil
1 clove garlic, crushed
1 teaspoon (5 ml) Dijon mustard

Salt and pepper
⅓ cup (3 fl oz; 75 ml) lemon juice, or more to taste
A sprig of fresh coriander, chopped

Bring to a boil in a medium-sized saucepan enough water to cover the artichokes. Add the flour and vinegar and stir, then add the artichokes. Cook for approximately 6 to 7 minutes, or until they are tender *but still firm.* Drain in a colander and cool. When completely cool, slice the artichokes thin and put them into a salad bowl, season with salt and pepper, and sprinkle with the chopped onion and fresh coriander leaves. Combine all the ingredients for the dressing and pour it over the salad.

CURRY SALAD

(CAN BE SERVED HOT OR COLD) SERVES 6

5 cups (2¼ pts; just over 1 l) water
1 teaspoon (5 ml) salt
1 tablespoon (15 ml) vegetable oil
2 cups (14 oz; 400 g) raw rice
1 ounce (25 g) butter
1 small onion, sliced
1 apple, peeled and sliced
2 stalks rhubarb, sliced
⅔ cup (¼ pt; 150 ml) chicken stock

1 teaspoon (5 ml) curry paste
1 teaspoon (5 ml) curry powder
Salt
Cayenne
1 large head cauliflower, cooked and separated into florets
1 pound (450 g) carrots, washed, cooked and sliced
1 pound (450 g) peas, shelled and cooked

In a medium-sized saucepan, bring the water to a rapid boil. Add the salt and oil, then add the rice and bring the water back to the boil. Cover the pan tightly and cook over low heat for 20 to 25 minutes, or until the water has been completely absorbed. Transfer the rice to a colander set over boiling water and steam, covered, for 15 minutes. In a small saucepan melt the butter and sauté the onion until it turns golden, then add the apple, rhubarb, stock, curry paste and powder. Cook the sauce and season it with salt and cayenne to taste. Before taking it off the fire, toss in the cooked vegetables. Let them heat through, and serve either hot or cold surrounded by a border of rice. Sprinkle some cayenne over the whole salad, including the rice.

A HERB SALAD

SERVES 4

*A handful of mixed fresh sage,
   thyme, tarragon, marjoram,
   winter savory and chives*
4 large tomatoes, quartered
A small handful of seedless raisins
Juice of ½ lemon

1 tablespoon (15 ml) olive oil
1 teaspoon (5 ml) Dijon mustard
*1 tablespoon (15 ml) superfine
   granulated (castor) sugar*
1 heaping teaspoon (6 ml) salt
1 teaspoon (15 ml) black pepper

Chop the herbs, which *must* be fresh, as fine as possible, and sprinkle them over the tomatoes. Add the raisins and lemon juice. Mix the olive oil and Dijon mustard together and add the sugar, salt and pepper.

EGGS

The composition of an egg is 13% protein, 9% fat and 60% water, the rest is blood, ash and minerals. Eggs contain vitamins A, B, and D. The shell consists entirely of carbonate of lime. The yolk stores fat in the form of an emulsion which is, therefore, easily digested. The yolk contains less water than the white, which is mostly albumen. When an egg is stored water evaporates, and the egg becomes lighter.

How eggs are kept is more important than how long. There is an air chamber at the blunt end of the egg which increases in size as the egg gets stale and begins to dry up. This is why eggs should always be stored in an egg carton with the pointed end down. They should be kept in a cold larder or in the refrigerator, not at room temperature. If the egg rests on the blunt end, eventually the yolk will break through to the air chamber and press against and stick to the shell. This will make the egg go bad quickly; if kept with the pointed end down, the yolk will rest on the white, and will stay fresh longer.

In order to prevent a fresh egg from cracking while boiling, you should prick the blunt end, thus releasing the air, which expands with heat. A fresh egg should sink at once in salted water. The older the egg, the more easily it will float. A week-old egg kept in cool conditions is better than one that is a day or two old kept in warm conditions.

Do not wash eggs. The shell has an invisible protective coating which, if washed off, will shorten the life of the egg. And do not store eggs near strong-smelling food as the eggshell is porous and will absorb the smell, thus affecting its taste.

Ideally, eggs should be removed from the refrigerator a few hours before using, but Madeleine Kamman in *The Making of a Cook* says: "If this is not possible, place the egg in warm water for 30 minutes. They must always reach room temperature while in their shells, otherwise when the shells are broken, the yolks will dehydrate and harden."

GENERAL HINTS

1. To peel shells from hard-boiled eggs, salt the cooking water and, when the eggs are done, rinse them quickly in cold water and crack the shell at either end instead of in the middle.
2. To keep a cracked eggshell intact while boiling, add 1 teaspoon (5 ml) salt to the water.
3. Fresh eggshells look rough and chalky; old eggs look smooth and shiny.
4. To make scrambled eggs fluffy, add a little carbonated water.
5. To keep egg yolks fresh for several days, cover them with cold water or salad oil and store in the refrigerator. Or beat up the yolks with a little cold water and store in the refrigerator. Or poach them until they are hard, sieve them and use in salads.
6. To cut hard-boiled eggs neatly, use a knife rinsed in hot water.
7. Egg whites will whip faster and thicker if the eggs have been kept at room temperature for at least 1 hour before whipping. A copper mixing bowl is best.
8. The reason for beating an egg yolk is to break it down to a condition where it will readily absorb fat and form an emulsion. This is how mayonnaise is made. Beat the yolk with a wire whisk for 2 to 3 minutes, or put it in a blender for about 30 seconds.
9. To prevent a skin from forming on sweet custards or soufflé sauces, sprinkle with sugar.

Egg Curdling

1. If a custard curdles, it can usually be brought back by beating briskly with an egg whisk. If this is not successful, mix some arrowroot (allowing 2 teaspoons [10 ml] to every pint [600 ml] of custard) with some milk

and a beaten egg, then mix into the curdled custard and reheat carefully; or quickly turn the custard into a cold bowl and beat it vigorously with an egg beater. This should work. If it doesn't, take a level teaspoon of cornstarch (cornflour), moisten it with cold water, add to the custard and place in a double boiler just long enough to cook the cornstarch (cornflour). Then strain.

2. Curdled Hollandaise Sauce—see page 239.
3. Curdled Mayonnaise—see page 240.
4. One of the main causes of eggs curdling in cooked mixtures is that the "chalaze," the two threads which bind the yolk to the middle of the white and protect it, has not been broken. Break the threads off over the sharp edge of the eggshell. Beaten whole raw eggs should be strained before adding them to custards or sauces, thus leaving behind the "chalaze."

Scrambled Eggs

Because albumen will hold a certain amount of liquid, melted fat and milk may be added to the eggs before cooking. Do not use milk if you are going to add tomatoes, as the acid in the tomato curdles the milk. Substitute a little stock instead. I sometimes add ends or cheap cuts of smoked salmon to scrambled eggs.

Common failures:

Watery and hard eggs result from overcooking. The albumen will hold only a given amount of liquid up to a certain temperature. When the cooking is carried to a point beyond that temperature, the albumen hardens and shrinks, thus giving up the liquid it has previously absorbed.

Poached Eggs

The reason for acidulating (adding vinegar) the water in which you poach eggs is that it keeps the white near the yolk instead of allowing white streamers (escaping albumen) to form. The older the egg, the more white streamers you get. The acid acts as a barrier and immediate coagulator. The poaching water must be at a rapid boil and salted (1 teaspoon [5 ml] to a quart [1.2 l]). Try shaking the pan to create a whirlpool just before lowering the eggs into it. The white will then be swept into a circle.

In a small saucepan, bring to the boil enough water to cover the eggs completely, add a teaspoon (5 ml) of vinegar or lemon juice and bring back to the boil. Stir the water rapidly and drop the egg into the center of the whirlpool. Lower the water to simmering. Cook for 4 minutes.

Broken eggs:

This is frequently a result of too quick boiling. The rough movement of the boiling water tears the albumen and can also cause the egg to become tough. On the other hand, too slow cooking can cause the failure of the white to set, so that it breaks apart when the egg is lifted out of the pan. If the egg is put into water *under* the boiling point, the temperature is further lowered by the addition of the egg. The egg must be put into *boiling* water, and the temperature *immediately lowered* to a simmer.

Omelettes

Omelettes should not be overcooked. The eggs must be evenly cooked and the underside just set to give the omelette a good shape. To achieve this result, three things are required:

1. A fairly quick, even heat is necessary.
2. Butter must be added in small pieces, both to the eggs when being beaten before pouring them into the pan, and to the pan itself. If added *only* to the pan, or *only* to the mixture in one large piece, the butter will not be thoroughly absorbed.
3. The omelette must be kept in motion by gently shaking the pan during cooking. This allows the heat to penetrate evenly and at the same time gives the typical flaked consistency of a French omelette.

When cooked, the omelette should be folded into two or three sections. *Note:* This should be done before the eggs set too firmly, otherwise the sides will crack.

Be sure to have the filling hot and ready, before the eggs go into the pan. Foods such as cheese, which must be cooked, should be added as soon as the eggs have begun to set. Additions such as cooked ham, tomatoes, kidneys, mushrooms, or herbs can be added when the omelette is cooked and just before it is folded over.

Hints:

1. Never mix milk with the eggs to be used for omelettes, as it will make them tough; a little water—1 tablespoon (15 ml) to 6 eggs—will make the omelette more tender.
2. Never use an omelette pan for cooking anything else; keep it for omelettes alone. Season it properly before the first use and never clean it with water. Wipe it with several changes of paper toweling, or even tissue paper, and remove any dry scraps with salt.
3. If serving more than two people, do not make one colossal omelette; use two pans and make a few small omelettes.

Common failures:

1. A cracked omelette occurs when the albumen has been overcooked and so loses its elasticity.
2. A greasy surface results when there is too much fat in the pan. Eggs can absorb only a certain amount and anything over that quantity will lie on the surface of the omelette. The same result will occur if the omelette has not been kept in motion during cooking. The eggs are not sufficiently broken up, and as a result the fat is not absorbed.
3. Sticking to the pan:
   a. The omelette pan has not been seasoned properly.
   b. The omelette pan has been washed instead of wiped with paper towels. In this case, season the pan again with cooking oil. Pour enough oil in the pan to just cover the surface, then place over medium heat until the oil just begins to smoke. Remove from the heat and leave for 1 hour. Then remove excess oil with paper towels.
   c. Margarine has been used instead of butter. Margarine contains a high percentage of water and exudes a certain amount of sediment when heated. Both the water and the sediment lower the proportion of fat, so that the omelette is more likely to stick. Butter is by far the best fat to use.

Soufflé Omelettes

These differ from omelettes both in texture, which is spongy, and in the cooking method.

1. The eggs are separated and the yolks thoroughly beaten together with sugar. This dissolves the sugar, which is then less apt to burn, while at the same time introducing air into the mixture.
2. The whites are whisked until they are very stiff. The albumen in the white is capable of holding a large quantity of air. The beaten whites are then folded lightly into the yolks and sugar. The mixture is now full of air.
3. *Important:* In order to preserve this lightness, the omelette is *never* stirred or disturbed by movement of any kind during cooking. It must be cooked over *moderate* heat. If the heat is too strong, the underside will burn and a hard layer of overcooked albumen will form, making it difficult for the heat to penetrate. To avoid overcooking, this kind of omelette should be placed over a flame for a short time in order to cook the underside. As the heat will not have had time to penetrate to the center, the rest of the cooking must be completed by placing the pan either in the oven or under

the broiler (grill). The heat then penetrates through the top, thus completing the cooking.

Common failures:

1. If there is a flat, close texture, the sugar and the yolks have not been sufficiently beaten. This mixture is then thin instead of being thick and creamy. When the well-whipped whites are added, it is impossible to incorporate them properly. They separate out in cooking, the air is lost, and the sugar, which is not well dissolved, falls to the bottom of the omelette and makes it stick to the pan. Or the whites are not beaten sufficiently stiff and the mixture does not contain enough air to make it light and fluffy.
2. The omelette is raw in the center. When this occurs, it indicates that the omelette has been cooked too quickly. The surfaces have hardened before the heat has had time to penetrate to the inside.

Soufflés

The basic mixture, whether flour-based or *crème pâtisserie,* should be thick enough to just drop off the spoon, and it must have a *strong* flavor, otherwise the egg whites will mask the flavor in the finished soufflé.

Egg whites: It is the glutinous nature of the egg white which allows it to stay in an almost permanent froth if carefully and properly whipped. The whites should increase their volume seven or eight times. To achieve the best results, the egg whites should be stale—the staler the better—up to six months old. They can be kept in open containers in the refrigerator or closed in the freezer. In this way, their water will evaporate and they will whip stiffer. When ready to use, the egg whites should be at *room temperature.* This will increase their volume. You can beat them with either an electric mixer or—the best way—a wire whisk in a copper bowl. It is the action of the wire whisk against the copper which oxidizes the albumen in the egg whites and keeps them firm. If you add cream of tartar to the egg whites for a savory soufflé, or sugar for a sweet soufflé, it will have a stabilizing effect, keeping the egg whites stiffer for a longer period of time. *Important:* Do not add salt. This will produce a softer foam that will not expand properly when subjected to heat. Egg whites foam when beaten, as do egg yolks, because the air bubbles are trapped within the expanding walls of the protein. The more you beat egg whites, the more air bubbles form and the firmer they become. The copper bowl should always be kept clean with either vinegar and salt, or lemon juice and salt. The acid gives the egg whites more body, resulting in a thicker and fluffier mixture.

With a flat pastry brush, paint the inside of the soufflé dish with softened butter. Then, if it is a savory soufflé, coat the butter with flour by putting some flour into the dish, shaking it so that it coats evenly, and pouring out the extra. If you are making a sweet soufflé, substitute sugar for the flour.

When incorporating the egg whites into the basic mixture, fold with your right hand, scraping under and up while continually turning the bowl to your right with your left hand. Fold in the egg whites little by little and *do not overfold*. Too much mixing will break down the albumen, allowing the air to escape.

Pour the soufflé into the dish, filling it either up to the rim or just below. Then, with a flat wooden spoon, spread it slightly away from the rim into the center, making a small peak.

If you are going to cook the soufflé in the ordinary way, preheat the oven and place a flat baking pan on the middle rack. Then, when the temperature is right, place the soufflé dish on top of the baking pan. This will provide instant underheat and make the soufflé rise more quickly.

Anton Mossiman, the *maître chef des cuisines* of the Dorchester Hotel, showed me a way to poach a soufflé for 1 hour, and then, when you are ready to serve, put it in a preheated oven—350° F (180° C; Mark 4)—for the last 10 minutes. To poach, put some newspapers in the bottom of a copper saucepan and add approximately 1 (2.5 cm) to 2 (5 cm) inches of water. Place the filled soufflé dish in the copper pan and place the pan over *very* low heat so that the water *just* simmers. The newspaper will keep the soufflé from boiling over into the pan.

Hints:

1. If you forget to preheat the oven, or some catastrophe happens in the house, cover the uncooked soufflé with an upturned mixing bowl while you heat the oven or deal with the crisis. Provided the egg whites were properly beaten, the mixture will hold well for approximately 20 minutes.
2. Flour-based soufflés may be frozen uncooked, and then cooked from the frozen state.

BAKING

YEAST BREADS

Ingredients

Flour: Most yeast cooking is done with flour milled from wheat. You can use other cereals, such as rye, barley and oats, but these contain very little or no gluten and, for best results, should be mixed with wheat flour. A variety of wheat flours are available on the market today—they are classified by their extraction rate: the percentage of the whole cleaned grain that is present in the flour. My preference is whole-wheat or wholemeal flours which have 100% extraction—nothing has been added or taken away. These produce a whole-wheat bread full of nutty flavor and texture, with a moist, close crumb. In fact, roughage and fiber are now recognized as essential to the diet and most doctors suggest eating wholemeal or whole-wheat bread. The next-best flours are brown or wheatmeal with an 85% to 90% extraction—10% to 15% of the bran and wheat germ of the grain have been removed, resulting in a bread that is lighter textured than wholemeal. White flours, with an extraction rate of 72% to 74%, have all the bran and wheat germ removed. These produce a bread that has good volume and texture, but the fiber (bran) and nutrients have been removed. Therefore, by British law, iron, thiamine (the vitamin B complex) and nicotinic acid must be added. In fact, by British law also, all flours except wholemeal must have added calcium as well.

The second important characteristic to look for in a flour is the quality and quantity of gluten-forming proteins present. When mixed with water the proteins combine to form gluten. Gluten is an elastic substance which expands when the moisture and gases present in the dough expand upon exposure to heat. The best quality elastic gluten appears in "strong" flours made from the hard spring wheat grown in North America and Russia, whereas the wheat grown in Britain and Europe is weaker, containing a lower protein content.

If, however, the flour is too strong and produces too much gluten you will have an unpleasant, over-tough bread. The "strong flour" sold on the market in Britain is milled from a mixture combining proportionally more strong wheat than the mixture in British all-purpose plain flour. Other things such as salt, acidity, and all kinds of handling, kneading and mixing can toughen the gluten so that it won't expand and the bread won't rise. However, fat, sugar, malt, bran, wheat germ and the enzymes in yeast can weaken it.

Yeast: Yeast is composed of plant protein and mineral matter, which grows by budding when provided with suitable food—i.e., the carbohydrates (starches and sugar) present in flour. One ounce (5 ml) of yeast contains thousands of cells which continually produce other small cells when given food and the right conditions for this food: moisture and warmth. The yeast will then produce carbon dioxide gas to "raise" the dough, making it spongy and light. Extreme heat kills the yeast plant, and extreme cold retards its growth. Too much sugar prevents budding and shrinks the yeast cells, and too much salt slows down growth and takes away its health, both resulting in a close-textured, heavy mixture. The ideal climate for yeast to grow and the dough to rise is 90° F (32° C).

Yeast for home baking is available in two forms: compressed fresh yeast, usually available from health-food shops, or dried active baking yeast, available in most grocery stores. 1 oz (25 ml) fresh yeast = 1 tablespoon (½ oz; 15 ml) dried yeast. Fresh yeast is quick and easy to use. It should be cool and firm to the touch. It will keep for up to 2 weeks in a refrigerator if stored in a small plastic container or in a plastic bag, or it may be frozen for up to 6 weeks. If you are freezing it, make sure that you do so in quantities you will use. Wrap each piece well in aluminum foil, label it, and freeze quickly. When you need it, remove from the freezer and blend it straight into warm liquid or allow it to thaw for 20 minutes before using. If you are making a soft dough, rub the fresh yeast directly into the flour as you would butter. Beat well after adding the liquid ingredient to insure even distribution.

Dried yeast, available in ½-ounce (15 g) sealed envelopes, will keep for up to 1 year. Once you open the envelope, it must be stored in a *small* airtight container where it should remain active up to 4 months; if there is too much airspace in the container the yeast will not keep. One half-ounce (15 g) of yeast will raise 1 pound (450 g) of flour. Dried yeast must be reconstituted before use: stir the dried yeast and a little sugar into "hand-hot" (100° F; 38° C) liquid and leave in a warm place until the yeast has dissolved and the mixture is frothy. This usually takes 10 minutes in water but a bit longer in milk. If the mixture does not froth, it means the yeast is stale and the dough will not rise.

SPONGING THE YEAST OR THE SPONGE-BATTER METHOD

As I have said before, growth in the yeast is started by the addition of carbohydrates (sugar and starch in the flour), warm water and air. During this process the yeast is liquefied and starts budding. When added to flour and put in a warm place, the growth of the yeast develops. This is noticeable when the volume of yeast increases and "sponges" through the flour.

To make a rich yeast dough of fat, sugar and eggs rise effectively, add the yeast and a little sugar to the "hand-hot" liquid. Then stir in a small proportion of the total amount of flour to be used to form a batter. If you are using dried yeast, leave the yeast/flour mixture for 5 minutes before adding the flour. Then add the flour and stand the batter in a warm place for about 20 minutes to become frothy. The yeast will then be able to work before the inclusion of the eggs, fat and salt, which would slow it down if added earlier. When the batter has frothed effectively, add the remaining ingredients (eggs, fat and salt) and mix it to form a soft dough.

Salt: Salt gives flavor to yeasted bread and prevents the yeast from working too quickly. Too much slows down the yeast, but too little results in a sticky, unmanageable dough. The ideal proportion is 1 or 2 teaspoons (5 to 10 ml) salt per 1 pound (450 g) flour. It is best to use fine-grained salt, but if you must use coarse-grained salt, dissolve it first in a little liquid from the recipe.

Sugar: Although, as seen above, yeast needs sugar as food, yeast is also able to convert starch in flour into sugar. Therefore, only a small amount of sugar is needed in the beginning to give the yeast a good start. For this, any type of sugar may be used, including corn syrup (golden syrup), honey, malt and molasses (treacle). The last should be used only for brown bread and should be slightly warmed to allow proper mixing. If you are making white bread, it is better to use white sugar.

Fat: Fat enriches the dough and improves the softness and the color of the crumb; it also serves to keep the bread fresh. Butter and lard give the best flavor and texture. You can use cooking oil, but it may give a grayish color to a white dough. If you are using oil, 15 ml = 1 tablespoon (½ oz; 15 ml) fat.

Liquid: Water, milk or a mixture of both may be used. Water is used for basic bread, however, milk will improve the nutritional quality of the baked loaf and will give a softer, browner crust. The temperature of the liquid should be 100° F (38° C). To achieve this, mix ⅓ boiling liquid with ⅔ cold water, i.e., 1¼ cups (½ pt; 250 ml) per 1 pound (450 g) of flour.

Eggs: Eggs improve the nutritional value, storage life and color of the finished bread.

The Stages in Making Bread with Yeast

Mixing and kneading: In order to speed up the rising of the dough, it is a good idea to warm both ingredients and utensils—particularly if you live in a cold climate.

If you are mixing the dough by hand: Add all the yeast liquid at one time to the flour and work the mixture with one hand until the dough is formed. The liquid and yeast are then more evenly distributed throughout the flour.

To knead: Turn the dough onto a lightly floured surface. Fold the dough in half toward you, then push down and away from you. Give the dough a quarter turn and repeat the folding and pushing action, developing a rocking rhythm and always using the heel of the hand. You will find the dough to be soft and sticky at first, but do not add too much flour at this point—the dough will improve its consistency through further kneading. Continue kneading in the same rocking motion until the dough has become silky-smooth and elastic and no longer sticks to your hands—approximately 4 minutes for whole-wheat (wholemeal) or brown dough; 10 minutes for white dough.

If you are mixing the dough in an electric mixer: Make sure you read the manufacturer's instructions before beginning to make yeast dough with the dough hook in your mixer. Place the yeast liquid in the bowl first and then add the other ingredients to it. Switch on the mixer at the lowest speed for 1 to 2 minutes to form the dough. Increase the speed a little and mix for a further 2 to 3 minutes. The dough will usually have a slightly rough appearance, even when fully kneaded. To make sure of a smooth finish complete the kneading by hand.

Rising: After kneading, the dough should be left in a warm place to rise to double its volume. Acids are formed which give flavor to the bread and certain other chemical changes take place. It is the carbon dioxide gas in the yeast that lightens the dough. Among the many constituents of yeast there is a ferment called diastase. This ferment acts on the starch in the flour, splits it up and produces a malt-sugar substance, called maltose, which is an important yeast food. The yeast also produces another ferment called maltase, which attacks the maltose, turning it into glucose. A third ferment, zymase, in turn attacks the glucose, liberating the gas—carbon dioxide—and alcohol, which adds flavor.

The bread becomes softer on rising because during the process described above the gluten becomes softer and is stretched by the carbon dioxide. If the bread is left to rise for too long, however, the gluten becomes over-stretched, collapses, and then liberates the carbon dioxide. The dough falls and a close, heavy-textured bread is the result. All yeast doughs must be risen at least once before baking to allow time for the yeast to work. Most bread doughs are risen twice, producing a better flavor than those which have risen only once.

When you are leaving the dough to rise, cover it with a large plastic bag which has been lightly oiled on the inside, or put the dough in a bowl and cover with a lid or plastic wrap.

The temperature at which the dough is risen will affect the time it takes for the dough to double in size. A long, slow rise will give better bread, as the yeast works more slowly and the alcohol produced (which gives the bread flavor) can be more fully developed. Also, if the temperature is too hot, the bread will have a crumbly texture and will not keep.

APPROXIMATE RISING TIME

1 hour in a warm place not above 90° F (32° C)
1½ hours at room temperature 65–70° F (18–21° C)
4 hours in a cool place

Preparation of baking pans: Tin baking pans or earthenware containers should be either greased with lard or butter (unsalted—salt will make the bread burn on the outside), or dusted well with flour.

For a particularly crisp crust and an unusually shaped bread, you can use a well-prepared clay flowerpot. For this, wash and dry the pot, then smear it, inside and out, with lard and bake it in a hot oven—425° F (220° C; Mark 7)—for about 5 minutes or until all the lard has been absorbed into the clay. Repeat this process several times before using; it need be done only before the pot is used for the first time. Before subsequent bakings grease the pots and wipe them out with a damp cloth. The amount of dough after the first rising should be sufficient to half fill the flowerpot.

The punching down or knocking back process: After rising, the dough must be "punched down" or "knocked back" and thoroughly kneaded again. This breaks the tenacity of the gluten, making the dough more elastic. The yeast buds are different sizes and so produce varying proportions of carbon dioxide. If you do not punch down the dough, the air bubbles will make large holes in the finished bread and will result in an uneven open texture. The kneading insures an even distribution of the gas. Punch the risen dough to deflate it and then knead until it becomes firm. You can also do this in a mixer at a very slow speed, but doing it by hand insures a better consistency.

The second rising (proving): As the result of the growth of the yeast and the subsequent kneading, the yeast cells have become shrunken. The budding after this becomes slower. The length of time for "proving" varies depending on the type of dough and the specific recipe. The richer the mixture the slower the budding. The sugar from fruit, for instance, will shrink the cells of the yeast and retard its growth, whereas in a plainer dough, where neither fruit nor sugar has been added, this is not true.

Place the dough in the utensil in which it is to be baked, cover with plastic wrap, place in a warm temperature as before, and allow it to rise again until doubled in volume. A large loaf may take 50 minutes, while rolls may take only 25. When risen, the dough should be light, puffy and double its size. It should feel spongy when touched with the hand, and on the point of collapsing.

Shaping bread:

1. When the dough is ready to be shaped into loaves, knead it down and cut with a sharp knife into two portions.
2. Form each portion into a smooth ball; cover and allow it to rest for 10 minutes. This will make molding easier and will improve the shape of the baked loaves.
3. Flatten the ball of dough with the palms of your hands until it becomes an oblong shape about 6 × 9 inches. DO NOT POUND OR PUNCH THE DOUGH.
4. Fold the long edge of the oblong farthest away from you to the center lengthwise and press gently to seal. Do the same with the edge nearest you.
5. Pick up the folded dough by both ends, and alternately stretch and slap it against the board until it is twice as long as the baking pan.
6. Bring the ends of the folded dough over to the center so that they overlap slightly, and press down to seal.
7. With the edge of your right hand make an indentation to mark the next fold.

BREAD SHAPING

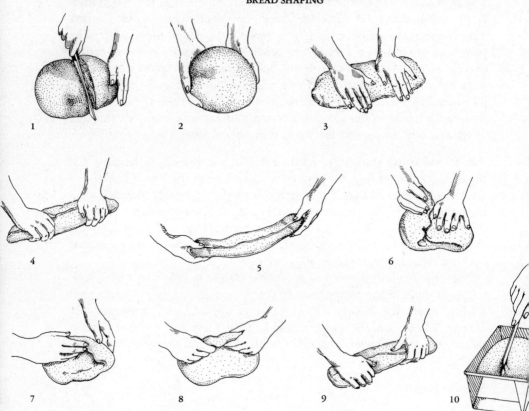

8. Using the indentation as a marker, fold over the edge near to you into the center. Then fold over the side away from you into the center.

9. Roll the dough gently back and forth with the palms of your hands to seal the edges and mold the loaf into a good cylindrical shape. Repeat this process with the second ball of dough.

10. Place each loaf, seam side down, into a greased bread pan. DO NOT WORK THE CORNERS OF THE BREAD INTO THE CORNERS OF THE BREAD PAN.

Baking: During this process the water and carbon dioxide expand and explode the gluten. The carbon dioxide is driven off and the starch in the flour cooks and is gelatinized. The interior of the bread never rises to any temperature higher than the boiling point because of the water present. This gives a soft dough. However, the outside of a loaf does rise above this temperature as the surface water evaporates.

A very hot oven is needed to kill off the yeast so that it will stop growing.

A basic bread dough would normally be baked in a preheated oven of 450° F (230° C; Mark 8) and the richer doughs at 400° F (200° C; Mark 6) in order to prevent overbrowning. In order to crisp the sides and base of bread, remove the loaf from its container 5 minutes before the end of baking.*

TO TEST FOR READINESS tap the bread or buns on their base. A hollow sound indicates that the gluten has exploded and set and the starch has been cooked.

YEAST BREAD RECIPES

ANADAMA BREAD

MAKES 2 LOAVES

2 cups (16 fl oz; 475 ml) cold milk
½ cup (3 oz; 75 g) yellow cornmeal
1½ teaspoons (7.5 ml) salt
½ cup (4 fl oz; 125 ml) molasses
3 tablespoons (45 ml) vegetable shortening
1 teaspoon (5 ml) sugar

¼ cup (2 fl oz; 50 ml) lukewarm water
1 package granulated yeast or 1 cake compressed yeast
4½ cups (2 lbs; 1 kg) all-purpose (plain) flour

Combine the milk, cornmeal and salt in a saucepan and bring to the boil, stirring constantly. Reduce to a simmer and continue to stir for 5 more minutes. Remove from the heat. Add the molasses and shortening and blend. Cool to lukewarm. Meanwhile, stir the sugar into the water, add the yeast and let stand for 10 minutes. Stir the yeast mixture to blend it, then add the cooled cornmeal mixture. Stir well, then add the flour gradually and mix it thoroughly.

Turn the dough onto a lightly floured board and knead it lightly but thoroughly for 10 minutes. Place the dough in a clean, greased bowl. Turn once to bring the greased side up. Cover and set in a warm place, away from drafts, until it has doubled its size—approximately 1 hour. Turn out the

---

* If you want a crusty finish to your bread, place a pan of hot water in the bottom of the oven during the baking. Remove the pan 10 minutes before the end of baking time.

dough again onto a lightly floured board and divide it in half. Form each portion into a round, cover and let it rest for 10 minutes. This improves the shape of the baked loaves and makes molding easier. Shape into loaves (see illustration, page 336) and place in two greased pans (8¼ × 4½ × 2¾ inches). Lightly grease the tops of the loaves, cover and set in a warm place until the dough has doubled in bulk—about 1¼ hours. Bake in a preheated oven at 400° F (200° C; Mark 6) for 45 to 50 minutes. Remove from the loaf pans and cool on a wire rack, uncovered and away from drafts.

FRUIT TEA LOAF

SERVES 8 TO 10

2¼ cups (12 oz; 350 g) mixed dried fruit (raisins, sultanas and apricots)

⅔ cup (6 fl oz; 175 ml) warm tea, strained

1½ ounce (7.5 g) fresh yeast or 3 packages granulated yeast

1 cup (6 oz; 175 g) soft dark brown sugar

2 cups (10 oz; 275 g) wholewheat flour (Granary Meal)

1 cup (5 oz; 150 g) all-purpose (strong white) flour

Soak the dried fruit in the tea for 1 hour. Cream the yeast with 1 teaspoon (5 ml) of sugar and 1 teaspoon (5 ml) of tea. Set in a warm place until it becomes frothy. Mix the remaining sugar, the tea, fruits and yeast in a large bowl. Gradually mix in the remaining ingredients to form a dough of firm dropping consistency, then turn out the dough onto a lightly floured surface. Knead for about 5 minutes until smooth. Place in a 8¼ × 4½ × 2¾ inch greased loaf pan and leave to rise in a warm place where there are no drafts for 1 to 2 hours or until it has doubled in size.

Preheat the oven to 400° F (200° C; Mark 6).

Sprinkle the dough with some additional Granary Meal and bake in the preheated oven for about 30 minutes. Lower the oven temperature to 350° F (180° C; Mark 4) and bake for a further 15 minutes.

NUT BREAD

MAKES 2 LOAVES

1 package granulated yeast or 1 cake compressed yeast

¼ cup (2 fl oz; 50 ml) lukewarm water

⅓ cup (3 oz; 75 g) sugar

1 cup (8 fl oz; 225 ml) milk, scalded

¾ teaspoon (3.75 ml) salt

3½ cups (1 lb; 450 g) all-purpose (plain) flour

2 tablespoons (30 ml) vegetable shortening, melted and cooled

1 egg white, beaten stiff

1¼ cups (7 oz; 200 g) coarse-chopped walnuts

Soften the yeast in the water with 1 teaspoon (5 ml) of the sugar. Let it stand for 10 minutes; stir it to blend. Combine the hot milk with the remaining sugar and the salt; stir and cool to lukewarm. Combine the yeast and milk mixtures and mix thoroughly. Add 1½ cups (7 oz; 200 g) of the flour and beat vigorously to a smooth batter. Add the cooled shortening and beat well. Fold in the egg white and the nuts. Add 1¾ cups (8 oz; 225 g) of the remaining flour and stir to form a stiff dough. (Use the ¼ cup [2½ oz; 62 g] remaining flour on the board for kneading and shaping the dough.) Turn the dough out on the board, and cover it with a bowl. Let it rest 10 minutes, then knead it quickly and lightly for 5 minutes. Round up the dough and place it in a greased bowl, turning the dough once in the bowl to bring the greased side up. Cover and set in a warm place away from drafts until the dough has doubled in bulk—approximately 1½ hours. Then turn it out onto a lightly floured board, divide the dough into two equal portions, round up each portion and cover with bowls to rest for 10 minutes. Shape into loaves (see illustration, page 336). Place the loaves in greased loaf pans (8¼ × 4½ × 2¾ inches), cover and let rise until they have doubled in bulk— about 1 hour. Bake in a preheated oven at 400° F (200° C; Mark 6) for 30 minutes, or until done. Remove the loaves at once to a wire rack and cool uncovered and away from drafts.

OATMEAL BREAD

MAKES 2 LOAVES

2½ cups (5 oz; 150 g) rolled oats
⅓ cup (7 fl oz; 200 ml) molasses
2 teaspoons (10 ml) salt
2 tablespoons (30 ml) vegetable
   shortening
1¼ cups (10 fl oz; 300 ml) boiling
   water
1 package granulated yeast or 1
   cake compressed yeast

¼ cup (2 fl oz; 50 ml) lukewarm
   water
1 teaspoon (5 ml) sugar
1 cup (8 fl oz; 225 g) lukewarm
   milk
5 cups (1½ lbs; 700 g) sifted all-
   purpose (plain) flour

Put the oats, molasses, salt and shortening into a bowl. Pour the boiling water over the mixture, stir well and let stand for 1 hour. Soften the yeast in lukewarm water with the sugar and let it stand for 10 minutes. Combine the yeast and milk and add it to the oatmeal mixture. Beat well. Add about 2½ cups (13 oz; 375 g) of the flour, beat it thoroughly and add 2¼ cups (11½ oz; 312 g) more flour. Stir to a stiff dough. Turn the dough out on a board sprinkled with the remaining flour. Cover the dough with a bowl, let it rest for 10 minutes, then knead it lightly and quickly until it becomes smooth and elastic—about 10 minutes. Place the dough in a greased bowl, turn once to bring the greased side up, cover and set in a warm place away from drafts to rise until doubled in bulk—about 2 hours.

Turn the dough out onto a lightly floured board, and divide it into two equal parts; quickly round up the portions and cover with bowls. Let it rest for 10 minutes on the board. Shape into two loaves (see illustration, page 336). Place the dough into two greased loaf pans (8¼ × 4½ × 2¾ inches), cover and let it rise again until it doubles in bulk—about 1 hour. Bake in a preheated oven at 400° F (200° C; Mark 6) for about 15 minutes. Reduce the heat to 375° F (190° C; Mark 5) and continue to bake for 30 to 40 minutes, or until the loaf is done.

PUMPKIN OR SQUASH BREAD

MAKES 3 LOAVES

*2 packages granulated yeast or 2
  cakes compressed yeast*
¼ cup (2 fl oz; 50 ml) water
¼ cup (2 oz) sugar
*1¾ cups (14 fl oz; 425 ml) milk,
  scalded*
1 tablespoon (15 g) salt
*8 to 8½ cups (2½ to 2¾ lbs; 1.1 to
  1.3 kg) sifted all-purpose (plain)
  flour*

*2 cups (16 fl oz; 475 ml) puréed
  cooked pumpkin or puréed baked
  squash*
*¼ cup (2 fl oz; 50 ml) vegetable
  shortening, melted and cooled*

Soften the yeast in the water with 1 teaspoon (5 ml) sugar. Let it stand for 10 minutes. Combine the hot milk, salt and the remaining sugar, stir and cool to lukewarm. Combine the yeast and cooled milk mixtures and stir to blend. Add 2½ cups (12 oz; 350 g) of the flour and beat until the batter is very smooth. Add the pumpkin and the cooled shortening and mix it well. Add enough of the remaining flour to make a stiff dough and use any left to sprinkle the board for kneading and shaping the dough. Turn the dough out onto a lightly floured board and cover the dough with a bowl. Let it rest for 10 minutes, then knead until it becomes smooth and elastic—about 10 minutes. Round up the dough and place it in a greased bowl, turning it once so that the greased side is up. Cover and let it stand in a warm place until it doubles in bulk—about 45 minutes. Turn it out onto the board and divide it into three equal portions. Quickly round up each portion, cover them each with a bowl and let the dough rest for 10 minutes on the board. Shape the portions into loaves (see page 336). Place them in greased loaf pans (8¼ × 4½ × 2¾ inches). Cover and let rise in a warm place until the loaves double in bulk, the sides of the dough reach the top of the pan, and the centers are well-rounded—1 hour. Bake in a preheated oven at 400° F (200° C; Mark 6) for 15 minutes; reduce the heat to 375° F (190° C; Mark 5) and continue to bake for 20 to 30 minutes or longer, until the loaves are well-browned. Turn them out onto wire racks to cool, uncovered and away from drafts.

CAKES

Ingredients

The combination of ingredients is most important in cakemaking, as it affects both the method of cooking and the oven temperature. The main ingredients are flour, fat, sugar, fruit and eggs, together with a leavening agent. When flour, which contains starch and a sticky substance known as gluten, is combined with all the other ingredients (which contain moisture) in the cake mixture, and heat is applied, the starch grains burst. The starch in the flour can then absorb and hold the moisture obtained from the other ingredients. When moist, the gluten in flour becomes tenacious; moisture when heated turns into steam and this steam expands the gluten. The application of further heat sets the gluten and holds it in this expanded condition. When this happens correctly, the cake has "risen" satisfactorily. It is what gives that open texture common to cakes with a high proportion of flour.

All the ingredients should be prepared before the actual cakemaking begins. The flour and other ingredients should all be measured out and ready to use when required. If the butter is to be creamed, always do this before the eggs are whisked, as beaten eggs deteriorate when left for a time, and the cake will lose its lightness. If the yolks and whites are to be beaten and added separately, beat the yolks and add them to the cake mixture before touching the whites. The whites should be whipped quickly at the last minute, together with a pinch of salt, and folded in.

Flour: In Britain, flour must be chosen with great care, as this has a decided effect upon the finished product. There are "hard" or "strong" flours, which contain a higher proportion of gluten, making them particularly suitable for breads, scones, buns and plain cakes, which should have an open texture. The gluten is expanded and set in position both by the air produced from the leavening agent and the steam from the liquid. Therefore, the more gluten there is in the flour the more liquid should be added to make it work. When making plain mixtures, such as those mentioned above, extra liquid should be added to compensate for the lack of fat and sugar which act as liquids when melted.

"Weak" or "soft" flours contain a smaller percentage of gluten than the "hard" or "strong" flours. Therefore, they are more suitable for rich cakes and plain pastrymaking. If you are making rich pastries, to obtain the proper texture you will need additional gluten, which can be obtained by a mixture of "hard" and "soft" flours.

In America, however, what is known as all-purpose flour, which is comparable to British "strong" flour, can be used for all baking unless cake flour is specifically called for in a particular recipe.

Fats: There are two kinds of fat: animal and vegetable. Butter and margarine are vegetable fats; lard is an animal fat.

Butter is ideal for cakemaking. Use only unsalted butter; salted butter will burn more quickly. Salt may always be added to the cake batter. A cake made with butter will stay moist longer than one made with margarine because butter has a lower melting point and all fats with a low melting point solidify in a much softer form than fats with a high melting point. Butter fats also have some property of reabsorbing moisture, which margarine does not.

Margarine has a higher melting point and contains more water than butter or lard. If you are cutting down on cholesterol and calories and feel you mustn't use butter, buy the best margarine available. Inferior makes, if used in rich cakes (when there is more than half as much fat as flour) give too much moisture to the mixture. The cake will then fall in the center. In plain cakes the case is a little different. The proportion of margarine is smaller, and there is sufficient starch and gluten provided by the flour to hold its moisture.

Lard is 100% animal fat. Therefore weight for weight it goes farther. But if used to any large extent in cakes requiring a high proportion of fat, its flavor predominates. If you must use lard, mix some margarine with it. But, basically, I am against using lard at all.

Sugar: There are various types of sugar.

Light brown sugar—clear, golden crystals with a sticky feel from the coating of natural molasses. Good for gingerbread, brides' cakes, or sprinkled on fruitcakes and cookies before baking to give a textured surface.

Dark brown sugar—moist brown sugar; soft, fine-grained with a sticky texture. Very good for rich fruitcakes, gingerbread and spice cakes.

Superfine granulated sugar (castor)—best for creamed mixtures. When fat is creamed with sugar in the making of rich cakes, the fat globules are broken up and the sugar slightly dissolved to form an emulsion which is capable of holding air. The mixture becomes whiter during the beating. A fine sugar hastens this process because the sugar grains dissolve more easily.

Granulated sugar—good for cakes in which the sugar is to be melted; for "rubbed-in" mixtures; and in cakes such as sponge, which can bear the coarser crystals because extra liquid, in which the sugar can more easily dissolve, is provided by the eggs.

Eggs: The chief constituents of eggs which affect baking are fat and albumen. Apart from having a nutritive value, eggs are valuable as leavening agents, because the albumen is capable of holding cold air, which expands when heated. When eggs are beaten alone or in conjunction with sugar, as for sponge cakes, meringues, etc., the albumen acts also as an adhesive liquid. Eggs used for cakes and meringues must be a minimum of two days old. When the eggs are too fresh the albumen is unable to hold a great deal of air. Do not overbeat egg whites; overbeaten eggs become very difficult to incorporate into the cake mixture.

Chemical leavening agents: These are acids or alkalis which effervesce when combined with moisture. A gas is given off which increases when heat is added. These agents should be stored in an airtight jar in a dry place, and they must be totally free of lumps before being added to the cake mixture. Mix the leavening agent with dry ingredients, which are then added to the liquid. Once the leavening agent is added to the liquid the gas spreads very quickly, so the mixture *must* be baked at once, particularly if it is a thin one. The most popular leavening agents are: *baking powder,* which combines acid and alkali (a fine starchy substance, usually rice flour, is added, which absorbs moisture from the atmosphere and prevents the gas from being given off during storage); *baking soda* (bicarbonate of soda), an alkali; and *cream of tartar,* an acid. Leavening agents are often used in combination to make plain cakes and scones. The proportions vary depending upon the amount of acid present in the other ingredients. For instance, if you are using a large amount of fruit, lemon juice or rind, molasses or sour milk, you need less cream of tartar, as the acid content of the other ingredients is very high.

Fruit: The most frequently used dried fruits are currants, raisins, sultanas, cherries, and almonds. Buy them in the autumn, when the new supplies arrive, wash them, dry thoroughly and store in clean jars. The more fruit you add, the better the cake will keep because the fruit adds sugar and moisture to the mixture.

Plain Cakes and Buns, Bread and Scones

General proportions:
To 3 cups (1 lb; 450 g) flour or any other farinaceous substance add:

> ½ to 1 cup (4 to 8 oz; 125 to 225 g) fat, preferably unsalted butter
> ½ to 1 cup (4 to 8 oz; 125 to 225 g) sugar
> 1 to 1¼ cup (4 to 8 oz; 125 to 225 g) fruit
> 2 to 6 eggs
> 2 teaspoons (10 ml) baking powder
> ½ cup (4 fl oz; 125 ml) liquid (milk)

Method: In a plain cake the proportion of fat should be half, or less than half, the amount of flour. If using unsalted butter, mix a pinch of salt with the flour. If using salted butter, omit the added salt. The fat should then be cut into the flour with a knife and rubbed with your fingertips until the mixture becomes like very fine bread crumbs. This is when the air is entering the mixture, and it is this fineness of texture which allows the fat to be absorbed easily by the flour. It will give a final even texture. The addition of liquid is extremely important, as the amount of liquid to be added depends upon the proportion of fat and sugar, which themselves act as liquids when heat is applied. In a plain cake, there must be a large proportion of fat and sugar, otherwise only a small amount of liquid will result from them and you will need more liquid in the form of either eggs or milk. The plainer the cake, the softer or more liquid must be the mixture, and the liquid should be added all at once, making a smoother batter and a more even texture. Add the fruit, if any, after the liquid has been incorporated.

Rich Cakes

In a rich cake the proportion of fat should be half, or more than half, the flour. A Madeira cake, which is quite often classed as a plain cake, is therefore in reality a rich cake.

General proportions:
To 3 cups (1 lb; 450 g) flour or any other farinaceous substance add:

1 to 2 cups (8 to 16 oz; 225 to 450 g) fat
1 to 2 cups (8 to 16 oz; 225 to 450 g) sugar
½ to 3 pounds (8 oz to 3 lbs; 225 g to 1.4 kg) fruit
6 to 14 eggs
1 teaspoon (5 ml) baking powder

Method: Because there is so much fat, it is obvious that you cannot rub it into the flour. Therefore the fat and sugar must be "creamed" together, making the mixture capable of holding air. The more the butter/sugar mixture is beaten, the greater capacity it will have for containing air. Never melt the butter; butter should be beaten to a cream, not melted to form one. Then beat the eggs thoroughly so they, too, will be able to hold air, and add them *slowly* to the butter/sugar mixture. If you add the eggs too quickly, the sugar/fat mixture will curdle. One way to avoid curdling is to add the eggs and flour alternately. If the mixture curdles, it loses the precious air you have beaten into it. However, flour, which is heavy, is also inclined to crush out the air when added alternately, so it is better to add the eggs carefully before mixing the flour in. This will give a more open texture to the final cake. Sift the baking powder into the flour to eliminate lumps, incorporate air and insure an even distribution of the leavening agent. Mix the flour into the egg/butter/sugar by heating thoroughly. If fruit is to be added, it should be cleaned and prepared according to kind (currants and other dried fruit should be washed to remove grit and stones, and raisins should be plumped by soaking in warm water or a liqueur), then dried thoroughly and dusted with flour before being added to the cake mixture. This will insure an even distribution in the cake batter, and will prevent the fruit from sinking to the bottom.

Sponge Cakes

This type of cake usually has no fat, although a small amount of melted fat can be added if desired. A sponge cake batter is so light that solid fat would not be distributed evenly.

General proportions:
To each egg add:

> 2 to 3 tablespoons (1 to 1½ oz; 25 to 32 ml) sugar
> ¾ to 1 tablespoon (1 to 1½ oz; 25 to 32 ml) flour
> 2 tablespoons (1 oz; 25 ml) optional fat
> Use 4 eggs for an average 8-inch (20.3 cm) cake.

Method: Whisk the eggs and sugar together until the air bubbles turn opaque; this occurs when air is blown into the albumen and the sugar dissolves, forming a thick mixture. The more you beat the mixture, the more air it will hold. You can beat it in a double boiler over hot water, which will help the sugar to dissolve more easily, and increase the capacity of the mixture to hold air. But be sure that the top of the double boiler is not actually in contact with the water below. The albumen in the eggs will set if overheated, and will not mix so well with the sugar. In addition, the flour will not absorb as easily and the cake will be brittle rather than moist. Always fold the egg mixture into the flour, do *not* stir or beat it in, as this will crush the air you have beaten into it.

If you are using three or more eggs, you will not need a leavening agent, as there is enough air in the albumen in the eggs to act as a leavening agent. If you are adding butter, it must be melted and still warm when folded into the flour to insure an even distribution.

Baking Pans

A pan must be strong. If it has a double bottom, so much the better—the bottom of the cake will be less likely to burn. Placing an asbestos pad between the pan and the oven shelf will achieve the same result. In a gas oven with bottom heat, or a small electric oven which radiates heat, it is best to protect the cake by lining the pan with greaseproof paper which does not conduct heat and therefore prevents burning. If the cake is going to be in the oven for a long time, it is *absolutely necessary* to line the pan. If you are using a thin pan, the heat will pass more quickly through the metal to the cake, and more layers of paper will therefore be necessary. In a rich cake, there is a larger proportion of fat, sugar and fruit, all of which burn very easily. Therefore, again, the more layers of paper used in the lining, the less likely it is that the cake will burn. When making a rich cake, you should not, however, grease either the pan or the lining paper, as the larger proportion of fat in the cake is sufficient to prevent it from sticking. Plain cakes, sponge cakes and gingerbread do *not* contain much fat, and the molasses in the gingerbread makes it particularly sticky. Therefore, in these instances the layer of lining next to the cake should be greased, but *not* the pan itself, as fat burns easily and there is no insulating paper between the pan and the heat source.

The Oven

To insure successful baking of large cakes, the heat should circulate from the bottom of the oven. It is the warmth which makes the air in the cake mixture rise, swelling out the starch in the flour and expanding the sticky and elastic gluten. As the heat inside the cake increases, the starch cooks and the gluten sets. Top heat browns the surface flour and also sets the surface gluten. If this happens too quickly, the warm air is unable to push up the hard-set top of the cake and it will not rise.

The middle shelf of the oven is the best place for large cakes because it allows for the best circulation of heat. Placing a cake too high or too low in the oven can result in burning either the top or the bottom before the center is cooked.

Oven temperatures:

Plain cakes. As we have seen, the proportion of flour in these cakes is high in comparison with the amounts of fat, sugar and fruit. The greater the heat, the greater the force of air from the leavening agent, and the better the cake will rise. Because of the small proportion of fat and sugar, plain cakes will not burn so easily, and can stand strong heat. The heat will penetrate to the inside and cook the cake without burning. Large cakes, which cook longer, should be baked at 350° F (180° C; Mark 4); small cakes need a hot oven, 400° F (200° C; Mark 6). The cooking time will depend upon the individual recipe.

Rich Cakes. The percentage of fat, sugar and fruit is higher in proportion to the flour. As a result, there is also a smaller proportion of gluten to hold the air, so that the gas from the leavening agent must evolve slowly. If the oven is too hot, the fat, sugar and fruit will burn and the outside of the cake will cook too quickly and possibly burn before the inside is cooked. The batter for a rich cake is thick and heavy, so it will take the heat longer to penetrate. The richer the cake, the slower the heat necessary to cook it evenly. The oven should be preheated to 400° F (200° C; Mark 6) when the cake goes in, and left at that temperature for 15 minutes to set the mixture. The heat should then be lowered to 300° F (150° C; Mark 2) to allow the cake to finish cooking gradually. A 2 to 3 pound (900 g to 1.4 kg) cake takes approximately 2½ to 3 hours.

Sponge Cakes. Here a *moderate oven* —350° F (180° C; Mark 4)—is absolutely essential, as the proportion of flour is small and the proportion of air should be high through the addition of the beaten eggs. If the heat is too high, the small amount of gluten in the flour will be unable to hold the large volume of hot air it creates. With moderate heat, on the other hand, the warm air will accumulate slowly, the gluten and the albumen in the eggs will set and will be able to hold the air, resulting in a sponge cake risen and set to perfection. If you are adding fat to the sponge-cake mixture, it is particularly essential that the oven be slow in order to prevent the cake from burning.

Gingerbreads should be baked in a moderate oven—350° F (180° C; Mark 4)—as they contain a great deal of molasses, i.e., sugar, which burns easily.

To Test for Readiness

One is always told that the test for whether a cake is cooked is to insert a skewer, but this is not the most accurate test. The cold metal put into the hot cake collects moisture, so that you may think the cake is not done. A better test is that when the cake is ready it will shrink from the sides of the pan, indicating the evaporation of any excess moisture.

If you are experienced, you can tell by touch, which will vary according to the kind of cake you are making.

Fruitcakes. Two good tricks for better fruitcakes are:
1. Place a dish of boiling water in the oven with the cake. The hot steam circling around the cake will keep it moist.
2. Place the cake pan in an old pan filled with sea salt to prevent the bottom of the cake from burning before the cake is cooked.

Common failures:

The fruit has sunk to the bottom of the cake:

1. The mixture was too moist. As fruit is heavy, it sinks before the starch cooks and the gluten sets.

In a plain cake, already a soft consistency, adding too much liquid will thin the mixture to such an extent that it will be unable to hold the weight of the fruit, which will sink immediately.

2. Fruit will also fall if it is added to the creamed butter and sugar before the flour is stirred in. It then becomes coated with fat and sugar, making it heavier and more likely to sink. Cherries in particular are difficult, as they are quite heavy in themselves. It is best to cut them into small pieces before adding to the mixture.

When making a Madeira cake, the batter must be partially cooked before adding the fruit peel, which will otherwise fall from the top to the center.

The cake has a close, heavy texture:

IN PLAIN CAKES

1. The fat was too warm and became oily while it was rubbed into the flour, thus making it incapable of holding air and mixing evenly with the other ingredients.
2. There was insufficient leavening agent which did not give off enough gas to make the texture open and spongy.
3. The mixture was put into too cool an oven; the air and moisture expanded too slowly and the elastic substance in the flour, i.e., gluten, did not stretch fully.

IN RICH CAKES

1. Insufficient beating of the fat and sugar made the mixture incapable of holding enough air.
2. The eggs were added too quickly, causing the mixture to curdle and resulting in a loss of air. You can correct a curdled mixture by adding some flour and stirring it in well.

IN SPONGE CAKES

1. The eggs and sugar were insufficiently beaten. As the lightness of a sponge cake is totally dependent on its air content, it is essential to beat the eggs and sugar well.
2. The mixture was beaten *after* the flour was added. The flour, which is heavy, will beat out the air already present.
3. You have used too much flour, making the cake too heavy.

The cake has a badly cracked top with a pronounced peak in the center and the inside boiled over:

1. The cake was put into too hot an oven, or placed too near the top or too near a heat-reflecting surface. The surface starch softened and browned,

with the gluten setting and burning before the mixture in the middle was heated. The inside then expanded, forcing its way through the cooked surface layer and boiling out.

The cake has fallen in the center:

1. Too much leavening agent was used, resulting in more air than the starch and gluten could hold. As most of the gas is given off during the first minutes of exposure to heat, the gluten is then stretched beyond its capacity. Thus, when the cake begins to set, the gas escapes and the gluten, with nothing to support it, falls.
2. The cake was put into too hot an oven. The gases in the leavening agent were released before the starch and gluten had expanded enough to hold them, with the results described just above. This is particularly true in sponge, gingerbread and rich cakes, which contain relatively little flour.
3. You slammed the oven door before the cake was set or cooked. A sudden inrush of cold air and change of pressure shook the air bubbles before the starch and gluten were set, resulting in a fallen cake.

General Hints

1. Before icing a cake, dust a little cornstarch (cornflour) or flour on top to prevent the icing from running off.
2. If eggs are in short supply, expensive, or if you wish to cut down on cholesterol, 1 egg and 1 tablespoon of vinegar will do instead of 2 eggs.
3. Cake icing will not sugar if a pinch of salt is added while the icing is cooking.
4. To keep unused cake fresh, cover the cut surface with a strip of waxed paper.
5. For making cookies: If you are using a regular baking sheet as opposed to one with a nonstick surface, grease it well with nonsalt fat, which will reduce burning. Baking sheets should have shallow sides, or no sides at all, to facilitate removal of the baked goods.

CAKE RECIPES

CHOCOLATE CAKE

This recipe was originally given to me by a Greek friend and I have adapted it to my own taste.

1 pound (450 g) semisweet (plain) chocolate
1 cup (8 oz; 225 g) margarine
5 eggs, separated
1 cup (¼ lb; 125 g) confectioners' (icing) sugar

1 cup (5 oz; 150 g) all-purpose (plain) flour
1 tablespoon (15 ml) baking soda (bicarbonate of soda)
2 ounces (50 g) almonds, chopped fine (almond nibs)

Preheat the oven to 350° F (180° C; Mark 4).

Melt the chocolate. Beat together the margarine, egg yolks and sugar, then mix with the melted chocolate. Mix the flour and baking soda and add to the sugar mixture, together with the chopped almonds. Whip the egg whites until stiff, then fold into the chocolate mixture. Pour into a buttered 8-inch (20 cm) cake pan and bake in the preheated oven for 1 hour or until the cake shrinks away from the sides of the pan. Turn out and cool on a wire cake rack. When cool, sprinkle with confectioners' sugar.

Preparation time: 25 minutes. Cooking time: approximately 1 hour.

RICE CAKE

4 eggs
1 cup (8 oz; 225 g) superfine granulated (castor) sugar

Zest of 1 lemon or 1 small orange
½ cup (4 oz; 125 g) rice flour (ground rice)

Preheat the oven to 300° F (150° C; Mark 2).

Beat the eggs for 5 minutes, then beat in the sugar for 5 minutes. Add the lemon or orange zest and the rice flour (ground rice), beating all together for

15 to 20 minutes. Pour into a well-greased 8-inch (20 cm) square baking pan and bake for 1 hour. Divide into small cakes.

Preparation time: 30 minutes. Cooking time: approximately 1 hour.

NUT CINNAMON CAKE

½ cup (4 oz; 125 g) butter, softened
½ cup (4 oz; 125 g) sugar
1 teaspoon (5 ml) ground cinnamon
1 tablespoon (15 ml) molasses (treacle)

1 cup (5 oz; 150 g) flour
1 teaspoon (5 ml) baking soda (bicarbonate of soda)
2 eggs
Coffee icing (see below)
¾ cup (4 oz; 125 g) chopped hazelnuts

COFFEE ICING

⅓ cup (3 oz; 75 g) butter, softened
½ teaspoon (2.5 ml) strong coffee

1¼ cups (6 oz; 175 g) confectioners' (icing) sugar

Preheat the oven to 350° F (180° C; Mark 4).

Grease two 8-inch (20 cm) round cake pans, then dust them with equal quantities of flour and sugar. In a bowl, cream the butter with the back of a wooden spoon, then add the sugar, cinnamon and molasses (treacle). Mix well for 5 minutes, sift the flour and baking soda together into a bowl, then beat the eggs into a stiff froth in another bowl. To the butter and sugar mixture, add alternately the sifted flour and the eggs, and mix for approximately 10 minutes. Divide the batter equally between the pans and spread it smooth. Place the pans in the preheated oven and bake for 20 minutes, or until the cake tests done. Turn them out on cake racks and allow them to cool completely. When cool, spread half of the coffee icing over one layer and sprinkle with half the nuts. Place the other layer on top and press lightly together. Spread the remainder of the coffee icing on top and sprinkle with the remaining nuts.

To make the coffee icing: Place the butter in a bowl and mix in the coffee. Sift the sugar into the bowl, then beat all ingredients together for approximately 15 minutes with a wooden spoon.

Preparation time: 20 to 25 minutes. Cooking time: approximately 20 minutes.

APRICOT AND ALMOND CAKE

THE TOPPING

¼ pound (125 g) dried apricots
2 tablespoons (30 ml) butter
¼ teaspoon (1.25 ml) ground
  allspice

⅓ cup (2 oz; 50 g) almonds, flaked

THE CAKE

1¼ cups (½ lb; 225 g) all-purpose
  (plain) flour
1 teaspoon (5 ml) baking powder
½ teaspoon (2.5 ml) salt
½ cup (4 oz; 125 g) butter or
  margarine

1 cup (4 oz; 125 g) superfine
  granulated (castor) sugar
6 tablespoons (90 ml) milk

In a small saucepan, pour boiling water to cover the dried apricots and soak for 2 hours. Then bring the water to the boil, simmer the apricots for 15 minutes, drain and chop them.

Preheat the oven to 375° F (190° C; Mark 5).

Grease and line a 7½-inch (19 cm) square cake pan with waxed or grease-proof paper, then grease it again.

In a small, heavy-bottomed saucepan, melt the butter for the topping. Remove it from the heat and stir in the allspice and almonds. Set the mixture aside.

Sift the flour, baking powder and salt into a large mixing bowl. Using a small spatula, cut the butter or margarine into the flour and rub it with your fingertips. Make a hollow in the center of the mixture, add the sugar and milk, and mix to a light and even consistency. Pour the batter into the greased pan and smooth the surface. Lightly press the apricots on to the top of the batter in an attractive pattern. Spoon the butter mixture over the fruit. If the butter has begun to set, reheat it gently until it becomes runny.

Bake in the center of the preheated oven for 40 to 45 minutes, or until the cake shrinks from the sides of the pan. When cooked, remove the cake from the oven and allow it to cool before turning it out onto a wire rack. Remove the lining paper, cut into slices and serve immediately.

Preparation time: soaking apricots, 2 hours. Cooking time: 1 hour.

COFFEE CAKE

---

2 cups (9 oz; 270 g) self-rising
    flour
½ teaspoon (2.5 ml) mixed spice
A pinch of salt
½ cup (4 oz; 120 g) butter
¼ pound (4 oz; 120 g) light (soft)
    brown sugar
3 egg yolks, well beaten

¾ cup (5 fl oz; 150 ml) molasses
    (treacle) or corn syrup (golden
    syrup)
¼ cup (2 fl oz; 60 ml) strong
    coffee or coffee extract (essence)
3 egg whites
Coffee Cream (see below)
1½ cups (3 oz; 90 g) walnuts

Preheat the oven to 350° F (180° C; Mark 4).

In a mixing bowl, sift the flour, mixed spice and salt together. In a large mixing bowl, cream the butter thoroughly, adding the sugar gradually. Cream until light and fluffy. Add the beaten egg yolks to the butter and sugar, and then add the molasses (treacle) and the coffee. Next add the flour mixture. Beat well until the batter is smooth. Beat the egg whites until they are stiff and fold them into the cake mixture. Pour the batter into two 8 × 2½-inch (20.3 cm × 6.3 cm) cake pans and bake in the preheated oven for 30 to 40 minutes, or until the cake shrinks from the sides of the pan. Turn out and cool on a wire rack. When cool, split the layers horizontally to make a 4-layer cake. Spread the coffee cream between each layer and over the top of the cake, and decorate with walnuts.

COFFEE CREAM

2 cups (9 oz; 250 g) confectioners'
    (icing) sugar
2 tablespoons (30 ml) warm water

4 tablespoons (60 ml) strong coffee
1¼ cups (10 fl oz; 300 ml) milk
¼ cup (2 oz; 50 g) butter

Melt the sugar in the water, add the coffee and milk, and boil until the mixture forms a ball when dropped into cold water. Add the butter and let stand for 10 minutes. Then beat until cool. If the frosting is too thick to spread easily, add milk until a spreading consistency is obtained.

Note: The cake and coffee cream may be frozen separately. Ice after both cake and cream have thawed completely.

Preparation time: approximately 20 minutes. Cooking time: approximately 40 minutes.

FLAPJACKS

These are *not* pancakes as in America. They are like chewy brownies, with rolled oats substituted for the chocolate.

MAKES 12 TO 16 FLAPJACKS

½ cup (4 oz; 125 g) butter or margarine

⅓ cup (4 oz; 125 g) dark brown (soft) sugar

2 tablespoons (30 ml) light corn syrup (golden syrup)

2 cups (4 oz; 125 g) rolled oats (Quaker oats)

1 teaspoon (5 ml) baking powder

A pinch of salt

Preheat the over to 350° F (180° C; Mark 4).

Melt the butter, sugar and syrup in a saucepan over low heat, stirring continuously. Remove the saucepan from the heat; mix the rolled oats with the baking powder and salt and then add to the mixture, blending well. Grease an 8-inch (20.3 cm) baking pan, press the dough into it, and place it in the center of the preheated oven. Bake for 25 minutes. Mark out the mixture into 2-inch (5 cm) squares and allow to cool. When cold, cut the divisions.

Preparation time: 15 minutes. Cooking time: 25 minutes.

GINGERBREAD CAKE

This is an old Yorkshire recipe which I have found will keep moist for months.

2⅔ cups (1 lb; 450 g) dark brown (soft) sugar
1 cup (8 oz; 225 g) butter
3 tablespoons (45 ml) black molasses (treacle)
3 cups (1½ lbs; 675 g) self-rising flour, mixed with
8 cups (1 lb; 450 g) oatmeal (not instant)
6 eggs
¼ cup (2 fl oz; 50 ml) milk
6 tablespoons (3 oz; 75 ml) candied citrus peel

⅔ cup (3 oz; 75 g) chopped blanched almonds
1 cup (4 oz; 125 g) sultanas (white raisins)
⅔ cup (3 oz; 75 g) currants
6 tablespoons (90 ml) caraway seeds
1 tablespoon (15 ml) ground ginger
1 tablespoon (15 ml) chopped preserved ginger
2 tablespoons (30 ml) syrup from preserved ginger

Preheat the oven to 325° F (170° C; Mark 3).

Melt the sugar and butter in a large saucepan, then add the molasses (treacle). Mix well together, then gradually add the flour and oatmeal by spoonfuls. Next add the eggs, one at a time, and beat well. When you have obtained a smooth paste, add the milk and other ingredients. Mix thoroughly. Pour into a well-greased 8-inch (20 cm) square cake pan and bake in the preheated oven for approximately 1½ hours, or until the cake is cooked through and shrinks away from the sides of the pan.

Preparation time: approximately 20 minutes. Cooking time: approximately 1½ hours.

DOUGHNUTS

In many parts of England doughnuts used to be eaten on Shrove Tuesday instead of pancakes. Some were plain, but most of the doughnuts contained currants, spices and chopped peel, others included shredded (dessicated) coconut, ground almonds and even minced ham. The main thing to remember about these doughnuts is to keep them small; then they will cook through without any trouble. If they are large, you will find they are cooked well on the outside but raw in the center. The fat must be deep enough to cover the doughnuts completely and must always be boiling fast when the doughnuts are put in.

MAKES 16 SMALL DOUGHNUTS

½ cup (4 oz; 125 g) margarine
1¾ cups (8 oz; 225 g) flour
2 eggs, beaten well
2 teaspoons (10 ml) currants
2 teaspoons (10 ml) mixed spice
2 teaspoons (10 ml) candied lemon
  peel, or whatever flavoring you
  prefer

2 teaspoons (10 ml) fine chopped
  blanched almonds
Superfine granulated (castor)
  sugar
Vegetable oil

In a bowl, rub the margarine into the flour. Make a well in the center and stir in the eggs, then all the rest of the ingredients except the sugar and oil. Make the dough into a ball by rolling the mixture in the palms of your hands, which have first been coated with sugar. (It could first be put in a food processor, then the final roll done with your hands.) Divide the dough into small balls.

In a deep frying pan, heat the oil until it is boiling fast, then drop the balls into the fat. Fry until they become a deep brown, drain and roll in sugar. Serve while hot.

Preparation time: approximately 20 minutes. Cooking time: approximately 20 minutes.

CHURROS

When we made a trip through northern Spain with friends five years ago, we stayed in *paradors,* government-owned hotels. The food on the whole was marvelous. But one of the things we especially looked forward to was breakfast, with delicious light, hot *churros,* a kind of Spanish "French cruller," only long instead of round, and twisted. That and strong hot coffee was something special.

This mixture will keep in the refrigerator for 24 hours, so you can make the dough the night before and cook it for breakfast.

MAKES 3 DOZEN

2 cups (16 fl oz; 475 ml) water
3 cups (15 oz; 425 g) flour
4 teaspoons (20 ml) salt
2 eggs
½ teaspoon (2.5 ml) almond
   extract (essence)

Olive oil
A little superfine granulated
   (castor) sugar

In a large saucepan, boil the water. Next, add the flour sifted with the salt and stir vigorously with a wooden spoon. Remove the pan from the heat and continue to stir the mixture. When the paste begins to stick to the sides of the pan, add the eggs and almond extract (essence) and beat the dough until a stiff ball is formed, like *choux* pastry (see page 380). Heat some olive oil in a deep frying pan until it begins to smoke. Fit a pastry tube with a 1½-inch (3.5 cm) rose nozzle. Fill it with the dough and press the *churros* out in long dollops, about the size and shape of a small sausage (*chipolata*), directly into the oil. Fry the *churros* until they are dark gold, remove with a draining spoon, sprinkle with sugar and serve immediately.

Preparation time: 10 minutes. Cooking time: approximately 20 minutes.

NORWEGIAN WALNUT WAFERS

MAKES APPROXIMATELY 2 DOZEN

1¼ cups (8 oz; 225 g) fine-chopped
   walnuts
1¼ cups (8 oz; 225 g) light (soft)
   brown sugar

2 tablespoons (30 ml) flour
A pinch of salt
2 eggs, well beaten

Preheat the oven to 350° F (180° C; Mark 4).
In a bowl, mix the walnuts with the sugar, add the flour, salt and eggs. Drop by spoonfuls onto a buttered baking sheet. Each drop should be about 2 inches wide. Bake in the preheated oven for about 15 to 20 minutes.

Preparation and cooking time: 20 to 25 minutes.

BOSTON BISCUITS

MAKES ABOUT 18 COOKIES (BISCUITS)

1½ cups (8 oz; 225 g) flour, sifted
1 teaspoon (5 ml) ground ginger
1 teaspoon (5 ml) ground
  cinnamon
⅔ cup (4 oz; 125 g) light (soft)
  brown sugar
Grated rind of ½ lemon
⅓ cup (3 oz; 75 g) butter

2 tablespoons (30 ml) light corn
  syrup (golden syrup)
2 eggs, well beaten
½ teaspoon (2.5 ml) baking soda
  (bicarbonate of soda)
1 tablespoon (15 ml) milk

Preheat the oven to 450° F (230° C; Mark 8).

In a large bowl, mix the flour with the ginger, cinnamon, sugar and lemon rind. In a small saucepan, warm the butter with the corn syrup (golden syrup). Add these gradually to the flour mixture, stirring constantly; then add the beaten eggs and, finally, the baking soda (bicarbonate of soda) dissolved in the milk. Make into a firm dough by kneading for 7 minutes. Roll the dough out thin and cut in squares or rounds. Prick the cookies all over, place them on a buttered baking sheet and bake in the preheated oven for 10 minutes.

Preparation time: 20 minutes. Cooking time: 10 minutes.

IRISH POTATO CAKES

These must be eaten straight from the oven. Marvelous on a cold afternoon.

MAKES 6 TO 8 CAKES

1½ cups (½ lb; 225 g) flour
½ pound (225 g) mashed potatoes
A good pinch of salt

¼ cup (2 oz; 50 g) butter (jam or
honey may be substituted)
2 tablespoons (1 fl oz; 25 ml) milk

Preheat the oven to 450° F (230° C; Mark 8).

In a bowl, mix the flour, mashed potatoes and salt. Rub in the butter and mix to a soft dough, adding the milk. Form into flat cakes about 3 inches (7.6 cm) in diameter (the size of a scone). Bake on a sheet in the preheated oven until brown. Split open, butter and eat immediately.

Preparation time: 10 minutes. Cooking time: approximately 15 minutes.

YORKSHIRE PARKIN

½ pound (8 oz; 225 g) margarine
or lard
⅔ cup (6 fl oz; 175 ml) molasses
(treacle)
1 pound (450 g) flour, sifted
2 heaping tablespoons (40 ml) dark
brown (Barbados) sugar
2 heaping tablespoons (40 ml) fine
oatmeal

2 eggs, beaten
1 teaspoon (5 ml) ground ginger
1 teaspoon (5 ml) mixed spice
1 teaspoon (5 ml) baking soda
(bicarbonate of soda)
¼ cup (2 fl oz; 50 ml) milk

Preheat the oven to 275° F (140° C; Mark 1).

In a medium-sized saucepan, melt the margarine or lard with the molasses (treacle). Then, in a large mixing bowl, stir the mixture into the flour. To this add the sugar and oatmeal, stirring well all the time, then the beaten eggs. Make a well in the center and add the ginger, mixed spice and baking soda (bicarbonate of soda) mixed with the milk. Stir well. Put the batter into a jelly (Swiss) roll pan and bake in the preheated oven for a good hour, or until the cake shrinks from the sides of the pan.

Preparation time: 10 minutes. Cooking time: 1 hour 15 minutes.

PASTRY

Pastry is composed of fat, flour and water, and sometimes eggs. Of these ingredients, the fat is the most important, and the variety and proportion of fat added to the flour governs the method of making and baking the pastry. It is the kind of fat used that classifies the pastry.

Suet Pastry

This can be used for both sweet and savory dishes and adds a particularly good taste and consistency as an accompaniment to either meat or fruit. Sometimes dripping is used as a substitute for suet, but even though it is a purer fat and less needs to be used, it lacks the moisture obtained in suet. Suet is the hard white fat surrounding the kidneys, heart and liver in beef or lamb. The former has a more open texture and a milder flavor and in general is the preferable of the two. Depending on how you mean to use the pastry, the proportion of fat can be varied from one-third to half the weight of the flour.

As suet is a very hard fat, it is essential that it be shredded or chopped very fine. When heat is applied to the pastry the fat melts, the starch in the flour bursts and absorbs the melted fat. Large lumps of suet will not melt thoroughly and the result will be an uneven texture. Commercially prepared suet is available and will keep for a while in the refrigerator, but butcher's suet should be used immediately.

With suet pastry you will need to add a leavening agent. You can use self-rising flour, or add baking powder—2 teaspoons (10 ml) to every pound (450 g) of ordinary flour. These quantities can vary according to the kind of flour being used. If you want a more open texture, bread crumbs can be added to the flour, in which case you will need only 1 teaspoon (5 ml) baking powder to 1 pound (450 g) of flour. The consistency of this pastry is governed largely by the quantity of liquid and the speed with which it is added. If the water is added too slowly, it is more difficult to distribute it evenly, which results in an uneven texture. Add the water quickly, stirring constantly. Depending on what you are making, regulate the quantity; a steamed fruit pudding needs a stiffer pastry, a baked jam pudding a softer one—the fruit in the former will give more moisture to the pastry. If you are using bread crumbs mixed together with the flour, it is necessary to mix a stiffer dough, since the bread has already absorbed moisture and therefore cannot hold the same quantity as flour.

In general, mix the pastry to a light elastic consistency and then handle it as little as possible.

To cook suet pastry: This type of pastry can be baked, steamed or boiled, but the most satisfactory method is steaming. Boiling is next best, but you may get a pastry with a heavy, close texture, particularly if you do not start it off at the boiling point. If it is not boiling, the starch does not cook quickly enough and thus cannot absorb the melting fat. The strong heat at the boiling point drives off the gas with terrific force and so expands all the gluten, which makes the pastry rise well. Baking is the least satisfactory method, since suet, being a hard fat, leaves a residue on baking, the result is a hard pastry.

Another reason you might get a heavy-textured pastry is that it is almost impossible to make a pudding cloth waterproof. If any water touches the outside of the pastry, it will become sticky.

SUET CRUST PASTRY

MAKES 12 CUPS (16 OZ; 450 g)

2 cups (16 oz; 450 g) self-rising flour, or
1½ cups (8 oz; 225 g) all-purpose (plain) flour and 1 tablespoon (15 ml) baking powder

½ teaspoon (2.5 ml) salt
½ cup (4 oz; 125 g) shredded suet
⅝ cup (5 fl oz; 150 ml) cold water

Sift the flour and salt into a medium-sized mixing bowl. Using a table knife, stir the suet and water into the flour mixture to form a firm dough. Form the dough into a ball. Sprinkle some sifted flour onto the working surface and turn the ball onto it. Knead the dough by drawing the outer edges lightly into the center with your fingertips. Continue kneading until the dough is smooth, with no cracks. Make a ball and wrap it in a plastic bag or wax paper and place it in the refrigerator for 10 minutes. Remove the dough from the refrigerator, remove and discard the paper. Roll out as needed.

Suet Pastry Roll:

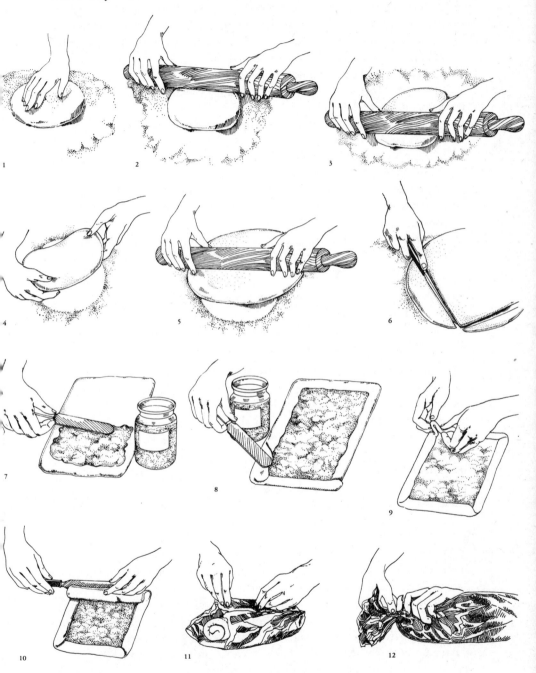

1. Flatten the ball of dough slightly with your hand.
2.-5. Roll out the dough by starting at the side nearest you and rolling away from your body. Turn the dough clockwise after each roll, and repeat the rolling away motion until the pastry measures 8 × 10 inches (20.3 × 25.4 cm) and is ¼ inch (0.6 cm) thick.
6. Trim the edges to make a neat rectangle.
7. Spread a thin layer of jam on the dough, leaving a ½-inch (1.25 cm) border all around the edge.
8. Turn the edges of the pastry over the jam pressing down lightly.
9. Make neat flat corners.
10. Starting from the short end, roll the pastry gently away from you, using a knife as backing to keep the roll neat.
11. Place the roll in the center of a piece of aluminum foil and fold over the top of the foil, leaving ample room for the dough to expand during cooking.
12. Twist the ends tightly, then place the pudding in a casserole or pudding dish half full of boiling water. Cover tightly and cook for 1½ to 2 hours, adding more water as needed.

If you don't want to steam the pudding, you could bake it by placing it in a preheated oven at 400° F (200° C; Mark 6) for 1½ hours. REMEMBER TO OIL THE ALUMINUM PAPER BEFORE WRAPPING THE SUET ROLL, if you are baking it, otherwise it will stick.

Suet Puddings: The basin in which you cook the pudding can be made of a variety of materials, but earthenware, or ovenproof glass or aluminum are the best. If you have a pudding bowl with a clip-on top, the lid *must* be removed while the pudding is cooking to allow for expansion during the cooking process. It is vital to use the right-sized basin for the correct amount of pastry—see chart (page 367). If the basin is too small, the pudding will expand out of it and will be ruined; if it is too large, condensation will form in the space between the top of the pudding and the covering, and drip down from the covering, resulting in soggy pastry. You should always allow a ½-inch (1.25 cm) space at the top for expansion during cooking.

Grease the inside of the basin all around—bottom and sides—with plenty of butter to prevent the pastry from sticking. Cover the pudding with aluminum foil, waxed paper or greaseproof paper and tie it on with string. You can use a steamer, a kettle or a saucepan as your cooking utensil, but you will need to put a trivet in the bottom of either of the second two so that the basin does not touch the bottom. Allow 1 inch (2.5 cm) of space between the widest part of the basin and the sides of the pan to allow the steam to circulate and cook the pudding. The whole process will take almost 3½ hours—particularly the first few times you do it:

Making the pastry, approximately 10 minutes;
Preparing the filling, approximately 10 minutes;
Lining and filling the basin, approximately 15 minutes;
Putting on string and tying on cover, approximately 5 minutes;
Cooking pudding to serve 4 people, approximately 2½ hours.

Fillings should always be made of raw ingredients, whether they are savory fillings such as finely chopped meat, onions, leeks, mushrooms, tomatoes; or sweet fillings, such as fruit, jam or honey.

The most successful savory fillings are made with a combination of meat and vegetables. The meat should be chopped coarsely, i.e., cut into cubes or strips. The best vegetables to combine with the meat are those which give off their own liquid during cooking, adding to that given off by the meat.

If you are using *beef:* chuck steak, flank, neck, shin, kidney or ground meat (mince) are the best. If *bacon:* slab or sliced bacon (streaky), and in England, gammon. If *pork:* belly, kidney, shoulder (blade), arm picnic (hand and spring). You can use chicken, but then combine it with a strong-flavored vegetable such as onion or leek. Vegetables should be chopped fine or sliced, then, together with the chopped meat, they should be tossed in seasoned flour in a plastic or paper bag. During cooking the flour will combine with the vegetable and meat juices to make a thick, rich gravy. Unless you are using tomatoes, which have a high liquid content, add a little luke-warm stock (*never hot*—it will make the pastry soggy) to the pudding before sealing it to allow the ingredients to cook, but not burn, before they begin to give off their own juices.

Sweet puddings are best when made with tart fruits, fresh or frozen, which, again, give off their own juices. Always add a little brown sugar between the layers and sprinkle it on the butter around the sides of the basin. Aside from adding sweetness to the pudding, sugar encourages the juices of the fruit to flow, and gives it color. Apples, rhubarb, plums, damsons, blackberries and black currants are my favorites for this pudding. Prepare them as you would for any dessert—berries can be used whole; plums, pricked and used whole; apples, peeled, cored and sliced; rhubarb, wiped and chopped.

It is extremely important when making savory-filled puddings that the pastry lid completely cover the filling and be firmly sealed. Turn the surplus folds of the pastry used to line the basin over the filling and brush the surface lightly with water to make it sticky. Next, cover it with the pastry lid and press lightly around the edges to seal. If not properly sealed, the filling will leak out during the cooking period and ruin the pudding. Savory puddings are always served in the bowl in which they were cooked, so they must look neat and appetizing on top when the cooking has finished.

Sweet-filled suet puddings, on the other hand, are turned out onto a dish, so that the lid becomes the base and the bottom is on top. In this case, when sealing the pudding, put the lid over the filling and brush the edges with water. Then turn the surplus folds of pastry over the lid and lightly press them down to seal.

To cover and cook the pudding

1. Cut a piece of aluminum foil, waxed or greaseproof paper into a round 3 to 4 inches (7.5 to 10 cm) larger than the top of the basin.
2. Grease one side of the covering with butter.
3. Pleat the covering ½ inch (1.25 cm) down the center to allow for expansion during cooking time, otherwise, when the pudding expands, the cover will blow off.
4. Place the covering, greased side down, on top of the basin, tuck in all the edges like a hem, and tie under the rim of the basin, twice around, then knot tightly.
5. Bring the water in the steamer, kettle or saucepan to the boil. The water should come up to the string. During cooking time you will have to add water as it evaporates. I keep a kettle on the stove simmering away, so that when it is time to add the water, it is hot. If you add cold water, the cooking temperature will drop and the cooking time will be put out of whack.
6. Place the basin on a large square of cheesecloth (muslin). Pick up the basin, holding the sides of the cloth firmly, lower the basin onto the steamer or trivet and tie the cloth *loosely* over the top of the pudding.
7. When the pudding is cooked, you can untie the cheesecloth (muslin) and lift the basin out of the container.
8. If it is a sweet pudding, have a plate large enough to hold the pudding warming in the oven. Run a spatula around the inside edge of the basin to loosen the pastry. Place the warm plate over the top of the basin. Put on a pair of oven gloves—both the basin and dish will be hot—and with your right hand holding the dish and the left holding the bottom of the basin, invert the basin onto the dish. Put the dish down on your working surface, then with both hands slowly lift off the basin, leaving the inverted pudding on the plate. Serve immediately.
9. If it is a savory pudding, tie a pretty napkin around the basin, place it on a dish and serve.

The following chart is a guide to the quantities of pastry needed for a filled pudding:

Size of basin	Quantity of pastry	Number of servings	Cooking time
1–1¼ pints (¾–1 pt; 500 ml)	1 cup (4 oz; 125 g)	2–3	1½ hours
2 pints (1½ pts; 900 ml)	1¼ cups (6 oz; 175 g)	3–4	2–2½ hours
2½ pints (2 pts; 1 l)	1½ cups (8 oz; 225 g)	4–6	2½–3 hours
3 pints (2½ pts; 1¼ l)	2¼ cups (12 oz; 350 g)	6–8	3–3½ hours
3¾ pints (3 pts; 1½ l)	3 cups (1 lb; 450 g)	8–10	4–4½ hours

Short Pastry

The point of this type of pastry is that it should be crisp, and this depends largely on the proportion and kind of fat used. Lard or vegetable fat are 100% fat, so that a smaller quantity need be used; however, because of their softness and low melting point they also oil easily, resulting in a tough rather than a crisp pastry. A better method is to use a 60–40 combination of butter to lard or vegetable fat for short pastry, and 100% butter in a rich shortcrust. The pastry should be handled as little as possible to avoid melting the fat. Cut the fat into the flour and rub with the fingertips until you achieve the consistency of fine bread crumbs.

As with suet pastry, the addition of liquid is most important. Because the proportion of fat is small, the less water added the easier it will be for the flour to absorb the fat, resulting in a good, stiff consistency. Once more, the liquid must be added quickly to achieve an even distribution and crispness. For a *rich* shortcrust pastry, add the yolk of 1 egg to the water. Because of the large proportion of fat in this pastry, it is essential that it be cool, and handled and rolled lightly. Remember, the friction of mixing causes heat.

Before rolling out, place the dough in a plastic bag in a cool place for about 30 minutes. This hardens the fat and generally cools the ingredients. The cold air will then expand when heated and make a light pastry.

Rolling the pastry is another important factor in achieving an even distribution of fat, flour and liquid. It should be done forwards and backwards with sharp, even strokes, turning the pastry as needed. Do *not* roll sideways, because this results in unequal pressure, and thus in uneven rising because of overstretching some of the gluten in the flour.

To cook short pastry: With all pastries it is necessary to have strong enough heat to cause the starch grains in the flour to cook quickly, thus enabling them to absorb the melted fat. The liquid, in the form of steam, and the air expand on heating, expanding the gluten in the flour and raising the pastry. Then the prolonged heat makes it set and retain its shape. The oven temperature should be regulated according to the thickness of the pastry and the amount of surface exposed. The thicker the pastry and the bigger the surface, the lower the oven temperature should be.

Various mistakes can happen:

THE PASTRY IS TOO HARD. It is either because not enough fat was used, or because the correct amount of fat was not well rubbed in, and thus not sufficiently mixed with the flour during the cooking. Or it could be that too much water was added, thus lowering the proportion of fat.

BLISTERS HAVE FORMED ON TOP OF THE PASTRY. The liquid has been added too slowly or unevenly. Then when the pastry was put into the oven, some parts contained more moisture than others, and there was not enough flour to absorb the extra water. The result is that the additional steam blows out the thin surface layer of gluten, forming a blister.

THE PASTRY COVERING A FRUIT TART IS SOGGY. When the fruit tart is first put into the oven the pastry cooks and sets, but the fruit gradually lets off steam. Unless there is an opening through which the steam can escape, the pastry will absorb this steam, resulting in a wet and heavy crust. To avoid this, make a slit on either side of the top of the tart as soon as the pastry is firm on the outside. The steam will escape through these openings. If you make the slits before the tart goes into the oven, the pastry will not get the support from the collected heat of the fruit, which helps to hold it in position while it is setting, and the pastry will sink. Another reason for a sinking top might be that the oven was too cool. Then the starch in the flour does not gelatinize quickly enough, the melted fat runs out, together with air, and the pastry subsides.

Do not sprinkle sugar on the surface of pastry before cooking it, nor mix granulated sugar into the pastry. The sugar loses its moisture, caramelizes and burns before the pastry has cooked, resulting in the pastry having a speckled appearance.

SHORTCRUST PASTRY

MAKES 1½ CUPS (8 OZ; 225 G), ENOUGH FOR ONE 12-INCH (30 CM) QUICHE

*1½ cups (8 oz; 225 g) all-purpose
  (plain) flour
½ teaspoon (2.5 ml) salt
¼ cup (2 oz; 50 g) cold butter*

*¼ cup (2 oz; 50 g) cold vegetable
  fat or lard
3 to 4 tablespoons (45 to 60 ml)
  iced water*

Sift the flour and salt into a medium-sized mixing bowl. Cut the butter and vegetable fat into small pieces. With your fingertips, rub the fat into the flour until the mixture resembles coarse bread crumbs.

Add 3 tablespoons (45 ml) of the iced water and, with a knife, mix it into the flour. With one hand, mix and knead the dough until it is smooth. Add more water if the dough is too dry. Form the dough into a ball, wrap it in a plastic bag or waxed paper, and chill it in the refrigerator for 30 minutes. Remove the dough and use as needed.

WHOLE-WHEAT SHORTCRUST PASTRY FOR DOUBLE PIE CRUST

MAKES 1 CUP (5 OZ; 150 G), ENOUGH FOR ONE 9-INCH (22.8 CM) PIE

*1 cup (5 oz; 150 g) all-purpose
  (plain) flour
1 cup (5 oz; 150 g) whole-wheat
  flour
1 teaspoon (5 ml) salt*

*½ cup (4 oz; 125 g) lard or ¾ cup
  (6 oz; 175 g) cold vegetable
  shortening
4 tablespoons (60 ml) iced water*

Preheat the oven to 450° F (230° C; Mark 8).

Sift the white flour onto a sheet of waxed paper before measuring. The whole-wheat flour need not be sifted. Combine the two flours and sift again into a mixing bowl. Add the salt to the flour and mix. Cut the fat into the flour with a pastry blender or two knives, or rub with your fingertips until it is well blended and resembles fine bread crumbs. Add the water gradually, a few drops at a time, and toss lightly with a fork to distribute evenly. Press the mixture gently into shape and then into a ball. Do not overhandle. Place some waxed or greaseproof paper around it and chill for 30 minutes.

Cut the ball of dough into two portions, one slightly larger than the other. Use the larger portion for the bottom crust. Place the large portion of dough on a lightly floured board and shape it quickly into a thick, flat disc with the hands. This shaping will form a small circle of dough. Then, lightly, roll out with a rolling pin to the size desired, rolling outward from the center and moving the pastry around so you are always rolling up and down. It should be about an eighth of an inch (0.3 cm) thick. Fold the sheet of pastry through the center and lift it carefully and quickly onto an ungreased pie pan so the fold is across the center of the pan. The fold makes it easy to center the pastry and the folded sheet is easier to move without cracking it.

Unfold the pastry without stretching and allow it to fall loosely into the pan. Lift the crust gently with one hand and ease it, without stretching, into the shape of the pan. At the same time, run the finger of your other hand around the inside. The pastry must fit snugly into the sides and bottom of the pan, particularly where the sides meet the bottom. Leave the edge of the lower crust untrimmed and put in the filling.

Roll out the rest of the pastry to the same thickness as the outer edge of the lower crust and in a circle large enough to fit over the top of the pie. Moisten the edges of the lower crust with water and lay the top crust carefully over the filling. Press lower and upper crusts together gently to seal them well. Then trim both together about ¼ inch (6 mm) beyond the rim of the pan. Fold the edge under and let rest for 10 to 15 minutes before baking. This will allow the gluten in the pastry, which has been stretched during the rolling, to relax, thus preventing the pastry from shrinking too much during the baking.

Place on the middle shelf in the center of the oven and bake in the pre-heated oven for 12 to 15 minutes, allowing the top crust to set. Then make neat cuts in several places to allow the steam to escape. Reduce the heat to the temperature required for the specific filling, and continue baking until filling is cooked.

Flaky Pastries

These are divided into three classes, according to the proportion of fat and the method of cooking.

Rough puff pastry is the plainest of this class. The fat—butter is best but half lard, half margarine can also be used—is usually one half or two-thirds the weight of the flour, and is cut into large pieces and rolled into the dough instead of being rubbed into the flour as in short pastry. Acid, either a pinch of cream of tartar or a squeeze of lemon juice, is added to the iced water.

This counteracts the richness of the larger proportion of fat and also makes the gluten elastic, which in turn makes it rise better. Be careful not to add too much acid; it will make the gluten so elastic it will not set. As usual, quickly and evenly poured liquid is essential; stir it lightly so that the fat remains unbroken in the mixing. *The dough should be lumpy*. The pastry is in rough flakes when cooked. As the fat is in large pieces, several—two or three—rollings are necessary before the dough will absorb the fat, and these rollings and foldings must be evenly executed. The number of rollings depends upon the coldness of the fat: If it is hard, more rollings will be necessary. With the increased quantity of fat, it is even more necessary for the pastry to cool before cooking.

TO COOK ROUGH PUFF PASTRY

Greater heat is required for this type of pastry than for suet and shortcrust. The starch in this flour must burst quickly so that the increased amount of fat may be absorbed. The edges of the pastry will rise better if you make slits around the perimeter of the top crust, because the hot air penetrates through the cut surface more quickly.

ROUGH PUFF PASTRY

Good for pie crusts and turnovers.

MAKES 1½ CUPS (8 OZ; 225 G) PASTRY

1½ cups (8 oz; 225 g) all-purpose (plain) flour
½ teaspoon (2.5 ml) salt
¾ cup (6 oz; 175 g) cold butter

A pinch of cream of tartar or 2 teaspoons (10 ml) lemon juice
4 to 6 tablespoons (60 to 90 ml) iced water

Sift the flour and salt into a cold, medium-sized mixing bowl. Cut the butter into walnut-sized pieces and add to the flour. Mix the cream of tartar or lemon juice with the iced water. Pour in 4 tablespoons (60 ml) of the water mixture and mix quickly with a knife to form a lumpy dough. Add a little more of the water if the dough looks too dry. Shape the dough into a ball with your hands, place in a plastic bag and refrigerate for 15 minutes.

On a lightly floured working surface and using a floured rolling pin, roll out the dough into an oblong. Fold the dough in three, turning it so that the open end faces you, and roll out the dough again into an oblong shape and fold it in three. Repeat the rolling and folding process once more. Wrap the dough in greaseproof or waxed paper and chill in the refrigerator for 30 minutes.

Remove the dough from the refrigerator. If it looks streaky, roll it out and fold it once more. The dough is now ready for use.

Flaky pastry: is used for meat pies, sausage rolls and other savories. The proportion of fat is two-thirds the weight of the flour. It is best to use a mixture of soft and hard fats, and it is essential that the two fats be mixed well together before they are rolled into the dough. One-quarter of the given weight of fat should be rubbed into the flour. Then a squeeze of lemon juice should be added to the mixing water, and the dough should be lightly kneaded to insure the complete distribution of the moisture and secure even rising. The remainder of the fat will be rolled rather than rubbed into the dough.

The point in flaky pastry is to keep the layers even, so even rolling is essential. Air and steam raise the pastry in cooking. If the layers of fat and dough are broken during the rolling, the air and steam escape on heating, and the pastry rises unevenly. At ordinary temperatures five rollings are necessary; six in cold weather. Because of the friction caused by this extra rolling, it is absolutely essential that the pastry rest in a cool place before use. If it is to be in a refrigerator overnight, it must be wrapped in greaseproof or waxed paper. This prevents it drying out. Because of the large amount of fat in this type of dough, an extremely hot oven is required.

TO MAKE FLAKY PASTRY

FLAKY PASTRY

MAKES 1½ CUPS (8 OZ; 225 G) PASTRY

⅜ cup (3 oz; 75 g) cold lard

⅜ cup (3 oz; 75 g) cold butter or margarine

½ pound (225 g) all-purpose (plain) flour

½ teaspoon (2.5 ml) salt

2 teaspoons (10 ml) lemon juice

7 tablespoons (75 ml) chilled water

1. Divide the fats into 4 equal pieces on four separate plates and put three of these in the refrigerator.

2. Sift the flour and salt into a mixing bowl and rub in the 1st quarter of the fats. Add the lemon juice and water to form a soft, pliable dough.

3. Turn out the dough onto a lightly floured surface and knead it into a oblong shape with a lightly floured rolling pin.

4. With short light strokes, roll the dough into an oblong 3 times as long as it is wide and approximately ¼ inch (6 mm) thick. Using a palette knife, mark the dough into 3 sections.

5. Cut up the 2nd quarter of fats into small pieces and dot them over one end and the middle marked sections, leaving the other end bare.

6. Fold the section WITHOUT fat over the middle section.

7. Fold the end with butter over the middle, making sure all the edges are straight.

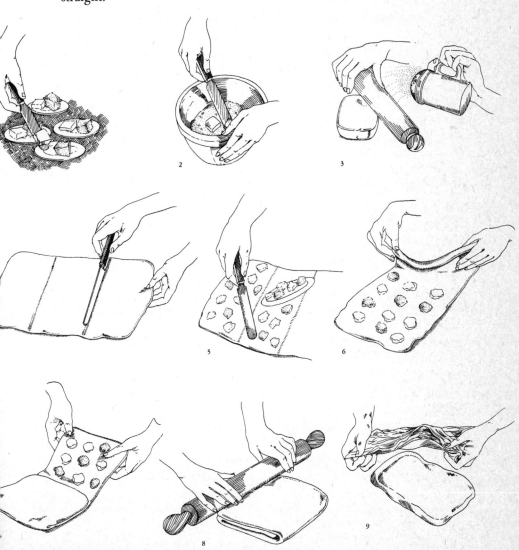

8. With a rolling pin, lightly roll over the dough to seal the edges. Brush off any excess flour. Wrap the dough in a plastic bag or plastic wrap (cling film) and refrigerate it for 30 minutes to 1 hour. Repeat the whole process with the 3rd quarter of fat, and then again with the 4th quarter.
9. Wrap the dough in plastic wrap and chill for ½ hour before using.

TO COOK FLAKY PASTRY

In order to obtain light, flaky pastry, it must be cooked on a shelf just *above* the center of the oven at 400° to 425° F (200° to 220° C; Mark 6 to 7) so that the impact of the heat causes the fats between the layers to melt, leaving empty spaces where the steam and air expand to lift the pastry and then quickly set it into its final shape. But do not make the oven *too* hot, otherwise the surface of the pastry will form a hard crust, stopping it from rising because it has become too heavy. If the oven temperature is too low, however, or if the pastry has not been put into a preheated oven, the fat will melt before the starch in the flour has had time to absorb it. Then the pastry will not rise and will be tough and dry.

A flaky pastry shell will cook unfilled in 25 minutes. Depending upon the individual recipe, pies with fillings will have varied baking times. A pie with a raw filling will take longer, as the filling cooks with the pastry. In this case you must lower the oven heat after the first 25 minutes so that the pastry does not overcook. If the pastry lid looks as though it is becoming too brown, put a piece of waxed or greaseproof paper over the lid and continue cooking for the prescribed amount of time. If you are putting a pastry lid on top of a cooked filling, allow the filling to cool first, then put it into the shell, place the lid on top and bake.

Puff pastry: This is the richest pastry of all, with equal quantities of fat and flour used; butter is the only acceptable fat. It is ideal for both its flavor and its hard consistency. A quarter of the butter should be rubbed into the flour for the reasons stated above (i.e., 1 oz [30 g] butter to 4 oz [225 g] flour), and once more a squeeze of lemon juice should be added to the liquid. The dough should be mixed to the same consistency as the butter, pliable but not sticky. The object is to produce thin layers of dough interspersed with thin layers of butter. When the dough is cooked, the butter is absorbed by the starch particles when they burst, and the result is a pastry of light, horizontal flakes. Light kneading after the first mixing will insure an even distribution of the moisture.

The large proportion of fat present in this pastry necessitates several rollings for even distribution. Even rolling out of the dough is absolutely essential. Using even pressure, avoid stretching the dough and keep the thickness of the dough the same all over. Undue pressure on any part of the dough will cause the layers to become misshapen, resulting in shrinkage and, thus, uneven rising. Roll out the dough between 4 to 6 times, depending on the temperature. During cold weather, with cold fat, you will need more rollings. The pastry must rest three times in a cool place during the process, once after it has been kneaded, once after the second time it has been rolled out, and again after the last time.

An important point to remember is not to use too much flour to keep it from sticking to the board while being rolled out, otherwise the proportions of butter to flour will alter and change the subsequent consistency of the pastry. Puff pastry may be frozen for up to 3 months.

TO COOK PUFF PASTRY

Puff pastry should always be baked *before* it is filled, and it should *never* be filled until the last minute, otherwise the pastry becomes soggy. It requires more heat at the beginning than any other pastry because of the high fat content. Bake it on a damp, *not greased,* sheet in a preheated oven 400° F (200° C; Mark 6). The cooking time depends upon what you are making and the individual recipe.

PUFF PASTRY

Use for *vol au vents, mille feuille* and *tranches.*

MAKES 4 CUPS (1 LB; 450 G) PASTRY

4 cups (1 lb; 450 g) all-purpose (plain) flour
½ teaspoon (2.5 ml) salt
2 cups (1 lb; 450 g) cold butter

1 cup (8 fl oz; 225 ml) iced water mixed with a squeeze of lemon juice

1. Sift the flour and salt into a large mixing bowl. With a table knife, cut ½ cup (4 oz; 120 g) butter into the flour, crumble the butter and flour with your fingertips, add the water and mix to a firm dough.
2. Knead the dough to make it pliable and form it into a ball. Cover with greaseproof or waxed paper and place the dough in the refrigerator. Chill for 15 minutes.
3. Put the remaining butter between two pieces of greaseproof or waxed paper and beat it with the back of a wooden spoon into a flat oblong slab about ¾ inch (1.9 cm) thick.
4. Unwrap the ball of dough, and, on a floured board, roll it into a rectangular shape ¼ inch (.6 mm) thick.

5. Place the slab of butter in the center of the dough.
6. Fold the dough over the butter to make a parcel. Place the dough in the refrigerator to chill for a further 10 minutes.
7. Place the dough with the long side facing you on the board and roll away from you into a rectangle.
8. Fold the rectangle in three.
9. Turn so that the open end is facing you and roll out again. Chill the dough in the refrigerator for 15 minutes.
10. Repeat the folding and rolling process until it has been rolled and chilled 6 times.

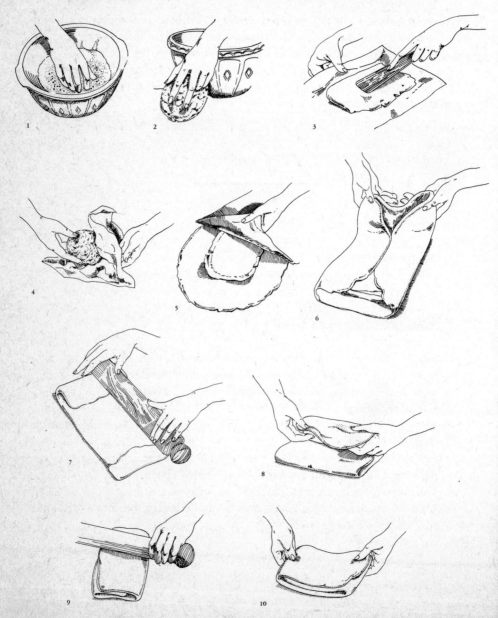

Hot-water Crust or "Raised Pastry," and Choux Pastry

Hot-water crust or "Raised Pastry": With all other pastries the main object is to keep the dough cool and the fat solid. With this pastry you do just the opposite. The fat and liquid are brought to the boiling point. When they are added to the flour, the starch grains will burst immediately and absorb the fat and liquid, so that this now takes place during the mixing process rather than during the baking process. The pastry should be crisp. It is molded by hand and therefore should be fairly stiff. If it is too soft, allow it to stand for a short time; the solidifying of the fat will cause the pastry to become stiffer.

Another difference between this and other pastries is in the addition of the liquid. Whereas with other pastries a quick addition of the liquid gives a better result, here care must be taken to add only a small proportion of liquid to fat. If you add a larger quantity than needed, all the liquid will not be used, thus making the proportions of fat to liquid inaccurate. After adding the small amount of boiling water to the fat, if you find the dough is too stiff, add a bit more liquid, but *make sure it is at the boiling point when added.* If you do not, the pastry will crack and be difficult to mold as a result of the premature solidifying of the fat. The starch grains will not have burst, so the fat will not have been absorbed.

Make sure the pastry does not become too cold after mixing, as this also will make the fat solidify and the pastry crack. If this does happen, put the pastry in a bowl, cover it, and put it in a warm place for a short time. *Warm, not hot,* otherwise the heat will cook the pastry and it will be impossible to mold.

TO COOK HOT-WATER CRUST PASTRY

Moderate heat is needed for most of the cooking time, since the starch has already been gelatinized and the liquid absorbed, but the pastry must be thoroughly cooked through to the inside and browned outside. For the first 30 minutes bake in a preheated 400° F (200° C; Mark 6) oven, then lower the heat to 325° F (170° C; Mark 3) for the remaining cooking time.

A metal raised-pie mold is a good investment—oval with a pattern embossed in the side which impresses itself on the pastry. This should have a 3¾-pint (3 pt; 1.7 l) capacity, with sides 8 inches (20.3 cm) long and 4 inches (10 cm) high, and serve 8 people. As the mold has no bottom, place it on a baking sheet before you start molding the pastry. The clips or hinges on the mold will facilitate removing the cooked pie. However, if you think you will not use it enough to warrant the expense, use a cake pan or a loaf pan. For sizes, see the chart on page 379. The cake pan should have a loose base—this will make removing the pie easier. A loaf pan will have to be inverted.

If you are going to make small pies, use jam jars. A 1-pound (450 g) jar is the best, because you can vary the height of the pie.

HOT-WATER CRUST PASTRY

ABOUT 3 CUPS (16 OZ; 450 G), ENOUGH FOR 1 DOUBLE-CRUST PIE

3 cups (16 oz; 450 g) flour
1 teaspoon (5 ml) salt
⅝ cup (5 fl oz; 450 ml) water

½ cup (4 oz; 125 g) vegetable fat
or lard
1 egg yolk, lightly beaten

Sift the flour and salt into a large mixing bowl. In a small saucepan, bring the water and vegetable fat or lard to the boil over high heat, stirring frequently until the fat or lard has melted. Remove the pan from the heat.

Make a well in the center of the flour and pour in the egg yolk and water and fat mixture. With a wooden spoon, gradually draw the flour mixture into the liquids. Continue until all the flour is incorporated and the dough is smooth. Turn out the dough onto a floured board, and knead it well with one hand until it is shiny and smooth. Roll out the dough to the required shape and use at once.

FILLINGS

Veal is an excellent filling, but as it is a dry meat it needs to be combined with bacon, which will also give it a better flavor. Pork is particularly good: Use the arm picnic (hand and spring) or the shoulder. Ham is usually combined with sliced chicken or sliced turkey or chunks of veal. The ratio is usually equal quantities of ham and poultry, or one-quarter ham to three-quarters veal.

At the end of the shooting season, when game birds are getting old and the prices have come down, you could use slivers of breast meat from pigeon, pheasant, partridge or grouse for a very special pie. Because raised pies are always eaten cold, they need a great deal of seasoning. Cinnamon, allspice, juniper, cloves and nutmeg are a particularly good marriage with basil and thyme for pork, tarragon for chicken, or rosemary for ham. Another delicious method for adding flavor is to marinate the meat in some wine or cider for a while before using it. Then add the liquid to the final filling.

Important: The filling should always be made *before* you make the pastry because there won't be time after. Quickness and preparedness are the secrets to making a successful raised pie.

Chart of Sizes for Raised Pies	Quantity of Pastry	Quantity of Filling	Serves
Raised pie mold	1 pound (450 g)	2½ pounds (1.1 kg)	8
Cake pan, 7½-inch (19 cm) diameter	1 pound (450 g)	2½ pounds (1.1 kg)	8–10
Loaf pan, 2 pound (1 kg)	1 pound (450 g)	2½ pounds (1.1 kg)	8–10
Six 1-pound (450 g) jam jars	1 pound (450 g)	2½ pounds (1.1 kg)	6
Cake pan, 6½-inch (16.5 cm) diameter	¾ pound (350 g)	1½ pounds (700 g)	6
Loaf pan, 1 pound (450 g)	½ pound (225 g)	1½ pounds (700 g)	4–6
2 jam jars	½ pound (225 g)	1¼ pounds (550 g)	4

Choux pastry: This is used mainly for profiteroles, éclairs and cream puffs. It is called *"choux"* because it puffs up during baking and resembles a cabbage. The important difference between *choux* and hot-water crust pastry is that with *choux* more eggs are added to the dough to make it lighter. The fat and liquid must be at boiling point when the flour is added. The dough is then put back over the heat to insure the complete cooking of the starch. The eggs should be beaten well and then slowly and thoroughly beaten into the mixture to distribute the air evenly. If you get a hard outside and soft inside, it is because the pastry has not risen well. This occurs when the starch has not been thoroughly cooked in the first mixture, or too much may have been added in proportion to the amount of eggs, which weakens their usefulness as a leavening agent.

TO COOK CHOUX PASTRY

The pastry should be covered while baking. This prevents the gluten on the outside of the pastry from becoming set too quickly, and allows the air inside the pastry to get warm gradually and expand to its full extent. If the oven is too hot, the starch becomes dextrinized too quickly and the gluten will set. The warm air inside will not expand because of the hard set outside the pastry; thus the mixture inside will not cook. *Do not remove the cover* before the pastry has cooked; if you do, the steam will escape, the pastry will fall and will never regain its shape. After the pastry has cooked and been removed from the oven, slit the *choux* puffs and allow the steam to escape.

CHOUX PASTRY

1½ CUPS (12 OZ; 350 G) PASTRY, MAKES 8 LARGE CHOUX PUFFS

1¼ cups (10 fl oz; 300 ml) water   *⅛ teaspoon (.75 g) grated nutmeg*
⅜ cup (3 oz; 75 g) butter, cut into   *2½ cups (12 oz; 350 g) flour*
  small pieces   *5 large eggs*
1 teaspoon (5 ml) salt

In a large, heavy saucepan bring the water to the boil over moderate heat. Add the butter, salt and nutmeg. When the butter has melted, remove the pan from the heat and beat in the flour. Return to the heat and continue beating until the mixture pulls away from the sides of the pan.

Remove from the heat, add the eggs one by one, beating each into the dough until it is well blended before adding the next. When the eggs have all been completely absorbed, the mixture should be thick and somewhat glossy. The dough is now ready for use.

CHOUX PUFFS

MAKES 8 LARGE OR 16 SMALL PUFFS

1 teaspoon (5 ml) butter   *1 egg, lightly beaten with ½*
1½ cups (12 oz; 350 g) Choux   *teaspoon (2.5 ml) water*
  Pastry

Preheat the oven to 425° F (220° C; Mark 7).
Grease two baking sheets with the butter. Fill a pastry bag with the warm pastry and using a ¼-inch (.6 mm) nozzle for small puffs and a ½-inch (1.2 cm) one for large puffs, squeeze the pastry onto the baking sheets in circular mounds. Small puffs should be roughly 1 inch (2.5 cm) in diameter and ½ inch (1.2 cm) in height; large puffs, 2 inches (5 cm) in diameter and 1 inch (2.5 cm) in height. The puffs will expand quite a bit during baking, so allow plenty of space between each mound. Using a pastry brush, coat each puff thoroughly but lightly with the beaten-egg mixture. Bake the puffs in the center of the preheated oven for 10 minutes. Reduce the temperature to 375° F (190° C; Mark 5) and continue to bake the small

puffs for a further 15 to 20 minutes; the large puffs for a further 25 to 30 minutes. By the end of the cooking the puffs will have doubled in size and should be light brown in color.

Remove from the oven and make a slit in the side of each puff with a sharp knife to allow the steam to escape, otherwise the moisture will permeate the baked shell, causing the puffs to collapse. Replace the puffs in the turned-off oven for 10 minutes, then transfer them to a wire rack to cool to room temperature. To fill the puffs, gently cut off the tops with a sharp knife and spoon in either a savory filling or some *crème pâtisserie* (see below) and melted plain chocolate. Replace the tops, gently pressing the two halves of the puffs together. Serve as soon as possible.

CRÈME PÂTISSERIE

MAKES 1½ CUPS (12 FL OZS; 350 ML), ENOUGH TO FILL 8 LARGE OR 16 SMALL CHOUX PUFFS

2 egg yolks
4 tablespoons (60 ml) sugar
1 tablespoon (15 ml) cornstarch (cornflour)
1 tablespoon (15 ml) plus 1 tea-spoon (15 ml) flour

1¼ cups (10 fl oz; 275 ml) milk
½ teaspoon (2.5 ml) vanilla extract (essence)
1 egg white

In a medium-sized mixing bowl, beat the egg yolks lightly with a fork. Add the sugar and beat the mixture until it is creamy. Sift in the cornstarch (cornflour) and flour a little at a time, beating constantly, then gradually mix in about one-quarter of the milk and the vanilla extract (essence).

In the top of a medium-sized double boiler, scald the remaining milk directly over high heat. Pour the hot milk into the egg and sugar mixture, beating well with a wire whisk. Return the mixture to the pan, set it over hot water and, stirring constantly, bring it back to the boil. Remove the pan from the heat and beat the mixture until it is smooth. Set it aside and allow it to cool. In a small bowl, whisk the egg white with a wire whisk until it is stiff. Transfer about one-quarter of the warm custard mixture to a medium-sized bowl. Carefully fold the egg white into the mixture, then carefully fold it back into the custard remaining in the saucepan. Return the saucepan to the stove and cook the mixture over low heat for 2 minutes, stirring occasionally. Pour the cream into a bowl to cool before using it.

French Pastry: Pâte Brisée, Pâte Sucrée and Pâte Frolle

Pâte brisée, (which is very short pastry that breaks up easily), *pâte sucrée* (sugared pastry), and *pâte frolle* (very lightly handled pastry with ground almonds) are very much richer than other shortcrust pastries. These are made with butter (rather than lard or shortening), eggs and sugar, which give a crisp, golden pastry—good for tart cases, flan rings, and making *barquettes* and *gateaux*. Though they are similar in some ways to an enriched shortcrust, the method of making them is entirely different. French pastry is made on a marble slab or board, rather than in a bowl, and the ingredients are worked in with the fingertips and using a metal scraper to scoop up the dough, instead of being rubbed in and then bound with water as in shortcrust. A marble slab is the best utensil to use as a work surface, as it remains cool.

The basic ingredients are *flour* (only all-purpose [plain] white flour should be used—never strong white flour or self-rising flour); *salt,* which is sifted with the flour to bring out the flavor of the other ingredients and to bring out the color of the egg yolks; and *butter*—for best results, use unsalted butter, but if you use salted butter, add less salt to the flour. It should be slightly softened to make it easy to mix with the fingertips, so remove it from the refrigerator approximately ½ hour before using. The quantity of butter is usually half that of the flour in *pâte brisée,* but this varies slightly with the other three pastries.

Sugar: If you are going to use the pastry for molding into flan or tartlette tins, superfine granulated sugar (castor sugar) should be used. If you are making galettes, the finer confectioners' sugar (icing sugar) should be used. The quantity of sugar is usually equal to the quantity of butter in the *pâte sucrée,* but this can vary.

Egg yolks are used in these sweet pastries: roughly 1 medium-sized egg yolk to ½ cup (2 oz; 50 g) of flour in *pâte sucrée*. Again, this will vary among the other pastries.

Vanilla extract (*essence*) is used only in *pâte sucrée*.

The amount of cold water used depends upon the age of the ingredients and the humidity in the air. But the minimum of water should be needed.

In general, the method for making all three of these sweet French pastries is the same, with small variation of ingredients in the individual recipes.

When you sift the flour and salt onto the marble slab, it should make a neat pile. Then make a well in the center of the flour; place the butter in the center of the well along with the sugar (if you are using confectioners' sugar [icing sugar], this must be sifted over the butter). Next add the egg yolks and vanilla extract (essence) beaten together in a bowl (for *pâte sucrée*), and poured into the well. For *pâte brisée* or *pâte frolle,* pour the egg yolks straight into the well and break them there with a fork. Then add 1 teaspoon (5 ml) or so of water.

At this point, with the fingertips of one hand, mix the butter and egg yolks, water and sugar well *before* drawing in any flour. Then, little by little, draw in the flour to the butter mixture with the fingertips of one hand until it is all incorporated and the dough forms a ball. When this is done, knead the dough with the heel of your hand in outward motions, pressing down lightly and quickly lifting off. Do this all over the pastry until it binds together. Gather it up with a dough scraper. It should become soft and pliable but not sticky. If it does become sticky, put it in some plastic wrap and refrigerate for 30 minutes until it becomes firm again. Then knead it again until it becomes smooth.

As with other kinds of pastry, French pastry needs to "rest" before being rolled out. It should be wrapped in plastic wrap, waxed paper, a plastic bag or aluminum foil, and put into the refrigerator. *Pâte brisée* needs 2 hours chilling time; *pâte frolle* and *pâte sucrée* need only 1 hour. If you wish to make these doughs ahead of time, they can remain, well-wrapped, in the refrigerator for up to 3 days, or they can be frozen.

When the dough is ready to be rolled out, make it into the shape it is meant to end up in—that is to say, a round ball for a circular shape, a square or rectangle for a square. Use a heavy, long, straight rolling pin without handles. Roll on a lightly floured surface, continually turning the pastry to the left so that it is not stretched and keeps its shape. *Pâte sucrée* should be the thickest—approximately ¼ inch (6 mm); the others should be slightly thinner.

To line a French flan ring, grease it first, then roll out the dough to about 2 inches (5 cm) larger than the flan ring or tart pan. Then roll the pastry around the rolling pin and lift it over the center of the ring. Unroll the pastry into the ring allowing it to rest over the edge, and carefully ease it into place. Then, with one hand, lift the dough slightly, and with the other gently press the pastry into shape against the sides as well as around the bottom edge. Run a rolling pin over the rim of the ring or pan to remove any excess pastry from the top. Then with your thumb and forefinger press the dough evenly around the rim beginning at the bottom so that the dough creeps up and into the fluted sides of the pan.

Next, with a fork, prick the base of the dough all over to allow the steam to escape and to prevent the dough from rising during baking. Chill it well, for about 2 hours, before using it—this will prevent most of the shrinkage and keep the dough firm while baking.

The same method can be used for lining tartlet pans. Group the pans together, and make the dough long enough and wide enough to overlap the outer pans. After you have pressed the dough into each pan, roll the rolling pin over the top to remove any excess pastry.

If you are using a precooked or soft filling, such as a custard or fruits, the pastry should be "baked blind"; that is, baked before the filling is put in, otherwise the result may be a soggy crust. Line the raw pastry with foil or waxed paper, fill it with raw beans to act as a weight, and put it into a preheated 400° F (200° C; Mark 6) oven for 6 to 10 minutes. Then remove the paper and beans. If you are partially baking the pastry shell, return it to the oven for a further 3 to 5 minutes, until it has set but has not become colored; if you are cooking the pastry shell completely, return it to the oven for a further 5 to 10 minutes, until it has completely dried and turned golden brown.

When you have added the filling, bake it in a preheated 375° F (190° C; Mark 5) oven for the amount of time indicated in the specific recipe.

When removing a baked-blind shell or a filled tart or a cooked flan from a flan ring, tilt the baking sheet or removable ring, and slide the pastry onto a wire rack. Allow it to stand for a few minutes so that the pastry will shrink away from the pan. Then remove the ring.

For removing tarts from tartlet pans, whether baked-blind pastry, cooked or filled shells, wait until it has completely cooled in the pan. Otherwise it may break. Remove it by sliding a palette knife between the pastry and the pan, then gently lifting up the tart and removing it with your fingers.

PÂTE BRISÉE

WILL LINE A 12-INCH (30 CM) FLAN RING OR 8 INDIVIDUAL 4-INCH (10 CM) TARTLET PANS

1½ cups (8 oz; 250 g) all-purpose
(plain) flour
1 teaspoon (5 ml) salt
½ cup (4 oz; 125 g) butter, cut
into pieces

2 egg yolks
3½ to 4 tablespoons (52 to 60 ml)
water

Sift the flour and salt onto a marble slab or board. Make a well in the center of the flour mixture and place the butter, egg yolks and 1 teaspoon (5 ml) water in the well. Using your fingertips, mix those ingredients, adding more water a little at a time and slowly drawing in the flour. Continue mixing in this way until all the flour is incorporated. The dough should first be in large crumbs, then as it is pressed firmly together, it should become soft but not sticky.

Knead the dough with the heel of your hand, pushing it away from you, then gathering it up with the metal scraper, until it becomes smooth and pliable and forms a ball. Roll it in a little flour, wrap in a plastic bag, plastic wrap, waxed paper or aluminum foil, and chill for a minimum of 30 minutes or up to approximately 2 hours, by which time it should become firm. It will keep like this in the refrigerator for 3 days, or you can freeze it. When ready to use, roll out only as much dough as you need.

I CUP (4 OZ; 125 G) OF DOUGH WILL LINE AN 8-INCH (20.3 CM) FLAN PAN OR RING OR 5 INDIVIDUAL 4-INCH (10 CM) TARTLET PANS. FOR THIS AMOUNT YOU WILL NEED:

1 cup (4 oz; 125 g) all-purpose (plain) flour
½ teaspoon (2.5 ml) salt
¼ cup (2 oz; 50 g) butter

1 egg yolk
1½ to 2 tablespoons (22 to 30 ml) water

1¼ CUPS (7 OZ; 200 G) OF DOUGH WILL LINE A 10-INCH (26 CM) FLAN PAN OR RING OR 7 INDIVIDUAL 4-INCH (10 CM) TARTLET PANS. FOR THIS AMOUNT YOU WILL NEED:

1¼ cups (7 oz; 200 g) all-purpose (plain) flour
¾ teaspoon (3.75 ml) salt
½ cup (4 oz; 125 g) butter

1 egg yolk
2½ to 3 tablespoons (37 to 45 ml) water

PÂTE SUCRÉE

WILL LINE AN 8-INCH (20 CM) FLAN PAN OR RING, OR 5 INDIVIDUAL 4-INCH (10 CM) TARTLET PANS

1 cup (4 oz; 125 g) all-purpose (plain) flour
A pinch of salt
¼ cup (2 oz; 50 g) butter, cut into pieces
¼ cup (2 oz; 50 g) superfine granulated (castor) sugar, or ½ cup (2 oz; 50 g) confectioners' sugar (icing sugar)

2 medium-sized egg yolks
½ teaspoon (2.5 ml) vanilla extract (essence)

Sift the flour and salt onto a marble slab or pastry board. Spread the flour into a circle and make a well in the center. Into this well put the butter and the sugar. In a bowl, mix the egg yolks with the vanilla extract (essence)

and add to the butter and sugar. Using the fingertips of one hand, mix these ingredients thoroughly (not yet touching the flour). Then work in the flour, a little at a time, drawing it in from the sides of the well. When all the flour is incorporated, knead the dough with the heel of your hand, pushing it away from you, then gathering it up with a dough scraper, until it becomes smooth and pliable and forms a ball. Wrap it in a plastic bag, plastic wrap, waxed paper or aluminum foil, and place in the refrigerator for 1 hour before rolling out. Continue as instructed on page 383. Because it contains quite a lot of sugar, you may find that the dough is less elastic but more crumbly than it should be. If so, chill it longer, then press it into shape rather than using a rolling pin. When you are baking the pastry, keep a good eye on it—the sugar in the dough makes it burn easily.

1¼ CUPS (6 OZ; 175 G) OF DOUGH WILL LINE A 10-INCH (26 CM) FLAN PAN OR
   RING OR 7 INDIVIDUAL 4-INCH (10 CM) TARTLET PANS. FOR THIS YOU WILL NEED:

1¼ cups (6 oz; 175 g) all-purpose (plain) flour
A pinch of salt
¼ cup (3 oz; 75 g) butter
⅓ cup (3 oz; 75 g) superfine granulated (castor) sugar or ¾ cup (3 oz; 75 g) confectioners' sugar (icing sugar)

½ teaspoon (2.5 ml) vanilla extract (essence)
3 medium-sized egg yolks

1½ CUPS (8 OZ; 225 G) OF DOUGH WILL LINE A 12-INCH (30 CM) FLAN PAN OR
   RING OR 8 INDIVIDUAL 4-INCH (10 CM) TARTLET PANS. FOR THIS YOU WILL NEED:

1½ cups (8 oz; 225 g) all-purpose (plain) flour
A large pinch of salt
½ cup (4 oz; 125 g) butter
½ cup (4 oz; 125 g) superfine granulated (castor) sugar or 1 cup (4 oz; 125 g) confectioners' sugar (icing sugar)

1 teaspoon (5 ml) vanilla extract (essence)
4 medium-sized egg yolks

PÂTE FROLLE

This dough should be used mainly for galettes.

WILL LINE A 7-INCH (18 CM) FLAN PAN OR RING OR 5 INDIVIDUAL 4-INCH
(10 CM) TARTLET PANS

½ cup (3 oz; 75 g) all-purpose (plain) flour

A pinch of salt

2 tablespoons (1 oz; 25 ml) ground almonds (hazelnuts or walnuts may be substituted)

¼ cup (2 oz; 50 g) butter, cut into pieces

2 medium-sized egg yolks

Grated zest of ½ lemon

¼ cup (2 oz; 50 g) superfine granulated (castor) sugar

Sift the flour, salt and ground almonds onto a marble working surface. Make a well in the center. Put the butter, egg yolks and lemon zest in the well. Add the sugar. With the fingertips of one hand, mix these last ingredients well, then draw in the flour and ground almonds, a little at a time, until the flour is totally incorporated. Knead the dough with the heel of your hand, pushing it away from you, gathering it up with a dough scraper, and kneading again until it becomes smooth and pliable and forms a ball. Wrap it in plastic wrap, a plastic bag, waxed paper or aluminum foil and place it in the refrigerator for 1 hour before rolling out as instructed on page 383.

1 CUP (5 OZ; 150 G) OF DOUGH WILL LINE A 10-INCH (26 CM) FLAN PAN OR RING
OR 7 INDIVIDUAL 4-INCH (10 CM) TARTLET PANS. FOR THIS YOU WILL NEED:

1 cup (5 oz; 150 g) all-purpose (plain) flour

A large pinch salt

4 tablespoons (2 oz; 50 ml) ground almonds

½ cup (4 oz; 125 g) butter

4 medium-sized egg yolks

Grated zest of 1 lemon

½ cup (4 oz; 125 g) castor sugar

Pâte à Pâté and Pâte Moulée

These are the French pastries used for savory flans, raised pies and *pâtés en croûte*. There is less elasticity in these pâtes, making it easier to mold them. The richest of the two is *pâte à pâté*, which is best for savory flans. *Pâte moulée* makes delicious pastry cases for meat, game or fish fillings and is perfect for lining pâté dishes. They are similar to *pâte brisée*, *pâte sucrée* and *pâte frolle* in that they consist of flour, butter and egg yolks. However, lard may be substituted for the butter to give the pastry more flavor, and an additional whole egg can be used. They are also made by the same method and the flan pan is lined in the same way.

Lining a Pâte Mold

1. Measure the mold with string, the width and length.

2. Measure the pastry ball, removing ⅓ out of which you will make the lid.
3. Roll out the remaining ⅔ of the pastry until it is rectangular in shape, slightly larger than the mold.
4. Fold the pastry in half, flour it and fold in half again.
5. Place the layered pastry in the bottom of the mold and fold out the layers.
6. Press each layer into the sides of the mold particularly along the base.
7. Lay the rolled-out lid of pastry over the filled mold.
8. Press the lid and sides together, crinkle the edges and brush with beaten egg or water.

Because when making pâtés and pies the filling has to cook, these need a lower oven temperature than the usual French savory pastry, which cooks at 400° F (200° C; Mark 6). Instead, preheat the oven to 375° F (190° C; Mark 5) and cook for the amount of time specified in the individual recipe; or put the pastry in at the hot temperature for 10 minutes to crisp, then lower the temperature, cover the pastry and continue to cook until done.

PÂTE À PÂTÉ

MAKES 2 CUPS (10 OZ; 275 G) OF DOUGH, ENOUGH FOR TWO 9-INCH (23 CM) FLAN PANS

2 cups (10 oz; 275 g) all-purpose (plain) flour
½ teaspoon (2.5 ml) salt
1 cup (8 oz; 225 g) butter or lard, cut into pieces

2 medium-sized egg yolks
1 tablespoon (15 ml) water

Sift the flour and salt onto a marble slab or board, making a well in the center. Into this put the butter, egg yolks and water. With the fingertips of one hand, blend the ingredients in the well, then gradually blend in the flour from the sides. You may need to add more water, but do this very carefully, adding the minimum amount each time. When the flour has been completely incorporated, press the dough firmly together to form a ball. Knead the dough with the heel of your hand, scoop it up with a dough scraper, and knead again until it becomes smooth and pliable. Wrap it in a plastic bag, plastic wrap, waxed paper or aluminum foil and place in the refrigerator to chill for 1 hour. Remove, roll out and line the flan pan as described on page 383.

PÂTE MOULÉE

MAKES I POUND (450 G) OF DOUGH, ENOUGH FOR A 2-POUND (I KG) RAISED
PIE OR PÂTE MOLD, SERVING FROM IO TO I2 PEOPLE

1 pound (450 g) all-purpose
  (plain) flour
1 teaspoon (5 ml) salt
1 cup (8 oz; 225 g) butter, cut into
  pieces

2 medium-sized eggs
4 to 6 tablespoons (60 to 90 ml) ice
  water

Sift the flour and salt onto a marble slab or board, making a well in the
center. Place the butter and eggs in the well and, using the fingertips of one
hand, blend the butter and the eggs. Add 1 tablespoon (15 ml) water and
begin to draw in the flour from the sides, little by little; blend in the flour,
adding a little more water when necessary until it forms a soft and pliable
dough. Form the dough into a ball and knead it with the heel of your hand,
pressing down and pushing it away from you. Gather it up again with a
dough scraper, form a ball and knead again, until it becomes smooth, without
cracks. Wrap the pastry in plastic wrap, a plastic bag, waxed paper, or
aluminum foil and chill in the refrigerator for 2 hours before rolling out.
Then roll out as mentioned on page 383, and line the pâte mold as illustrated
on page 388.

GENERAL BAKING HINTS

1. To make slicing meringue pies easier, sprinkle a little granulated sugar
   over the meringue before browning.
2. To keep dough that is rising from becoming crusty or dry, put the dough
   in an *unheated* oven with a pan of boiling water. Also put a pan of boiling water in the oven while baking bread.
3. To avoid soggy pie crust, rub the bottom of an unbaked pie shell generously with shortening (vegetable fat). Then fill and bake.
4. Flour is sifted in order to allow air into it to make the pastry lighter.
5. Rest pastry dough in a polyurethene bag for 25 minutes in the refrigerator
   before rolling out. This will insure a smooth dough that does not crack.
6. To make an extra-flaky upper pie crust, brush it lightly with cold water
   or milk before baking.

JAM-MAKING AND PRESERVING

EQUIPMENT

It is very important to sterilize preserving jars properly, otherwise your jam will spoil and all your hard work will be a waste of time. Wash the jars well in hot soapy water and then rinse them in hot water. Dry and turn them upside down in a warm oven so that they will be hot and dry when the jam is ready. Pour the jam in while it is still hot; this prevents it from turning moldy.

Choose a heavy-bottomed pan, preferably of aluminum or stainless steel. The food will burn too quickly in enamel, and the acid in the fruit will corrode galvanized iron. Brass or copper preserving pans are fine, but are likely to give a greenish tinge to pale jams or jellies.

As jam foams up during cooking, the pan must be large enough to allow the fruit to boil without boiling over. In fact, the pan should be no more than half full after the sugar has been added.

To prevent sticking and excessive scum, rub a knob of butter or margarine, or a little glycerine, over the base of the pan before making the jam. A knob of butter put in as soon as the jam begins to boil also prevents the jam from boiling over, and gives it a delicate flavor as well.

A long-handled wooden spoon is best for stirring jam. Metal spoons become hot and uncomfortable to hold; plastic spoons or rubber spatulas may become misshapen with the heat.

TO COOK

A well-set and full-flavored jam is dependent on the amounts of acid and pectin in the fruit. Cooking apples, black currants, gooseberries, damsons and cooking plums are rich in both. Next are apricots, blackberries, greengages, morello cherries, loganberries and raspberries. Dessert cherries, pears, some strawberries, eating apples, rhubarb and end-of-season blackberries have poor setting qualities and should either be combined with fruits known to be abundant in acid and pectin, or cooked with additional acidic juice and/or commercial pectin. Allow 2 tablespoons (30 ml) lemon juice or ½ level teaspoon (2.5 ml) citric or tartaric acid to every 4 pounds (2 kg) fruit. With commercial pectin, follow the directions on the package.

Fruit for jam-making should be slightly underripe or *just* ripe, and *dry*. Bruised or overripe fruits rarely give good results. Pick over the fruit very carefully and make sure it is clean before boiling.

All fruit should be cooked gently in water *before* the sugar is added to extract as much acid and pectin as possible. Those fruits which cook down quickly need less water than fruits such as currants, plums, damsons and gooseberries which soften and break down more slowly. If too much water is used, the jam will take a long time to set, and the color and flavor may be spoiled. Use just enough to stop the fruit from sticking; up to 1 pint (500 ml) for 3 pounds (1½ kg) cooking apples and about 3 pints (3¾ pts; 1¾ l) for every 4 pounds (2 kg) black currants.

Use preserving sugar or superfine granulated (castor) sugar. The preserving sugar gives a clearer look to both jam and jelly. Warm sugar will dissolve more quickly when added to the fruit, so 15 minutes before you need it, place it in a cool oven, 225° F (110° C; Mark ½). Once the sugar has been added to the fruit pulp, stir until it is dissolved (otherwise it may crystallize later in the preserve), then bring the jam to the boil. Boil it briskly, stirring occasionally, for 5 to 20 minutes (depending on the fruit), until it has set.

Never allow the jam to boil before the sugar has been dissolved. The best plan is to draw the pan to one side until the sugar has been dissolved, then return it to the heat and allow it to boil. Tart fruits, such as currants, gooseberries, damsons and rhubarb require 1 pound (450 g) of sugar to 1 pound (450 g) of fruit, whereas blackberries, raspberries and strawberries need only ¾ pound (350 g) of sugar to 1 pound (450 g) of fruit. In any case, I always use just a bit less sugar than is usually required because I prefer a bit of tartness rather than a terribly sweet taste.

There is no need to skim continuously while the jam is boiling. Wait until the end of cooking before removing the scum. To do this use a perforated spoon or a flat skimmer dipped in hot water. If you are making pit-fruit jam, lift out the pits as they rise to the top.

There are two methods by which to test for setting. The most accurate is to use a candy or sugar thermometer. Place the thermometer in the pan and when it reads 225° F (110° C) the jam or jelly should be ready. If you haven't got a thermometer, an alternative method is to put a little jam on a saucer which has been chilled in the freezing compartment of your refrigerator and leave it for 2 minutes. If a skin forms on top, it wrinkles when touched, and the knob of jam separates when a finger is passed through, then it has reached setting point. Remove the pan from the heat and leave for about 5 minutes. Then stir and carefully spoon the jam or jelly into the prepared, clean, dry and warm jars. Since jam shrinks on cooling, each jar should be filled to the brim. To prevent fruit rising in the jars, leave jam made from whole fruit, such as strawberries, in the pan for about 15 minutes until a skin forms on top. Stir gently then spoon it into the clean jars. This is particularly necessary with marmalade.

When the jars have been filled, place a waxed disk on top of the jam itself—this must be an exact fit. As soon as the jam is completely cold, cover with cellophane, then with waxed or greaseproof paper cut to size and dipped on one side in either hot water or milk. Place this on top of the jar, wet side up; smooth it down with a cloth, and secure it with either string or an elastic band.

Store all preserves in a dry place and in an even temperature, and make sure the covers on the jam are airtight.

What Has Happened When

1. *The skins of the fruit are tough and rubbery.* This means the fruit was not cooked long enough in the water *before* the sugar was added.
2. *The jam is brownish, cloudy and/or dull.* Either the quality of the fruit was poor or the jam was cooked too long after the sugar was added. Other possible reasons are: the scum was not removed properly or the jam was stored in too light and/or warm a cupboard.

3. *The jam has shrunk.* The jam was inadequately covered and/or stored in a warm place.
4. *The jam has crystallized.* One of three things has happened: there was not enough acid in the jam, or it was either over or underboiled after the sugar was added.
5. *Mold on top of the jam.* The fruit was either of poor quality or wet. It was inadequately covered, it was stored in a damp place, or the jars were not filled full enough.
6. *The jam is syrupy.* The fruit was too ripe, or the jam was either under or overboiled after the sugar was added.

MUSHROOM CATSUP

(ADAPTED FROM AN 1826 RECIPE)

2 tablespoons (30 ml) sea salt
1 pound (450 g) large, fresh
    mushrooms
4 dried mushrooms
2 tablespoons (30 ml) boiling water
1 tablespoon (15 ml) whole black
    peppercorns

2 blades mace or 2 tablespoons
    (30 ml) ground mace
3 cloves
1 tablespoon (15 ml) fresh-grated
    nutmeg
1 bouquet garni

Rub the salt well into the fresh mushrooms, and allow them to stand for 3 or 4 days until all the liquid has drained. On the last day of the soaking put the dried mushrooms to soak in the boiling water for 3 hours. Drain the fresh mushrooms and squeeze them through a piece of cheese-cloth (muslin) into a saucepan and add the dried mushrooms and their liquid. Simmer, taking off the scum as it rises. When the liquid is perfectly clear, add the herbs and spices and let them simmer together for 30 minutes. Remove the bouquet garni. Allow the mixture to cool, then bottle it when cold and cover it tight.

MR. WOOD'S MUSTARD

This is a most delicious homemade mustard, which was given to me by a charming gentleman, Mr. Wood, who taught himself to cook while he was living in Malaya. I make it continually. Some friends like it so much, they spread it on bread without any meat!

MAKES APPROXIMATELY 2 POUNDS (900 G)

4 tablespoons (2 oz; 50 ml) black mustard seeds

4 tablespoons (2 oz; 50 ml) white mustard seeds

White wine vinegar

Clear honey(preferably Rumanian lime)

1 teaspoon (5 ml) good quality coarse salt

Olive oil (optional)

Grind together the black and white mustard seeds until they form a paste (a small coffee grinder is ideal for this). Place them in a bowl and pour the vinegar over them until the seeds can absorb no more. Add an equal amount of honey, then the salt. Leave to ferment for a few days. If the mustard is too strong, add 1 to 2 tablespoons (15 to 30 ml) of olive oil. Store in a cork-topped jar.

MR. WOOD'S APRICOT CONFITURE

Another of Mr. Wood's imaginative recipes is this:

MAKES APPROXIMATELY 1 POUND (450 G)

½ pound (8 oz; 225 g) dried apricots, chopped fine

Brandy

Clear honey (preferably Rumanian lime)

In a bowl, place the apricots and add brandy until they can absorb no more. Add an equal amount of honey and mix well. Place in a glass preserving jar and leave in a cool place, *not* the refrigerator, for 2 weeks or more before using.

PEAR KETCHUP

MAKES 3 POUNDS (1.4 KG)

4 pears, peeled, cored and chopped fine

4 medium-sized onions, peeled and chopped fine

6 tomatoes, peeled and seeded

1 tablespoon (15 ml) salt

1 tablespoon (15 ml) pickling spices

1 sweet red pepper, chopped fine

2 cups (12 oz; 350 g) light brown sugar

2¼ cups (1 pt; 600 ml) malt vinegar

Place all the ingredients in a jamming pan and boil up. When the fruit becomes soft, pass it through a wire sieve and simmer the purée for 2 hours. Remove it from the heat and cool. Then bottle.

CRAB APPLE CONSERVE

MAKES APPROXIMATELY 2 POUNDS (1 G)

4 pounds (1.8 kg) crab apples, washed, cored and chopped

Preserving sugar or superfine granulated (castor) sugar

Cloves

Fresh mint

1 tablespoon (15 ml) brandy

2 tablespoons (30 ml) red currant jelly

Place the apples, barely covered with water, in a jamming pan. Simmer the mixture until the fruit is soft. Place the pulp in a jelly bag overnight or put it directly through a wire sieve. Measure the juice and for every pint of juice add 1 pound (450 g) of sugar, a dozen cloves and a sprig of mint. Boil until the syrup gels, or reaches 225° F (110° C). Then add the brandy and red currant jelly.

PUMPKIN AND WALNUT CONSERVE

MAKES ABOUT 6 POUNDS (2.7 KG)

1 large pumpkin
Preserving sugar or superfine
granulated (castor) sugar

Orange juice
Lemon juice
Walnuts, chopped

Cut up the pumpkin into small squares, and to every 3 pounds (1.4 kg) pumpkin, add 3 pounds (1.4 kg) sugar, the juice of 3 oranges and 3 lemons. Put into a jamming pan and leave overnight to soak. The next day boil up the mixture until the pumpkin becomes soft and the mixture thickens. Add the walnuts to taste.

SLOE GIN OR VODKA

MAKES ABOUT 5 CUPS (2 PTS; 1 L)

1 pound (450 g) sloes, washed
½ cup (4 oz; 125 g) sugar
5 cups (2 pts; 1 l) gin or vodka

¼ teaspoon (1.25 ml) almond
extract (essence)

With a tapestry needle prick each sloe about 5 times, to allow the juices to run out. Take a large glass container—large enough to hold all the liquid plus the sloes and sugar—and put the sloes, sugar, gin or vodka, and almond extract (essence) into this. (Keep the empty gin or vodka bottles.) Put on the top of the container, give it a good shake, then lay it on its side. Once a week for 3 months shake it, then lay it back on its side. At the end of 3 months, put a funnel into the original gin or vodka bottles and syphon the liquid into them.

The longer you keep the sloes soaking the stronger will be the taste.

ENTERTAINING

"You must reflect carefully beforehand with whom you are to eat and drink, rather than what you are to eat and drink. For a dinner of meats without the company of a friend is like the life of a lion or wolf."

EPICURUS, *Fragments*

I am a firm believer that the hour before dinner should be peaceful, with a long hot bath and a cool drink, alcoholic or not. There should be no frenetic rush in the kitchen. What can be done beforehand should have been done, with only the last-minute cooking to finish. The table can be set well ahead of time, while waiting for something to finish cooking, so that you'll be spared doing it at the last moment. If you are serving a roast, put it in the oven, then take your bath.

Several days before a luncheon or dinner, write down a menu which is seasonal, using the best fresh ingredients within your budget. Check supplies on hand and make a list of what to buy. As it is usually impossible to give an entire day to preparation, try to choose a menu in which you have at least one, if not two courses which may be prepared ahead, either the night before or in the morning. "The secret of leisure is careful planning," to quote Nell Heaton.

It is madness to attempt to serve a meal to more guests than you can cook for or serve comfortably. Much better to give two or three informal dinners which are successful, than one large formal dinner for which the food is cold or not cooked properly, and with too few people to serve.

These days, entertaining being more relaxed and help more difficult to find—not to mention pay for—friends are quite happy to help themselves from the sideboard rather than wait for the hostess or host or one helper to move slowly around the table, so that the meat is cold by the time the vegetables arrive, the sauces likewise. We put sauces on the dining-room table and everyone passes them around; in the country, my husband will often carve and serve the meat while I look after the vegetables.

When preparing for a dinner party, one of the most important considerations must be to build a setting and ambiance in which your guests will relax and wish to talk. Furniture should not only be comfortable and good-looking, but should be arranged to encourage tête à têtes as well as general conversation. A sofa—or even two—are the best focal points, with two or three armchairs and perhaps a floor cushion or ottoman which can be moved about easily.

Dining rooms tend to be less important these days, with casual entertaining more and more taking the place of formal dinners. A table in the corner of the living room or a table and banquette of chairs in the kitchen are comfortable, attractive alternatives to a table in a room which is used at the most twice and rarely three times a day. Alternatively, if you do have a separate dining room, it is a good idea to make it double as a library, dressing room or spare bedroom. Then, when it is not being used for a dinner or luncheon, it has a life of its own with bookcases and tables and a sofa (which may be made into a bed). A lived-in room, I find, gives an added appeal when used as a dining room.

Round or oval dining tables are more conducive to good conversation than the long, narrow ones. I prefer tablecloths to place-mats. They bring the table together, whereas place-mats seem to draw inhibiting boundaries between people.

As to numbers, I find eight people, including the host and hostess, ideal, twelve maximum. More than that and the dinner becomes too formal, unless you have a big enough room to take two or three small tables—but even then you will find yourself staying with one group for most of the evening.

Your cutlery, glass, china and linen need not be expensive, or even of the same period. Antique and modern mixed can be interesting and amusing, but keep everything simple and blending easily in a pretty way, so that once seen the setting will be taken for granted with no one object so outrageous or exotic that it intrudes. This, incidentally, should be true of the food as well.

CHINA

Buying china can be expensive or not, depending on your taste. It is always best to choose by place settings, so buy what you can afford and add to it little by little. How much you need depends, naturally, on the kind of entertaining you intend to do. Eight, as I have said, is the ideal number in my opinion. So you will need eight of each of the following:

dinner plates (11 inches [27.9 cm] in diameter)
side plates (6 inches [15 cm] in diameter)
dessert plates, which can also substitute for fish plates
soup plates, or soup cups and saucers
salad plates
fruit (or cereal) bowls
after-dinner coffee cups and saucers
and:
2 vegetable dishes
1 large meat dish
2 sauceboats and stands
If you are using the same set of china for everyday you will also need:
large coffee cups and saucers
tea cups and saucers

Pieces such as meat and vegetable dishes can be in a different pattern from the rest of the china, or you might have a silver platter. Also, dessert plates can be in another pattern; their number can be built up gradually, and those in the set used for the first course. This will, of course, eliminate having to wash dishes during a dinner party. Most important, buy what you think will go with the surroundings, and a pattern which is not so extraordinary that you will soon tire of it. Above all, choose a design which is in open stock, so that when the inevitable breakage occurs it will be easy to replace. China is an investment with which one will want to live for many years. A further consideration is whether your china can go into the dishwasher. You don't want to be up all night washing dishes after a dinner party.

The word "china" is applied as a generic term to porcelain, china and earthenware alike. However, there are two main groupings: ceramics and china; and these in turn are subdivided into:
Stoneware is very hard with a pitted surface requiring no extra glaze.
Earthenware, or faience, is pottery made out of properly proportioned clay which is well mixed before firing.

Soft porcelain is not very plastic and difficult to shape.

Hard porcelain—the natural hard porcelain is so hard it does not scratch.

Bone china is midway between soft and hard porcelain. It is a special combination of china clay, stone and bone ash, and is the English term for porcelain.

Biscuit is the term denoting earthenware or porcelain after the first firing, but before decoration and the second firing.

Slip denotes the thick and semisolid fluid composed of clay and water which is used as crude underglaze decoration.

Underglaze is the decoration applied to the article before coating with liquid glaze.

Overglaze is the decoration, or printing, which is painted or printed onto the china after the glaze has been applied.

Salt-glaze—this finish is obtained by throwing salt into the kiln, causing fine layers of glaze to be deposited on the objects undergoing the firing process.

CUTLERY

Whatever kind of cutlery you buy, whether it is silver or not, remember that you need more than you think. You may need a small fork for the first course as well as for the dessert, or small knives for the first course and the cheese. There is nothing more annoying than having to wash cutlery during the meal. Again, as entertaining is much more informal now, many people don't go to the trouble and expense of silver cutlery. There are some beautiful designs in wood, metals and even plastic, all of which are dishwasherproof.

I have found that the following amounts are necessary for eight people:

table knives—8 large, 16 small
table forks—8 large, 16 small
8 soupspoons
4 serving spoons
4 large serving forks
8 dessert spoons
8 coffee spoons
3 ladles, for gravies and sauces
salad set—a fork and spoon for serving, if you are not using wooden ones
Optional:
a carving set—fork, knife and steel, if you like carving at table
8 pointed fruit spoons, for grapefruit

GLASSWARE

Glasses should add to the delicacy and taste of the dinner wine. I prefer plain, long, thin-stemmed glasses with a thin rim on a large bowl, although many people's favorites are beautiful English cut crystal. Whichever you like, buy the best you can afford but from a stock pattern so that breakages can be replaced. I spend more money on wine glasses, and then compensate by spending less on highball glasses, or tumblers which are broken more often and which needn't be at all expensive. Some of the cheapest are the best looking, but they should have broad, semiheavy bases which cannot be overturned easily, and they should fit the hand. No matter how smart they may look, huge, oversized glasses that require two hands to lift are more trouble than they're worth. Eating and drinking should never require unnecessary effort on the part of the guest.

For eight people you will need:

8 water goblets—larger versions of the red wine glasses
8 red wine glasses with a curved lip and plenty of room in the bowl. These can be used for both Burgundy and claret. Chablis graves or Sauternes may also be served in them if they are being drunk throughout the meal.
8 white wine glasses with long stems and a smaller bowl than for claret. For hock or Moselle, to go with the first course. Some people like colored bowls, or white glasses with colored stems. I like them plain.
8 "balloons" for brandy
8 liqueur glasses
8 port or Madeira glasses—these are usually smaller versions of the red wine glasses, and could also be used for sherry.

Glasses can be arranged either in a triangle with the water glass behind, the white wine in front on the left, the red on the right, or graded according to height from left to right, with the water goblet at the left, ranging down to the liqueur glass on the right.

Planning the table decoration with the comfort of your guests in mind shows that you care more about giving them pleasure than about showing off your possessions or your elaborate flower arrangements. An overloaded table gives a claustrophobic feeling. Equally, a skimpy table setting looks as though you couldn't be bothered. Candles are important for giving an intimate atmosphere and undoubtedly the most flattering light. Nothing is more off-putting than the glare of an electric bulb in one's face while eating good food or trying to carry on a conversation. In fact, there are many good restaurants where I have eaten delicious food whose effect has been destroyed by brilliant lamps glaring down at one. The flame of the candles should never be at eye level—making it impossible to see across the table—and the candles themselves should be placed symmetrically upon the table. I prefer white or off-white candles, as they will go with any table linen, and, more important, they will never clash with the flowers. But if you are using colored candles, be sure they coordinate not only with the table linen and flowers, but also with the color scheme of the room. If your candles tend to soften quickly and drip wax on the table, put them in the refrigerator to harden for a few hours before using them. More important, avoid placing the candles in a draft, which will immediately cause them to drip.

Flowers can either add to a dinner or become a hindrance. If you are arranging a centerpiece, be sure the flowers are low, providing an unobstructed view across the table. If placed too high, they will act as a barrier between sides and ends of the table, thereby destroying any chance of general conversation. Flowers can make an informal dinner become too formal if they are stiffly arranged; equally they can make a formal dinner more cosy if arranged naturally. My favorite arrangements are spring flowers and greens in a dark brown basket, looking as though they have just been picked.

If your table is a long one, a nice epergne made of several small glass vases in varying sized holders can be very pretty. If you have a small table, a vast centerpiece can make it too overcrowded. Then you might use two to five tiny individual vases of varying heights in the center, each holding one or two flowers, or even an individual vase of one or two flowers at each place.

Autumn flowers, such as lilies, lose their beauty when cut down. In the spring my favorites are anemones, violets and lilies of the valley in a basket, as well as pansies, freesias and irises. During the summer, sweetpeas, old-fashioned pinks and fuchsia look beautiful together. Narcissus and daffodils massed together in a bowl with berried ivy give a fresh look as well as a delicious smell. In the winter the berried ivy mixed with white and yellow spider chrysanthemums give a bright color on cold days, as do potted tulips. Or you can make a centerpiece of a combination of fruits in varied colors.

If you eat out of doors in the summer there is a natural setting of trees and flowers. Therefore, it is desirable to add complementary colored table linen, such as apple green, pale yellow or pink. If you must have a design on the linen, it should be a delicate one, picking up the colors of the surroundings. By choosing a bold design, you are fighting the natural elements. The food, too, ought to be thought out with color in mind, coolness in color being of paramount importance.

The appearance of the food you serve, whether in or out of doors, formal or informal, should be considered as part of the table setting. Almost all food colors look well on purely white china, but take even greater care the way they are arranged on the plate as there is no design to distract the eye. Although a multicolored china does not show a mistake so glaringly, food should always be presented attractively.

Coffee is as important a course as any other. It is worth spending money on good-quality beans as they have a high extraction rate and retain more essential oils. Cream or cool milk—never boiled—should always be served after dinner. Dr. Edouard de Pomiane said in his *Cooking with Pomiane:*

> . . . to prepare a dinner for a friend is to put into the cooking pot all one's affection and good will, all one's gaiety and zest, so that after three hours' cooking a waft of happiness escapes from beneath the lid.

Dr. Pomiane was a professor at the Institut Pasteur in Paris. He enjoyed good food and cooking, and knew all the nutritive and medicinal values. He regarded "cookery as an art which expressed the warmth of human kindness." He also thought of it as a technique and as a psychological satisfaction. His ideas about the "Duties of a Host" blend so much with mine that I would like to share them with the reader.

> . . . To invite relations, friends or business contacts to a meal is a most complicated business. You must, according to Brillat-Savarin's formula, be responsible for their entire happiness whilst they are under your roof.
>
> But the guest's happiness is a matter of infinite complexity. It depends on the host himself, on his humour, his health, his business interests, his pastimes, the character of his wife, his education, his appetite, his attitude towards his neighbour at table, his artistic sense, his inclination to mischief, his good nature, and so on and so forth.
>
> So it is not really worth worrying too much, or the problem of inviting guests to dinner would become insoluble. . . .

However, the table setting, the flowers, the light, the wine and, most important, the food should combine to make guests return home with a happy glow of contentment, having felt wanted and cosseted.

RECIPES FOR ENTERTAINING

The following selection of recipes is a reflection of personal choice. I have not included any main courses such as fish, poultry, game or meat in the following recipes as these will be found in other sections of this book.

Soups

HAZELNUT SOUP

We had this delicious soup on our trip through the north of Spain a few years ago, as we had the Caracoles (see page 409). Both dishes were very special, so I asked the patron for the recipe. He gave me the basic recipe, but later a Spanish friend added some more touches and, finally, I added mine.

SERVES 4

1½ pints (1¼ pts; 750 ml) chicken stock or broth
⅓ cup (2 oz; 50 g) toasted bread crumbs
A pinch of saffron

1 clove garlic, peeled
4 tablespoons (2 oz; 50 ml) hazelnuts
Salt and pepper

Pour the chicken stock or broth into a saucepan; add the bread crumbs and heat over a moderate flame. Grind the saffron, garlic and nuts in a mortar or in an electric blender until the mixture becomes a smooth paste, then stir it into the saucepan. Season with salt and pepper to taste and simmer slowly for 10 minutes.

Preparation time: 10 minutes. Cooking time: 10 to 15 minutes.

TAMASIN'S BLACK LENTIL SOUP

SERVES 12

1 large or 2 medium onions,
chopped coarse
3 large carrots, chopped coarse
1½ pounds (675 g) black lentils
3¾ pints (3 pts; 1.8 l) good beef
stock

1½ teaspoons (7.5 ml) ground
cumin
1 teaspoon (5 ml) celery salt
10 coriander seeds, crushed
Sea salt and black pepper
Juice of 1 lemon

In a large saucepan, put the onions, carrots and lentils, then add the stock. Bring this to the boil and then skim. Add all the seasonings except the lemon juice, cover and simmer gently for 40 minutes. Add the lemon juice and put the mixture into the blender. If the soup is too thick for your liking, add a little milk. Reheat before serving.

Preparation time: 15 minutes. Cooking time: approximately 45 minutes.

First Courses

SPINACH, RAISIN AND PINE NUT CRÊPES

SERVES 8

16 Entrée Crêpes (see below)
1 pound (450 g) frozen spinach,
chopped fine, or
2 pounds (900 g) fresh spinach,
washed, trimmed and chopped
fine
1 cup (5 oz; 150 g) raisins

½ cup (3 oz; 75 g) pine nuts,
roasted
⅔ cup (6 fl oz; 175 ml) sour cream
or plain yogurt
1 teaspoon (5 ml) salt
1 teaspoon (5 ml) grated nutmeg
Fresh-ground black pepper

GARNISH

¼ cup (2 fl oz; 15 ml) sour cream
or yogurt

2 tablespoons (30 ml) pine nuts,
roasted

Preheat the oven to 350° F (180° C; Mark 4).

Make the entrée crêpes. These may be made the night before and kept in the refrigerator, or make them well in advance and freeze them.

In a large mixing bowl put all the filling ingredients and mix well. Take each crêpe and lay it flat. Place 3 tablespoons (45 ml) of the spinach mixture in the middle of the crêpe and roll it up. Place the crêpes in an ovenproof dish and heat slowly in a preheated oven for about 6 or 7 minutes. Garnish each crêpe with a tablespoon (5 ml) of sour cream or yogurt and sprinkle them all with pine nuts.

Preparation time (if crêpes are already made): 10 minutes. Cooking time: 6 to 7 minutes.

BASIC ENTRÉE CRÊPES

MAKES 18 TO 25 CRÊPES; SERVES 6 TO 8

4 eggs
1 cup (5 oz; 150 g) flour
½ teaspoon (2.5 g) salt
1¼ cups (½ pt; 300 ml) milk

1¼ cups (½ pt; 300 ml) water
1 tablespoon (½ oz; 15 ml) melted butter
Clarified butter (see page 243)

In a bowl, beat the eggs with a wire whisk. Add the flour, sifted, with the salt, and beat until smooth. Gradually add the milk, water and melted butter, stirring the batter until it is well blended and has the consistency of heavy cream. Allow to stand for at least 30 minutes before using and, if necessary, thin it again with a spoonful of water or milk.

Heat a small iron or aluminum frying pan until it is very hot and brush it with clarified butter. Pour in about 3 tablespoons (45 ml) of batter, tilting and rotating the pan to distribute it evenly. Cook the crêpe until it is lightly browned on the underside. Lift one edge with the fingers or with the aid of a spatula, and flip the crêpe over to brown the other side. Continue making crêpes in this manner, stacking them to keep them moist, until all the batter is used. If you use two crêpe pans at once, it will save time.

Preparation time: 30 minutes. Cooking time: 30 minutes.

CAVIAR PIE

This is the ultimate luxury first course, and these days with caviar as out-rageously expensive as it is, there is little chance you will want to make it often. However, if you are lucky enough to be given some fresh caviar, you can make a small amount go further by using it in the following manner.

SERVES 6 TO 8

8 to 10 hard-boiled eggs
1 cup (8 oz; 225 g) butter, melted
½ cup (4 fl oz; 125 ml) sour cream

6 to 8 ounces (175 to 225 g) fresh
caviar (lumpfish or salmon eggs
may be substituted)

Place the eggs in a food processor or pass them through a food mill until they are smooth. In a bowl, mix them thoroughly with the melted butter, then press the mixture into an 8- to 9-inch (20.3 to 22.8 cm) china quiche or pie plate. Spread a thick layer of sour cream over the top. Put the dish in the refrigerator and chill for 1 hour. When the mixture has thoroughly chilled, remove it from the refrigerator and spread the caviar over the sour cream. Return the pie to the refrigerator until you are ready to serve it. This should be served cold but *not* frozen. Cut as you would a pie and serve.

Preparation time: 5 to 8 minutes. Chilling time: 1 hour.

SNAILS WITH ALMONDS IN MUSHROOMS

SERVES 4

2 cloves garlic, chopped fine
2 shallots, chopped fine
2 tablespoons (30 ml) fine-chopped
  parsley
½ teaspoon (2.5 ml) salt
Pepper to taste
1 cup (8 oz; 225 g) butter, softened

One 4½-ounce (140 g) can snails
  (24 snails)
26 large button mushrooms
3 tablespoons (45 ml) fine-chopped
  almonds (almond nibs)
2 tablespoons (30 ml) dry
  vermouth

Preheat oven to 450° F (230° C; Mark 8).

In a food processor or in a large bowl, combine the garlic, shallots, parsley, salt and pepper with half the butter. Drain the snails and rinse them under cold water. Pat dry. With a small, blunt knife, like a grapefruit knife, spread some of the garlic butter in the bottom of the mushroom caps. Then place one snail in each mushroom and cover with some more butter mixture. Place the filled mushrooms on a baking sheet or in a flat ovenproof dish, sprinkle with the almonds, and place the sheet or dish in the refrigerator for about 15 minutes. *Note:* The mushrooms can be prepared up to this point a few hours in advance; if they are, wrap the dish or sheet in plastic wrap or foil to prevent the smell of garlic pervading the rest of the food in the refrigerator.

When ready to serve, remove the mushrooms from the refrigerator, sprinkle some dry vermouth over them and place in the preheated oven for 6 to 7 minutes. To serve, put 6 mushrooms on each hot plate and spoon the juice over the mushrooms. Serve with French bread to mop up the juices.

Preparation: 10 minutes. Cooking time: 6 to 7 minutes. Chilling time: at least 15 minutes.

CARACOLES (SNAILS)

SERVES 4

One 4½-ounce (140 g) can of snails (24 snails)
4 tablespoons (60 ml) olive oil
One 1-pound (450 g) can of plum tomatoes in their juice
1 tablespoon (15 ml) flour
2 tablespoons (30 ml) cold water
8 thick slices jamón serrano, prosciutto or Parma ham
⅓ cup (2½ oz; 65 g) chopped walnuts

½ chorizo or garlic sausage, chopped
4 tablespoons (60 ml) fine-chopped parsley or fresh coriander
Fresh-ground black pepper
1 dried chili pepper (optional)
½ cup (4 fl oz; 125 ml) dry white wine

Drain the snails in a colander, rinse them and pat dry. Put the oil into a deep frying pan, heat slowly, then add the tomatoes and stir. Mix the flour and water and add to the pan, stirring continuously over a low flame. Mix in the ham, walnuts, chorizo, parsley or coriander, black pepper and chili pepper and simmer for 5 to 7 minutes. Then add the white wine and simmer for an added 5 minutes. Now add the snails and simmer for a further 5 minutes. Serve in small earthenware dishes which will retain the heat and keep the sauce sizzling while you are eating the snails.

Preparation time: 15 minutes. Cooking time: 25 minutes.

CURRIED AVOCADO WITH SHRIMP (PRAWNS)

SERVES 6

3 large ripe avocados, halved and pits removed	*¼ teaspoon (1.25 ml) ground ginger*
2 tablespoons (30 ml) sour cream	*1 teaspoon (5 ml) cumin seeds, roasted*
1 tablespoon (15 ml) lemon juice	
1 tablespoon (15 ml) ground coriander	*1 large clove garlic, peeled and crushed*
1½ teaspoons (7.5 ml) hot chili powder	*1 pound (450 g) cooked shrimp (prawns)*
2 teaspoons (10 ml) garam masala	*6 lemon wedges*

Preheat the oven to 400° F (200° C; Mark 6).

Using a teaspoon, scoop out the avocado flesh into a bowl, leaving the skins intact. Set the skins aside. Mash the avocado with the back of a spoon. Stir in the sour cream, lemon juice, herbs and spices and beat until the mixture is smooth. Then add the garlic and shrimp (prawns) and pile the mixture back into the avocado skins. Place the avocado halves in a baking dish and bake in the preheated oven for approximately 15 minutes, or until the tops of the fillings are golden brown. Serve immediately on individual plates, each garnished with a lemon wedge.

Preparation time: approximately 20 minutes. Cooking time: approximately 15 minutes.

GALETTES AU FROMAGE

---

28 GALETTES

1½ cups (6 oz; 180 g) flour
¼ teaspoon (1.25 ml) dry mustard
⅛ teaspoon (.75 ml) cayenne
  pepper
¾ cup (6 oz; 175 g) butter, cut into
  small pieces

1 cup (4 oz; 125 g) Gruyère cheese,
  grated
1 cup (4 oz; 125 g) grated Cheddar
  cheese
1 egg, beaten lightly with 1
  teaspoon (5 ml) water

Preheat the oven to 400°F (200° C; Mark 6).

Sift the flour, mustard and cayenne pepper into a medium-sized bowl. Add the butter and cheeses and mix them into the flour mixture to form a firm dough. Cover and chill the dough in the refrigerator for 20 minutes.

On a lightly floured surface, roll out the dough to a circle about ¾ inch thick. With a 2-inch pastry cutter, cut out circles of dough and transfer them to a baking sheet.

Brush the circles with the egg mixture and place the baking sheet in the preheated oven. Bake for 15 minutes or until the galettes are pale golden brown. Remove the galettes from the oven and cool them for 5 minutes before serving, or leave them to cool completely on a wire rack.

Serve them hot as hors d'oeuvre or cold with salads.

Preparation time: approximately 45 minutes. Cooking time: 15 minutes.

PASTA VERDE

When I am in North Wales, I make my own pasta because there I have the time, and because there are no shops which sell it. Now I have become addicted to it and have been given some added tuition by Italian friends who own a pasta shop.

SERVES 6, MAKES APPROXIMATELY 1½ POUNDS

¼ pound (4 oz; 125 g) spinach,
  washed and trimmed
4 eggs, lightly beaten

1 pound (450 g) flour, preferably
  unbleached or semolina, sifted
  with a pinch of salt

Blanch the spinach for 2 minutes in boiling water. Drain thoroughly, squeezing out all the liquid by putting it in a tea towel and squeezing dry. Then chop it fine or put it in a food processor or Mouli-Légumes. Mix the spinach and eggs. If the spinach is not totally dry, you may need to add a little flour.

On a pastry board put the flour in a mound and make a well, then pour the spinach and egg mixture into the center. With a fork work the flour from the outside of the mound into the middle and over the eggs; work this well into a smooth dough, kneading until it is smooth, firm and has an elastic consistency. This should take about 10 minutes. Roll into a ball and place in a plastic bag to rest in a cool place for 30 minutes.

If you are using a pasta machine, divide the dough into two pieces, dust with flour and, starting with widest opening, run the piece through the machine. Then fold the piece into three, like an envelope, and run it through again always turning it around so that it never goes through the same way twice in succession. Each opening, usually three, should be used *4 times,* until the dough is thin enough to be cut into narrow strips. Sprinkle it with flour. Then run it through either the tagliatelle or fettucine cutter. The flour keeps the strips from sticking to one another.

Or, roll the dough by hand as thin as possible, and cut it with a knife to the desired width.

Put the pasta on a platter lightly sprinkled with flour and allow it to dry for at least 10 minutes before using. If you have made more than you need at the moment, either make nests of the strips, allow to dry completely and keep in a sealed tin or dry on a pasta rack and place the extra in a plastic bag and freeze. Some experts maintain that pasta should *not* be frozen, but I have always had excellent results by doing so. However, when it is placed in boiling water you must stir it with a fork so that strips do not stick together forming a lump.

To cook

Fill a large pot with water—the pasta must have plenty of room in which to cook, otherwise it will stick. Add 1 tablespoon (15 ml) salt and 1 teaspoon (5 ml) olive oil. Bring the water to a rapid boil, and add the fresh pasta. Cook for 2 or 3 minutes, until it is *"al dente,"* and empty it into a colander.

TAGLIATELLE WITH SPICY OLIVE OIL, GARLIC AND PINE NUTS

SERVES 4

1 pound (450 g) tagliatelle or fettucine, white or green (see above)
3 to 4 hot dried chili peppers
5 ounces (¼ pt; 250 ml) good olive oil

4 to 5 cloves garlic, peeled and crushed or chopped fine
6 tablespoons (3 oz; 75 ml) roasted pine nuts (kernels)
1 cup (3½ oz; 90 g) fresh chopped basil or parsley

In a large saucepan or a deep frying pan, heat the chili peppers in the olive oil over very low heat for 5 minutes, then remove the peppers with a slotted spoon. (I keep a good supply of olive oil with chili peppers in a large bottle for use in this dish and in Gambas al'Ajillo; see page 106.) Add the garlic and roasted pine nuts. Just before the pasta is ready, simmer this mixture for 2 to 3 minutes. Add the drained pasta and mix thoroughly. Turn into a heated dish and top with fresh basil or parsley.

Cooking time: 3 minutes.

ALDO'S TAGLIATELLE WITH SMOKED SALMON AND CREAM

Use ends of smoked salmon or lox for this dish.

SERVES 6 AS A FIRST COURSE, 4 TO 5 AS MAIN COURSE

¼ pound (125 g) sliced smoked salmon, freshly chopped
1¼ cups (10 fl oz; 300 ml) light (single) cream

Fresh-ground black pepper
1 pound (450 g) fresh tagliatelle verde

Place the smoked salmon and the cream in a bowl. Grind quite a bit of black pepper over the mixture and leave for 2 hours, if possible, so that the cream takes on the taste of the smoked salmon.

Drop the tagliatelle into rapidly boiling salted water. Stir with a fork to separate the strands. Continue boiling over high heat for 7 minutes.

Meanwhile, place the smoked salmon and cream in a double boiler over hot water and warm gently over very low flame. *Do not boil.*

When the tagliatelle is cooked, drain it in a colander and turn into a warm serving dish. Pour the smoked salmon and cream over the pasta and top with a lot of fresh-ground black pepper. Serve immediately.

Note: Very salty smoked Virginia or Baltimore ham is also delicious when substituted for smoked salmon.

Cooking time: 3 minutes.

Desserts

FIONA'S AVOCADO ICE CREAM

SERVES 6

1 avocado, peeled and pit removed	*¾ cup (5 fl oz; 150 ml) heavy*
Juice of 1 lemon	*(double) cream, whipped*
1 teaspoon (5 ml) sugar	
2 tablespoons (30 ml) Madeira or	
port	

Place all the ingredients except the whipped cream in a food processor, and process until thoroughly mixed and smooth. Pour into a bowl and add the whipped cream. Mix well. This can then either be chilled and eaten, or put into the freezer for 4 hours and eaten as an ice cream.

Preparation time: 15 minutes.

TREACLE PUDDING

SERVES 6

¼ cup (2 oz; 50 g) flour
4 tablespoons (2 oz; 50 ml) butter
1 tablespoon (15 ml) molasses
   (treacle)
4 tablespoons (2 oz; 50 ml) superfine granulated (castor) sugar

2 eggs, separated
1 small teaspoon (4 ml) baking
   soda (bicarbonate of soda)
Whipped cream

In a bowl, mix the flour with the butter, molasses, sugar, egg yolks and baking soda. Beat the egg whites stiff and add to the mixture. Stir well. Pour
into a buttered mold and boil for 1 hour (see page 364). Serve with sweetened
whipped cream. Marmalade may be substituted for the molasses.

Preparation time: 15 minutes. Cooking time: 1 hour.

BLACKBERRY PUDDING

SERVES 6 TO 8

1½ pounds (700 g) blackberries,
   black currants, raspberries or
   green grapes
Kirsch or marc (for grapes)

Juice of 1 lemon
2¼ cups (1 pt; 300 ml) heavy
   (double) cream
Light brown (demerara) sugar

Preheat the broiler (grill).
   Soak the fruit in kirsch or marc and lemon juice and place in a dish that
can withstand heat. Whip the cream and spread it over the fruit. Sprinkle
a thick layer of brown sugar over the cream and place the dish under the
broiler (grill) until the sugar has melted. Remove and cool. Then place in
the refrigerator—or in a cool place, as the heat moistens the top.

Preparation time: 12 to 15 minutes. Cooking time: 1 to 2 minutes.

FIONA'S COLD GINGER/MANGO SOUFFLÉ

SERVES 8 TO 12

5 good ripe mangoes, peeled and
  pitted, or one 14½-ounce (410 g)
  can of mangoes, drained and
  syrup reserved
Juice of 1 lemon
A pinch of ground ginger
1¼ cups (8 oz; 225 g) superfine
  granulated (castor) sugar

1 envelope unflavored gelatin
2 tablespoons (30 ml) water
5 eggs, separated
A pinch of salt
5 pieces of crystallized ginger or
  the syrup from the canned
  mangoes

In a food processor or blender (liquidizer), purée 4 of the mangoes with the lemon juice and ground ginger. In a saucepan, combine the purée with the sugar. Cover the pan and cook the mixture over low heat, stirring, for 10 minutes. Remove the lid and cook for 5 minutes more. Allow to cool.

Melt the gelatin in the water, over low heat. Beat the egg whites with a pinch of salt until they are stiff. Beat the yokes and add them to the fruit mixture, followed by the melted gelatin and then the crystallized ginger or mango syrup. Finally, fold in the egg whites and pour the mixture into an 8-inch (20.3 cm) soufflé dish. Cover the dish with foil and place it in the refrigerator for 6 hours. When ready to serve, slice the remaining mango and use it to decorate the top of the soufflé.

Preparation time: 10 minutes. Cooking time: 15 minutes. Chilling time: 6 hours.

GREEN GRAPES IN HONEY AND COGNAC
WITH CARAMEL CRUNCH

This recipe was in my last book, but since then I have improved upon it by adding the caramel crunch, which adds a touch of crisp sweetness to the light coldness of the grapes. A good dessert to serve after a rich dinner.

SERVES 8

*1¼ pounds (575 g) green seedless
  grapes
½ cup (11 oz; 325 m) honey*

*3 tablespoons (45 ml) Cognac
1½ teaspoons (7.5 g) lemon juice
Caramel Crunch (see below)*

Wash the grapes and drain them thoroughly. Remove the stems and toss the grapes gently in a mixture of honey, Cognac and lemon juice. Chill for at least 5 hours, stirring occasionally. Serve in a chilled bowl with caramel crunch sprinkled on top.

CARAMEL CRUNCH

*½ cup (4 oz; 125 g) granulated or
  lump sugar*

¼ cup (2 fl oz; 50 ml) water

Put the sugar and water into a saucepan and place it over low heat. Stir the mixture with a metal spoon until the sugar dissolves. Then increase the heat to high and *do not stir again.* Boil the syrup for 5 minutes, until it reaches 293° F (146° C; hard crack) on a candy thermometer, or until it becomes a rich brown color. Pour it on some waxed or greaseproof paper and allow it to cool and harden. Then place another piece of paper on top and hit it with a wooden mallet, breaking it into small pieces.

This dessert can be made ahead of time, the grapes and the caramel crunch kept in separate bowls in the refrigerator until it is time to serve them.

Preparation time: 20 minutes. Cooking time: 5 to 10 minutes. Chilling time: 5 hours.

OLD-FASHIONED HOT FUDGE SAUCE

SERVES 4

*Two 1-ounce (30 g) squares
  unsweetened chocolate
½ cup (4 oz; 125 ml) corn syrup
A pinch of salt*

*½ teaspoon (2.5 ml) vanilla
½ teaspoon (2.5 ml) butter or
  margarine*

Melt the chocolate over hot but not boiling water. Add the syrup and cook over hot water until the chocolate is melted and blended. Add salt, vanilla and butter. Serve hot over ice cream.

Cooking time: 10 minutes.

MY MOTHER'S CINNAMON CUBES

SERVES 6

½ cup (2¼ oz; 55 g) superfine
　granulated (castor) sugar
3 tablespoons (45 ml) ground
　cinnamon

½ loaf fresh unsliced white bread
½ pound (225 g) butter or
　margarine

Mix the sugar and cinnamon thoroughly in a dish. At least 1 hour before using, remove the crust from the bread and cut it into 1½-inch (3.8 cm) cubes. Over very low heat, melt the butter in a frying pan. Put the bread cubes in the pan and turn them, making sure that all sides of each cube are covered in butter. Leave them in the butter long enough for the fat to penetrate to the center; then take each cube out and roll it in the cinnamon/ sugar mixture to cover completely. Leave the cubes in the sugar and cinnamon until ready to serve, allowing them to absorb the mixture. This can be done in the morning or several hours in advance, but in any case, they should be left for at least 1 hour. When ready to serve, put the cubes back in the frying pan with the melted butter, adding more butter as needed. Heat on all sides and serve very hot.

Preparation time: 10 minutes. Cooking time: 10 minutes.

DESSERT AND SWEET HINTS

1. Shave chocolate with a potato peeler.
2. To substitute cocoa for chocolate in a recipe, use 3 level teaspoons (15 ml) cocoa and 1 extra tablespoon (15 ml) butter for each square or ounce of chocolate.

3. To eliminate waste when measuring molasses, butter the measuring cup slightly.

4. To cut marshmallow easily, dip a pair of scissors into hot water, then cut the marshmallow.

5. To prevent a steamed pudding from breaking: When the pudding is cooked, remove the pudding bowl from the saucepan and leave it for a few minutes to settle, then turn it out.

6. To brown sugar on a *crème brûlée:* If the brown sugar does not brown evenly, light a long match and hold it over the nonburned patches; the sugar will melt instantly.

7. To keep cookies (biscuits) crisp: Place some crushed tissue paper in the bottom of the cookie jar (biscuit tin).

8. Never store cookies (sweet biscuits) in the same tin as crackers (dry biscuits). The sugar in the former makes the latter go soggy.

BIBLIOGRAPHY

SOURCES AND FURTHER REFERENCES

"Knowledge," said Dr. Johnson, "is of two kinds. We know a subject as our own, or we know where we can find information on it."

Adamson, Helen Lyon. *Grandmother's Household Hints*. London: Frederick Muller Ltd., 1976.

Anderson, Jean, and Hanna, Elaine. *The Doubleday Cookbook*. New York: Doubleday & Co., 1975.

Beaty-Pownall, S. *The "Queen" Cookery Books*. London: Horace Cox, 1902.

Beeton, Isabella. *Beeton's Book of Household Management*. New York: Farrar, Straus and Giroux, 1977.

Brody, Jane E. A Polyunsaturate Guide to Fats. *The New York Times,* Oct. 5, 1977: C1, 12.

Broughton, K.F. *Pressure Cooking Day by Day.* 9th ed. London: Kaye & Ward Ltd., 1976.

Brown, Marion. *The Southern Cookbook*. Chapel Hill: University of North Carolina Press, 1968.

Camrass, Zoe. *The Only Cookbook You'll Ever Need*. London: Mitchell Beazley, 1977.

Cassell's Book of the Household. Vols. I–IV. London, Paris and Melbourne: Cassell and Company Ltd., 1895.

Chafin, Mary. *Original Country Recipes*. London: Macmillan London Ltd., 1979.

Child, Theodore. *Delicate Dining*. London: J.R. Osgood, McIlvaine & Co., 1891.

Chitty, Susan. *The Modern Household Encyclopaedia*. London: Spring Books.

Claiborne, Craig and Lee, Virginia. *The Chinese Cookbook*. New York: J.B. Lippincott, 1972.

Conran, Caroline and Wickham, Cynthia. "A Plain Cook's Guide to Fancy Curry Spices." *The Sunday Times Magazine* (London) 11.27.77.

Cox, Pat M. *The Home Book of Food Freezing*. Rev. ed. London: Faber and Faber Ltd., 1977.

Craig, Elizabeth. *Keeping House with Elizabeth Craig*. London: Collins, 1936.

Cutts, Sue. *The Prestige Book of Crock-Pot Cookery*. London: Octopus Books, 1977.

Emlee, Josephine. *Cooking for Texture*. London: Faber and Faber Ltd., 1957.

Farmers' Weekly. *Home Made Country Wines, Recipes from Country Housewives*. London: Hulton Press, 1955.

Francatelli, Charles Elmé. *The Cook's Guide, and Housekeeper's and Butler's Assistant*. London: Richard Bentley and Son, 1884.

Garrett, Theodore Francis, ed. *The Encyclopaedia of Practical Cookery*. 8 vols. London: L. Upcott Gill, 1899.

Gerrard, Frank and Mallion, F.J. *The Complete Book of Meat*. London and Coulsdon: Virtue and Co. Ltd., 1977.

Giobbi, Edward. *Italian Family Cooking*. New York: Random House, 1971.

Greenberg, Florence. *Cookery Book*. London: The Jewish Chronicle, 1947.

Grieve, M. *A Modern Herbal*. 1931. Edited by C.F. Leyel. Reprint. London: Jonathan Cape, 1977.

Grigson, Jane. *Vegetable Book*. New York: Atheneum, 1979.

Hamilton Talbot, Mary. *Remedies for Cooking Disasters*. London: 1930.

Hanbury-Tenison, Marika. *Deep Freeze Sense*. London: Pan Books Ltd., 1976.

Heaton, Nell. *The Complete Hostess*. London: Cresta Books.

Jack, Florence B. *Cookery for Every Household*. London: T.C. and E.C. Jack Ltd., 1914.

Jekyll, Lady. *Kitchen Essays*. Edited by Lady Freyberg. London: Collins, 1969.

Jerome, Helen. *The Fine Art of Cooking*. 1935. Reprint. London: Sir Isaac Pitman and Sons Ltd., 1956.

Jones, Beverly. "To Thaw or Not to Thaw." *The Freezer Family*, March/April 1975.

Kamman, Madeleine. *The Making of a Cook*. New York: Atheneum, 1971.

Leeming, Janet. "The Meat in Your Freezer." *The Freezer Family*, February/March 1973.

Lindsay, Jessie and Tress, Helen M. *What Every Cook Should Know*. London and New York: Nisbet and Co., 1933.

Lowenfeld, Claire. *Herb Gardening*. London: Faber and Faber, 1970.

McLane, A.J. *The Encyclopaedia of Fish Cookery*. New York: Holt, Rinehart and Winston, 1977.

Marshall Cavendish. *The Marshall Cavendish Handbook of Good Cooking*. 8 vols. London: Marshall Cavendish Ltd., 1976–77.

Montagné, Prosper, ed. *Larousse Gastronomique, The Encyclopaedia of Food, Wine and Cookery*. New York: Crown Publishers Inc., 1961.

Owen, Sri. *Indonesian Food and Cookery*. London: Prospect Books, 1980.

Pasadena Art Alliance. *All Things Wise and Wonderful*. Pasadena: Pasadena Art Alliance, 1975.

————. *To Talk of Many Things*. Pasadena: Pasadena Art Alliance, 1977.

Paterson, Margaret. *The Craft of Cooking, A Digest of the Hows and Whys of Cookery*. London: Macdonald and Jane's Publishers Ltd., 1978.

Pomiane, Edouard de. Edited and translated by Peggie Benton. *Cooking with Pomiane*. Oxford: Bruno Cassirer, 1976.

Reader's Digest Association. *Food from Your Garden*. London: Reader's Digest Association Ltd., 1977.

————. *Household Manual*. London: Reader's Digest Association Ltd., 1977.

Reynolds, Mary. "Fish Cooking." *The Freezer Family*, August 1978.

Roy, Mike. *The Mike Roy Cookbook No. 2.* Los Angeles: The Ward Ritchie Press, 1968.

Senn, Charles Herman. *Dictionary of Foods and Culinary Encyclopaedia.* London: Ward Lock, 1930.

Sherson, Erroll. *The Book of Vegetable Cookery.* London and New York: Frederick Warne and Co. Ltd., 1931.

Silvester, Elizabeth. *Silvester's Sensible Cookery.* London: Herbert Jenkins Ltd.

Simms, A.E., ed. *Fish and Shell-fish.* London and Coulsdon: Virtue and Co. Ltd., 1973.

Smith, Henry. *The Master Book of Poultry and Game.* London: Spring Books, 1949.

Supercook. 8 vols. London: Marshall Cavendish Ltd., 1975.

Webb, Jenny M. *Microwave, The Cooking Revolution.* London: Forbes Publications Ltd., 1977.

Wells, Patricia. "Tips for Lowering Fat in the Diet." *The New York Times,* Oct. 5, 1977: C12.

Which? Magazine "All About Fish." August 1979: 473–480.

Willis, Eva. *Sauce and Sage.* London and New York: Frederick Warne and Co. Ltd., 1933.

Wright, Jeni, ed. *The Complete Encyclopaedia of Home Freezing.* London: Octopus Books Ltd., 1977.

INDEX